U.S. Policy on Palestine
From Wilson to Clinton

U.S. Policy on Palestine
From Wilson to Clinton

edited by
Michael W. Suleiman

Association of Arab-American University Graduates, Inc.
Normal, Illinois, 1995

First published in the United States of America by
 PRESS

© Copyright 1995
The Association of Arab-American University Graduates, Inc.
All rights reserved

Library of Congress Cataloging-in-Publication Data

U.S. Policy on Palestine from Wilson to Clinton / Michael W. Suleiman, editor.

    p. cm.
Includes bibliographical references and index.
ISBN: 0-937694-88-6
    1. United States—Foreign relations—Palestine. 2. Palestine—Foreign relations—United States. I. Suleiman, Michael W. II. Association of Arab-American University Graduates.
E183.8.P19U15 1995
327.7305694—dc20   94-36125 CIP

ISBN: 0-937694-88-6

Contents

Preface . . . vi

Introduction
    Michael W. Suleiman . . . 1

1 Palestine and the Palestinians in the Mind of America
    Michael W. Suleiman . . . 9

2 Roots of Denial: American Stand on Palestinian Self-Determination from the Balfour Declaration to World War Two
    Hisham H. Ahmed . . . 27

3 The Truman Administration and the Palestinians
    Fred Lawson . . . 59

4 Missed Opportunities and Roads Not Taken: The Eisenhower Adminstration and the Palestinians
    Deborah J. Gerner . . . 81

5 The Kennedy-Johnson Administrations and the Palestinian People
    Zaha Bustami . . . 113

6 Nixon's Middle East Policy: From Balance to Bias
    Donald Neff . . . 133

7 The Carter Administration and the Palestinians
    Janice J. Terry . . . 163

8 The Reagan Administration's Policy toward the Palestinians
    Ann M. Lesch . . . 175

9 The Bush Administration and the Palestinians: A Reassessment
    Cheryl A. Rubenberg . . . 195

10 The Clinton Administration and the Palestine Question
    Joe Stork . . . 223

11 America's Palestine Policy
    Ibrahim Abu-Lughod . . . 233

Selected Bibliography . . . 245

Contributors . . . 255

Index . . . 257

Preface

The need for a detailed and comprehensive study of American policy on Palestine became particularly evident when the earlier publication in the form of a special issue of the *Arab Studies Quarterly*, vol. 12, nos. 1 & 2 (Winter/Spring 1990) quickly went out of print. Continued demand for such information prompted the AAUG to request that I edit an expanded and updated volume on the subject. I accepted the challenge and was gratified with the results. Apart from the chapters on the Truman and Nixon administrations, whose authors saw no need for revision, all other material is new or much revised and brought up to date. The chapter on American perceptions of Palestinians provides an added dimension to studies of the foreign policies of the various American administrations, including the most recent ones, namely those of Bush and Clinton.

As for transliteration of Arabic and Hebrew words and names, I have generally followed the usage common in general surveys of the Middle East. This practice makes it much easier for the general reader to recognize these foreign words and names.

It is appropriate here to record my gratitude to all the authors in this volume for their cooperation and prompt response to queries and suggestions for revision. Also, Jamal Nassar, Director of Publications for AAUG, was most helpful in all aspects of the book production process. I am also grateful to Lory Eggers for her efficient typing of the manuscript.

Samia Halaby generously donated a beautiful painting for the cover of this book. The cover design is the work of Fayez Husseini. I am most grateful to both individuals for their contribution.

Michael W. Suleiman
November 1994

Introduction

Michael W. Suleiman

THE MAKING AND EXECUTION of foreign policy decisions are affected by a number of factors of unequal weight. Which particular factor plays a more critical part depends on the actual situation. The detailed studies in this volume illustrate the variety of factors affecting American policy on Palestine. For instance, the personalities and backgrounds of the decision makers, especially those in the highest positions, certainly influence foreign policy decision-making. Thus, Ronald Reagan, Jimmy Carter, and Dwight D. Eisenhower, for instance, would not be likely to handle any specific world crisis, including the Palestine-Israeli conflict, in the self-same manner or approach it from the same perspective. Their differing personality traits, motivational factors, and perceptions would lead them to somewhat varied decisions.

Another factor affecting American foreign policy on Palestine is the American "style" in foreign policy. Thus, it is frequently suggested that American policy makers favor a pragmatic and short-term approach to problem solving in any area — an approach that leads Americans to adopt a "reactive" policy in international politics. American pragmatism is very much in evidence in the cases presented in this volume.

A country's history and its people's ideology are also important aspects of foreign policy making. In the case of the United States, long periods of isolationism have been followed by periods of forceful interventionism. This latter stance, which has characterized American policy since World War II, is often accompanied by a strong missionary zeal and a tendency to rationalize foreign policy decisions with legal and moral arguments, rather than with those citing material needs or the national interest. As the various authors in this text indicate, U.S. decisions on Palestine have often been rationalized on the basis of Israel's democratic system, American public support for Israel, or the strong interest of many Americans in Palestine as the Holy Land.

Economic factors are also held to be a very important element in foreign policy decisions. In the specific case of the Middle East, Americans are most interested in securing for themselves, and denying the enemy, the tremendous oil and gas supplies available in the region. This is a major factor in almost all the cases discussed in this volume.

The size and power of states also affect the kind of foreign policy they pursue. The United States generally views the Middle East from the point of view of its larger strategic interests and power balances. On the other hand, smaller powers tend to be involved in regional disputes over territory and security. As illustrated in several of the cases in this volume, quite often the United States has misinterpreted the nature of the conflict in the Middle East and has acted as if global concerns or superpower rivalry were the only issues of consequence.

The international system, international organizations, and third parties also play roles in specific regional disputes. In fact, in the Middle East and specifically in the Palestine-Israel conflict, the United States is in a very real sense a third party, albeit one that has repeatedly played a partisan role supportive of Israel. Detailed discussion in the following chapters will provide information about the extent of this partisanship, the possible reasons for it, and under what circumstances it might change.

Most of the discussion, however, will naturally focus on specific U.S. policies and how these policies were developed, i.e. on the foreign policy decision-making process itself. Much attention will center on the actions of the executive, particularly the president and his associates, as the major foreign policy actor in the American system. But other branches of the U.S. government, and non-governmental agencies as well, have an impact on the making of foreign policy. Hence, the studies will include pertinent discussion of the roles played by the U.S. Congress, political parties, pressure groups, the military, the media, and public opinion in the shaping of American policy on Palestine and the Palestinians.

HIGHLIGHTS OF THE VOLUME

The volume opens with a general essay on American views of Palestine and the Palestinians. Michael W. Suleiman reports the impact which popular American attitudes have had on the development and execution of U.S. policy on Palestine. Up to the end of the nineteenth century, and as a result of both specifically American factors and attitudes "inherited" from the Europeans, Palestinians either did not register on the consciousness of Americans or they were seen in a negative light. In particular, Palestinians suffered from the fact that Americans viewed Palestine as the Holy Land associated with Christians and Jews. Especially among millenarian evangelical Protestants, Palestinian Arabs (both Muslim and Christian) were dispensable and disposable since what mattered was the "return" of Jews to Palestine prior to the Second Coming of Christ. After World War I, Palestinian wishes for self-determination were ignored both by political leaders and in public discourse. A review of American views of Palestinians in the twentieth century reveals a generally anti-Palestinian and pro-Israeli bias. This negative orientation has had an impact on American policy toward Palestine and Palestinians.

American policy toward, and involvement in, Palestinian affairs began during World War I. As early as 1916, President Woodrow Wilson asserted in general terms that every people has the right to self-determination. In his study of this important period, Hisham Ahmed discusses in detail how the United States has supported in principle the notion of self-determination, but has subverted in practice Palestinian efforts to attain self-determination. On this issue, American policy seems to have been the product of several interrelated factors. President Wilson was pressured by some of his pro-Zionist friends and aides to accept the idea of a Jewish homeland in Palestine. In addition, America's European allies, namely Britain and France, were not interested in ascertaining the wishes of the peoples emerging from under Ottoman control (including the Palestinians) concerning independence. Under such circumstances, Wilson in 1919 sent an American-only delegation (the King-Crane Commission) to ask the people what they wanted. However, the commission's report was suppressed for three years, most likely because it suggested self-determination for the Palestinians and might have influenced the deliberations at the Paris Peace Conference. Later, the American government supported the British mandatory regime in Palestine which also undertook to support the establishment of a Jewish homeland. The presumably universal application of the principle of self-determination was denied to the Palestinians.

In the next chapter, Fred Lawson argues that domestic political considerations and the Zionist lobby were not the only, or even the most important, factors affecting American policy toward Palestine under the Truman administration. Lawson suggests that the main concerns of American policy at the time were the economic recovery of a capitalist Western Europe, the attempt to keep the Soviets out of the Middle East, and the desire to inherit the political and trade privileges the British had in the area. As long as actions toward Palestinians or Israelis did not threaten these general objectives, the American authorities were willing to push for policies supportive of one side or the other, depending on where economic aid was most needed. Also, when it seemed as though the severity of the Palestinian refugee situation would provide the Soviet Union with an opportunity for intervention, the U.S. administration made an effort (albeit an unsuccessful one) at pressuring the Israelis for concessions. The examples that Lawson presents primarily deal with humanitarian issues affecting the area *after* the establishment of Israel. In any case, Lawson argues that the special circumstances facing the United States after World War II had a strong influence on American policy concerning Palestine and caused "Truman's vacillation."

Deborah Gerner next argues that opportunities arose when solutions to the Palestine-Israel problem could have been possible. However, for various reasons, the Eisenhower administration missed these opportunities. Among the reasons for this, Gerner cites a basic flaw in the way many American governments have viewed the situation: the United States has looked upon Palestinians not as a people seeking a homeland, but only as refugees needing to be settled. In other words, *economic* solutions were sought for a definitely political problem. Furthermore, America dealt only with the states in the region and, therefore, not with the Palestinians. In any case, the overall approach was dictated by America's strategic interests. Those, once more, were the defense and growth of Western Europe and the containment of communism, goals which entailed the need for a steady flow of oil supplies from the Middle East and the need for stability for the pro-Western Arab states. If Israeli actions or obduracy threatened these objectives (as they did during and after the 1956 Suez invasion), then the Eisenhower administration did not hesitate to criticize Israel. None of this, however, was of much help to the Palestinians, who were seen, if they were seen at all, as refugees and not as a people with national aspirations and the right to self-determination.

During the Kennedy and Johnson administrations, according to Zaha Bustami, the Palestinians continued to be no more than a problem of refugees. Even on this level, however, Kennedy's attempt at a solution of the "refugee problem" was not successful exactly because other American interests in the region were deemed to be more important. Then, under Johnson, hardly any attention of any sort was paid to the Palestinians — but paradoxically, although Palestinians were seen as insignificant or nonexistent as actors on the political scene, they were also seen as a significant force capable of setting in motion the events which led to the 1967 war! In 1968 a feeble attempt was made to settle the refugee problem — an attempt that ignored the major changes taking place concerning Palestinian organization and commitment to nationhood, exemplified by the growing stature of the Palestine Liberation Organization (PLO). In part, this situation reflected President Johnson's lack of interest in foreign policy issues, his concerns about Vietnam, and the fact that both Johnson and many of his top advisers were very pro-Israeli.

The policies of the Nixon/Ford administrations are outlined by Donald Neff. He states that Richard Nixon came to the presidency very well informed on the Arab-Israeli situation, but mostly ignorant of the Palestinian aspect. He was not indebted to Jewish-American voters for his political success, and wanted to find a solution to the Arab-Israeli problem, but in the end he failed. This failure is attributed to four main factors: first, his appointment of two incompatible aides, namely William Rogers at the State Department and Henry Kissinger as National Security Advisor; second, his misreading of the Middle East problem as a global conflict with the Soviet Union; third, Nixon's political weakness as a result of the Watergate scandal; and finally, Kissinger's strong pro-Israeli sympathies, which were eventually translated into such policies as the restriction on recognition of or negotiation with the PLO until it recognized Israel's right to exist and accepted UN Security Council resolutions 242 and 338 — a condition that was not resolved until twenty years later. This delay not only hurt the Palestinian cause but the chances of a peaceful settlement as well.

Janice Terry discusses the Carter presidency and its dealings with the Palestinians. She states that Jimmy Carter wanted a comprehensive settlement of the Palestine and Arab-Israeli disputes. Consequently, his administration initiated contacts and indirect discussions with the PLO — in fact, it came very close to recognizing the PLO. In the end, however, the Camp David accords and process were basically a continuation of the step-by-step approach advocated and practiced by Henry Kissinger. The failure to reach a comprehensive settlement that would include the Palestinians is attributed to strong lobbying by Zionist groups who interpreted the Palestine-Israel dispute as a zero-sum game, to Anwar Sadat's personal diplomacy and trip to Jerusalem, and to the fact that the Carter administration ignored or chose to misinterpret the reality that in the Arab world no solution would be acceptable that denied self-determination to the Palestinians. Another reason for the failure was the strength of pro-Israeli sentiment among members of the White House staff, in Congress, in the press, and in general public opinion. However, the fact that the Palestinians were not included in an overall comprehensive settlement meant that the Israelis continued to dominate the West Bank and Gaza. It also led to the 1982 Israeli invasion of Lebanon, and the continuation of the Palestinian struggle for self-determination.

Next, Ann Lesch explores American policy on Palestine under the Reagan administration. She states that Ronald Reagan's overriding preoccupation was with the Soviet Union. In the Middle East, Israel was viewed as an asset and the PLO was labeled as a terrorist organization. With this perspective, the Reagan administration moved quickly to establish Israel as a strategic ally and generally ignored the Palestinian issue, insisting that King Hussein of Jordan negotiate on behalf of the Palestinians. After the PLO recognized Israel's right to exist, renounced terrorism in the exact language the United States requested, and accepted UN Security Council resolutions 242 and 338, the United States opened a "substantive dialogue" with the PLO. According to Lesch, it was the *intifada*, the Palestinian uprising against Israel, that really changed American policy on the Palestine issue.

The next chapter, by Cheryl A. Rubenberg, analyzes the Bush administration's policy on Palestine. Her assessment is that, contrary to the common perception that the Bush administration was more even-handed than previous executives on the Palestine question, this was not the case. In fact, the Bush administration maintained previous U.S. policy by rejecting the Palestinian right to self-determination, to an independent state or to leaders of their own choosing. Furthermore, there is no evidence that U.S.-Israeli relations deteriorated to the extent of jeopardizing the close partnership between the two countries. What did happen, however, was that the rhetoric heated up at times and some remarks sounded openly hostile. Otherwise, the Bush administration continued to accept Israel as a strategic asset, cooperated closely with it on military and intelligence issues, and provided it with huge amounts of financial aid.

Bill Clinton, both as presidential candidate and as president, has been extremely pro-Israeli, writes Joe Stork. However, the main focus of U.S. strategy as Clinton entered the White House was the Gulf and how to maintain and advance American interests there. The 1990-91 war in the Gulf had resulted in the destruction of Iraq as a major military power and assured the U.S. its ability to set the political agenda there. With this major objective achieved, the Clinton administration moved to obtain a Palestinian (and other Arab)-Israeli settlement in order to avoid any problems there impacting negatively on the American position in the Gulf. However, Clinton's appointment of pro-Israelis to the White

House and the State Department was designed to accord Israel strong American support and to provide it with the most favorable outcome in the Palestinian-Israeli (and Arab-Israeli) negotiations. In fact, the pro-Israeli slant was so strong that the Israelis and the PLO worked out the outline of a peaceful settlement in Norway, i.e. away from American pressure and delaying tactics. Once that happened, Clinton embraced the agreement. However, there is no evidence that the Clinton administration has changed its pro-Israeli stance.

The final essay, by Ibrahim Abu-Lughod, studies the Question of Palestine, as reflected in American foreign policy. Abu-Lughod first provides a cursory survey of America's Palestine policy and then discusses the factors contributing to that policy. Writing in 1990, Abu-Lughod states that the United States has consistently subsumed the Palestine question under the Arab-Israeli issue, which it treats as the main issue. Furthermore, American policy makers have attempted to deconstruct the Question of Palestine, in order to treat it as a collectivity of minor issues related to "autonomy," refugees, resettlement, and so on. Also, American policy is oriented to the *states* in the Middle East, thus side-stepping the Palestinians. Abu-Lughod points out that the United States has consistently denied the Palestinians their right to self-determination and has refused to accept the PLO as the representative of the Palestinian people. Three main factors underlie the particulars of American policy on Palestine: first, hostility rooted in cultural, ethnic, and racial values; second, a negative orientation to Third World peoples, including Palestinians; and third, an antipathy to the Palestinian struggle as a movement of national liberation. In a 1994 update, Abu-Lughod argues that recent developments, including the Madrid Conference, the Oslo agreement, and the Palestinian-Israeli accords, demonstrate continuing American opposition to Palestinian self-determination.

To conclude, although many factors affect American policy making on Palestine, a few stand out as most important. Thus, the United States as a superpower has major strategic interests in the Middle East which it constantly defends. Although there is general agreement as to what constitutes American national interest in the region, the policies designed to advance those interests have been flawed by errors of perception and ideology. These misperceptions, which in good part derive from the American historical experience, have become the main issues militating against an equitable policy toward the Palestinians — and can be viewed as frustrating the very objectives of defending and advancing American interests in the Middle East.

Also, over the years, there has been a predominant view that American interests are better served through an Israeli state. Because supporters of Israel, especially American Zionists, have viewed the Israeli-Palestinian struggle as a zero-sum game, and because these supporters have been very well organized and politically powerful, American political leaders and decision makers have generally accepted their view of the Middle East, its peoples, and the main issues of the region. The consequence has been an American policy that has, especially since 1967, strongly favored Israel and provided it with enormous support.

Simultaneously, American policy makers have looked at and treated the Palestinians in nonpolitical and nonnationalist terms. They have often acted as if Palestinians were either nonexistent or politically insignificant, yet somehow troublesome! These views have also led American officials to divide up the Palestine question into smaller units which are then treated as primarily economic or humanitarian in nature — but not as political or national. Under such circumstances, American policy makers have generally (and especially during the long Cold War period) adopted the following stance: The main issue in the Middle East is a global conflict between the United States (West) and the Soviet Union (East); the less important regional issue is the Arab-Israeli conflict, only a smaller and less significant part of which is an Israeli-Palestinian conflict. Therefore, until recently, the main effort was focused on the support of strong, friendly states in the area, and on the resolution of the Arab-Israeli conflict through negotiations between Israel and individual Arab states. Any nonstate action, such as the Palestinian national struggle, was labeled "terrorism," and the Palestine Liberation Organization was denied any status as a representative of the Palestinians and was also labeled "terrorist."

In December 1987, the Palestinians on the West Bank and Gaza intensified their long fight for a homeland in an uprising (*intifada*) against Israeli rule. Then in December 1988, the PLO expressed more explicitly what it had been advocating for some fifteen years, namely the recognition of Israel, the acceptance of UN Security Council resolutions 242 and 338, and the renunciation of terrorism. The United States then initiated a "substantive dialogue" with the PLO. However, until it was suspended in June 1990, the "dialogue" turned out to be a general discussion about minor and mostly procedural issues.

When the American-Palestinian dialogue resumed in September 1993, it was because the situation on the ground had dictated a reorientation of American policy toward acceptance of the reality and significance of the Palestinians and toward the realization that a peaceful settlement would be in the best interest of the United States as well as regional and world peace. While the situation is in flux and negotiations continue, there is a strong temptation to exploit the weakness of the Palestinians at this juncture in order to block their objective of self-determination. If that happens, the seeds of future and further conflict will have been sown.

1

PALESTINE AND THE PALESTINIANS IN THE MIND OF AMERICA

Michael W. Suleiman

AMERICAN FOREIGN POLICY IS THE product of many forces. Domestic factors, including the press and media in general, public opinion, and interest group lobbying have at times been dismissed as having little or no impact on foreign policy decision-making in the United States. This school of thought suggests that the press in particular is no more than a reflection of the views of foreign policy decision makers. An opposing view is presented by those scholars who argue that the press plays the role of a fourth estate or branch of government, i.e. it contributes to the policy-making process on foreign affairs.[1] Similar dichotomous views are found about public opinion and pressure groups concerning their impact on foreign policy-making.[2] Additional scholarship on this issue, however, suggests that a third alternative or viewpoint is more descriptive of what actually happens in foreign policy-making in the United States. Thus, in the case of the press, it is argued that it is an autonomous institution which performs both "active" and "reflective" roles under different conditions. When there is consensus among the main foreign policy decision-makers on a particular policy, the press acts as a reflector of that policy. However, when there is disagreement among the foreign policy-making elites, the press performs as a participant, siding with one group against the other — primarily guided by the particular ideological bias of the specific newspaper involved. In other words, and in the case of the Middle East, the *New York Times* and the *Los Angeles Times*, for instance, will follow their traditional pro-Israeli bias in choosing the side to support. A more neutral newspaper, however, such as the *Christian Science Monitor*, is more likely to offer a balanced or less pro-Israeli view.[3]

It follows from the above that the way Americans view Palestine and Palestinians is a factor which needs to be considered in the discussion of American foreign policy on Palestine.

ORIGIN AND DEVELOPMENT OF AMERICAN VIEWS ON PALESTINE

Numerous factors may be cited in the development and formation of the image of Palestinians in the United States. These can be grouped into two major sources. One relates to Europe's relations with, and attitudes toward, Palestinians as part of Arabs/Muslims/Turks, since these views were then transferred to America with the European settlers. The other source is specifically American and especially relates to attitudes and orientations first articulated by the Puritans concerning their perception of their own role in the unfolding of God's plan for humankind. In particular, this perception is important because it specifically relates to Jews and the Holy Land, and ignores any reference to, or recognition of, Palestinians (whether Christian or Muslim).

The European view, inherited by Americans, was shaped by mostly hostile encounters with Middle East peoples beginning with the rise of Islam. Before the Crusades, however, European hostility toward Muslims was mixed with indifference and ignorance. Then the Crusades changed indifference into xenophobia and zealotry, and intensified the hostility by whipping up emotions against Islam and Muslims. An anti-Muslim ideology developed which painted a dark picture of Islam, Mohammed and Muslims in general, including the people of Palestine, most of whom were Muslim. Palestine, the Holy Land, was in the hands of non-Christian infidels and had to be "rescued". However, the carnage that accompanied the Crusaders' capture of Palestine certainly did *not* spare the non-Muslim population of Christians and Jews, as these suffered the same fate as that of the Muslim residents.[4]

The prevailing European Christian notion in the Middle Ages of Jews as alien people, to be shunned and persecuted changed radically after the Reformation and the establishment of Protestant churches and movements. As a result of the Reformation, the Bible was translated into the vernacular and people were encouraged to read it, which they did, often as the only worthwhile text. Emphasis on the Old Testament, the study of Hebrew as the language of the Bible, interest in Biblical prophesy and Messianism, and the new idea that the Bible was truly the word of God and that, therefore, the text should be taken literally, all combined to change Europe's ideas about Jews and the Holy Land. Whereas before, Palestine was viewed as a *Christian* holy land which had to be liberated from Islamic control, now Palestine was seen as the homeland of the Jews who were expected to convert to Christianity before their return to the Holy Land, in fulfillment of the divine plan. Later, it was suggested that Jewish conversion to Christianity need not take place until they get to Palestine but before the Second Coming of Christ. Eventually, the more popular view among fundamentalists and millenarians accepted the notion that Jewish conversion to Christianity would not take place until after the return of the Messiah.[5]

The changed focus and this new idea of Christian Zionism also meant that Palestine and its Palestinian-Arab inhabitants did not at all register on the consciousness of the Protestant, especially evangelical, churches and members. Palestine's history was also reduced to the history of the Jewish presence in Palestine. In particular, the Protestant Christians used the Bible, especially the New Testament, to recreate the physical setting in which Christ lived and preached. The Palestinian inhabitants were either viewed as non-existent, did not matter, or as the bands that despoiled the countryside of the Holy Land by their ignorance and backwardness. These views were also reflected in literature, travel accounts of Europeans, and in the popular imagination of Europeans generally, including influential politicians. Thus, it was Lord Shaftesbury who in 1839 suggested that Palestine was an empty land and formulated the slogan: "A country without a nation for a nation without a country."[6] As various European travelers, geographers, archaeologists, etc. visited palestine, they came with definite and well-developed pre-dispositions toward the people and the land. Consequently, the Palestinians were either viewed as part of the landscape or as lazy people unworthy of sympathy or support. By 1917, Lord Balfour could openly deny the existence of the Palestinian people by avoiding to refer to them as anything positive, merely calling them "the existing non-Jewish communities," when in fact they constituted over ninety percent of the population at the time.[7] Their "desires and prejudices" were unimportant and they were not to be consulted — Zionism was what mattered to the West.[8]

These and similar themes were propagated in most of the reports by Western merchants and travellers who visited the Middle East in the sixteenth and seventeenth centuries. Arabs were viewed as wild, cruel, savages or robbers, in greater or lesser degree. Also, once the *Arabian Nights* was translated into Western languages, in the eighteenth century, Arabs became identified with the book, and the traits and life-styles of the characters in these tales were automatically and repeatedly transferred to "the Arabs". To Westerners, the Arabs (including Palestinians) were now viewed as "very superstitious . . . indolent, excessively obstinate, submissive to authority, and sensual."[9]

While Americans inherited this image of Palestinians, Arabs and Muslims from Europe, they added other specifically American ingredients — influenced by distinctly American factors. These included a greater emphasis on the Bible as a literal representation of what happened in the Middle East.[10] Furthermore, the earliest European Christian settlers in America, i.e. the Puritans of New England, brought with them the Zionist idea of Jewish settlement in Palestine long before the notion was taken up by Jewish Zionists as a potential solution to Jewish persecution, especially in Europe. These Americans believed that their new country was part of a divine plan and that they were chosen to fulfill God's providence. As God's people, they were partners in a divine mission in which they had a duty to enlighten and save the world. They saw a definite similarity between their situation and that of the early Israelites, and viewed their country as "God's American Israel."[11] Despite the separation of church and state in the constitution, Christianity was the pervasive religious and moral force in the country. The new political system, democracy, was strongly associated with Christianity to produce a unique and great experiment — one that is worthy of emulation and export to the rest of the world.

Protestant Christianity, viewed as the hope of the world, was to be spread with missionary zeal. American missionaries began arriving in the Holy Land and the Levant generally early in the nineteenth century. Their encounter with Islam and Muslims was a big failure, as hardly any converts were won for Christ.

The missionaries then concentrated on converting Eastern Christians to the "true" Christian faith as practiced by American Protestants. Muslims as well as Christians in Palestine (and in the Middle East generally) were viewed as backward, corrupt, immoral — and in need of salvation.[12]

By the late nineteenth century, general American interest in the Holy Land became immense, being both reflected in, and reinforced by, travel accounts, stories in the popular press, missionary reports, seminars, Sunday school lectures and discussions, and outdoor models displaying the topography of Palestine. Unfortunately for the Palestinians, this tremendous interest was not at all focused on them as a people or, for that matter, on their country as they experienced it. Rather, the primary interest of Americans focused on Palestine's past, at the time of Christ — as this past was recorded in the Bible and told in Sunday school classes.[13] This image severely clashed with nineteenth century reality where Palestine was under Muslim Turkish control, mostly inhabited by Muslim and Christian Arabs and some Jews. The idyllic image was shattered by the reality of an economically impoverished country inhabited by a people of non-Western culture. Even Eastern Christians were alien unrecognizable and unacceptable Christians to American Protestants. While the condition of Jews in Palestine at that time was not much different from the rest of the population, they were often viewed more favorably, especially as the Messianic and millenarian element among Protestant evangelicals became stronger and more pronounced.[14]

To Americans of the last century, Palestine was a representation of "geopiety," i.e. a place of reverence, the land where Jesus was born and where Christianity began, a holy land, unlike any other on earth. In stark contrast with this was the view of Palestinians (both Muslims and Christians) who were seen as having contributed little to the development of the country. Beyond the image of a glorious past and an unpalatable reality soon emerged the vision of a future of hope and redemption with the expected Second Coming of Christ.[15]

Americans did not have to belong to Messianic sects or be practicing fundamentalist Christians to hold the above views of Palestine and the Palestinians. Until World War I, Protestantism was the dominant force in America and shaped almost all aspects of American life. It most certainly molded the American view of the Holy Land and its Palestinian inhabitants. Bible reading and Sunday school lectures and discussions had a major impact on Americans' views of Palestine. So much was this the case that there developed among the people a strong desire to visit, read or write about, or be a missionary to, the Holy Land. Some, anticipating the "End Times," went and settled in Palestine. For almost all of these, the orientation and emphasis was Jewish or Christian, i.e. neither Palestinian nor Muslim or Arab. It was more Christian than Jewish in that the sacredness of Palestine was attributable to Christ's birth and preachings there. The Jews came into the picture as part of the belief in fulfillment of prophecy which was believed to necessitate Jewish "return" to Palestine before the coming of the Messiah. According to this scenario, Palestinians were, and are, at best, unnecessary and can be ignored or their existence can be wished/willed away. At worst, the Palestinians might be viewed as a hindrance in the way of God's plan and the eventual redemption of humanity. Either way, they did not matter; Jews did, albeit for the specific purpose of eventual conversion to Christianity.

While American Protestants had a negative view of the native inhabitants of Palestine and the Levant in general, two main orientations may be distinguished concerning what could be done (and what the United States could and should do) to "help" these people. The fundamentalist, millenarian group, as already indicated, either completely ignored the Palestinian Arabs and acted as if they did not exist or else thought of them as an obstacle to the fulfillment of God's plan for humanity. The opinions of this group never changed and they continue to be inimical to Arabs/Muslims in general and to the Palestinian Arabs in particular.[16]

The other group, i.e. the missionaries, who sought to enlighten the world by spreading the good news about true Christianity, eventually proposed a different solution. Members of this group started out with very negative views about Islam and Muslims, as well as about the Eastern Christians who were generally seen as corrupt or as nominal Christians, or members of the "Romish" church.[17] However, the longer they stayed in the Middle East and interacted with the people there, the less hostile they became. When the Ottoman Empire was about to fall and Western powers were scheming to carve up pieces of it for themselves, many of the missionaries and their churches showed sympathy and support for the view that the Arabs should be consulted to determine their desires for independence or for which foreign country would be appointed as the Mandatory power under the League of Nations. While this view was consistent with Woodrow Wilson's celebrated Fourteen Points, it ran counter to the wishes of the Zionists who sought and eventually received Western (including American) support for the establishment of a Jewish homeland/state in Palestine. Furthermore, many of the descendants of these American missionaries who were born, raised and often educated in the Middle East, learned Arabic and later joined the U.S. foreign service. These Arabists, whose knowledge of Arabic and expertise on the Middle East were unrivaled among the foreign policy staff of the U.S. State Department, often clashed with pro-Zionist forces especially at the White House, as to what policies were in the best interest of the United States on the Palestine question.[18]

Apart from the Protestant evangelical view of the Holy Land and its inhabitants, other factors contributed to the American orientation toward, and relationship with, Palestine and the Palestinians. As already noted, early American settlers associated themselves with the ancient Hebrews and drew an analogy between the American Indian and the Arabs of Palestine. That analogy was also made in the nineteenth century by some of the American travelers to the Middle East. In the view of these writers (a view also internalized by their readers), American Indians and Palestinian Arabs were allegedly lazy, uncivilized, backward and inferior. Palestinians and American Indians also were supposedly similar in their dispensability and (eventual) demise — a convenient assumption as it would facilitate their replacement by "more important" people, performing a great, if not divine, mission.[19]

AMERICAN POLITICAL INVOLVEMENT IN PALESTINE

By the turn of the century, Americans generally saw Palestine as the Holy Land. As such, the Palestinian Arabs had by then been written and read *out* of the history of the area. For most Americans, what mattered was the history of Christ and Christianity in Palestine, even though that era ended several hundred years earlier. Any other group or people associated (or wanting to be associated) with that land had to somehow relate to the Protestant conception of the role the Holy Land was to play in God's providential design. In this scheme, there was no place for the Palestinian Arabs, not even the Christians among them. On the other hand, the Zionist political idea of a Jewish homeland in Palestine coincided with, and was reinforced by, the Christian Zionist idea of a Jewish "return" to Palestine as a prelude to the Second Coming of Christ.

Until World War I, there was very little political American involvement in Palestine or the Middle East in general. That world conflict was focused on the Middle East and the break-up of the Ottoman Empire. In the scramble for power, control, or possession of any part of the defeated Ottoman Empire, the Palestinians (and the Arabs in general) found themselves in a weak position. In the United States, President Woodrow Wilson's idealism and the call for self-determination of the peoples of the Middle East clashed with, and was opposed by, the Zionist movement which sought a Jewish homeland in Palestine. At the time, the United States had no major political interests to defend or advance in that region. Zionist pressure and the popular American notions which associated the Holy Land with the Jews were instrumental in suppressing the Arab demand for independence and/or for keeping the Zionists out of the region. Thus, President Wilson kept the contents of the King-Crane Commission report a secret until after political arrangements were made which incorporated the Balfour Declaration into the British Mandate for Palestine. In the end, Woodrow Wilson's pro-Zionist sentiment proved to be stronger than his devotion to the supposedly universal principle of self-determination which he had enunciated as part of his Fourteen Points.[20]

With World War I, the U.S. began, albeit slowly and cautiously, to be involved in Middle East politics. Consequently, more Americans were drawn to the area, as political officials, writers, tourists or journalists. There was also more reporting on the area. During the war, reporting about the Arab uprising against the Ottomans (and in alliance with Britain), their colorful campaigns and desert fighting provided Americans with the first extensive coverage of the people of the area. The reporting presented Arabs, especially the bedouin, in a fairly positive light. However, this transformation "dissolved in the wake of peace and they [Arabs] reappeared in the post-war media in the familiar visages of the exotic and alien Levantines."[21] This, of course, included Palestinian

Arabs. In order to present a somewhat more detailed picture, American views of Palestine and Palestinians as they emerged and developed since World War I will be discussed in terms of the press, literature, textbooks, television, movies, religious groups, and public opinion surveys.

AMERICAN LITERATURE

At least up to the beginning of the twentieth century, the development of American ideas on Palestine were not based on the Palestinian reality but rather on American views of themselves and a conception of an imagined or imaginary Holy Land. This concept was mostly metaphysical in the seventeenth century when New England Puritans thought of themselves as the New Israel. In the eighteenth century, the American conception of Palestine became rather metaphorical as the American scene witnessed major changes including greater denominationalism, separation of church and state, and the rise of romantic humanitarianism as a substitute for theology. In the nineteenth century, the millenarian view became most dominant. Throughout all these phases, however, there was hardly any change in the overall perception of Palestine and Palestinians in that Palestine was viewed as a Christian Holy Land or, later, as a place for the Jews to return to prior to the Second Coming of Christ. Palestinians were not part of the formula and were either not seen, ignored, or viewed as a nuisance and a hindrance.[22]

American literature, especially fiction, about the Middle East in the twentieth century, not unlike earlier writings, continued to portray Palestinians and Arabs in negative stereotypical terms. However, it was only after World War II and the violent encounter between the Palestinians/Arabs and the Israelis that Palestinians and Arabs generally became pervasive subjects in popular literature, i.e. adventure, romance, mystery, crime and espionage novels. Viewed as "the prototype for contemporary [American] fiction based on Middle Eastern themes," *Exodus* (1958), written by Leon Uris, propounds practically all the negative stereotypes about Palestinians in the United States.[23] To begin with, Palestinians are not mentioned but subsumed under the designation "Arab," in order to deny their existence as a people.[24] As "Arabs," they are presented as inherently violent, religiously fanatic, hopelessly backward, dirty and lazy. They belong to hate-mongering and discredited movements, like Arab nationalism, and are led by corrupt and self-serving leaders.[25] *Exodus* was extremely popular, and was then made into a successful movie. Even though the propaganda themes were obvious to any objective or knowledgeable reader or viewer, the American public evidently enjoyed reading the book and seeing the movie. This is clearly a case where the stereotypes presented in this work reflected and reinforced popular American views of Palestinians and Arabs.[26] These stereotypes have been used repeatedly, especially after the 1973 Arab-Israeli war, in a large number of fictional works and particularly in mysteries, novels and thrillers in which Palestinians and Arabs generally appear as villains.[27]

SCHOOL TEXTBOOKS

Studies of school textbooks by individual scholars and also by the Middle East Studies Association of North America (MESA), which is the professional organization of scholars on the Middle East, have clearly shown the inadequacy, ignorance and bias of authors and texts about Palestine and the Arab-Israeli conflict.[28] Among the distortions found in many of the textbooks are the following. Palestinians are not seen as the underdogs in their fight with Israel, since they are presented as part of a large, rich and powerful Arab world. Palestinians are presented as having caused their own refugee status by heeding the call of Arab leaders to leave Palestine, when the Israelis supposedly wanted them (and asked them) to stay. Palestinian backwardness, a perennially popular theme, is continually emphasized and contrasted with Israeli diligence and progressivism which has made the desert bloom. Finally, the Palestinian reaction to, and defense against, Zionist and Israeli attempts to take over Palestine are often presented as representing anti-Jewish sentiment in contrast with Zionism which is presented as a basically liberal philosophy.[29]

THE PRESS

American press coverage of the 1917 Balfour Declaration hardly mentioned the Palestinians, except as they were referred to in that declaration, namely as "existing non-Jewish communities in Palestine."[30] In the 1920s, the Palestinian struggle for independence was primarily reported negatively, i.e. as opposition to the Zionist attempt to convert Palestine into a Jewish homeland/state. As incoming Zionists were also presented as progressive and bent on development of the area, Palestinian opposition was viewed as an obstacle to progress and development.[31]

In the 1930s and 1940s, the American press ignored the King-Crane Commission report which clearly stated the Palestinian and Arab desires for independence and their opposition to Zionism. Furthermore,

> Despite the fact that there was considerable evidence of the extreme nationalistic drive behind the Zionist movement, which was its motivating force, American journals gave a good press to the Zionists' alleged goal of building a democratic commonwealth in Palestine. How this would be possible when the Arabs constituted two-thirds of the population and were opposed to Zionism, did not seem to be a relevant question to many of the magazines.[32]

The author concludes the above study by stating that the magazines he researched, especially the liberal *Nation* and *New Republic*, condemned imperialism as immoral when "practiced by the British in India, the Dutch in the East Indies, and the French in Indo-China, but . . . strangely insisted that Zionist colonialism in Palestine was moral."[33]

In the 1948-49 war over Palestine, the American press focused primarily on Israel. "When mentioned, the Palestinians were described as an anonymous, helpless mass of Arab refugees. They were portrayed as a problem and not as real individuals."[34] In another study of the same conflict, it was found that: "The Jews in Palestine were depicted in a humanitarian manner, as people struggling to build a flourishing life, while the Palestinians were dehumanized and denied identity and political recognition."[35]

In 1956, the Palestinians were hardly acknowledged except as "Arab refugees." In 1967, the Palestinian desire for a homeland was mentioned. However, they also began to be seen as terrorists. By 1973, in addition to the terrorist label, the American press began to present the Palestinians as a distinct entity, and the idea of a Palestinian homeland/state was broached. Once the Palestinians emerged as a significant political force, especially following the Rabat Arab Summit and Yasir Arafat's speech at the United Nations, greater coverage ensued.[36] During the 1982 Israeli invasion of Lebanon, where the fighting was primarily between Israel and the PLO, Israel received the most coverage by far.[37] However, for the first time, the Palestinians (not the Arabs as a whole) were presented as the underdog fighting the Israeli super-power of the region.[38] American press coverage of the *intifada* since 1987 improved as Israeli violence against Palestinians was presented more openly and more critically. Nevertheless, there has not been adequate coverage of the forces behind the uprising or of the Palestinian conditions under occupation. Also, the editorials have tended to follow U.S. official guidelines, failing to explain adequately the Palestinian political objective and the push for a peaceful settlement.[39]

TELEVISION AND MOVIES

There have been relatively few studies of television coverage of Palestine and the Palestinians. Most of these were done in the 1970s and may be divided into three categories, namely news, documentaries, and entertainment. Studies of the news show that, during that period, "the hub of Middle East coverage has been Israel. News from the region has largely been defined in terms of Israel's perils."[40] Also, Israel received the most favorable treatment. "Israel emerged as the 'good' guy while the PLO emerged as the 'bad' guy," although there was also some decrease in unfavorable coverage of the PLO in 1979.[41]

Documentaries about Palestine and the Palestinians have been either balanced or pro-Israeli. However, when they are balanced, television networks are pressured into refusing to air them or they arrange to have pro-Israeli commentary follow the presentation.[42]

Television entertainment shows have presented many episodes depicting Palestinians and Arabs as terrorists or as villains generally.[43]

American movies have overwhelmingly depicted Arabs in a very bad light. These also reflect badly upon Palestinians as an Arab people. However, movies about Palestine and the Arab-Israeli conflict have been among the worst where Palestinians are depicted as terrorists and are often compared to Nazis. Palestinians are presented "not as individuals within their own culture, but as a 20th-century scourge, rooted in a fossilized culture, indelibly molded by a violent mentality."[44] In these films, Palestinians are not made to speak for themselves; neither does anyone speak for them and for their aspirations for peace, security and self-determination.[45]

CHRISTIAN CHURCHES

While practically all Christian church groups in the United States recognize and support the right of Israel to exist as a sovereign state, there are differences among them in their attitudes toward specific aspects of Palestine and the Palestine-Israeli conflict. In general, however, all the major established church groups recognize the right of Palestinians to self-determination. Also, the National Council of Churches and the World Council of Churches, as well as several church groups, have argued for the inclusion of the PLO in peace negotiations.[46] On the other hand, fundamentalist, evangelical, millenarian church groups have generally avoided any reference to the Palestinians, speaking and behaving as if Palestinian Arabs (Christian and Muslim) do not exist or as if they are dispensable and disposable. These groups have been much politicized and have provided a great deal of support (moral and financial) to Israel. They are basically Christian Zionists who encourage Jewish emigration to the Holy Land in preparation for the Second Coming of Christ at which time Jews would either convert to Christianity or be condemned to hell. Such groups have looked upon Palestinian Arabs as a hindrance to the divine plan and should, therefore, leave or be dispossessed. Obviously, these groups do not countenance self-determination for Palestinians.[47]

PUBLIC OPINION

Many factors affect the formation of attitudes. Some of these have been discussed above and show that Palestinian Arabs are not a priority concern in the literature, school textbooks, the press, television or the movies. It should not be surprising, therefore, to discover that in answer to the question, "In the Middle East situation, are your sympathies more with Israel or more with the Arab nations?," most Americans state that their sympathies are more with Israel.[48] However, it is worthwhile to point out that the results represent an inflated positive view of Israel and a concomitant more negative view of Palestinians and Arabs because of polling bias or sloppy survey practices. One factor contributing to the bias, for instance, is the centrality of the Jewish question and Israel to American polling agencies. Also, until the last decade or so, there appeared to be almost total ignorance, or deliberate negligence, of the fate of Palestinian Arabs. When one looked up "Palestine" or "Arabs in Palestine" in the index of the typical public opinion reports, for instance, one was referred to "Jews: Colonization" or to "Israel."[49] As was the case in the media coverage, public opinion polls also typically ignored, until recently, the existence of Palestinians in their own country, or spoke of them only in relation to Jews or Israelis. Even though American public opinion was divided over the proposed partition of Palestine in 1948, Palestinians were practically dropped from public opinion polls in the U.S. until the mid-1960s. After the 1967 war, some polls asked Americans about their attitudes concerning Jerusalem and the return of occupied territories. In general, compared with questions dealing with Israel and its people, there have been far fewer questions about Palestinians and their concerns. Also, question-wording has been a problem, where the pollster has often provided information favorable to Israel and/or unfavorable to the Palestinians.[50] In response to such biasing tactics, an Arab-American group began to commission its own surveys about Palestine and the Palestinians, with fairly different results, i.e. ones showing somewhat greater sympathy for the Palestinians and for their desire and need for a homeland on the West Bank and Gaza.[51]

SUMMARY, CONCLUSIONS AND IMPLICATIONS

The above survey of American attitudes and orientations concerning Palestine and the Palestinians generally shows a negligence of, or antipathy toward, Palestinians. Such views have definite implications which also affect American foreign policy toward the region and its inhabitants.

1. Until recently, Palestinians did not register much on the consciousness of Americans. This is particularly true for evangelical Protestant Christians. But it is also true generally, because of the Biblical association of the land with Jews and Christians. Palestinian Arabs, including Christian Palestinians, have generally been viewed as non-existent or alien. For the millenarians, the Arab presence in Palestine interferes with God's plan or, at best, postpones the Second Coming of Christ.

2. From the perspective of the Americans, Palestinians are a people who have lived outside of history.[52] If they have any history at all, it is recorded in negative terms. They are the "non-Jews" in Palestine or, as presented in Biblical movies produced in the United States, they are the people who fight with the Jews, Zionists or Israelis and kill and maim their people. They are the outgroup, while the Jews, Zionists and Israelis are part of the ingroup. Even though Palestinians are the victims, i.e. the people who lost their homeland and are fighting to regain some part of their patrimony, they are the ones who are most often blamed for the conflict.[53]

3. American views of Palestine and the Palestinians are based less on the basis of the actual reality in Palestine and are more the product of American history, environment and culture. In this respect, Orientalist views and American Orientalism in particular have played a major role in shaping such views.[54]

4. Because these attitudes are so pervasive, writers on the subject, either deliberately or out of ignorance can and often do distort the Palestinian position and weaken or demolish it by attributing their actions to a faulty character or cultural trait when in reality it is based on a solid political foundation. For example, Palestinians supposedly oppose Israelis because they are opposed to

progress and to the West — when in fact they are fighting to defend themselves and their political rights. Also, Islam or Islamic revivalism did not cause the intifada, as some assert. The intifada is a response to continued Israeli occupation.[55]

5. Because of their alleged backwardness and opposition to progress, Palestinians are often not deemed worthy of self-determination.

6. Palestinians are not allowed to speak for themselves. Justifications for this position are found in their presumed backwardness, non-democratic practices or terrorism. Palestinian sources are often ignored or rejected as biased or irrational.[56] Often only "moderate" or evangelical Palestinians, other Arabs, or the Israelis are accepted as spokespeople for the Palestinians.[57]

7. These attitudes make it possible for American political agencies to restrict or infringe the political rights of Palestinian Americans or their supporters. This can take the form of FBI investigation/harassment of activists on the Palestine issue or of U.S. Department of Justice and Immigration and Naturalization Service (INS) restrictions on the entry and residence in the U.S. of Palestinians or Arabs. While these are not regular/continuing practices, their occasional use serves to intimidate large sectors of the community into silence or reduced activity.[58]

8. In the end, the most important element in pursuing specific policies on Palestine or any other region is the view of American leaders as to how best to advance American interests. However, the very process of arriving at what the national interest is on any issue or how best to achieve a specific objective is very much influenced by the attitudes of the political leadership, which is also influenced by the above factors. Also, the American political process itself makes the presentation of an objective or pro-Palestinian position (which by definition is not in the mainstream) a *controversial* issue and, therefore, a very costly political position for a political candidate or leader to espouse.[59]

Furthermore, while decision-makers claim that they are acting in the national interest rather than in response to domestic pressures, the nature and diversity of American interests in the region and the fact that some of the objectives are either incompatible or contradictory means that "domestic forces can serve to define priorities and to facilitate the determination of trade-offs."[60] This is exactly where pro-Israeli groups have been most successful. In particular, they have made Israel a high priority issue in American foreign policy.[61] This has been the result of several factors, including the effective role they have played in the American political system, the electoral process, pressure group tactics, and close personal contacts with political officials, especially the president and members of Congress. However, the pro-Israeli impact on American politics has, at the very least, been much enhanced by the development of popular attitudes and public opinion that are favorable toward Israel. Such attitudes and domestic factors "do seem to enter into consideration by defining boundaries beyond which it seems imprudent to step."[62] The end result is that pro-forma support for Israel and public concern for Israel's "security" are now expected from national political candidates and government officials. In other words, Israel's interests as expounded by its leaders and by pro-Israeli supporters in the United States define the way American politicians view the Palestine-Israeli conflict. Consequently, Palestine and the Palestinians are either ignored, considered unimportant, viewed as dispensable and disposable, or seen only in relation to Israel and Israelis. Palestinians, in other words, to the extent that they register on the consciousness of Americans, including American political leaders, do so only in negative terms, i.e. as non-Jews, non-Israelis, anti-Jewish, anti-Israeli, an impediment to Israeli development and progress or, in general, as the people who cause Israel problems.

Within the above framework, however, American political leaders have at times found it necessary to respond to Palestinian concerns, interests and needs, precisely because that was seen as the best way to advance American interests in the region. This has happened on at least three occasions. The first time was in response to the rise of the Palestinian guerrilla movement and the emergence of the PLO as a significant Palestinian political force in the Middle East in the 1960s and 1970s. The second time followed the 1982 Israeli invasion of Lebanon and the attendant publicity concerning the massacres at the Sabra and Shatilla refugee camps. Finally, the eruption and continued effectiveness of the Palestinian intifada against Israeli occupation also moved the American leadership to propose a comprehensive settlement, a situation later greatly impacted by the Gulf crisis of 1990-91.[63] In all of these situations, whenever the American leadership moved to propose a solution deemed unacceptable to the Israelis, the result was the mounting of major opposition by pro-Israeli supporters in the U.S., which in essence caused a breakdown of leadership consensus on the issue. Overall, such confrontations have ended with half-hearted actions, flip-flops on positions, and slow progress toward a comprehensive settlement. In other words, the strong pro-Israeli lobbying was greatly aided by generally positive public American attitudes toward Israel and Israelis. On the other hand, the weak Palestinian political position in the U.S. was hurt further by the absence of positive American views of Palestinians. This was indeed the case during the long period of negotiations which were initiated in Madrid in October 1991, primarily sponsored by the United States. That process seems to be moving toward a denouement in 1994 which envisages a comprehensive Middle East peace. In the event of an overall successful political settlement of the Palestine-Israeli conflict, some improvement in the American view of Palestinians is likely. However, such change will not occur quickly nor will it be radical in nature.[64]

NOTES

1. There is much scholarship on this issue. In particular, see Fred S. Siebert, Theodore Peterson, and Wilbur Schramm, *Four Theories of the Press* (Urbana: University of Illinois Press, 1956); Bernard C. Cohen, *The Press and Foreign Policy* (Princeton, NJ: Princeton University Press, 1963); William A. Dorman and Mansour Farhang, *The U.S. Press and Iran: Foreign Policy and the Journalism of Deference* (Berkeley: University of

California Press, 1987); Daniel Hallin *The "Uncensored War": The Media and Vietnam* (New York: Oxford University Press, 1986); and Montague Kern, Patricia Levering and Ralph Levering, *The Kennedy Crisis: The Press, the Presidency, and Foreign Policy* (Chapel Hill: University of North Carolina Press, 1983).

2. For a bibliography and a review of the literature on this issue, see Shanto Iyengar and Michael Suleiman, "Trends in Public Support for Egypt and Israel, 1956-1978," *American Politics Quarterly*, vol. 8, no. 1 (Jan. 1980), pp. 34-60.

3. See, in particular, Osman Mohammed Araby, "The Press and Foreign Policy: A Comparative Study of the Role of the Elite Press in U.S. Foreign Policies in the Middle East, the Sale of AWACS Arms Package to Saudi Arabia, the Deployment of U.S. Marines to Lebanon, and the U.S. Air Raid on Libya." Ph.D. diss., University of Minnesota, 1990. Many studies have documented the pro-Israeli bias of the *New York Times*, and the *Los Angeles Times*. For general accounts, see Joseph C. Goulden, *Fit to Print: A.M. Rosenthal and His Times* (Secaucus, NJ: Lyle Stuart, 1988); and Marshall Berges, *The Life and Times of Los Angeles: A Newspaper, a Family and a City* (New York: Atheneum, 1984).

4. On medieval European views of Arabs and Muslims, see Norman Daniel, *Islam and the West: The Making of an Image* (Edinburgh: The University Press, 1966); R.W. Southern, *Western Views of Islam in the Middle Ages* (Cambridge, MA: Harvard University Press, 1962); and Albert Hourani, *Islam in European Thought* (New York: Cambridge University Press, 1991).

5. For details, see Regina Sharif, *Non-Jewish Zionism: Its Roots in Western History* (London: Zed Press, 1983).

6. *Ibid.*, p. 42.

7. For a text of the Balfour Declaration, see Fred J. Khouri, *The Arab-Israeli Dilemma* (Syracuse, NY: Syracuse University Press, 1985), p. 526.

8. These were the views of Lord Balfour. See Sharif, *Non-Jewish Zionism*, p. 78.

9. Sari J. Nasir, *The Arabs and the English* (London: Longman, 1979). 2d ed., p. 65.

10. In the Bible, the Arabs are portrayed as nomadic bedouin, wily politicians, and "lurking" mercenaries. They were also seen as a continual threat to the Hebrews. See James A. Montgomery, *Arabia and the Bible* (Philadelphia, PA: University of Pennsylvania Press, 1934), pp. 27-36; and Terry Brooks Hammons, "'A Wild Ass of A Man': American Images of Arabs to 1948." Ph.D. diss., University of Oklahoma, 1978, pp. 20-22.

11. Fuad Sha'ban, *Islam and Arabs in Early American Thought: The Roots of Orientalism in America* (Durham, NC: The Acorn Press, 1991), p.16.

12. According to Helen Kearney, most missionary accounts blurred the distinction between Muslims and Christians in the area and viewed both negatively: "Both religious communities were believed to share moral and intellectual deficiencies which locked the Oriental races into a state of semi-barbarism." Helen McCready Kearney, "American Images of the Middle East, 1824-1924: A Century of Antipathy." Ph.D. diss., University of Rochester, 1976), p.176.

13. One of the most widely-read books on the Holy Land, which clearly illustrates these themes, was William M. Thomson, *The Land and the Book*, in three volumes (New York: Harper & Bros., 1880, 1882, 1886).

14. Sha'ban, *Islam and Arabs in Early American Thought*, pp. 161-66.

15. See Lester I. Vogel, *To See a Promised Land: Americans and the Holy Land in the Nineteenth Century* (University park, PA: Pennsylvania State University Press, 1993).

16. See Grace Halsell, *Prophecy and Politics* (Westport, CT: Lawrence Hill, 1986).

17. See the many publications of Henry Harris Jessup and, in particular, his *The Mohammedan Missionary Problem* (Philadelphia, PA: Presbyterian Board of Publications, 1879; and *The Setting of the Crescent and the Rising of the Cross* (Philadelphia, PA: The Westminster Press, 1898).

18. Zionist and pro-Israeli writers have actively sought to undermine the Arabists, especially because they did not always view American support for Israel as in the best interest of the United States. See, for instance, Robert D. Kaplan, *The Arabists: The Romance of an American Elite* (New York: The Free Press, 1993).

19. Sha'ban, *Islam and Arabs in Early American Thought*, pp. 189-90. See also George William Curtis, *Nile Notes of a Howadji* (New York: Harper, 1851).

20. Sharif, *Non-Jewish Zionism*, pp. 93-96.

21. Kearney, "American Images of the Middle East, 1824-1924," p. 372.

22. See Samuel H. Levine, "Changing Concepts of Palestine in American Literature to 1867." Ph.D. diss., New York University, 1953.

23. See Janice J. Terry, *Mistaken Identity: Arab Stereotypes in Popular Writing* (Washington, DC: American-Arab Affairs Council, 1985), p. 15.

24. Americans and others saw Palestinians as "Arab refugees" exactly because that was the way they were frequently referred to in the press and literature, not only in the U.S. but even in the Arab World as well. See G.H. Jansen, "Palestinian D.P.s: Victims of Terminological Inexactitude," *Sunday Times* (London), 10 Dec., 1969.

25. Terry, *Mistaken Identity*, pp. 15-33. See also, Aziz S. Sahwell, *Exodus: A Distortion of Truth* (New York: Arab Information Center, 1960).

26. As it turns out, Leon Uris was in fact commissioned to write a novel about Israel as a public relations attempt to improve American views of Israel. The result was *Exodus*. See Art Stevens, *The Persuasion Explosion* (Washington, DC: Acropolis Books, 1985), pp. 104-5.

27. See Reeva S. Simon, *The Middle East in Crime Fiction: Mysteries, Spy Novels and Thrillers from 1916 to the 1980s* (New York: Lilian Barber Press, 1989).

28. See William J. Griswold, *The Image of the Middle East in Secondary School Textbooks* (New York: Middle East Studies Association of North America, 1975). See also, Ayad Al-Qazzaz, "Images of the Arab in American Social Science Textbooks," in Baha Abu-Laban and Faith T. Zeadey, eds., *Arabs in America: Myths and Realities* (Wilmette, IL: Medina University Press International, 1975), pp. 113-32; and Glenn Perry, "Treatment of the Middle East in American High School Textbooks," *Journal of Palestine Studies*, vol. 4, no. 3 (Spring 1975), pp. 46-58.

29. See Elizabeth Barlow, ed., *Middle East Studies Association/Middle East Outreach Council Text Evaluation Project* (Ann Arbor, MI: Center for Middle Eastern and North African Studies, University of Michigan, 1991).

30. Lawrence R. Davidson, "Historical Ignorance and Popular Perception: The Case of U.S. Perceptions of Palestine, 1917." Paper presented at the Middle East Studies Association meeting, Research Triangle Park, North Carolina, 11-14 Nov. 1993. It is forthcoming in *Middle East Policy*, vol. 3, no. 2 (1994).

31. These are some of the findings from a lengthy study in progress on popular American perceptions of Palestine from 1917-1948 as reflected in the major American newspapers. These images will be compared and contrasted with the views of American foreign policy personnel. A book-length manuscript is being prepared by Lawrence R. Davidson. See also Issam Suleiman Mousa, *The Arab Image in the U.S. Press* (New York: Peter Lang, 1984).

32. Michael A. Dohse, "American Periodicals and the Palestine Triangle, April, 1936, to February, 1947." Ph.D. diss., Mississippi State University, 1966, p. 240. For the findings of the King-Crane Commission, see Harry N. Howard, *The King-Crane Commission* (Beirut: [Khayat], 1963).

33. Dohse, "American Periodicals and the Palestine Triangle," p. 250.

34. Beverly S. Marcus, "The Changing Image of the Palestinians in Three U.S. Publications: 1948-74." M.A. Thesis, University of Wisconsin, Madison, 1976, p. 135.

35. Abdelkarim A. Abuelkeshk, "A Portrayal of the Arab-Israeli Conflict in Three U.S. Journals of Opinion: 1948-82." Ph.D. diss., University of Wisconsin, Madison, 1985, p. 258.

36. Marcus, "Changing Image of the Palestinians," p. 138.

37. Badran Abdel-Rizz Badran, "Editorial Treatment of the Arab-Israeli Conflict in U.S. and European Newspapers: 1980-1982." Ph.D. diss., University of Massachusetts, 1984, p. 227.

38 Abuelkeshk, "Portrayal of the Arab-Israeli Conflict," p. 265.

39. Khalil Jahshan, "U.S. Media Treatment of the Palestinians Since the *Intifada*," *American-Arab Affairs*, no. 28 (Spring 1989), pp. 81-88.

40. William Adams and Phillip Heyl, "From Cairo to Kabul with the Networks, 1972-1980," in William C. Adams, ed., *Television Coverage of the Middle East* (Norwood, NJ: ABLEX Publishing Corporation, 1981), p. 12. See also, Montague Kern, *Television and Middle East Diplomacy: President Carter's Fall 1977 Peace Initiative* (Washington, DC: Center for Contemporary Arab Studies, Georgetown University, 1983).

41. Morad O. Asi, "Arabs, Israelis and U.S. Television Networks: A Content Analysis of How ABC, CBS, and NBC Reported the News between 1970-1979." Ph.D. diss., Ohio University, 1981, p. 142.

42. Jack G. Shaheen, *The TV Arab* (Bowling Green, OH: Bowling Green State University Popular Press, 1984). See also, "Public Television Faulted for Anti-Arab Bias," *ADC Times*, vol. 15, no. 2 (Feb. 1994), p. 11.

43. Shaheen, *TV Arab*.

44. Jack G. Shaheen, "Palestinians on the Silver Screen in the 1980s," *American-Arab Affairs*, no. 28 (Spring 1989), p. 77.

45. Ibid. See also, Laurence Michalak, *Cruel and Unusual: Negative Images of Arabs in American Popular Culture* (Washington, DC: ADC, 1988). 3d ed.

46. See Robin Madrid, ed., *Statements and Position Papers of Major American Organizations on Middle East Peace* (Washington, DC: Washington Middle East Associates, 1986).

47. See Ruth W. Mouly, *The Religious Right and Israel: The Politics of Armageddon* (Chicago: Midwest Research, 1985). See also, Ronald R. Stockton, "Christian Zionism: Prophecy and Public Opinion," *The Middle East Journal*, vol. 41, no. 2 (Spring 1987), pp. 234-53.

48. See Michael W. Suleiman, *The Arabs in the Mind of America* (Brattleboro, VT: Amana Books, 1988); Eytan Gilboa, *American Public Opinion and the Arab-Israeli Conflict* (Lexington, MA: D.C. Heath, 1987); and Richard H. Curtiss, *A Changing Image: American Perceptions of the Arab-Israeli Dispute* (Washington, DC: American Educational Trust, 1986). 2d ed.

49. See Hadley Cantril, ed., *Public Opinion, 1935-1946* (Princeton, NJ: Princeton University Press, 1951), pp. xvi, xlii; and George H. Gallup, *The Gallup Poll: Public Opinion, 1935-1971*, vol. 3 (New York: Random House, 1972), p. 2365.

50. This issue is discussed in Michael W. Suleiman, "American Public Support of Middle Eastern Countries, 1939-1979," in Michael C. Hudson and Ronald G. Wolfe, eds., *The American Mass Media and the Arabs* (Washington, DC: Center for Contemporary Arab Studies, Georgetown University, 1980), pp. 13-36.

51. See the 1982 survey by Decision/Making/Information and others conducted in 1985 by the Survey Research Center of the University of Michigan. The results of those surveys and others in Canada were published in Elia Zureik and Fouad Moughrabi, *Public Opinion and the Palestine Question* (New York: St. Martin's Press, 1987).

52. This observation applies to Arabs in general. See William E. Leuchtenburg, "The American Perception of the Arab World," in George N. Atiyeh, ed., *Arab and American Cultures* (Washington, DC: American Enterprise Institute for Public Policy Research, 1977), pp. 15-25.

53. See the various studies in Edward W. Said and Christopher Hitchens, eds., *Blaming the Victims: Spurious Scholarship and the Palestinian Question* (London: Verso, 1988).

54. See Edward W. Said, *Orientalism* (New York: Vintage Books, 1979); Edward W. Said, *Culture and Imperialism* (New York: Alfred A. Knopf, 1993); and Thierry Hentsch, *Imagining the Middle East* (Montreal, Canada: Black Rose Books, 1992).

55. See John L. Esposito, *The Islamic Threat: Myth or Reality?* (New York: Oxford University Press, 1992), p. 182.

56. See Elias H. Tuma, "The Palestinians in America," *The Link*, vol. 14, no. 3 (July/Aug. 1981), p. 4.

57. This is true for Palestinians in general as well as for Palestinians in the United States. For an account of the Palestine-Israeli conflict by an "acceptable" evangelical Palestinian, see Anis A. Shorrosh, *Jesus, Prophecy, and the Middle East* (Nashville, TN: Thomas Nelson Publishers, 1982). Other Arab Americans seen as "acceptable" spokesmen on the Palestine issue are Fouad Ajami and Kanan Makiya (pseud. Samir al-Khalil). Both of them are generally viewed by the Arab-American community as anti-Arab in their sentiment and writings on Arab nationalism and other Arab causes.

58. See Elaine Hagopian, "Minority Rights in a Nation-State: The Nixon Administration's Campaign Against Arab-Americans," *Journal of Palestine Studies*, vol. 5, nos. 1-2 (Autumn 1975/Winter 1976); pp. 97-114; U.S. Congress. House. Subcommittee on Criminal Justice of the Committee on the Judiciary. *Hearings on Ethnically Motivated Violence Against Arab-Americans* (Washington, DC: U.S. Government Printing Office, 1988); M.C. Bassiouni, *The Civil Rights of Arab-Americans* (Detroit, MI: AAUG, 1974); and Nabeel Abraham, "The Gulf Crisis and Anti-Arab Racism in America," in Cynthia Peters, ed., *Collateral Damage: The New World Order at Home and Abroad* (Boston: South End Press, 1992), pp. 255-78.

59. See James Zogby and Helen Hatab Samhan, *The Politics of Exclusion : A Report on Arab-Baiting in the 1986 Elections* (Washington, DC: Arab American Institute, 1987); and *The Deadly Silence: A Report on the 1988 Presidential Candidates and Where They Stand on the Middle East* (Washington, DC: Arab American Institute, 1988).

60. William B. Quandt, *Domestic Influences on U.S. Foreign Policy in the Middle East: The View from Washington* (Santa Monica, CA: The Rand Corporation, 1970), p. 23.

61. *Ibid.*, p. 23.

62. *Ibid.*, p. 17. See also William B. Quandt, *United States Policy in the Middle East: Constraints and Choices* (Santa Monica, CA: The Rand Corporation, 1970).

63. See Joseph Massad, "Palestinians and the Limits of Racialized Discourse," *Social Text*, vol. 11, no. 1 (1993), pp. 94-114.

64. Changes in public attitudes take place rather slowly and gradually. Dramatic events, such as the signing of a peace settlement, cannot produce lasting attitude changes by themselves. If good relations with a future Palestinian entity develop and are sustained for a long time (10-20 years, for instance) changes in attitude will follow. See M. Abravanel and B. Hughes, "The Relationship between Public Opinion and Governmental Foreign Policy: A Cross-national Study," in J. McGowan, ed., *Sage International Yearbook of Foreign Policy Studies*, vol. 4 (Beverly Hills, CA: Sage Publications, 1973); and K.W. Deutsch and R.L. Merritt, "Effects of Events on National and International Images," in H.C. Kelman, ed., *International Behavior* (New York: Holt, Rinehart & Winston, 1965), pp. 132-87.

2

ROOTS OF DENIAL: AMERICAN STAND ON PALESTINIAN SELF-DETERMINATION FROM THE BALFOUR DECLARATION TO WORLD WAR TWO

Hisham H. Ahmed

THEORETICAL SYNTHESIS

THE RECORD OF ORGANIZED political structure, dating back to the city-states of Mesopotamia, Greece and Rome, demonstrates that the right to self-determination has been asserted and cherished by all peoples. The concept of self-determination, although fraught with difficulties of definition, has always connoted the right of a people to establish a government of their own choice.[1] The underlying theme is that the established political structure in any given political entity has to be consented to by the people concerned. It follows that a country's establishment, or assistance in the establishment, of a regime in another country, while ignoring or suppressing the wants of the majority of the people, is a contravention of the latter's legal right to assert their national and territorial identity, to enjoy national independence, as well to choose its own representatives.[2] Insofar as impediments to the exercise of a people's right to self-determination represent a denial of the right of the people affected to express its will, they also constitute a violation of international consensus.[3]

The idea that a people should be governed by its own consent is one of the tenets of American political thought. This theme was elucidated most clearly by Thomas Jefferson in the Declaration of Independence:

> We hold these truths to be self-evident, that all men are created equal, that they are endowed by their Creator with certain inalienable Rights, that among these are Life, Liberty and the pursuit of Happiness. That to secure these rights, Governments are instituted among Men, deriving their just powers from the consent of the governed, that whenever any Form of Government becomes destructive of these ends, it is the Right of the People to alter or to abolish it, and to institute new Government, laying its foundation on such principles and organizing its powers in such form, as to them shall seem most likely to effect their Safety and Happiness.[4]

The brilliance of Jefferson's political thought was echoed more than a century later in the rhetoric of another statesman, Woodrow Wilson. With the advent of World War I, the principle of self-determination was popularized when championed by President Wilson as a war aim. As early as 27 May 1916 he proclaimed that "every people has a right to choose the sovereignty under which they shall live."[5] In his memorable "Peace Without Victory" address to the United States Senate on 22 January 1917, Wilson emphasized that "no peace can last, or ought to last, which does not recognize and accept the principle that governments derive all their just powers from the consent of the governed, and that no right anywhere exists to hand people about from sovereignty to sovereignty as if they were property."[6]

A more explicit reference to the idea of self-determination was made by President Wilson in his Fourteen Points, announced in a speech to the U.S. Senate on 8 January 1918. Point Five, concerning "colonial claims," provided that "the interests of the populations concerned must have equal weight with the equitable claims of the government whose title is to be determined." In Point Twelve, Wilson stated: "The other nationalities which are now under Turkish rule should be assured an undoubted security of life and an absolutely unmolested opportunity of autonomous development."[7]

In another speech, known as the Four Points address, delivered on 11 February 1918 before a joint session of the Senate and House of Representatives, President Wilson further clarified his position: "National aspirations must be respected; peoples may now be dominated and governed only by their own consent." He affirmed: "'Self-determination' is not a mere phrase. It is an imperative principle of action, which statesmen will henceforth ignore at their peril."[8] Wilson's utterances were repeated in speeches he made on 4 July 1918, Independence Day in the United States, [9] on 14 February 1919, while in attendance at the Paris Peace Conference,[10] and as late as 24 February 1920, after he returned from the conference.[11]

During World War II, the principle of self-determination was reaffirmed by Franklin D. Roosevelt and Winston Churchill in the Four Freedoms Declaration and in the Atlantic Charter. They asserted that international justice rests on the premise that nations should determine their internal affairs without outside aggression.[12] Furthermore, the United States was one of the major participants in drafting the Charter of the United Nations after World War II. In Article 1(2) of the UN Charter, the United States committed itself to promoting the development of friendly relations based upon respect for "the principle of equal rights and self-determination of peoples."[13]

The Wilsonian pronouncements constituted a general platform for a foreign policy that seemed to advocate the right of other peoples to self-determination. The popularization of the idea of self-determination by Wilson led experts on international law to engage in a vigorous debate regarding the meaning as well as the status of that principle.

One school of thought maintains that self-determination is a fundamental principle of international law, that it is the right of all peoples freely to exercise this principle and, further, that its denial will result in international instability, as well as in the impediment of the national will of the people concerned. Most legal scholars, jurists, text writers, and international bodies hold this view.[14]

Others have been less enthusiastic about considering self-determination as a recognized principle of international law,[15] and these views have greatly influenced American policy making toward other peoples. Ironically, despite the fact that the championing of the principle of self-determination has always been claimed by the United States, some American policy makers have led in a direction opposing its universal, consistent application.[16] Even on its own territory, while the American colonists were working to free themselves of British control, they simultaneously launched their unabashed conquest of the Native Americans, in the process endangering the latter's very existence.

Jefferson's ideas clashed on several occasions with the desire for expansion of American influence. The Monroe Doctrine of 1823, while claiming to rid Latin America of European interference, actually intended to consolidate U.S. interests in territories outside the American republic. Theodore Roosevelt's Corollary to the Monroe Doctrine, enunciated at the beginning of this century, was an even more concrete step toward instituting American involvement in Latin America.

The underlying motivation in both instances was the drive to advance the national strategic interests of the United States. That the peoples of the region aspired to govern themselves, free of outside intrusion, be it American or European, was of lesser concern to the power whose objective was to impose its hegemonic influence.

In light of what has been said, one can detect that U.S. motives for enunciating the principle of self-determination as the governing principle of international relations were not entirely genuine. Wilson intended to apply the principle only to peoples living in countries with whom the United States and its allies were in conflict: self-determination was applicable to Central Europe only.[17] With the consent of the United States, the principle was denied application in the case of peoples under British and French colonization.[18] Even Wilson himself admitted that there was partiality in the way self-determination was to be applied. He denied that it had a general application. Wilson seemed to be content as long as the application would serve colonial interests.[19] When the principle was denied to certain countries, Wilson did not express dismay.

Perhaps Wilson's following words best describe his stand on self-determination for peoples outside Europe: "Undeveloped peoples and peoples ready for recognition but not yet ready to assume the full responsibilities of statehood were to be given adequate guarantees of friendly protection, guidance, and assistance."[20] In actuality, this view was not different from British and French colonial pronouncements of the time, particularly regarding the placing of certain peoples under the guardianship of more "civilized" nations.

The U.S. involvement in Mexico during World War I cast further doubts on Wilson's sincerity in applying the principle of self-determination. "The same Woodrow Wilson who argued for the self-determination of peoples after World War I as one way to 'make the world safe for democracy,' also supported the Allied intervention against the Bolshevik revolution in 1919."[21]

The goal of the allied powers was to dissolve the territorial hegemony of the Austro-Hungarian, German, and Ottoman empires.[22] Furthermore, in enunciating his notion of self-determination, Wilson was concerned about presenting a countermeasure to the ideas of the Bolshevik Revolution of 1917 in Russia, for the Bolsheviks had been vigorously championing the right of self-determination for other peoples and nationalities.[23] The success of the Bolshevik Revolution in November 1917 added extra momentum to the already inspiring notion of self-determination. Wilson did not utter that principle before it was declared by the Russians in their internal and external relations.

Wilson's Secretary of State, Robert Lansing, maintained that the idea of self-determination was not Wilson's own creation.[24] Questioning the sincerity of American policy makers in advocating it, Lansing went so far as to argue that adherence to that principle by the United States was unlikely, illustrating his point by citing precedents from American history: "If the right of 'self-determination' were sound in principle and uniformly applicable in establishing political allegiance and territorial sovereignty, the endeavor of the Southern States to secede from the American Union in 1861 would have been wholly justifiable; and, conversely, the Northern States, in forcibly preventing secession and compelling the inhabitants of the States composing the Confederacy to remain under the authority of the Federal Government, we have perpetrated a great and indefensible wrong against the people of the South by depriving them of a right to which they were by nature entitled."[25]

Wilson's selectivity in the application of the principle of self-determination following World War I constituted the basis for subsequent U.S. actions. Although the United States did not join the League of Nations at the time of its establishment in June 1919, Wilson was one of the main authors of the League's Covenant. Significantly, no mention of the principle of self-determination appeared in that covenant. Furthermore, after the Treaty of Versailles, the United States did not object to the acquisition of territory from the enemies by the victorious powers.[26] Two decades later, although the Atlantic Charter of 1941 seemed to call for the respect of the right of each people to govern itself independently, its application was to be limited.[27] British colonies were prevented from exercising this right. The United States consented to the deliberate exclusion of peoples colonized by the British from enjoying what was claimed as a ruling principle in the conduct of international relations. Furthermore, despite the fact that the United States played a major role in the drafting of the United Nations Charter, it was not the United States but the Soviet Union that proposed to make it an express purpose of the United Nations "to develop friendly relations among nations based on respect for the principle of equal rights and self-determination of peoples."[28]

Later, concern over the "national strategic interests" of the United States once again clashed with the aspirations of another people, the Vietnamese. That the Vietnamese were entitled to choose their own representatives, to determine the style of government they desired, to preserve their national identity, and to protect the territorial integrity of their country was of secondary significance, if considered at all, in the minds of American foreign policy makers. Here it is important to note that the U.S. disregard for the right of the Vietnamese to exercise self-determination did not commence when the United States began its war in Vietnam. When Ho Chi Minh came to Versailles to advocate the right of his people to self-determination at the 1919 Peace Conference, "United States Marines, guarding President Wilson in his quarters, chased the would-be petitioner away, 'like a pest.'"[29]

The case of Native Americans, Mexico and Vietnam are not isolated incidents in the conduct of American foreign policy making. The record shows the United States as "voting against or abstaining on United Nations resolutions on self-determination . . . and refusing to participate in or recognize the jurisdiction of international organs concerned with self-determination."[30] "Self-determination has frequently been used by American policymakers to justify, rather than limit or prevent, intervention in other countries' affairs."[31] "Self-determination is acceptable [to the United States], provided it evolves toward a political system approximating the American model."[32]

In view of the above, it can be argued that the premise that it is impossible and unrealistic to apply the principle of self-determination in all circumstances and at all times is primarily advanced to serve as a justification for the lack of observance of that principle as a central guarantor of world stability and order. The following assessment of the role played by the United States in determining the fate of Palestine from World War I until 1947-48 will investigate the way in which American foreign policy makers have — in theory and in practice — applied the principle of self-determination to the Palestinian people.

WILSON BETWEEN IMAGE AND REALITY

The prolongation of conflict in the Middle East is mainly caused by Israel's denial of the right of the Palestinian people to exercise self-determination in their historic homeland. The United States, because of its unconditional political, moral, economic and military support of the Israeli occupation of Palestine, must bear heavy responsibility for the continuing state of unrest in the region.[33]

Before the defeat of the Ottomans during World War I, Palestine was part of their empire. Upon the dissolution of the Ottoman Empire in the war's aftermath, its territory was divided into spheres of influence among the victorious allied powers.

During the war, in 1916, Britain and France had secretly concluded the Sykes-Picot Agreement whereby, at the end of the war, Syria and Lebanon were to be put under French control and Transjordan and Iraq were to be placed under British domination. According to this secret agreement, Palestine was to be assigned an international status. The motivation for assigning an international status to Palestine became clear when, on 2 November 1917, British Foreign Secretary Arthur James Balfour, declared that "His Majesty's Government will use their best endeavors to facilitate the achievement [of] the establishment in Palestine of a national home for the Jewish people."[34] His statement, which was the product of Zionist efforts,[35] was issued in the form of a letter to the Zionist leader, Louis de Rothschild.

Before the American declaration of war in April 1917, the British were greatly concerned about the course of the war without U.S. participation.[36] The British saw in American Zionists a potentially influential force in convincing the American public to accept the idea of U.S. entry into the war. In 1916, the war situation for the Allies was especially disastrous. Losses on the western front were three men for every two German casualties and German submarines were inflicting heavy damages on allied shipping.[37]

This difficult situation was grasped by an Oxford-educated Armenian, James Malcolm, who had privileged contacts with high British officials. His special friendship with Sir Mark Sykes of the Foreign Office was of particular significance. Sir Mark informed him that the British were anxiously looking for U.S. intervention in the war. Malcolm replied: "You are going the wrong way about it. You can win sympathy of certain politically-minded Jews everywhere, and especially in the United States, in one way only and that is, by offering to try and secure Palestine for them."[38] For the Zionists, this was an opportune moment.

The British hoped that in promising the establishment of a national home for the Jews in Palestine, American Zionists would reward England by paving the way for the entry of the United States into the war. This was meant, among other things, to fill the vacuum resulting from Russia's withdrawal from the war.[39]

During World War I, American Zionists, represented by Wilson's Supreme Court Justice, Louis Brandeis, carefully monitored talks conducted in London between the British government and English Zionists. Combining his position as a U.S. Supreme Court justice with his influence in Zionist circles, Brandeis began to transmit Zionist political ideas from Washington to London. In May 1917, six months before the Balfour Declaration was issued, Brandeis transferred a document of Zionist thinking from London to the State Department in Washington. This document was accompanied by a brief note which read as follows: "I think you will be interested in enclosed formulation of the Zionist program by [Chaim] Weizmann and his associates and which we approve."[40] In summary, the document proposed that "Palestine is to be recognized as the Jewish National Home; Jews of all countries [are] to be accorded full liberty of immigration; Jews [are] to enjoy full national, political and civic rights according to their place of residence in Palestine; a Charter [is] to be granted to a Jewish Company for the development of Palestine; the Hebrew language [is] to be recognized as the official language of the Jewish Province."[41]

This document represented Brandeis' thinking on Palestine. Almost every provision denied the right of the indigenous people of Palestine to self-determination. The same language, with minor variations, was later incorporated into the Balfour Declaration and the British Mandate over Palestine.

When Balfour visited the United States in May 1917, he discussed his proposed declaration with Brandeis. The *New York Times* reported that Balfour conferred with Justice Brandeis on a Zionist republic in Palestine.[42] He also informed Wilson, in a private talk, of the existence of secret treaties between the Allies. It was Brandeis, however, who took the lead in discussing the matter of Palestine further with the president. On 15 May 1917, he cabled Lord Rothschild in London that he had had "satisfactory" talks with Balfour and with the President, but this news was "not for publication."[43]

Wilson was greatly influenced by Brandeis' Zionist ideas. "It was said that Brandeis was regarded by Wilson as the man to whom he owed his career."[44] Stressing the impact of Brandeis on Wilson's policy toward Palestine, Frank Edward Manuel wrote: "His [Wilson's] interest in Zionism was being slowly nurtured by Louis Brandeis, one of the men who stood closest to him in the early years of the administration and who became the key figure in future American intervention in Palestine."[45]

Brandeis' influence on the president was such that it allowed him to prevail upon Wilson to adopt Zionist ideas as part of his foreign policy. According to Reuben Fink, Wilson was not only sympathetic to Zionism, but he actually referred to himself as a Zionist in discussions with Brandeis, Felix Frankfurter, Judge Julian Mack, Rabbi Stephen Wise and other American Zionist leaders.[46]

In June 1917, Balfour asked Colonel Edward House, a Wilson confidante, for his views on a proposed declaration of sympathy with the Zionist program. Balfour stressed that the British War Cabinet was seriously concerned about the German attempt to capture the support of the Zionist movement.[47]

On 4 September 1917 House wrote Wilson that he had received the following cable from Lord Robert Cecil, the British minister of blockade (1916-1918): "We are being pressed here for a declaration of sympathy with the Zionist movement, and I should be very grateful if you felt able to ascertain unofficially if the President favors such a declaration." Three days later, House reminded Wilson of the Cecil message: "Have you made up your mind regarding what answer you will make to Cecil concerning Zionist Movement?" On 13 October 1917 Wilson replied to House's original note: "I find in my pocket the memorandum you gave me about the Zionist Movement. I am afraid I did not say to you that I concurred in the formula suggested from the other side. I do, and would be obliged if you would let them know it." House confirmed in writing to Wilson on 16 October, "I will let the British Government know that the formula they suggest as to the Zionist Movement meets with your approval."[48]

Weizmann was desirous of a simultaneous formal statement from the United States to accompany the Balfour Declaration at the time of its issuance. However, because the United States was not at war with Turkey, Wilson did not favor issuing a formal pronouncement.[49] Yet with his message to House, Wilson had given his unequivocal support to the issuance of the Balfour Declaration. Therefore, it was no surprise that the declaration was issued shortly after Wilson wrote his note to House.

Wilson probably was not fully aware of the precise version of the declaration he had supported, especially as it had been subjected to changes prior to its formal issuance. However, through his support, Wilson allowed the declaration to be promulgated as policy. When the Balfour Declaration was issued, celebrations were held in front of American consulates in the Soviet Union, Greece, Egypt, Australia and China. Bundles of telegrams reached Wilson thanking him for his efforts as if he were the one who had issued the declaration.[50]

Although the Balfour Declaration was issued by the British government, it was drafted primarily by Zionist figures in the American government in a coordinated effort between the United States and Britain. Although the declaration was not issued by the United States, Brandeis, through his influence on Wilson, paved the way for its issuance and later, its implementation. Colonel House, as has been seen above, also played a major role on the American side. An early collaborator of Theodor Herzl, Jacob de Haas, who became executive secretary of the Provisional Executive Committee for General Zionist Affairs, maintains that American Zionists were responsible for the final text of the declaration.[51]

By Lloyd George's own admission, the issuance of the Declaration was essentially a war measure, designed to thwart the efforts of the Central Powers to win the support of world Jewry and to enlist Jewish sympathies and financial power in support of the Entente.[52] Testifying before the Palestine Royal (Peel) Commission in 1937, Lloyd George was even more explicit as to the reasons which had motivated the British government to issue the Balfour Declaration. In the Peel Commission's report, Lloyd George is quoted as saying: "The Zionist leaders . . . gave us a definite promise that, if the Allies committed themselves to giving facilities for the establishment of a national home for the Jews in Palestine, they would do their best to rally Jewish sentiment and support throughout the world to the Allied cause. They kept their word."[53]

Samuel Landman, a London solicitor and legal adviser to the World Zionist Organization, described the Balfour Declaration as follows in his *Great Britain, The Jews and Palestine* (London, 1936): "The best and perhaps the only way . . . to induce the American President to come into the War was to secure the cooperation of Zionist Jews by promising them Palestine, and thus enlist and mobilize the hitherto unsuspectedly powerful forces of Zionist Jews in America and elsewhere in favor of the Allies on a *quid pro quo* contract basis."[54]

At the time of the declaration, 91 percent of the people in Palestine were Arabs and 9 percent were Jews, half of whom were recent arrivals.[55] For the Palestinian people, the Balfour Declaration constituted a flagrant denial of their right to exercise self-determination. They were not consulted, nor was their existence as a national unit considered. Even after the issuance of the Declaration, Wilson was informed of the detrimental consequences which would be suffered by the indigenous people of Palestine if their country were transformed into a homeland for the Jews. As will become evident, Wilson showed as much receptivity to Zionist ideas after the issuance of the Declaration as he had before.

On 27 August 1918 Rabbi Stephen Wise wrote a letter to Wilson, asking for the president's support of the Zionist program on the Jewish New Year, and on 31 August Wilson replied favorably.[56] Wilson reiterated his support of Zionist plans in a 13 January 1919 letter to Lord Rothschild in which he confirmed that he was "greatly interested in the development of the plans for Palestine." He went on to say: "I hope with all my heart, that they can be given satisfactory form and permanency."[57]

Contrary to Wilson's public utterances contained in his Point Twelve on 8 January 1918, and in his address on 4 July of the same year, Palestine was, in fact, handled precisely "upon the basis of the material interest" and "advantage" of other nations and was not based upon "the free acceptance of" or consultation with "the people immediately concerned." The fate of Palestine was determined in accordance with what the Allies had already planned, in contradiction to Wilson's publicly declared opposition to the implementation of the secret treaties arrived at during the war.

Palestinian self-determination could not be, to use the words of Wilson's Secretary of State Robert Lansing, "harmonized with Zionism, to which the President is practically committed."[58] When he arrived in Paris for the peace conference in December 1918, President Wilson started to sense the complexity of reconciling the application of the principle of self-determination in Palestine with the Zionist plans there. At one point in January 1919, he was specifically advised by his legal counselor, David Hunter Miller, that "the rule of self-determination would prevent the establishment of a Jewish state in Palestine."[59] On the other hand, the report of the intelligence section of the American delegation to the peace conference, on 21 January 1919, suggested, *inter alia*, that a separate Jewish state of Palestine be established, with Britain as the mandatory.[60] In practical terms, the Report reinforced the provisions of the Balfour Declaration, and provided a clear interpretation for the meaning of a "national home" for the Jews. It explicitly stated that the national home meant nothing less than the transformation of the *whole* of Palestine into a Jewish state.

On 27 February 1919 representatives of the Zionist movement presented their program for Palestine to the peace conference. On that day, Nahum Sokolov argued that the Jews desired a "national home" on the basis of the Balfour Declaration, and that the safeguarding of Jewish immigration required a mandatory system supervised by the British. His argument was a further reinforcement of the suggestion contained in the report of the intelligence section, submitted to the American delegation approximately one month earlier. As we shall see, this was to be precisely the outcome of all the political maneuvers before and after the conference.

Although Wilson was not in attendance at the conference in late February and early March, his reconfirmation of support for Zionist plans could not have been stronger. During a short visit to the United States, Wilson wrote his most important chapter in Zionist history. In Chicago on 2 March 1919, he met a delegation headed by Judge Julian Mack of the American Jewish Congress. After the meeting, the following statement was issued in Washington: "I am . . . persuaded that the Allied nations with the fullest concurrence of our own Government and people, are agreed that in Palestine shall be laid the foundations of a Jewish Commonwealth."[61] Frank Edward Manuel perceptively noted that "these words were far more of a commitment than the letter to Rabbi Stephen Wise on 31 August 1918; they outstripped the British promise in the Balfour Declaration. That amorphous word 'homeland' had become a Jewish Commonwealth."[62]

From the Arab side, the Allies consented to have the son of Sherif Hussein of Mecca, Emir Faisal, present the Arab position to the peace conference. While Emir Faisal presented the so-called Arab position, no representative from Palestine was allowed at the conference.

However, during the Paris Peace Conference debates on Palestine, the American commission received a steady flow of reports on the grave dangers of the Zionist policy from Otis Glazebrook, the U.S. consul in Jerusalem. His main argument was that the implementation of Zionist goals would lead to bloodshed in the area. "There is no difference of opinion," Glazebrook dispatched, "that the opposition of the Moslems and Christians to granting any exceptional privilege to the Jews in Palestine is real, intense and universal."[63] Further, Howard Bliss, President of the American University in Beirut, and William Linn Westermann, an aide to Wilson, on 13 February 1919 managed to convince Wilson to dispatch a commission to investigate the situation in the former Ottoman Empire. Westermann expressed many misgivings about Zionist policies, most important of which, according to him, was the fact that those policies were in conflict with the Wilsonian principles of self-determination. Zionist policies, he perceived, were, in contradiction to the wishes of the overwhelming majority of the people of Palestine, a violation of that vaunted principle.

After numerous delays, Wilson, under pressure from the American Peace Conference commissioners themselves, as well as from some of his aides, such as Westermann and Henry White, felt compelled to dispatch the investigatory commission, although without the participation of Britain and France. The Commission was composed of two prominent American figures, Henry C. King (president of Oberlin College in Ohio and a former religious director for the American Expeditionary Forces), and Charles Crane (a Chicago manufacturer of valves, vice-chairman of the Finance Committee in Wilson's 1912 campaign, and treasurer of the American Committee for Armenian and Syrian Relief). By 22 May 1919, the King-Crane Commission was prepared for action.[64] Its goal was to meet representative individuals and delegations, in order to ascertain, as far as possible, "the opinions and desires of the whole people" of Syria and Palestine.[65]

During its visit to Palestine in the period between 10 and 25 June 1919 the commission found that only the Jewish minority (one-tenth of the entire population) favored the establishment of a Jewish national home in Palestine. The majority of the inhabitants, both Muslims and Christians, opposed the usurpation of their homeland, and preferred either independence or unity with Greater Syria.[66]

On 12 June 1919 the commissioners sent a cablegram to President Wilson from Jaffa, which was then transmitted from Jerusalem on 20 June, in which they warned: "Here the older inhabitants, both Moslem and Christian, take a united and most hostile attitude toward any extensive Jewish immigration or toward any effort to establish Jewish sovereignty over them." The commissioners continued: "We doubt if any British Government or American official here believes that it is possible to carry out the Zionist program except through the support of a large army." The commissioners sent another cable on 12 July from Beirut in which they confirmed the desire of the indigenous people for complete independence. They reported that the wishes of the indigenous people had been expressed on 2 July by the democratically elected Syrian National Congress, composed of sixty-nine regularly elected representatives from Syria, Lebanon, and Palestine.[67]

On 28 August 1919 the King-Crane Commission presented its findings to the American delegation which remained in Paris after Wilson's departure on 28 June. The fifth recommendation of the report explicitly dealt with Palestinian self-determination. In its report, submitted to the Council of Four of the Paris Peace Conference, the King-Crane Commission demonstrated beyond doubt that the establishment of a Jewish national home in Palestine would constitute a flagrant violation of the right of the indigenous people to self-determination. The commission recommended in favor of the independence and unity of Syria. Regarding Zionist entanglement in Palestine, the Commission found that the Zionist program was incompatible with the principle of self-determination and Arab rights. The commissioners had examined the situation in Palestine thoroughly and comprehensively. They realized that increasing colonial immigration into Palestine would deprive the indigenous people of their right to self-determination and would destabilize the situation in the country and thus endanger Palestinian lives.[68]

In conducting its inquiry, the King-Crane Commission had relied on the Anglo-French Declaration of 9 November 1918 and the resolutions of the Council of Four of 30 January 1919, as well as on the oft-pronounced Wilsonian notion of self-determination. The first document explicitly provided for "the complete and definite freeing of the peoples so long oppressed by the Turks and the establishment of national governments and administrations deriving their authority from the initiative and the free choice of the native populations." The second provided "that the well-being and development" of the peoples involved formed "a sacred trust of civilization" and that "securities for the performance of this trust shall be embodied in the constitution of the League of Nations."[69]

SUPPRESSION OF THE KING-CRANE COMMISSION REPORT

Since Wilson had left Paris on 28 June 1919, and in order to communicate to the President the findings of the commission, Crane sent a cable from Paris which arrived at the White House on 1 September, in which he summarized the information the commissioners had gathered. In this cable, Crane emphatically recommended "that the extreme Zionist Program be seriously modified."[70]

On 25 September, Wilson fell ill; he suffered a massive stroke on 4 October which left him bed-ridden until April of the following year.[71] Three years later, in July 1922, Wilson's biographer, Ray Stannard Baker, asked the president to give him permission for the publication of the King-Crane Commission's report. Wilson gave his approval, noting that it was "a very timely moment for its publication." The "very timely moment" Wilson spoke of has confronted scholars with serious questions as to the reasons for his agreeing to the release of the King-Crane Commission report three years after its submission.

Was it the case that he had not understood the contents of the report at the time of its presentation by the commission? Did he, even for a moment, forget that he had given his consent to the Balfour Declaration, which the commission's report challenged and considered as a violation of his principle of self-determination? Or could it be the case that Wilson underwent feelings of guilt, knowing that the contents of the report had been suppressed for so long?

Perhaps the commission's report was not officially considered at the peace conference because it reflected only the American view on the issue. Earlier, Britain and France had refused to participate in the work of the commission. It follows that they would be equally unreceptive to the idea of having the report disclosed. Britain understood that had the findings of the report been made known, Zionist plans in Palestine would have been endangered. The French, for their part, desired to suppress the report because its findings concerning Syria, where the French had earlier colonial interests, were not favorable to their position. It appears that both Britain and France were able to convince the United States that keeping the report secret would be the least unfavorable option. The overriding concern for Britain, France and the United States was the maintaining of their alliance, which would have been compromised had their disagreements over the publication of the report been allowed to intensify.

While there could be uncertainty as to the reasons for concealing the King-Crane Commission report, there is little disagreement that certain important principles were violated in the process. Wilson's claimed attempt to release peoples from the domination of others was not implemented in the case of Palestine. Palestine was removed from the Ottoman Empire only to be handed over to the Zionists, with British and American orchestration.

Significant to the understanding of the complex process which led to the suppression of the King-Crane Commission report is an analysis of Wilson's role in contributing to the suppression of the facts about Palestine, both before the commission embarked on its task and after the submission of its report, as well as of his dedication to defending the provisions of the Balfour Declaration, even during his illness. In the discussion that follows, an attempt will be made to highlight the significance of the role played by Wilson's close Zionist associates in ensnaring the president to support their position before the facts about Palestine were disseminated, and the impact of this entrapment on the president after the facts were reported.

It seems that the likeliest scenario is that the president desired to divest himself of all responsibility and decouple himself from disclosing or suppressing the report, knowing that either undertaking would have great impact on the course of the history of the world. Let us assume for a moment, as many scholars do, that Wilson never read the full contents of the report. Let us also suppose that had he been familiar with the contents of the report, Wilson would have broken his promise to support the Balfour Declaration. The fundamental question that remains irreconcilable with these two assumptions is whether the president acted in accordance with the information he received from the commission while he was in Paris. In their cabled summaries of 20 June to Wilson and of 12 July to the American delegation to the peace conference, the commissioners clearly indicated that the implementation of the Zionist program would be a flagrant violation of the right of the Palestinian people to self-determination. Was it not Wilson's responsibility to act upon the information he received while in attendance at the peace conference? Is it not also the case that the president is responsible for properly channeling important information such as that contained in the commission's report?

Arriving at answers to these questions is indeed an arduous task. In order to dissipate the confusion surrounding this matter, it is important to examine the connection between first, Wilson's stand on Palestinian self-determination at the time he gave instructions to his commissioners as to the scope of their mission; second, Wilson's probable response to the commission's report had he been in full control of his office when the report was submitted; and third, Wilson's engagement in the complexities surrounding the political status of Palestine while he was ill.

By enumerating the developments that led to Wilson's accentuation of his stand in opposition to the Palestinian people's right to exercise self-determination, both *before* and *after* the commission's report was submitted, it is possible to deduce his probable reaction had he been in full command of his office at the time of the report's submission. As we shall see, Wilson played a leading role in concealing the facts about Palestine. From the outset, Wilson did not object to excluding consultation of the people of Palestine from "those regions" assigned to his commissioners. When on 3 May 1919, in a discussion between the Big Three, Lloyd George referred to the problems that would arise as a result of allocating the mandate for the Turkish provinces, Wilson agreed. He observed that Palestine might be especially difficult because of the Zionist question, on which the British, the United States, and he thought also the French, were "to some extent committed."[72]

A leading Zionist figure, Harvard law professor Felix Frankfurter, who was at the scene in Paris, worked diligently to ensure the incorporation of the provisions of the Balfour Declaration into the final settlement before the findings of the commission could be reported.[73] Frankfurter, a close associate of Justice Brandeis, and later a Supreme Court Justice himself, hastened to the office of Colonel House, complaining that the commission's undertaking was nothing more than a vehicle to "cheat Jewry of Palestine."[74] House did not concur in this assessment. He assured Frankfurter that the president would fully honor the terms of the Balfour Declaration. Frankfurter requested that House ensure that Palestine be excluded from the field of inquiry of the commission as its fate had already been decided in earlier treaties and particularly in the Balfour Declaration. He also cabled Brandeis and asked that he wire Crane to secure his cooperation in coordinating the study with Zionist representatives.[75]

On 14 May, Frankfurter sent a letter to Wilson asking for "a reassuring word, written or spoken, even though it be repetitive — that you are proposing to have the Balfour Declaration written into the Treaty of Peace, and that you are aiming to see that declaration translated into action before you leave Paris." Frankfurter, who had already written to Colonel House on 30 April, suggesting that Palestine be excluded from the scope of the inquiry as territory concerning which there was no dispute, had previously written to President Wilson on 8 May: "The controlling Jewish hope has been — and is — your approval of the Balfour Declaration and your sponsorship of the establishment of Palestine as the Jewish National Home." To Wilson, Frankfurter further noted: "The appointment of the Interallied Syrian [King-Crane] Commission and the assumed postponement for months, but particularly beyond the time of your stay here, of the disposition of Near Eastern questions, have brought the deepest disquietude to the representatives of the Jewry of the world."

Frankfurter thus attempted to sway the President from sending the commission to investigate the situation in Palestine. His primary goal was to get a renewed commitment from Wilson in support of the Balfour Declaration. Such a commitment, he thought, would provide a countermeasure for whatever conclusions the commission might transmit. The purpose of Frankfurter's writing to Wilson was to obstruct conveying the realities of Palestinian suffering to the conscience of the world. Through his lobbying efforts, Frankfurter wanted to prevent the dispatching of the King-Crane Commission to Palestine because he correctly anticipated that the commission would return with an accurate picture of Zionist exploitation and demoralization of Palestine.

On 13 May 1919 Wilson assured Frankfurter of his appreciation of "the importance and significance of the whole matter." Still, Frankfurter was not satisfied, particularly since Wilson's response had not been immediate. His language to Wilson became more explicit and strident: "Your note of acknowledgement to my letter of May 8th has occasioned almost despair to the Jewish representatives now assembled in Paris, who speak not only for the Jews of Europe but also for the American Jewish Congress, the democratic voice of three million American Jews."

On 16 May 1919 Wilson acquiesced. He reaffirmed his "adhesion to the Balfour Declaration." This assertion represented the third triumph to be scored by the Zionists since Wilson's letter to Rabbi Wise of 31 August 1918. Solidifying the victory, Frankfurter hastened to send Wilson's confirmation to Brandeis and to transmit all of the memoranda to the American delegation at the conference. Frankfurter's strategy was to "have the Balfour Declaration written into the Treaty of Peace," and to ensure that the declaration be "translated into action" before Wilson left Paris. His intent was to have Wilson's confirmation channeled as official United States policy.[76]

Although in his final instructions to King and Crane, Wilson informed them that their investigation was not bound by any preconference agreements, he nonetheless emphasized that the questions of Palestine and Mesopotamia were "virtually" closed by the powers.[77] By this statement, Wilson acceded to the Zionist demand put to him by Frankfurter and Brandeis. In essence, Wilson's full acquiescence to Zionist demands was institutionalized before the commission took off. Wilson's contradictory statements rendered the task of the commission ambiguously defined — even obsolete. How could the commission be sent to inquire about the aspirations of the indigenous peoples in the former Ottoman provinces, of which Palestine was a part, and at the same time be informed beforehand that the fate of Palestine had already been decided? Precisely this had been Frankfurter's request of Colonel House and of the president himself. As can be discerned, through subtleties of language conveyed to Wilson and by discreetly penetrating the decision-making apparatus, Frankfurter managed to institutionalize in American foreign policy in particular, and in American political thought in general, misinformation about Palestine as well as the denial of the right of the Palestinian people to self-determination.

To further consolidate his position, Frankfurter proposed, and in fact insisted, that Louis Brandeis go to Palestine in order to offset the presence as well as the findings of the King-Crane Commission.[78] Reacting to this plea, the Supreme Court justice sailed on 14 June 1919.[79] Upon his arrival in Paris, which coincided with the period in which the commission was investigating the situation in Palestine, Brandeis conferred with Wilson and others.[80] Coordination between Brandeis and Balfour took place in the latter's apartment in Paris prior to Brandeis' departure to Palestine. Balfour asked Brandeis how President Wilson could reconcile his principle of self-determination with the Zionist program. Brandeis replied that Wilson could do so by arguing that the Jewish condition was a world problem which transcended the desire of any "existing community."[81] In Brandeis Balfour had found the right conduit to get his ideas regarding Palestine across to Wilson.

In Palestine, Brandeis was confronted with the reality of the situation. He realized that the achievement of the Zionist program would entail massive problems. Even more determined than Frankfurter, he viewed none of these problems as insoluble.[82] While in Palestine, Brandeis took the first concrete step to neutralize the report of the King-Crane Commission even before it was compiled. Visiting the British military headquarters on the Mount of Olives in Jerusalem, Brandeis is reported to have told General Louis Bols, the chief administrator, that "ordinances of the military authorities should be submitted first to the Zionist Commission." The general replied: "For a government to do that would be to derogate its position. As a lawyer you realize this." But Brandeis proceeded to lay down the law as he saw it almost as if Palestine were under his jurisdiction. "It must be understood," he warned, "the British Government is committed to the support of the Zionist cause. Unless this is accepted as a guiding principle," he asserted, "I shall have to report it to the Foreign Office."[83]

Brandeis, who visited only Zionist colonies during his trip, managed to influence American foreign policy making toward Palestine to the extent that one could say that his above-mentioned remarks were adopted as America's policy toward Palestinian self-determination. Brandeis' predetermined conception carried far more weight than the carefully researched and responsibly deliberated report of the King-Crane Commission.[84] It is important to note here that Zionist propaganda tried to convey the image that the King-Crane Commission was one-sided and that its conclusions were predetermined. The fact of the matter though, as stated in the commission's report (recommendation 5[1]), was that before they embarked on their mission, the commissioners had held pro-Zionist views and that it was firsthand observation on the scene that convinced King and Crane to revise their views in favor of Palestinian self-determination. In reality, it was Brandeis and Frankfurter who persistently tried to predestine the fate of Palestine before the commission had even started its examination of the facts.[85] The findings of the King-Crane Commission were reconfirmed by a dispatch of 12 December 1919, sent to the White House by Glazebrook, the American consul in Jerusalem.[86]

It is believed that Wilson, who himself sent the commission to investigate the situation in the provinces of the former Ottoman Empire, never saw the report of the King-Crane Commission in its entirety, whether because of his failing health or due to Zionist pressure on him.[87] Although there is no conclusive evidence that Brandeis and Wilson thoroughly discussed the commission's report, it is difficult to refute the fact that the report was suppressed due to Zionist opposition.

Wilson did, in fact, come under tremendous pressures from American Zionist leaders, who, both before and after the commission's inquiry, were determined to sway the president from acting upon its findings. Even in February 1920, while he was ill, Wilson received a letter from Justice Brandeis in which the latter exerted pressure on the president to support the economic boundary lines of Palestine as outlined by the Zionists. In a formal communication to Lansing, Wilson instructed the American delegation in Paris "to do their utmost towards the fulfillment of Brandeis' request."[88] Wilson wrote: "All the great powers are committed to the Balfour Declaration, and I agree with Mr. Justice Brandeis regarding it as a solemn promise which we can in no circumstance afford to break or alter."[89]

In light of the above, it is unrealistic to imagine that, had Wilson read the King-Crane Commission report in its entirety at the time of its submission, he would have complied with its recommendations. Perhaps Wilson found it difficult to reconcile the King-Crane Commission's presentation of facts with his earlier commitments to the Zionist program. In this context, one should recall Wilson's earlier assurances given to the Zionists in support of their colonial program, particularly his statement of 2 March 1919, that "in Palestine shall be laid the foundations of a Jewish Commonwealth." Wilson's reconfirmation of his dedication to the colonization of Palestine, even while he was convalescing, leaves little doubt in projecting his probable course of action, had he become familiar with the details of the King-Crane Commission report at the time of its submission. His failure to act upon the recommendation he received in the King-Crane telegram while he was in Paris is an additional element in substantiation of this hypothesis.

The King-Crane Commission report brought out the details of the colonial interests of Britain, France, and the Zionist movement in the provinces of the former Ottoman Empire; contradicted Zionist allegations, namely, that Palestine was uninhabited and that the Zionists would be developers of the area; and provided firsthand information about the demographic and political structure in Palestine. In fact, had the report been immediately published, it would have proven Wilson's duplicitous stand since he, on the one hand, claimed that his entry into World War I was motivated by his commitment "to keep the world safe for democracy" on the basis of the right of peoples to national self-determination and, on the other hand, unceasingly supported the implementation of the Zionist goal that "in Palestine shall be laid the foundations of a Jewish Commonwealth." Given all this it would be naive to rule out the possibility that Wilson actually was familiar with the report but chose not to act upon it. In so choosing, Wilson demonstrated consistency: he reacted in the same manner upon receiving advice from his legal counselor, David Hunter Miller in January 1919 that "the rule of self-determination would prevent the establishment of a Jewish state in Palestine"; upon receiving Glazebrook's information from Jerusalem during the deliberations of the peace conference in February 1919; as well as upon receiving the King-Crane telegram in June of the same year. Although one might not be able to confirm the specific date or manner in which Wilson took cognizance of the report, one would be safe in concluding that Wilson would not have consented to the publication of such a document in July 1922 before having read it.

Wilson might have felt seriously constrained not only to ignore the right of the people of Palestine to self-determination during his presidency, but also to suppress the King-Crane Commission report while he was in office. The fundamental question then remains: Why did Wilson finally come to authorize the publication of the report? To imagine that Wilson at last became concerned about the rights of the Palestinian people is delusory, particularly since his action came too late.

Consonant with what has already been stated, it is quite likely that Wilson envisaged publishing the report after he left office. Perhaps he allowed its publication in 1922 as evidence of the sincerity of his idealistic pronouncements. Possibly he hoped to assuage his conscience somewhat by letting the facts be known. Or, most likely, he may have realized that historians studying his statesmanship during the period of World War I and its aftermath would one day embark on analyzing the complex factors leading to the suppression of the King-Crane report, and by granting of permission for its publication, even belatedly, his responsibility would be evaluated less harshly.

The publication of the report, just several weeks after the House of Representatives Committee on Foreign Affairs had concluded a four-day hearing (18-22 April 1922) on a congressional resolution pertaining to the fate of Palestine, makes us skeptical of the possibility that Wilson was acting out of good will toward the Palestinian people. Because of the timing of its publication, the report contributed nothing to providing with the sorely needed information about Palestine and its people, thus leaving the floor open to Zionist supporters to bring up Wilson's statements in which he committed himself to the Zionist colonization of Palestine.

Could it then be presumed that Wilson's soul-searching about violating the right of the Palestinian people to self-determination led him to grant permission for the publication of the King-Crane Commission report? Perhaps! If this assumption is held to be true, however, then one would expect, recognizing Wilson's perspicacity and the excellence of his rhetorical skills, that he would have found some way to express support for Palestinian self-determination without ambiguity. Up until his death in 1924, he never did such a thing, neither before the publication of the report nor after. Even upon his granting permission to disclose the report, it was published only *unofficially* by the State Department.

Wilson's pronouncements in support of Zionist colonialism, not the contents of the King-Crane Commission report, constituted the tenets upon which subsequent U.S. policies were formulated and advanced.

U.S. LEGITIMATION OF THE BRITISH MANDATE

On 21 September 1918, Secretary of State Robert Lansing had prepared a memorandum for the guidance of the American Peace Commission to the Paris Peace Conference in which he suggested, *inter alia*, that Palestine be put under an autonomous authority, international protectorate, or a mandatory power.[90]

On 24 April 1920, the San Remo Agreement was concluded by the Supreme Council of the European Allies, whereby Syria, Palestine, and Mesopotamia were abandoned by Turkey. The San Remo Conference assigned to France the mandate for Syria and Lebanon, and to Britain that for Palestine and Mesopotamia.[91]

The United States had instructed Robert Underwood Johnson, the American ambassador in Rome, to serve as an observer at the San Remo conference. When Johnson was asked by the European ministers what his function was, his reply was that it was only reportorial. In reality, however, his presence gave at least tacit American consent to the resolutions of the conference, as he raised no objections.

The actual disintegrating mechanism of the Turkish Empire was prescribed some months later by the Treaty of Sèvres. Article 95 of the treaty gave force to an earlier request made of the allied powers by Wilson, under pressure from Brandeis, as we have seen, to put into effect the Zionist scheme for the colonization of Palestine as spelled out in the Balfour Declaration.[92] Wilson's silence on the provisions of the treaty signified his acceptance of the allied powers' actions. Britain, France, Italy, and Japan thus proceeded to sign the Treaty of Sèvres with Turkey on 10 August 1920.[93]

On 24 July 1922, in fulfillment of Article 95 of the Treaty of Sèvres, and in compliance with Article 22 of the Covenant of the League of Nations, Britain submitted a draft mandate for Palestine to the Council of the League of Nations. A text was agreed upon and confirmed by the council on 29 September 1923.[94]

Although the British government was the executor of a colonial plan in Palestine after World War I, the Zionist movement in the United States was its legislator. Zionist goals, adopted in the provisions of the mandate, had been formulated primarily by Zionist personalities in the United States. In the discussion between Brandeis and Balfour held in the latter's apartment in June 1919, Brandeis, who was tenacious in his denial of Palestinian rights, made three proposals for the projected mandate through which he envisaged the realization of the Zionist program. The first was that Palestine should be *the* Jewish homeland and not merely that there be *a* Jewish homeland in Palestine. This meant that the whole of Palestine was to be transformed into a Jewish state and that all Palestinians already living there were to make room for Zionist colonists. The second called for the securing of an enlarged territorial base, one which would allow control of the water resources in the north of Palestine to serve colonial economic purposes.[95] Third, Brandeis insisted on full-scale colonization of Palestinian land and natural resources.

The mandatory's commitment to the protection, sustainment, and preservation of Jewish political, economic and development rights, while denying those same rights to the indigenous people of Palestine, was a policy engineered in the highest political circles of the United States and Britain: The content of the June 1919 discussion between Brandeis and Balfour was later embodied in the British Mandate over Palestine. American encouragement of Brandeis' proposal was explicit in a January 1922 correspondence from U.S. Secretary of State Charles E. Hughes to Balfour in which he maintained that the United States interpreted the idea of a homeland for the Jews to mean the establishment of a Jewish state in Palestine.[96]

The people of Palestine strongly resisted the imposition of the British Mandate over them. Orchestrated by influential American figures, the provisions of the mandate contradicted the policy enunciated earlier during World War I by the Allies, namely, that each people should be governed by its own consent.

CONGRESS ENDORSES THE ZIONIST COLONIZATION

At the urging of the Zionists, on 12 April 1922, Henry Cabot Lodge, chairman of the Senate Foreign Relations Committee, introduced a resolution into the Senate essentially reaffirming the Balfour Declaration.[97] On 4 April, Representative Hamilton Fish, Jr. had introduced a similar resolution in the House of Representatives, favoring the establishment in Palestine of a national home for the Jewish people and advocating the adoption of the Zionist program by the United States. On 31 May, the House Committee on Foreign Affairs, to whom that resolution was referred, recommended that the resolution pass.[98] The committee reported its understanding of the concept of the Jewish homeland to mean the eventual creation of a Jewish state.[99] Despite the strong tendencies toward isolationism in the United States during this period, the House of Representatives passed the Fish resolution on 30 June 1922, embodying the terms of the Balfour Declaration.[100] For the British this was a clear indication of America's legitimation of the mandate. For the Zionists this was an important milestone in advancing the program for the colonization of Palestine.

It is not entirely accurate to assume that the members of the House committee were not aware of the dire consequences that would be suffered by the Palestinian people as a result of the adoption of the resolution. They were informed that conflict would erupt upon the usurpation of Palestine. However, they conspired to deal with the Palestinians in the same way as their forebears had dealt with the Native Americans: by absorbing them, exterminating them, or confining them to reservations.

In a four-day hearing, from 18 to 21 April 1922, Congress had ample opportunity to be informed of the implications of passing Fish's resolution.[101] Albert B. Rossdale, a representative from New York, recognized the intricacy of the issue, as evidenced in his statements before the hearing on 19 April: "The *reestablishment* of a *Jewish Palestine* is not without difficulties and recently there has been some opposition by Arabs against the Jewish colonists." Nonetheless, Rossdale extolled a rationale for the Zionist colonization of Palestine:

> The resettling of Palestine has created a situation somewhat akin to that of the American colonist in his *struggle* with the American Indian. For like the early American settler on this continent, the Jewish colonist frequently *has to till the soil with a rifle in one hand and a hoe in the other*. The nomadic Arab raiders, on a smaller scale are fighting the civilization of the Jewish settler as the Indian fought the American settler on this continent in the early days.[102]

Conscious of the harm the Zionist program would inflict on the Palestinian people, Professor Edward Bliss Reed[103] was one of the few who testified in ardent opposition to the resolution: "I am . . . trying to do all I can to keep my country from making what I think would be a bad blunder." Reed explained:

> "The Balfour Declaration . . . struck these people like a bolt from the blue. President Wilson had promised all people in subjection to Turkish rule an 'absolutely unmolested opportunity for autonomous development.' . . . If that phrase means anything at all, it means that people in a country such as Palestine should have an unmolested chance to develop themselves. They really believed that opportunity would be theirs; they believed that this was true; and then suddenly came the Balfour declaration."[104]

Professor Reed warned the members of the House Committee on Foreign Affairs that the Balfour Declaration was illegal:

> Now, here is a country of 700,000 people and the Zionists compose just about one-tenth of the country, and here is a declaration that is going to change absolutely the whole status of the people of that country. Have they one word to say about it? Are they consulted about it in any way? Are they asked about it, or do they know anything about it? They did not even know it was coming, or from where it was coming. Where does it come from? It comes from the Zionist offices in America as well as in England.

> One thing is certain, it [the Balfour Declaration] was submitted to President Wilson through Justice Brandeis, and it was submitted to the Zionist organization in New York. However, one other thing is certain, it was not submitted to the people of the country that it affects. If you believe that the people of that country had any right at all in their own country, or were entitled to any consideration at all in its disposition, it is certain that you can have nothing to do with Mr. Fish's resolution.

Reed then put the committee members to the fundamental test:

> Do you think that the United States has not the right to control immigration into the United States . . . ? Have the people of Palestine no right to control immigration? Do you mean to say that if immigration should come . . . with the avowed purpose of establishing a majority so as to rule the country, they cannot say, "no"? These people have been pillaged by the Turks and Germans; they have been reduced to poverty and should we now say that they shall be kept down and deprived of their rights in their country in order to build up this Jewish State? I do not think that is the way to build a State.

After that admonishment, Reed cautioned:

> If we pass this resolution it is a pressure on England to hurry up the mandate. The mandate is much worse than this. . . . The whole Palestinian constitution is drafted with the aid and consent of the Zionists. . . . This resolution will be used as America's approval, as a powerful weapon abroad to say that America believes in this proposition.[105]

The following case illustrates the belief that, had the contents of the King-Crane Commission report been made public, Congress might have been better informed on this important issue. On Thursday, 20 April 1922, Stephen J. Porter, chairman of the Committee on Foreign Affairs in the House of Representatives, questioned Abraham Goldberg, a representative of the Zionist Organization of America: "Do the Arabs oppose immigration?" Goldberg replied: "The Arabs, if you speak of them, are often inarticulate. There are a few agitators who speak in their name." The chairman then asked: "Some of the Arab people. Are they opposed to the immigration of the Jews?" Goldberg then answered: "Some of them are opposed, but not all of them. The trouble is that you deal here with a people which is inarticulate."[106]

Defying the allegations made by Goldberg was Reed's testimony concerning the King-Crane Commission and its report. In the course of the hearing, Reed informed Congress of this commission. He had been in Palestine at the time of King and Crane's arrival there. He testified: "I was there engaged in relief work . . . I leaned over backwards to give the Zionists a chance, because I believed in Zionism when I went there; and it is only because I saw what they were doing that I am fighting as hard as I can now."

Astonished at Goldberg's remarks, Reed informed the committee that King and Crane

> went up and down that country, and what has happened to their report? That report has absolutely disappeared. I wrote down to the State Department, asking them if I could not get that report. That was before Mr. Wilson went out. I was told that there was no chance of seeking that report, and that it probably never would come out . . . I applied for that report and was told that there was no probability or possibility of the Government publishing it. Now, it is very strange that President Weizmann . . . could see what I cannot see. He can see that report. I, an American citizen and tax payer cannot know what is going on there, but President Weizmann can. . . .
>
> I ask you, before you do anything, before you indorse the Zionist organization, before you get into this mandate business, that you find out what those two Americans of standing think about the situation in Palestine . . . If President Weizmann can find out, I do not see why a committee from the American Congress cannot find out.[107]

Professor Reed made a passionate appeal to the members of the committee: "That is why I think this Balfour declaration is very un-American and that is why I think we want to go very slowly before we underwrite it." He posed the question: "Why in the world should we depart from our American principle of giving to people of a country the right to be heard, the right to a representative government; Why should we do this? . . . Why should we do this to that country?"[108]

In the concluding part of the hearing, Professor Reed strongly warned against the adoption of that Zionist Resolution: "I wish to say that if you pass this . . . resolution you indorse the Balfour declaration, because that is what this resolution virtually is. . . . If you indorse the Balfour declaration, you are caught absolutely in the mandate. . . . What I want to warn you against is getting caught by the mandate in what I consider an impasse. It will bring disaster on this country of Palestine. . . . I want to prevent my country from doing something that will bring it untold trouble."[109]

After all the insights provided by Reed, one would not expect Congress to have passed the resolution. However, in addition to the fact that some members of Congress showed ignorance and lack of awareness regarding Palestine and the intricacy of the situation, the Congress of 1922, as is the case at the time of this writing, was subjected to Zionist pressures, a campaign of misinformation about Palestine. Congress preferred to adopt Goldberg's racist views on Palestine and its people, ignoring the well-substantiated position of Professor Reed. The House passed Fish's resolution on 30 June 1922. Later, on 11 September 1922, Joint Congressional Resolution No. 322, expressing sympathy for the idea of the creation of a Jewish homeland in Palestine, was also adopted and signed by President Warren Harding.[110]

Like the Balfour Declaration, these resolutions were statements of policy which were to have serious repercussions. The United States was on its way to continuous involvement in the question of Palestine.

THE UNITED STATES COMPETES WITH BRITAIN

The Anglo-American Convention of 3 December 1924 could be considered the first legal, official endorsement by the United States of all the provisions embodied in the British Mandate over Palestine.[111] The United States, not being a member of the League of Nations, did not have legal control or official participation in the administration of Palestine before signing this convention. Its main concern in signing was to compensate for its absence from the League of Nations: to establish some form of political legalism whereby the United States would be able to safeguard its colonial interests in Palestine on an equal footing with Britain. The United States sought to participate in, and later dominate, the determination of the political status of Palestine. In addition to the inclusion in this document of all the articles of the British Mandate, several articles were added with the intent of legitimizing the U.S. role. Article 7 of the convention conditioned any change in the status of Palestine by the British upon U.S. assent. Through this treaty, the United States committed itself, as did Britain in the Balfour Declaration, to deprive the people of Palestine of their right to self-determination. The Anglo-American Convention emphasized the protection of the rights of American missionaries in Palestine, whereas the rights of the Palestinians were denied. No mention was even made as to the assent required from the Palestinian people themselves as to any possible change in the politico-legal status of their country. This convention laid upon the United States a further share of the responsibility for the denial of Palestinian self-determination, a responsibility which heretofore had been borne primarily by the British. As the political and military status of the United States began to rise to preeminence in the global arena, the American government began to play a more and more substantial role in the denial of Palestinian rights.

In the 1940s, the United States cited the 1924 Anglo-American Convention in an attempt to legalize its involvement in policies pertaining to the future of the demographic structure of Palestine.[112] Zionist plans continued to determine American foreign policy toward Palestine. Between 1943 and 1945, in reaction to the Zionist Biltmore Program of May 1942, Congress responded with a series of resolutions and declarations in favor of unrestricted immigration and the establishment of a Jewish state in Palestine.[113] In October 1944, in a message to a convention of American Zionists, President Franklin D. Roosevelt reiterated his party's commitment to the achievement of Zionist goals.[114] Roosevelt's statement of support of those goals contradicted the principle of a people's right to self-determination that he claimed in the Atlantic Charter; his negation of that right as applicable to the Palestinian people was further evidenced by the fact that he chose to discuss the future of Palestine not with Palestinian representatives, but with Abdulaziz al-Saud, the Saudi Arabian monarch.[115]

Significantly, Roosevelt explicitly identified himself with Zionism, as revealed in a conversation which took place between Roosevelt and Joseph Stalin at Yalta.[116] Roosevelt, as had Wilson before him, ignored the existence of the Palestinian national identity in formulating his policy toward Palestine. The principles enunciated in the Atlantic Charter were denied application in the case of the people of Palestine, as had been the case with the principles of the Fourteen Points. The end result was the negation of Palestinian rights for many years to come.

NOTES

1. For a good synthesis, see Umozurike Oji Umozurike, *Self-Determination in International Law* (Hamden, CT: Shoe String Press, 1972), pp. 3-6. See also Malcolm N. Shaw, *International Law*, 2d ed. (Cambridge: Grotius Publications, 1986), p. 130.

2. For an excellent analysis of the meaning of the right of peoples to self-determination, see Ibrahim Abu-Lughod, "Retrieving Palestinian National Rights," in Ibrahim Abu-Lughod, ed., *Palestinian Rights: Affirmation and Denial* (Wilmette, IL: Medina Press, 1982), pp. 3-10.

3. See D.B. Levin, "The Principle of Self-Determination of Nations in International Law," *Soviet Year Book of International Law* (Moscow: Soviet Association of International Law, 1962), p. 48.

4. Henry Steele Commager, ed., *Documents of American History*, 9th ed. (New York: Meredith, 1973), 1:100-2.

5. *Congressional Record*, 64th Congress, 1st sess. (Washington, DC: U.S. Government Printing Office, 1916), 53, pt. 9:8854.

6. *Congressional Record*, 64th Congress, 2nd sess. (Washington, DC: U.S. Government Printing Office, 1917), 54, pt. 2:1742.

7. For text of Wilson's Fourteen Points, see Commager, ed., *Documents*, 2:137-39. See also U.S. Department of State, *Foreign Relations of the United States*, supp. 1 (Washington, DC: U.S. Government Printing Office, 1936), pp. 55-56; Geoffrey Malcolm Gathorne-Hardy, *The Fourteen Points and the Treaty of Versailles* (Oxford: Clarendon Books, 1939), p. 10.

8. *Congressional Record*, 65th Congress, 2d sess. (Washington, DC: U.S. Government Printing Office, 1918), 56, pt. 2:1952-53.

9. Woodrow Wilson, "Four Factors of World Peace, Address at Mount Vernon, July 4, 1918," in Albert Bushnell Hart, ed., *Selected Addresses and Public Papers of Woodrow Wilson* (New York: Boni & Liveright, 1918), pp. 266-69.

10. U.S. Department of State, "Preliminary Peace Conference, Protocol No. 3, Plenary Session of February 14, 1919," *Papers Relating to the Foreign Relations of the United States: The Paris Peace Conference, 1919* (Washington, DC: U.S. Government Printing Office, 1943), 3:213-14.

11. See Ray Stannard Baker and William E. Dodd, eds., *The Public Papers of Woodrow Wilson, War and Peace: Presidential Messages, Addresses, and Public Papers (1917-1924)* (New York: Harper & Brothers, 1927), 2:469.

12. For excerpts of President Roosevelt's Four Freedoms address to Congress of 7 January 1941, and the Atlantic Charter of 14 August 1941, see U.S. Department of State, *Making the Peace Treaties 1941-1947: A History of the Making of the Peace Beginning with the Atlantic Charter, the Yalta and Potsdam Conferences, and Culminating in the Drafting of Peace Treaties with Italy, Bulgaria, Hungary, Rumania, and Finland* (Washington, DC: U.S. Government Printing Office, 1947), pp. 1-2.

The Atlantic Charter was issued following shipboard meetings between Churchill and Roosevelt off the coast of Newfoundland in August 1941.

13. Article 55 of the UN Charter also called for respect of the right of self-determination.

For text of the United Nations Charter, see Burns H. Weston, et al., *Basic Documents in International Law and World Order* (St. Paul, MN: West Publishing, 1980), pp. 6-23.

14. This school of thought is represented by, among others, Philip M. Brown, Edward Hallett Carr, Alfred Cobban, Rosalyn Higgins, Ann V.W. Thomas and A.J. Thomas, Harold S. Johnson, Mohammed Cherif Bassiouni, Umozurike Oji Umozurike, D.B. Levin, Lawrence T. Farley, Manfred Lachs, Ian Brownlie, Claude Cheysson and Ibrahim Abu-Lughod. Its tenets have also been asserted by the United Nations on many occasions.

See Philip Marshal Brown, "Self-determination in Central Europe," *American Journal of International Law*, 1920, 14:235; Edward Hallett Carr, *Conditions of Peace* (London: Macmillan, 1942), p. 37; Alfred Cobban, *National Self-Determination*, rev. ed. (Chicago: University of Chicago Press, 1947), p. 4; Rosalyn Higgins, *The Development of International Law through the Political Organs of the United Nations* (London: Oxford University Press, 1963), p. 105; Ann Van Wynen Thomas and A.J. Thomas, Jr., *Non-Intervention: The Law and Its Import in the Americas* (Dallas, TX: Southern Methodist University Press, 1956), p. 369; Harold S. Johnson, *Self-Determination within the Community of Nations* (Leyden: A.P. Sijthoff, 1967), p. 94; Mohammed Cherif Bassiouni, "'Self-Determination' and the Palestinians," *American Journal of International Law* (October 1971), 65(5):33; Umozurike, *Self-Determination*, pp. xiii, 3, 202-3; Levin, "Principle of Self-Determination," pp. 46, 48; Lawrence T. Farley, *Plebiscites and Sovereignty: The Crises of Political Illegitimacy* (Boulder, CO: Westview Press, 1986), p. 3; Manfred Lachs, "The Law in and of the United Nations: Some Reflections on the Principle of Self-Determination," *Indian Journal of International Law*, 1961, p. 432; M. Lachs, "Some Reflections on the Problem of Self-determination," *Law in the Service of Peace* (December 1957), 2:61; Ian Brownlie, *Principles of International Law* (Oxford: Clarendon, 1966), p. 484; Claude Cheysson, "The Right to Self-Determination," interview conducted by

Elias Sanbar, *Journal of Palestine Studies* (Autumn 1986), 16(1):9; Abu-Lughod, "Retrieving Palestinian National Rights". See also Shaw, *International Law*, p. 130.

15. This school is represented by, among others, Leslie C. Green, Georg Schwarzenberger and Rupert Emerson.

See *Report of the Forty-Seventh Conference of the International Law Association, 1956* (London: International Law Association, 1957), p. 58; Georg Schwarzenberger, *A Manual of International Law*, 5th ed. (New York: Frederick A. Praeger, 1967), p. 74; Rupert Emerson, *From Empire to Nation: The Rise of Self-Assertion of Asian and African Peoples* (Cambridge, MA: Harvard University Press, 1960), p. 307; Emerson, *Self-Determination Revisited in the Era of Decolonization*, Occasional Papers in International Affairs, no. 9, December 1964, Harvard Center of International Affairs, pp. 63-64; *Proceedings of the American Society of International Law at its Sixtieth Annual Meeting* (Washington, DC: American Society of International Law, 1966), p. 135.

16. For illustration, see Dean Rusk, "The Winds of Freedom," in Ernest K. Lindley, ed., *Selections From the Speeches and Statements of Secretary of State Dean Rusk, January 1961-August 1962* (Boston: Beacon Press, 1963), p. 227.

17. See Wilson's address relative to the treaty of peace with Germany delivered on 10 July 1919, in "Treaty of Peace With Germany," 66th Congress, 1st sess., *Sen. Doc.* no. 50 (Washington, DC: U.S. Government Printing Office, 1919), p. 6.

18. See Herbert Adams Gibbons, "The Armistices and Peace Negotiations," *The Century* (February 1919), 97(4):534-43, reprinted in 66th Congress, 1st sess., *Sen. Doc.* no. 27 (Washington, DC: U.S. Government Printing Office, 1919), pp. 32-42.

19. On this point, see the statements made by Wilson as cited in Baker and Dodd, eds., *Public Papers of Woodrow Wilson*, 2:244.

20. Cited in Farley, *Plebiscites and Sovereignty*, p. 7.

21. Melvin Gurtov and Ray Maghroori, *Roots of Failure* (Westport, CT: Greenwood Press, 1984), p. 5.

22. Farley, *Plebiscites and Sovereignty*, pp. 4-5. See also Erich Hula, *Nationalism and Internationalism: European and American Perspectives* (Lanham, MD: University Press of America, 1984), p. 4.

23. Vladimir Ilytch Lenin, "Imperialism and the Right of Nations to Self-Determination," in V.I. Lenin, *Collected Works, Volume 39, Notebooks on Imperialism*, trans. Clemens Dutt, ed. M.S. Levin (London: Lawrence & Wishart and Moscow: Progress Publishers, 1968), pp. 735, 737, 739-41, 787.

24. Robert Lansing, *The Peace Negotiations: A Personal Narrative* (London: Constable, 1921), pp. 85-86.

25. *Ibid.*, pp. 89-90.

26. Quincy Wright, *Mandates under the League of Nations* (Chicago: University of Chicago Press, 1930), p. 49.

27. It is worth noting that Churchill maintained that the Atlantic Charter applied only to European nations occupied by the Germans and to the British colonial empire. See Umozurike, *Self-Determination*, pp. 60-61.

28. Hula, *Nationalism and Internationalism*, p. 238.

29. Noam Chomsky, *Turning the Tide* (Boston: South End Press, 1985), pp. 46-47.

30. John F. Murphy, "Self-Determination: United States Perspectives," in Jonah Alexander and Robert A. Friedlander, eds., *Self-Determination* (Boulder, CO: Westview Press, 1980), pp. 43-44.

31. Gurtov and Maghroori, *Roots of Failure*, p. 5.

32. M. Gurtov, *United States against the Third World* (New York: Praeger, 1974), p. 8.

33. For an analysis of the legal aspects of this issue, see Mark P. Cohen, "U.S. Legal Involvement in Violations of Palestinian Rights," *Journal of Palestine Studies* (Spring 1989), 28(3):76-95.

34. The Balfour Declaration is reproduced in Leonard Stein, *The Balfour Declaration* (London: Vallentine, Mitchell, 1961), Frontispiece.

35. For background on British-Zionist relations which led to the issuance of the Balfour Declaration, see Stein, *Balfour Declaration*, pp. 3-94, 97-305, 309-556; Isaiah Friedman, *The Question of Palestine, 1914-1918: British-Jewish-Arab Relations* (New York: Schocken Books, 1973), pp. 1-7, 25-118, 259-81.

36. Josephus Daniels, *The Wilson Era: Years of War and After, 1917-1923* (Chapel Hill: University of North Carolina Press, 1946), pp. 31-40.

37. Figures cited in Sami Hadawi, *Bitter Harvest: Palestine 1914-1979* (Delmar, NY: Caravan Books, 1979), p. 13. See also Abdallah Frangi, *The PLO and Palestine*, trans. Paul Knight (London: Zed Books, 1983), pp. 41-43; David Lloyd George, *Memoirs of the Peace Conference* (New Haven, CT: Yale University Press, 1939), 2:545-55; Paul Guinn, *British Strategy and Politics 1914 to 1918* (Oxford: Clarendon Press, 1965), pp. 166-67; Daniels, *Wilson Era: Years of War*, pp. 41-125, 145-156; J. Daniels, *The Wilson Era: Years of Peace, 1910-1917* (Chapel Hill: University of North Carolina Press, 1944), pp. 413-15, 565-85, 591-96; Herbert Asquith, *Memories and Reflections, 1852-1927* (Boston: Little, Brown, 1928), 2:147-49.

38. James A. Malcolm, *Origins of the Balfour Declaration: Dr. Weizmann's Contribution* (London: Zionist Archives, 1944), pp. 2-3.

39. For a discussion of the British motives for issuing the Balfour Declaration, see Anthony Nutting, *The Tragedy of Palestine from the Balfour Declaration to Today* (London: Arab League Office, 1969).

40. Quoted in Frank Edward Manuel, *The Realities of American-Palestine Relations* (Washington, DC: Public Affairs Press, 1949), p. 165.

41. *Ibid.*, pp. 165-66.

42. *The New York Times*, 11 May 1917, p. 3.

43. Manuel, *Realities*, p. 166.

44. Mohammed K. Shadid, *The United States and the Palestinians* (London: Croom Helm, 1981), p. 25. See also Daniels, *Wilson Era: Years of Peace*, p. 543.

45. Manuel, *Realities*, p. 116.

46. Reuben Fink, ed., *America and Palestine: The Attitude of Official America and of the American People toward the Rebuilding of Palestine as a Free and Democratic Jewish Commonwealth* (New York: American Zionist Emergency Council, 1944), p. 30.

47. See Friedman, *Question of Palestine, 1914-1918*, p. 216.

48. For details on this episode, see Manuel, *Realities*, pp. 167-69.

49. *Ibid.*, p. 170.

50. Shadid, *United States and the Palestinians*, p. 25.

51. Manuel, *Realities*, pp. 168-69.

52. David Lloyd George, *The Truth about the Peace Treaties* (London: V. Gollancz, 1938), 2:1119-20, 1134. See also H.W. Temperley, ed., *The History of the Peace Conference* (London: Henry Frowde and Hodder & Stoughton, 1920-24), 6:171-73.

53. Cited in Hadawi, *Bitter Harvest*, pp. 13-14, whose source is *Cmd. 5479*-Palestine Royal (Peel) Commission Report, p. 17.

54. Cited in Issa Nakhleh, "The Liberation of Palestine is Supported by International Law and Justice," in John Norton Moore, ed., *The Arab-Israeli Conflict: Readings and Documents*, abr. and rev. ed. (Princeton, NJ: Princeton University Press, 1977), p. 122.

55. Joseph M. N. Jeffries, *Palestine: The Reality* (New York: Longmans, Green, 1939), p. 177.

56. Manuel, *Realities*, p. 176.

57. Cited in Seth P. Tillman, *Anglo-American Relations at the Paris Peace Conference of 1919* (Princeton, NJ: Princeton University Press, 1961), p. 225.

58. Lansing, *Peace Negotiations*, p. 87.

59. David Hunter Miller, *My Diary at the Conference of Paris, With Documents* (New York: Appeal Printing, 1928), 15:104-08.

60. Harry N. Howard, *The King-Crane Commission: An American Inquiry in the Middle East* (Beirut: Khayats, 1963), pp. 11-12.

61. Manuel, *Realities*, pp. 233-34.

62. *Ibid.*, p. 234.

63. Cited in *ibid.*, p. 238.

64. For details, review *ibid.*, pp. 222-24, 228, 237, 244. See also Richard Cottam, "The United States and Palestine," in Ibrahim Abu-Lughod, ed., *The Transformation of Palestine: Essays on the Origin and Development of the Arab-Israeli Conflict* (Evanston, IL: Northwestern University Press, 1971), pp. 387-94.

65. Howard, *King-Crane Commission*, pp. 24-27, 74, 89.

66. *Ibid.*, p. 100.

67. U.S. Department of State, *Papers Relating to the Foreign Relations of the United States: The Paris Peace Conference, 1919* (Washington, DC: U.S. Government Printing Office, 1947), 12:748-50.

68. For full details, see *ibid.*, pp. 751-863. See also Walid Khalidi, ed., *From Haven to Conquest: Readings in Zionism and the Palestine Problem until 1948* (Washington, DC: Institute for Palestine Studies, 1971), pp. 213-18.

69. Hadawi, *Bitter Harvest*, p. 17; Jeffries, *Palestine: The Reality*, pp. 237-38.

70. Cited in M. Thomas Davis, "The King-Crane Commission and the American Abandonment of Self-Determination," *American-Arab Affairs* (Summer 1984), 9:62, whose source is Library of Congress, *The Papers of Woodrow Wilson*, Cablegram, Crane to Wilson, dated 31 August 1919.

71. See John K. Winkler, *Woodrow Wilson: The Man Who Lives On* (New York: Vanguard Press, 1933), pp. 284-86; Edwin Weinstein, *Woodrow Wilson: A Medical and Psychological Biography* (Princeton, NJ: Princeton University Press, 1981), pp. 353-55.

72. Manuel, *Realities*, p. 242.

73. *Ibid.*, pp. 232-33.

74. Quoted in Howard, *King-Crane Commission*, p. 37.

75. Melvin I. Urofsky and David W. Levy, eds., *Letters of Louis D. Brandeis: Mr. Justice Brandeis* (Albany: State University of New York Press, 1971-78), 4:373-98; Alpheus Thomas Mason, *Brandeis: A Free Man's Life* (New York: The Viking Press, 1946), pp. 451-58.

76. See E.L. Woodward and Rohan Butler, eds., *Documents on British Foreign Policy 1919-1939*, 1st ser. (London: H.M. Stationery Office, 1952), 4:260-62. See also Howard, *King-Crane Commission*, pp. 73-74; Manuel, *Realities*, pp. 242-44; Davis, "King-Crane Commission," p. 61, n18.

77. Howard, *King-Crane Commission*, p. 79.

78. Manuel, *Realities*, p. 245.

79. Davis, "King-Crane Commission," p. 61.
80. Manuel, *Realities*, p. 246.
81. See "An Interview in Mr. Balfour's Apartment, 23 Rue Nitot, Paris, on June 24th, 1919, at 4:45 p.m.," in Khalidi, ed., *From Haven to Conquest*, pp. 195-99. See also "Memorandum by Mr. Frankfurter of an Interview in Mr. Balfour's Apartment, Paris, June 24, 1919, 4:45 p.m.," in John Norton Moore, ed., *The Arab-Israeli Conflict: Volume III, Documents* (Princeton, NJ: Princeton University Press, 1974), pp. 45-48.
82. Manuel, *Realities*, p. 247.
83. Jeffries, *Palestine: The Reality*, p. 314; Hadawi, *Bitter Harvest*, p. 41.
84. Brandeis visited only Zionist colonies, twenty-three in all, averaging two per day. The commission, on the other hand, spent much time meeting with local inhabitants of all three religious affiliations and from all walks of life, as well as with British officials in the country. See *Papers Relating to the Foreign Relations of the United States*, 1919, 12:752-57.
85. Davis, "King-Crane Commission," pp. 64-65.
86. Manuel, *Realities*, pp. 257-58.
87. For the differing, often contradictory, arguments on whether Brandeis persuaded Wilson not to accept the report of the commission and whether Wilson saw the report, see Davis, "King-Crane Commission," pp. 62-64; Bruce Allen Murphy, *The Brandeis/Frankfurter Connection: The Secret Political Activities of Two Supreme Court Justices* (New York: Oxford University Press, 1982), p. 63; Ezekiel Rabinowitz, *Justice Louis D. Brandeis: The Zionist Chapter of His Life* (New York: Philosophical Library, 1968), p. 99.
88. Manuel, *Realities*, p. 256.
89. *Ibid.*, pp. 256-57. See also Tillman, *Anglo-American Relations*, p. 227.
90. Charles Seymour, *The Intimate Papers of Colonel House* (Boston: Houghton Mifflin, 1928), pp. 157, 199. See also D.H. Miller, *My Diary*, doc. 85, pp. 428-57; Howard, *King-Crane Commission*, p. 6.
91. For text of the San Remo Agreement, see U.S. Department of State, *Papers Relating to the Foreign Relations of the United States: The Paris Peace Conference*, 1919 (Washington, DC: U.S. Government Printing Office, 1942), 2:655-58.
92. For text of Article 95, see U.S. Department of State, *The Treaty of Versailles and After: Annotations of the Text of the Treaty* (Washington, DC: U.S. Government Printing Office, 1944), pp. 95-96. See also 67th Congress, 1st sess., "Peace Treaties," Sen. Doc. no. 7 (Washington, DC: U.S. Government Printing Office, 1921), p. 349. For an informative interpretation of the treaty, see William Linn Westermann, "The Armenian Problem and the Disruption of Turkey," Edward Mandell House and Charles Seymour, eds., *What Really Happened at Paris: Story of the Peace Conference, 1918-1919* (New York: Charles Scribner's Sons, 1921 and London: Hodder & Stoughton, 1921), p. 176.
93. The Treaty of Sèvres was the peace agreement between Turkey and its World War I opponents, excluding the United States and the USSR. Turkey never ratified the treaty, which was superseded by the Lausanne pacts. The Lausanne Treaty was concluded as a result of meetings held in Lausanne, Switzerland (21 November 1922-24 July 1923), between the allied powers and Turkey. By the signing of this treaty, World War I was officially ended between the Allies and Turkey.
94. For text of the Covenant of the League of Nations, see Manley O. Hudson, ed., *International Legislation: A Collection of the Texts of Multipartite International Instruments of General Interest, Beginning with the Covenant of the League of Nations* (Washington, DC: Carnegie Endowment for International Peace, 1931), 1:2-17.

95. This Zionist desire for control of water resources was clearly spelled out in a speech delivered by Herbert Samuel, the man who would be appointed Britain's High Commissioner in Palestine, on the second anniversary of the Balfour Declaration at a meeting held in London under the auspices of the English Zionist Federation. He stated:

There is plenty of water in Palestine . . . . It is a question of storing and of utilizing it. For that purpose it is essential that the rivers and streams should be made available, particularly in the North-the Litani River and the streams that flow down the Southern slopes of Mount Hermon. Zionists therefore press and urgently demand that the Northern boundaries shall be so drawn as to secure for Palestine the water resources without which it cannot fully prosper. Further, the industries of Palestine will depend for their success and prosperity in future in no small degree upon electric power; for that, again, water power is necessary; and for that reason also the Northern boundary must be rightly drawn.

See Herbert Samuel, *Zionism: Its Ideals and Practical Hopes* (London: The Zionist Organization, 19[19]), p. 5.

96. Manuel, *Realities*, pp. 273-74.

97. *Congressional Record*, 67th Congress, 2d sess., S.J. Res. 191 (Washington, DC: U.S. Government Printing Office, 1922), 62, pt. 5:5376.

98. House of Representatives, 67th Congress, 2d sess., "National Home for the Jewish People in Palestine," *Report No. 1038, May 31, 1922* (Washington, DC: U.S. Government Printing Office, 1922).

99. *Ibid.*

100. *Congressional Record*, 67th Congress, 2d sess. (Washington, DC: U.S. Government Printing Office, 1922), 62, pt. 10:9799.

101. House of Representatives, 67th Congress, 2d sess., Subcommittee of the House Committee on Foreign Affairs, *Hearings Before the Committee on Foreign Affairs on H. CON. RES. 52* "Expressing Satisfaction at the Re-creation of Palestine as the National Home of the Jewish Race" 18, 19, 20, 21 April 1922 (Washington, DC: U.S. Government Printing Office, 1922), 318:5-119.

102. *Ibid.*, p. 20 (emphasis added).

103. Reed was a professor of English Literature at Yale University. He visited Palestine between the signing of the armistice and the signing of the peace treaties, and was engaged in relief work there as deputy commissioner for the American Red Cross for three-and-a-half months.

104. Subcommittee of the House Committee on Foreign Affairs, *Hearings*, pp. 22, 24.

105. *Ibid.*, pp. 25, 28, 32.

106. *Ibid.*, pp. 49-50.

107. *Ibid.*, pp. 69-70.

108. *Ibid.*, p. 32.

109. *Ibid.*, p. 68.

110. *The Statutes-at-Large of the United States of America* (Washington, DC: U.S. Government Printing Office, 1923), 62, pt. 1:1012; 67th Congress, 2d sess., 11 September 1922, reprinted in Ralph H. Magnus, ed., *Documents on the Middle East* (Washington, DC: American Enterprise Institute for Public Policy Research, 1969), p. 40. See also "U.S. Policy Statements: 1922-1970," *Fateh* (March 14, 1970), 2(5):8; Shadid, *United States and the Palestinians*, p. 27; Manuel, *Realities*, p. 282.

111. For text of the Anglo-American Convention of 3 December 1924, see Division of Near Eastern Affairs of the U.S. Department of State, *Collected United States Documents Relating to the League of Nations Mandate for Palestine, to the Possible Future*

Independence of Palestine and to the Need for the Creation of a Separate Jewish State (Salisbury, NC: Documentary Publications, 1977), pp. 107-14.

112. See Nadav Safran, *The United States and Israel* (Cambridge, MA: Harvard University Press, 1963), pp. 35-38.

113. *Congressional Record*, 78th Congress, 2d sess. (Washington, DC: U.S. Government Printing Office, 1944), 90, pt. 1:815. See also Manuel, *Realities*, p. 309.

114. Manuel, *Realities*, p. 312.

115. For information on the correspondence between Roosevelt and Ibn Saud, see U.S. Department of State, *Foreign Relations of the United States: Diplomatic Papers, 1945* (Washington, DC: U.S. Government Printing Office, 1969), 8:678-704.

116. U.S. Department of State, *Foreign Relations of the United States: The Conferences at Malta and Yalta, 1945* (Washington, DC: U.S. Government Printing Office, 1955), p. 924.

3

THE TRUMAN ADMINISTRATION AND THE PALESTINIANS

Fred H. Lawson

TRUMAN ADMINISTRATION POLICY toward Palestine has generally been explained in terms of three aspects of American domestic politics during the later 1940s. In the first place, contemporary scholars emphasize the intensive lobbying that took place on behalf of the Zionist movement by influential individuals with close personal ties to the president. Steven Spiegel argues that Truman exhibited a predilection to support the creation of a United Nations trusteeship for Palestine in March 1948, in response to which "a group of B'nai B'rith leaders contacted Eddie Jacobson, Truman's old haberdashery partner, who then tried to arrange a meeting between [Chaim] Weizmann and the president." In response to this appeal, "the president met the aging Zionist leader secretly at the White House on 18 March. Weizmann appealed again for Truman's support and the President reiterated his backing of partition as long as the United Nations did not approve a temporary trusteeship."[1] Peter Grose indicates that far from being an isolated incident, Jacobson's action represented part of a concerted effort by American Jews to persuade Truman to ignore or override the advice of officials in the departments of State and Defense who opposed unequivocal American support for the establishment of a Jewish state in Palestine.[2]

Second, the classic historical accounts of the period underline the importance that Truman's closest advisers attached to pro-Zionist Jewish voters as potential bases of electoral and financial support for the Democratic party in the presidential election of 1948 — an election in which the president's chances of winning were universally regarded as slim. John Snetsinger reports that party leaders "wrote to Truman early in 1948 and suggested that a pro-Jewish policy in the Middle East would brighten the domestic political situation." Clear backing for a Jewish state was considered particularly crucial for a Democratic victory in New York, "since 47 percent of the country's Jews live there, and approximately 17 percent of the state's voters were Jewish." Furthermore, Henry Wallace's candidacy on the American Labor party ticket posed a direct challenge to the Democrats in New York in light of the fact that in the previous election "Roosevelt won New York's electoral votes but only as a result of the half-million votes he received as the ALP candidate."[3] Michael Cohen's variation of this line of argument — "that Truman, given his superficial understanding of Palestine and the Middle East, really did believe, as he stated in his memoirs, that he could at one and the same time support Zionism, protect his own political future, and safeguard the national interest in the Middle East" — eliminates the more Machiavellian assumptions rejected by the president's defenders.[4]

Finally, most later observers spell out a pervasive conflict of interest between top officials in the departments of State and Defense on the one hand and many of Truman's senior staff on the other. In Spiegel's view, "the low priority given the Palestinian issue and the strong divisions within the government and American political system account for the inconsistency of the Truman administration in its Palestinian policy. At critical points, individuals who favored the Zionists and were respected by the president outweighed the efforts of cabinet officials and the bureaucracy." For the most part, however, "Truman took a position between the two groups, favoring one or the other according to his own view of national security, his preoccupation with other matters, events in the Middle East, domestic politics, or arguments made to him by key aides."[5] Zvi Ganin argues that the coalition of officials in the Office of Near Eastern and African Affairs, high-ranking civilians in the Pentagon, and senior military officers successfully reversed the president's policy supporting the partition of Palestine into separate Jewish and Arab states:

> By early March 1948 President Truman was then faced with diametrically opposed policy recommendations. His trusted advisers counseled continued support for partition while the State Department, the Pentagon and the intelligence community were adamantly opposed to it and recommended its abandonment and replacement by some formula which would ensure continued and effective British (or Anglo-American) control over Palestine. The internal fight between the White House and the bureaucracy raged for several more days until the State Department pulled off a surprise coup which resulted in one of the worst crises (but a well-kept secret) of the Truman administration, and plunged the Jews into despair.[6]

Similarly, Shlomo Slonim explains the consistent American support for an embargo of armaments to Palestine in terms of bureaucratic political factors.[7]

The combination of these three internal political dynamics is taken as an irresistible force driving U.S. policy in the direction of support for the creation of the Zionist state in Palestine at the expense of — or in complete disregard for — the interests of the territory's Arab population. This position has been neatly summarized by Cheryl Rubenberg in her recent survey of Israel and the American national interest:

> For the majority of American government officials, Washington's policy in [the Middle East] was intimately bound up with the global power situation. For other individuals involved in the policy-making process, the immediacy of domestic political concerns outweighed calculations of long-term consequences of national interest. In the end, the arguments of the latter prevailed. . . .

"Indeed," she continues, "it is questionable whether Truman thought through the long-term international consequences for American interest of his position on Palestine or if he simply responded to the pressure of the moment. . . . [T]he president did not demonstrate any awareness of the humanitarian problems his policies were creating for the indigenous Arab inhabitants of Palestine."[8]

This conventional wisdom is compelling on a variety of different grounds; but it is seriously problematic in several crucial aspects. First, the historical record does in fact indicate considerable awareness on the part of senior officials within the Truman administration, including the president himself, of the growing difficulties facing Arab Palestinians as Jewish immigration to Palestine accelerated in the last years of the British Mandate. Second, positing any sort of continuous American support for the Zionist project creates a number of central analytical puzzles regarding important aspects of U.S. policy toward Palestine: why, for instance, did Washington persist in its embargo of military supplies and armaments to all combatants in the fighting that preceded and culminated in the 1948 war? And why did the Truman administration refuse to play a role in the tug-of-war for jurisdiction over Jerusalem that took place among Israeli, Jordanian, and United Nations representatives in the wake of that war?[9] But third — and most crucial of all — focusing upon the interplay between State Department officials and Truman's personal advisers obscures the underlying objectives of American policy in the Middle East in the years immediately following World War II, goals that remained remarkably consistent despite the presumed differences that separated prominent U.S. decision makers.

AMERICAN ECONOMIC ASSISTANCE FOR ARAB PALESTINE

As World War II drew to a close, the general shape that U.S. economic assistance to other parts of the world should take became the subject of intense debate among senior officials in the American government. Some agencies — in particular the State Department — favored expanded state-to-state aid to assist areas ravaged by the war. Others opposed such governmental aid on the grounds that it would tend to interfere with the free operation of the international market and would thereby produce inefficient use of the country's relatively depleted resources. With regard to areas of crucial strategic importance to the United States, this debate was generally resolved in favor of the former position. Thus U.S. aid to western Europe took the form of direct state grants to continental governments.[10]

But with respect to other parts of the world, those considered more "peripheral," the outcome of this controversy was considerably less clear-cut. In June 1945 Undersecretary of State Dean Acheson and the Office of Near Eastern Affairs of the State Department proposed that Congress set up a $100 million annual fund to be used in support of American political and strategic interests in the Middle East. This proposal was vetoed by Secretary of State James Byrnes, however, on the grounds that Congress would never approve a plan that entailed such extensive government involvement in economic affairs.[11] In the wake of this episode, according to Nathan Godfried, "the State Department . . . decided that private and public financial aid for Arab development would be made on a commercial basis — on the nature of the projects and the ability of the country to repay the loan. A successful program would depend on vigorous world trading in general and on increased trade between the United States and the Middle East in particular."[12]

Nevertheless, at the end of July 1946, President Truman announced his intention to ask the Congress for monies to create a fund to provide loans to Palestine and other Middle Eastern states. Such loans would only be approved "for some development projects if for any reason such projects cannot adequately be financed through the International Bank [for Reconstruction and Development]."[13] The announcement drew immediate fire from the Jewish Agency, whose leadership opposed linking economic assistance to Palestine to aid for other Arab governments.

Zionist opposition postponed the president's proposal but did not kill it. On 5 September Truman announced the granting of a $300 million loan to improve the living conditions of the Arab population of Palestine.[14] Following the disbursement of this loan, the president wrote to King Abdulaziz of Saudi Arabia that, "In supporting the establishment of the Jewish National Home in Palestine the United States had not thought of embarking upon a policy which would be prejudicial to the interests of the indigenous population of Palestine, and it has no such thought at the present time." In his words, the primary aim of U.S. policy was to ensure that "the fundamental rights of both the Arab and Jewish population of Palestine shall be fully safeguarded and that in Palestine Arabs and Jews alike shall prosper and shall lead lives free of any kind of political or economic oppression."[15] But despite Truman's protestations, subsequent assistance was slow in coming.

In mid-August 1948, the State Department notified the president that, "As a result of the recent fighting in Palestine, approximately 330,000 Arab inhabitants of that country residing in areas now under occupation of the Provisional Government of Israel or the military forces of Israel precipitately fled from their homes and are now scattered either in the Arab portions of Palestine or in neighboring countries, including Syria, Transjordan and Egypt." Although both Jewish and Arab refugees were facing considerable hardships, "the plight of the Arabs . . . is much more grave. They are destitute of any belongings, are without adequate shelter, medical supplies, sanitation and food. . . . Once the rainy season commences and winter sets in, tragedy on the largest scale will be inevitable unless relief is forthcoming." The State Department recommended as an appropriate American response to the situation:
1. That the Department continue its efforts to secure immediate donations from American private relief organizations.

2. That the Department be authorized to approach other agencies of this government with a view to assuming some share of the international burden of relief for refugees in the Near East.
3. That, as part of this government's diplomatic participation in securing a peaceful settlement of the Palestine problem, it urge upon the Provisional Government of Israel and to other governments concerned the need for repatriating Arab and Jewish refugees under conditions which will not imperil the internal security of the receiving states.[16]

A month later the Joint Chiefs of Staff went on record as recommending that the secretary of defense create a comprehensive aid program for Palestine's Arab population. In their view, "the present distress of some 300,000 Arab refugees from Palestine and the inability of the Arab nations to provide for their urgent needs present an opportunity for the United States to strengthen the friendship of the Arab people for the people of the United States and to enhance the prestige of the United States, both of which have suffered as the result of recent events in connection with the Palestine situation."[17] Consequently, the Department of State urged the president on 15 October "under his authority as Commander-in-Chief" to order

> the National Military Establishment . . . to release to the extent available from stocks on hand or which may be quickly obtained from other departments or agencies: 100,000 blankets; 5,000 tons of wheat; cloth or appropriate clothing for 200,000 persons; typhus vaccine, atebrine and other urgently needed medical supplies; and to provide transportation facilities for shipment of these supplies to the Near East. The total value of supplies and transport should not exceed $1,500,000 to cover the period from now until the end of the year.[18]

At almost exactly the same time, the new U.S. envoy in Tel Aviv, James G. McDonald, was writing the president to report that the "Arab refugee tragedy is rapidly reaching catastrophic proportions and should be treated as a disaster." In McDonald's opinion, the "situation requires [the] same comprehensive program and immediate action that dramatic and overwhelming calamities such as [a] vast flood or earthquake would invoke. Nothing less will avert horrifying losses."[19] Recognizing that the president's counsel, Clark Clifford, might attempt to block any appeal from the State Department on behalf of the Arab refugees, Undersecretary Robert A. Lovett sent Clifford a lengthy telegram from Paris arguing that the United Nations General Assembly was about to approve economic assistance to the Arab population of Palestine anyway and that Great Britain had taken the lead in sponsoring such a resolution to that point. "The US delegation," Lovett concluded,

> strongly recommends that the resolution be handled as a joint US-UK project since it will not be possible for us to sit silent on the matter and since we do not feel that we should permit the British to get the full credit for the introduction of a resolution in which we will undoubtedly later concur.[20]

McDonald in Tel Aviv cabled in support of such a move on 10 November. He further recommended that the Truman administration cooperate with the American Red Cross to provide desperately needed food and clothing to the refugees in Palestine. In addition, he offered to fly to Paris to give public testimony before the Third Committee of the General Assembly in the capacity of a "refugee expert." "Such an appearance by the American special representative in Israel," he confided to the White House, "would help answer Arab criticism that the US is disproportionately interested in Jewish welfare."[21]

Faced with such a consensus on the part of his subordinates, the president authorized the State Department to carry out a two-pronged effort to provide relief supplies to both Arab and Jewish refugees displaced by the fighting in Palestine. On the one hand, the department was authorized to contact other governments in an attempt to determine the scale of potential multilateral assistance. On the other, it was directed to solicit private foundations for funds and material that would be shipped to Palestine immediately. In early October, officials at State reported back that they had been unable to gather enough funds and supplies to form a credible relief effort.[22] Consequently, Lovett, as acting secretary of state, urged Truman to ask Congress for $16 million to cover half of the total relief monies estimated by the UN General Assembly to be necessary to provide food, shelter, and medical supplies to the Palestinian refugees. The president approved this course of action on 6 November and announced his decision to the Congress two weeks later.[23]

By March 1949, the failure of the UN Conciliation Commission for Palestine to persuade the Provisional Government of Israel to repatriate the Palestinian Arabs who had fled during the course of the fighting prompted a reassessment of American policy toward the refugees. The U.S. representative to the commission, Mark Ethridge, joined George C. McGhee, a senior State Department adviser on Near Eastern affairs, in recommending that Washington induce Tel Aviv to accept 250,000 Arab returnees, implying that the remainder could be handled by surrounding governments.[24] Undersecretary of State Acheson pressed the Israeli foreign minister to repatriate "say a fourth of the refugees," or some 200,000, when they met in New York on 5 April. When this suggestion was parried, President Truman himself confronted the Israeli head of state on the issue; as Truman told Ethridge at the end of April, "I am rather disgusted with the manner in which the Jews are approaching the refugee problem. I told the President of Israel in the presence of his Ambassador just exactly what I thought about it. It may have some effect, I hope so."[25] Continuing American pressure led the Israeli provisional government to announce in mid-June that it would "consider favorably" requests by Arabs within Israeli borders to bring back their wives and young children. According to Benny Morris, "Israeli officials widely described and trumpeted this scheme as a 'broad measure easing the lot of Arab families disrupted as a result of the war.'"[26]

U.S. officials immediately expressed their "disappointment" with the family reunion proposal, noting that such minimal steps were "causing [a] delay in [finding a] refugee solution."[27] After heated debate, the Israeli cabinet then signaled Washington that it would consider repatriating 100,000 refugees. The State Department responded that this offer was still insufficient and repeated its recommendation that Tel Aviv be forced to accept 250,000 returnees. But President Truman, in a last-ditch effort to find a compromise solution to the refugee problem, informally approved the plan as a way of breaking the "deadlock" surrounding the issue.[28]

These moves, inadequate as they must appear in retrospect and in comparison with official American programs in support of the new State of Israel, demonstrate that U.S. policy toward Palestine and its Arab population during 1947-48 was more complex than has been depicted by conventional accounts. Not only did the Truman administration undertake a series of programs to provide economic assistance and emergency relief to the Palestinians, but it also appears to have exerted some pressure on the Israeli government to allow Arab refugees to return to their homes after the fighting came to an end. These programs, combined with Washington's remarkable persistence in maintaining an embargo on arms and military materiel coming into mandatory Palestine, should prompt us to reevaluate the utility of a domestic political explanation for U.S. policy in the eastern Mediterranean at this time. I would offer as an alternative a structural explanation for these events that is somewhat more nuanced than the rather simplistic realpolitik model usually tossed off as a prelude to studies primarily concerned with decision-making in Washington or with American electoral politics.

FOUNDATIONS OF U.S. MIDDLE EAST POLICY

As World War II drew to a close, it became increasingly evident that the structure of the international arena was undergoing a profound transformation. The multipolar order that had been in place since at least the last third of the nineteenth century collapsed during the course of the war, as first France, then Germany and Japan and finally Great Britain exhausted their respective industrial capacities and financial reserves. The shift in world power that accompanied the gradual exhaustion of these states was clear to American officials as early as 1943. According to a report prepared in the Pentagon that fall:

> The successful termination of the war against our present enemies will find a world profoundly changed in respect of relative national military strengths, a change more comparable indeed with that occasioned by the fall of Rome than with any other change occurring during the succeeding fifteen hundred years. . . . After the defeat of Japan, the United States and the Soviet Union will be the only military powers of the first magnitude. This is due in each case to a combination of geographical position and extent, and vast munitioning potential.[29]

The subsequent development of the atomic bomb by American scientists and difficulties encountered by western European governments in carrying out autonomous economic recovery programs only reinforced the emerging bipolar configuration of the postwar international arena.

Under these circumstances, four interrelated principles came to provide the guidelines determining the general shape of American policy toward the Middle East during the late 1940s. In the first place, Washington predicated its actions upon a determination not to permit developments in this part of the world to threaten either the security of western Europe from attack by Soviet forces or the continent's postwar economic recovery. By relying upon their continuing monopoly of nuclear weapons and extending the network of strategic air and naval bases encircling the USSR, U.S. officials for the most part expected to be able to deter the first of these threats.[30] But the second appeared more problematic, particularly as the European economy continued to deteriorate throughout 1946 and 1947.

Virtually all of the countries in western Europe faced a peculiar sort of economic crisis by the summer of 1947. As Alan Milward has demonstrated, this crisis was not so much characterized by declining industrial output, lower standards of living, or shortages of foodstuffs; it was instead related to the growing importance of industrial imports as a basis for continued economic expansion. "Given the uninterruptedly rising trend of output," Milward observes, "imports were crucial, and as western European production climbed rapidly towards and in many cases above pre-war levels the volume of imports necessary to sustain it seems on all the evidence to have been greater per unit of output relative to pre-war."[31] U.S. officials thus became increasingly concerned that disruptions in the flow of machine tools, raw materials, and fuel to the continent would produce a widespread recession that could be exploited both by indigenous communist parties and by Moscow.

Among the most significant of the imports vital to European economic recovery was petroleum. Throughout the war, the United States had served as the primary supplier of both crude and refined oil to the continent; according to Robert Pollard, it "supplied about 80 percent of the petroleum products that the Allies consumed from December 1941 to August 1945."[32] With the end of the conflict, and the attendant lifting of wartime price controls in early 1946, petroleum prices on the international market jumped, causing a severe drain on the dollar reserves of most European governments. As a result, "oil became one of the key commodities in the European Recovery Program (ERP). More than 10 percent of the total aid extended under ERP was spent on oil, more than for any other single commodity."[33] Furthermore, growing competition for petroleum products produced in the Western Hemisphere left Washington worried about the future security of supplies to the American domestic market. These worries intensified in early 1948, when "the United States became a net importer of oil for the first time."[34] Reconciling their efforts to promote European economic recovery with rising American dependence on imported minerals represented one of the most salient strategic puzzles confronting U.S. officials in the immediate postwar period.

As one way of solving this puzzle, Washington began encouraging private firms to augment their exploration and production operations in the oil-producing regions of the Middle East. These moves were to some degree intended to supplement the existing sources of supply for the United States itself; but they were more immediately designed to provide western Europe with a secure flow of petroleum products. According to a report prepared by George F. Kennan, the director of the Policy Planning Staff of the State Department, the European Recovery Program announced in June 1947 would require an additional 1.2 million barrels of oil per day to achieve its initial objectives, all of which was to come from Middle Eastern producers.[35] As Michael Stoff has observed, the need to increase oil production in the Persian Gulf after 1945 "followed with greater compulsion from expanding conceptions of national security, conceptions that encompassed the reconstruction of western Europe and the maintenance of stability in the Middle East."[36] So although neither the Gulf nor the eastern Mediterranean represented a major focus of U.S. military or economic policy during these years, averting political disorder in these areas remained a consistent priority of U.S. leaders throughout the late 1940s.

Second, Washington determined that the transition from British imperial rule in the Middle East be accomplished in a way that would allow the United States to inherit the most important strategic advantages previously held by British forces in the region. American forces took control of air bases at Abadan in Iran, Salalah and Masirah island in Oman, and Shaikh Uthman in southern Arabia during the course of the war, while gaining rights to use pivotal Royal Air Force installations at Habbaniyyah in Iraq, Muharraq in Bahrain, Khartoum in the Sudan, and Karachi in India.[37] In addition, the U.S. Army Air Force began constructing a new strategic airfield at Dhahran in the eastern province of Saudi Arabia in the fall of 1945, even as the RAF was shutting down bases on Socotra island and at Riyan in the Aden protectorate, on Masirah island, and at Sharjah in the Trucial States.[38] As nationalist sentiment in Egypt and Iraq rose during 1946-47, it became impossible for British forces to continue using their main bases in the Suez Canal Zone and around Habbaniyyah and also impossible for U.S. personnel to replace them after they had evacuated. Consequently, American planners began looking to more peripheral areas of the Middle East as potential basing and staging areas. The most significant of these prospective bases were to be located in newly independent Arab North Africa.[39]

Third, U.S. officials were adamant that the Soviet Union be given no opportunity or pretext to become directly involved in Middle Eastern affairs in the years just after World War II. This principle lay at the heart of the program of containment articulated by Kennan in the winter of 1946 and presented in his anonymous article, "The Sources of Soviet Conduct," the following summer.[40] According to John Lewis Gaddis, the American policy of containing potential Soviet expansionism had three distinct components. For present purposes, the most basic of these involved focusing U.S. effort on a limited number of geographical areas whose retention would be crucial to Western defense. This assumption soon transformed itself into a conception of "strongpoint defense," which Gaddis defines as a "concentration on the defense of particular regions, and means of access to them, rather than on the defense of fixed lines." In Gaddis' view, "the 'strongpoint' concept permitted concentration on areas that were both defensible and vital, without worrying too much about the rest. The assumption was that not all interests were of equal importance; that the United States could tolerate the loss of the peripheral areas provided that this did not impair its ability to defend those that were vital."[41] The industrial heartlands of western Europe, North America, and Japan made up the most vital of these "strongpoints," although Kennan considered the oil-producing areas of the Gulf only a little less important to ensure the success of containment.

What is most striking about the policy of containment as it was applied to the postwar Middle East is its strongly Wilsonian cast: containing Soviet expansionism in truly peripheral parts of the world — such as the eastern Mediterranean — entailed enforcing a strictly noninterventionist order. In Gaddis's words,

> The objective of "strongpoint" defense . . . was not so much control as denial: the American interest was not to dominate other power centers itself, but to see to it that no one else did either. This was a goal consistent both with the principle of non-intervention in the internal affairs of other nations, and with the fact that the United States had only limited capabilities to bring to bear in their defense. It did not mean insistence on particular forms of government; only that governments not be changed arbitrarily in such a way as to upset the world balance of power.[42]

U.S. policy makers reiterated the country's commitment to self-determination in a variety of different contexts. The most obvious of these concerned the Greek and Turkish crises of 1946-47; but American insistence that London abide by the terms of the 1936 Anglo-Egyptian treaty and reduce the British military presence in the Suez Canal Zone after the war arose from similar premises.[43] Washington did in the end acquiesce in London's plans to create a substitute for this military complex in Cyrenaica, but only as a way of thwarting Soviet attempts to obtain a trusteeship over the former Italian territory.

Finally, U.S. policy toward the Middle East during the late 1940s was rooted in the principle that American commercial and financial prospects in the region should be encouraged wherever possible, particularly by concerted efforts to dismantle the network of preferences and trade barriers that had accompanied British and French imperial rule. This principle was evident as early as mid-1944, when the State Department and Foreign Economic Administration drew up plans to dispatch to the region a fact-finding mission charged with scouting out potential areas for U.S. trade and investment in the postwar era. This mission, led by Lieutenant-Colonel William S. Culbertson of the U.S. Army Industrial College, visited Tehran and Baghdad that October. Its final report noted that "real barriers exist to the participation of American trade and capital in the economic life of the Middle East countries," even though neither Great Britain nor France practiced "avowed and open discrimination against American economic activity" in this part of the world.[44] In an effort to circumvent these barriers, an Executive Committee on Economic Foreign Policy made up of representatives of the departments of State, Commerce, and the Treasury recommended a concerted program of "financial, commercial, technical, and regional means to improve Middle East economies and living standards" and thereby provide a basis for greater, mutually beneficial trade with the United States.[45]

Despite the enthusiasm generated by the executive committee's report, the Truman administration devoted little attention to developing Middle Eastern economies in the immediate postwar period. As Godfried remarks, Washington found itself "preoccupied with other regions" during the latter half of 1946: "Assistant Secretary Will Clayton's economic divisions directed most of their energy and resources toward Europe and Asia. Secretary of State George Marshall and his successor, Dean Acheson, insisted that the economic development of areas like the Arab East fell under the responsibility of the UN."[46] As a result, direct U.S. aid and investment monies to the region remained scarce until the adoption of the Marshall Plan in mid-1947.

Even with the implementation of that plan, however, the extent of American foreign direct investment and economic assistance to Middle Eastern countries failed to spread beyond the relatively narrow confines of the petroleum sector. By 1949, U.S. firms had invested some $114 million in the region, $98 million of which was devoted to oil operations.[47] These investments soon proved incapable of generating economic development in their respective host countries, partly due to persistent shortages of the hard currency needed to purchase goods on world markets and partly as a result of ineffective linkages between this relatively capital-intensive sector and other "less developed" sectors of the indigenous economies. But along with these deficiencies went a pervasive shortfall in the level of funding appropriated by U.S. agencies to support new development projects in the region. According to Godfried, "American government aid to Egypt from 1945 to 1950 amounted to only $19.9 million in credits and grants," most of which came in the form of loans by the Export-Import Bank. Lebanon, Jordan, Iraq, and Syria received considerably fewer monies than Egypt, although Saudi Arabia fared substantially better.[48]

AMERICAN POLICY TOWARD PALESTINE

These four underlying principles — of support for European recovery, displacement of British predominance, containment of the Soviet threat, and encouragement of U.S. commercial interests — provided the basis for a broad consensus among American officials across a wide range of governmental agencies regarding the appropriate orientation for U.S. policy toward Palestine. U.S. policy makers agreed, first and foremost, that no American military forces should be sent into the eastern Mediterranean in the years following World War II. Any deployment of U.S. forces to this part of the world was, in Washington's view, sure to destabilize local affairs in ways detrimental to Western security. At the same time, American officials agreed that the United States should do all it could to offset Soviet strategic gains in the Middle East with equivalent or countervailing American ones. These overlapping objectives provided the foundation for the U.S. response to Britain's increasingly desperate efforts to devolve its responsibility for administering Palestine during the late 1940s.

Washington had worked hard to ensure that the fighting against communist guerrillas in Greece would be done by British soldiers during the uncertain months after March 1946; and when London became convinced that the country could not be rescued by a limited military intervention, the Truman administration authorized unprecedented levels of economic assistance to the government in Athens rather than dispatching U.S. troops. Even after the British signaled their intention to withdraw their military personnel from Greece in the early autumn of 1947, American officials refused to consider replacing them with U.S. forces. Secretary of War Kenneth C. Royall noted in a top secret memorandum to Secretary of State George C. Marshall on 11 September that "Even if Congress approved, we would be presented with a serious question as to whether the introduction of United States forces into Greece would really help the situation or would be disturbing and provocative."[49] By early 1948, the Joint Chiefs of Staff were arguing that even though "from the point of view of the military consideration . . . the security of the Eastern Mediterranean and the Middle East is of critical importance to the future security of the United States, any deployment of appreciable military strength in this area will make a partial mobilization a necessity."[50] Similar reservations surfaced in discussions of whether or not U.S. troops might be sent to assist the Turks in the event that they were attacked by the Red Army.

Direct military intervention in Palestine was thus out of the question. The Joint Chiefs of Staff informed the State-War-Navy Co-ordinating Committee in June 1946 that its members opposed the use of any U.S. armed forces to enforce the recommendations of the Anglo-American Committee of Inquiry on Palestine. In their view, "the political shock attending the reappearance of U.S. armed forces in the Middle East would unnecessarily risk such serious disturbances throughout the area as to dwarf any local Palestine difficulties," pushing the region "into anarchy" and turning it into "a breeding ground for world war."[51] One month later a terse memorandum drafted by the *ad hoc* Cabinet Committee on Palestine listing "Matters Regarding Palestine To Be Considered Before the London Conference" included as its first item: "Is [the] U.S. willing to employ military forces?" This question was given the unequivocal answer, "No."[52]

A determination to avoid committing American military units to Palestine continued to underlie U.S. policy in the eastern Mediterranean during the succeeding two years. In its first survey of "Policies of the Government of the United States of America Relating to the National Security," the newly created National Security Council (NSC) concluded its brief discussion of events in Palestine with the injunction: "In any event the United States should not accept any proposal for a Jerusalem police force which calls for the provision of armed force contingents by any of the following: the United States, the USSR, or the Soviet satellites."[53] A draft position paper that was circulated in the State Department in mid-February 1948 reported that "The Joint Chiefs of Staff have emphasized their view that, of all the possible eventualities in the Palestine situation, the most unfavorable in the security interests of the United States would be the intrusion of Soviet forces and, second only to that, the introduction of US troops in opposition to possible Arab resistance."[54] At about the same time, the NSC advised the president that any direct U.S. military involvement in Palestine would force substantial revisions in American policy toward Greece, which was only then beginning to show some signs of succeeding.[55]

By the spring of 1948, Washington's resolve to avoid sending American military units to Palestine had merged with widespread fears that the Soviet Union would manipulate the continuing disorder in the territory to its own advantage. John D. Hickerson, director of the State Department's Office of European Affairs, told Undersecretary of State Lovett in mid-April that "If the question of a UN security force in Palestine arises at the forthcoming special session of the General Assembly, a proposal for the participation of a Soviet contingent may be expected." As all previous episodes of Soviet participation in military occupations had involved "a consistent policy of conducting military occupation upon a zonal basis under the exclusive command of its own military authorities," it was his opinion that "it appears highly improbable that the Soviet Union would agree to participate in a security force in Palestine under any other conditions." Hickerson continued:

> The record of Soviet military occupation is clear. Soviet military occupation of Latvia, Lithuania and Estonia in 1940 led to the forcible incorporation of these countries into the Soviet Union. It has given Moscow complete control of the administration of the Soviet zones in Germany, Austria and Korea. In addition, it has proved a determining factor in establishing Communist-controlled governments in Poland, Hungary, Rumania and Bulgaria and in influencing their immediate neighbors to create governments of a similar political complexion. Wherever Soviet military occupation has occurred, it has consistently been accompanied by the political reorganization along Communist lines of the Soviet occupied zone. It is therefore axiomatic that if a Soviet contingent were permitted to participate in a UN security force in Palestine, the same pattern of communist control might be expected to emerge within the area occupied by Soviet troops.[56]

The Policy Planning Staff had reached a similar conclusion the previous January; in their view, American participation in any international peacekeeping force sent to Palestine under United Nations auspices would prompt Soviet participation, with the result that "further opportunities would be provided for the exercise of Russian influence in the whole Near Eastern area."[57] Analysts at the Central Intelligence Agency (CIA) concurred:

> In the present state of international security, probably no nation will send its troops to fight the Arabs in Palestine for the purpose of establishing a Jewish state unless its national interests are threatened by the failure of partition or unless it can hope to enlarge its sphere of influence. The USSR is the only nation that would gain from sending troops to Palestine. Since both the UK and the US have strong strategic reasons for refusing to allow Soviet or Soviet-controlled troops to enter Palestine, it is highly improbable that an international police force will ever be formed.[58]

Thus virtually every agency within the U.S. government opposed the deployment of American military units to Palestine on the grounds that U.S. intervention would prompt Soviet intervention.

But direct military involvement was not the only means by which Washington believed that Moscow could extend its influence in the eastern Mediterranean during the late 1940s. In its first "Review of the World Situation as it Relates to the Security of the United States," the CIA observed that the creation of an independent Jewish state in Palestine "would precipitate Arab armed resistance possibly assuming the proportions of a Holy War against Europeans and Americans as well as Jews." In the course of this struggle, Arab governments could be expected to cancel the concessions they had made to American and British oil companies; and "since the Arabs could not operate the oil properties themselves, and since, in these circumstances, they would be in desperate need of powerful support, it is probable that they would eventually transfer these concessions to the Soviet Union."[59] By May 1948 the agency had revised the basis for its assessment: "The termination of the mandate will also open the way to unlimited Jewish immigration and to the importation of heavier armament. There is every reason to suppose that the USSR will actively support the Jewish state, infiltrating Soviet personnel into Palestine and seeking to establish there a lodgment in the Eastern Mediterranean."[60] Such activities, CIA analysts later concluded, would be much more efficient than any sort of "direct intervention" by units of the Red Army.[61]

President Truman's senior advisers therefore posed a true dilemma concerning U.S. policy toward Palestine. Under no circumstances should American troops be sent into this part of the world. At the same time, active U.S. support for the creation of a Zionist entity would most likely result in greater Soviet influence throughout the region. But on the other hand any effort by Washington to block or delay the formation of a Jewish state might open a floodgate allowing Russian and eastern European communists to spread first to Palestine and then to surrounding countries. The latter possibility became more salient in early February 1948 when the British Foreign Office officially confirmed reports that "a considerable number of Communist party members had been found among some 15,000 Jewish immigrants attempting to enter Palestine without visas aboard the ships *Pan Crescent* and *Pan York*, which sailed from Burgas, Bulgaria, on December 27."[62]

Under these circumstances, the only prudent course for the United States to adopt resembled what Edward Ingram has called a policy of "masterly inactivity."[63] Because any direct American intervention in Palestine was almost certain to precipitate some sort of Soviet countermeasure that would most likely improve Moscow's position in the area, Washington opted instead to remain largely uninvolved in regional affairs. Eugene Rostow has described the operation of this policy in the following terms:

> While the British quandary in Greece triggered an American response of remarkable dimensions, the British quandary in Palestine resulted only in American hand-wringing, dithering, ineffectiveness, and indeed irresponsibility. For the Middle East, unlike Greece or Turkey, or Iran for that matter, our motto remained the old isolationist battle-cry, "Let the British do it."[64]

Only when local developments seemed about to go out of control did the United States take a direct role in determining the outcome of events.

Despite the scale of the fighting in Palestine throughout 1947-48, American officials never came to the conclusion that the situation was spiraling out of control. On 13 August 1948, Secretary of State Marshall cabled the U.S. ambassador in London to say that

> we agree with Bevin that [the] Palestine situation is serious, . . . but feel that his references to Russian threats against Iraq are somewhat of the red herring variety. As for his notion of building up RAF munitions in Iraq and Transjordan, . . . we feel that you should caution him to go very slowly. From this point of view [the] danger of Britain appearing as military guarantor of [the] Arabs against [the] Jews, which would invoke popular outcry here for [the] US to lift [its] arms embargo in favor of Israel, is much greater than Bevin's qualms over Soviet machinations against Iraq.[65]

Six weeks later, Secretary Marshall met with an Israeli delegation in Paris, who informed him "that a great deal had happened during the past five months and it was now clear that the State of Israel had been able to establish its government and to defend itself against its enemies." The secretary replied: "I said that I agreed with Mr. Shertok's view that Arab leaders now seemed to be taking a more realistic approach toward the Palestine case, but observed that the reaction on the other side had been as I expected. . . . I said that I had been criticized by both Arabs and Jews for our support of the Bernadotte plan which was probably the best evidence of our impartiality."[66] A clearer statement of American complacency regarding the situation could hardly have been made.

Washington's view that matters were for the most part under control in Palestine during the fall of 1948 coincided with a marked reduction in tension between the United States and the Soviet Union. On 26 April the U.S. ambassador in Moscow cabled the secretary of state to say that "We are inclined to believe that [the] Kremlin has already taken its immediate decision regarding Western Europe (less Germany and probably Austria) and that this decision is not to press [its] present line of policy to [the] point of provoking actual hostilities."[67] Three months later, the embassy in Moscow reported that its staff

> has long considered [the] likelihood of [the] Soviets turning to [the] Far or Middle East if temporarily stopped in west Europe. . . . While we are inclined to agree with Bevin . . . that at present [the] Middle East [is a] more likely target than [the] Far East, it seems to us even here that such [an] action [is] likely [to] be covert rather than overt. The Soviets['] position for any direct action has deteriorated due [to the] Yugoslav defection and [the] failure [of] Markos in Greece, while at [the] same time Palestine has opened up opportunities for exploitation that will not be neglected.[68]

In his end-of-the-year overview of events, the ambassador reiterated this rather optimistic assessment of Soviet intentions. In his opinion, the most likely trouble spots for the coming year were Berlin and the "Near East (notably Iran)," where there was a "certainty that Soviet plans would be altered to exploit any disruption [of] Western unity [or] reduction [of] Western strength."[69]

By the beginning of 1949, however, this relatively sanguine assessment of Soviet intentions in the Middle East was beginning to crumble. The Syrian foreign minister visited Moscow in mid-January and reportedly received "further intimation from the Soviet authorities of a possible shift in Soviet policy toward Palestine and the Arab states"; five weeks earlier, the Syrian government had publicized a purported "offer to reverse Soviet Palestine policy in return for a demonstration on the part of Syria and other Arab countries that they are not instruments of Anglo-American policy." The U.S. chargé in Moscow downplayed the Syrians' claims. In his words, "we do not believe there will be any sudden public shift in [the] Kremlin's Palestine policy. We should rather expect that the new line will be implemented somewhat later and gradually, with direct approaches to the Arab Governments timed to take advantage of developments connected with [the] UN effort to effect a Palestine settlement."[70]

British officials at the time were considerably more alarmed at the possibility of a new Soviet diplomatic initiative concerning Palestine than was the U.S. Department of State. On 24 January 1949 the American chargé in London informed Secretary Acheson that "When I saw Bevin on other matters this morning it was evident that he is deeply preoccupied with Palestine. He referred to Moslem resentment toward the West generated by Palestine developments and expressed [his] belief that [the] USSR would 'switch to the Arabs.' If it did so he thought this should be [a] matter of grave concern to both [the] US and [the] UK."[71] By early March, these misgivings were reinforced when Soviet forces in the Balkans initiated moves menacing both Yugoslavia and Greece. The British embassy in Washington passed along to the State Department a memorandum on 17 March noting that:

> The British Government has recently received reports of Russian troop movements and other military activities in South-East Europe, of which the following are typical:

The Truman Administration and the Palestinians

a) The arrival of fresh Soviet troops from the Soviet Union at Constanza, which has been "evacuated" by Roumanian troops;

b) The southward movement of Soviet occupation forces in Roumania towards Bulgaria;

c) The introduction of partial mobilization measures (blackout precautions, etc.) in Roumania;

d) The arrival of Soviet troops at Szombathely near the Austro-Hungarian frontier;

e) The massing of guerrillas, said to number from 10,000 to 15,000 on the Greco-Bulgarian frontier;

f) The movement of Soviet men and arms by sea to Albania.

"The British military authorities," the memorandum continued, "are not disposed to consider the reported Soviet movements abnormal. . . . They do not consider that these reports connote anything in the nature of military action. On the contrary there are indications that such reports are being deliberately disseminated with a psychological motive."[72]

Despite this disclaimer, the news of Soviet troop movements along the Greek border accompanied growing expectations in Washington of Soviet-sponsored insurgencies breaking out in various regions of the world. The embassy in Moscow cabled on 17 March that even though the USSR was unlikely to "make any aggressive move with armed forces this year likely to embroil it in major hostilities with [the] west[ern] powers," the Kremlin could be expected to "organize, support and supply so-called local and liberation forces, notably Greco-Macedonians in north Greece and south Yugoslavia, Barzani Kurds in Iran-Iraq, North Korean bands in South Korea, etc., all calculated to weaken local governments and contribute to [a] worldwide war scare."[73] As U.S. concern regarding the potential for greater Soviet involvement in the Middle East was rising, the Israeli government petitioned Moscow for a concessionary loan equivalent to the one approved by the U.S. Export-Import Bank in February 1949.[74]

The conjunction of these events, superimposed upon the persistent Israeli refusal to discuss the repatriation of Palestine's Arab refugees, convinced both Secretary of State Acheson and President Truman to announce in late March that "From the political point of view, the stabilization of the Near East is a major objective of American foreign policy. The refugee problem, therefore, as a focal point for continued unrest within the Arab states, a source of continuing friction between Israel and the Arabs, and a likely channel for Soviet exploitation, is directly related to our national interests." As a way of solving the refugee problem, the State Department recommended a comprehensive program designed:

1. To stimulate the adoption of plans to expedite the transfer of the problem from its present unproductive relief basis to a basis for a definitive settlement;

2. To persuade Israel to accept the principle of repatriation of an agreed number or category of refugees, with provision by Israel for appropriate safeguards of civil and religious rights and on condition that those repatriated desire to live at peace within Israel and to extend full allegiance thereto;

3. To persuade Israel to initiate the gradual repatriation of an agreed number or category as soon as possible;

4. To urge the Israeli Government to make equitable compensation for the property and assets of those refugees who do not desire to return and of those whose property and assets have been expropriated or otherwise disposed of by the State of Israel;

5. To provide for the permanent settlement in Arab Palestine in the near future of as large a number of the refugees as appears economically practicable.[75]

These guidelines provided the basis for the Truman administration's concerted effort during the succeeding two months to pressure the Israeli government to change its position concerning the rights of Arabs who had fled the fighting in Palestine the year before.

CONCLUSION

Domestic political explanations for American policy toward Palestine during the late 1940s obscure several key aspects of the Truman administration's foreign policy program, most notably the attention it paid to satisfying the needs of the territory's Arab inhabitants as a means of stabilizing regional affairs. As President Truman (perhaps apocryphally) remarked to a group of visiting dignitaries in 1945, "I do not have hundreds of thousands of Arabs among my constituents."[76] Consequently, any account of his administration's actions that looks only at domestic political factors is virtually certain to focus exclusively on the Jewish dimensions of the Arab-Israeli dilemma.

But by situating American policy toward Palestine in the context of broader U.S. efforts to resurrect a stable capitalist order in western Europe, to succeed Great Britain as the predominant strategic actor in Middle Eastern affairs, to prevent the Soviet Union from extending its influence in the eastern Mediterranean, and to encourage the expansion of American commercial and financial prospects, particularly in the oil-producing areas of the Gulf, one is forced to take a more comprehensive view of Washington's foreign policy program *vis-a-vis* this part of the world. And by thus broadening one's focus, it becomes possible to discern a marked concern on the part of the Truman administration for the plight of the Palestinian Arabs in general and for the refugees displaced by the 1948 war in particular.

This concern was no doubt partly inspired by the same sort of humanitarianism that engendered U.S. support for a Jewish national homeland. It was also, and arguably more fundamentally, dictated by considerations of

Western security. As long as developments in Palestine remained for the most part within bounds, the likelihood that direct American involvement in the region would precipitate Soviet intervention precluded any attempt by Washington to shape the course of events. When it appeared possible, however, that the severity of the refugee situation would generate substantial disorder in Middle Eastern affairs, thereby providing Moscow with the pretext or the opportunity to take a more active role in the region, the Truman administration pressed the Provisional Government of Israel to take a more conciliatory line regarding the Arab population of Palestine. This effort failed — but not for the obvious reasons. Just as the administration could not allow the difficulties confronting the Palestinians to de- stabilize local politics, so it could not (or rather, elected not to) push Tel Aviv to the point that the new status quo would be disrupted. The logic behind U.S. postwar policy in the Middle East led Washington to relinquish the initiative in regional affairs during the late 1940s. "Truman's vacillation" regarding Palestine[77] resulted neither from the president's indecisiveness nor from the activities of the Zionist lobby: it arose from the ambivalent strategic circumstances in which the United States found itself in the years immediately following World War II.

NOTES

1. Steven L. Spiegel, *The Other Arab-Israeli Conflict* (Chicago: University of Chicago Press, 1985), pp. 33-34.
2. See Peter Grose, "The President and the Diplomats," in William Roger Louis and Robert W. Stookey, eds., *The End of the Palestine Mandate* (Austin: University of Texas Press, 1986); Grose, *Israel in the Mind of America* (New York: Knopf, 1984).
3. John Snetsinger, *Truman, the Jewish Vote and the Creation of Israel* (Stanford, CA: Hoover Institution Press, 1974), pp. 79-80.
4. Michael J. Cohen, *Palestine and the Great Powers* (Princeton, NJ: Princeton University Press, 1982), pp. 53-54. For the views of a prominent defender of Truman, see Clark M. Clifford, "Recognizing Israel," *American Heritage* (April 1977), 28(3):4-11.
5. Spiegel, *Other Arab-Israeli Conflict*, p. 19.
6. Zvi Ganin, "The Limits of American Jewish Political Power: America's Retreat from Partition, November 1947-March 1948," *Jewish Social Studies* (Winter-Spring 1977), 39(1-2):20.
7. Shlomo Slonim, "The 1948 American Embargo on Arms to Palestine," *Political Science Quarterly* (Fall 1979), 94(3):495-514.
8. Cheryl A. Rubenberg, *Israel and the American National Interest* (Urbana: University of Illinois Press, 1986), p. 31.
9. See Slonim, "1948 American Embargo"; Yossi Feintuch, *U.S. Policy on Jerusalem* (Westport, CT: Greenwood, 1987).
10. See Michael J. Hogan, *The Marshall Plan* (Cambridge: Cambridge University Press, 1987).
11. Nathan Godfried, *Bridging the Gap between Rich and Poor: American Economic Development Policy toward the Arab East, 1942-1949* (Westport, CT: Greenwood, 1987), p. 124.
12. *Ibid.*

13. *Ibid.*, p. 170.
14. Cohen, *Palestine*, p. 157.
15. *Foreign Relations of the United States 1947* (Washington, DC: U.S. Government Printing Office, 1971), 5:1012. Hereinafter this source will be abbreviated *FRUS* followed by the appropriate year and volume number.
16. *FRUS 1948*, 5:1324-26.
17. *FRUS 1948*, 5:1427-28.
18. *FRUS 1948*, 5:1479-80.
19. *FRUS 1948*, 5:1486.
20. Lovett to Clifford, memorandum dated 26 October 1948, reproduced in *Declassified Documents* (Woodbridge, CT: Research Publications, various dates), reference number 803 720B. Hereinafter this source will be abbreviated *Declassified Documents* followed by the reference number of the document cited.
21. Lovett to Truman, cable dated 10 November 1948, *Declassified Documents*, (75) 202A.
22. *FRUS 1948*, 5:1478-79.
23. *FRUS 1948*, 5:1554-55.
24. Benny Morris, *The Birth of the Palestinian Refugee Problem, 1947-1949* (Cambridge: Cambridge University Press, 1987), pp. 258-59.
25. As quoted in Donald Neff, "U.S. Policy and the Palestinian Refugees," *Journal of Palestine Studies* (Autumn 1988), 18(1):105.
26. Morris, *Birth of the Palestinian Refugee Problem*, p. 277.
27. *Ibid.*, p. 278.
28. *Ibid.*, p. 279.
29. As quoted in Paul Kennedy, *The Rise and Fall of the Great Powers* (New York: Random House, 1987), p. 357.
30. See Michael S. Sherry, *Preparing for the Next War: American Plans for Postwar Defense, 1941-45* (New Haven, CT: Yale University Press, 1977).
31. Alan S. Milward, *The Reconstruction of Western Europe 1945-51* (Berkeley: University of California Press, 1984), p. 19.
32. Robert A. Pollard, *Economic Security and the Origins of the Cold War, 1945-1950* (New York: Columbia University Press, 1985), p. 199.
33. David S. Painter, *Oil and the American Century* (Baltimore, MD: Johns Hopkins University Press, 1986), pp. 155-56.
34. Pollard, *Economic Security*, p. 201.
35. Aaron David Miller, *Search for Security: Saudi Arabian Oil and American Foreign Policy, 1939-1949* (Chapel Hill: University of North Carolina Press, 1980), pp. 151-52; Cohen, *Palestine*, p. 346.
36. Michael B. Stoff, *Oil, War, and American Security* (New Haven, CT: Yale University Press, 1980), p. 212.
37. J.E. Peterson, *Defending Arabia* (New York: St. Martin's Press, 1986), pp. 58-59.
38. See James L. Gormly, "Keeping the Door Open in Saudi Arabia: The United States and the Dhahran Airfield, 1945-46," *Diplomatic History* (Spring 1980), 4(2):189-205.
39. See Melvyn P. Leffler, "The American Conception of National Security and the Beginnings of the Cold War, 1945-48," *American Historical Review* (April 1984), 89(2):352-53, 372-73.
40. X [George F. Kennan], "The Sources of Soviet Conduct," *Foreign Affairs* (July 1947), 25(4):566-82.

The Truman Administration and the Palestinians 79

41. John Lewis Gaddis, *Strategies of Containment* (New York: Oxford University Press, 1982), pp. 58-59.
42. *Ibid.*, p. 64.
43. William Roger Louis, *The British Empire in the Middle East, 1945-1951* (Oxford: Clarendon Press, 1984), pt. 3, ch. 6.
44. John A. DeNovo, "The Culbertson Economic Mission and Anglo-American Tensions in the Middle East, 1944-45," *Journal of American History* (March 1977), 63(4):923.
45. Godfried, *Bridging the Gap*, p. 123.
46. *Ibid.*, p. 128.
47. *Ibid.*, p. 133.
48. *Ibid.*, pp. 156, 160-61, 174.
49. *FRUS 1947*, 5:335.
50. *FRUS 1948*, 4:8.
51. *FRUS 1946*, 7:632.
52. *FRUS 1946*, 7:644.
53. National Security Council, "Policies of the Government of the United States of America Relating to the National Security," report dated 31 December 1948, *Declassified Documents*, (80) 377B.
54. U.S. Department of State, "The Position of the United States with Respect to Palestine," draft report dated 17 February 1948, *Declassified Documents*, 135A.
55. *FRUS 1948*, 4:51.
56. *FRUS 1948*, 4:825-26.
57. *FRUS 1948*, 5:549.
58. *FRUS 1948*, 5:673.
59. Central Intelligence Agency, "Review of the World Situation as it Relates to the Security of the United States," report dated 26 September 1947, *Declassified Documents*, (77) 179A.
60. Central Intelligence Agency, "Review of the World Situation as it Relates to the Security of the United States," report dated 12 May 1948, *Declassified Documents*, (77) 179D.
61. Central Intelligence Agency, "Review of the World Situation," report dated 19 August 1948, *Declassified Documents*, (77) 180C.
62. Arnold Krammer, *The Forgotten Friendship: Israel and the Soviet Bloc 1947-53* (Urbana: University of Illinois Press, 1974), p. 25.
63. See Edward Ingram, *The Beginning of the Great Game in Asia* (Oxford: Clarendon Press, 1979).
64. Eugene V. Rostow, "Israel in the Evolution of American Foreign Policy," in Clark M. Clifford, Rostow, and Barbara W. Tuchman, *The Palestine Question in American History* (New York: American Historical Association, 1978), pp. 56-58.
65. *FRUS 1948*, 5:1310.
66. *FRUS 1948*, 5:1452-53.
67. *FRUS 1948*, 4:837.
68. *FRUS 1948*, 4:909.
69. *FRUS 1948*, 4:943-47.
70. *FRUS 1949*, 6:656.
71. *FRUS 1949*, 6:694.
72. *FRUS 1949*, 6:265-66.
73. *FRUS 1949*, 5:596.

74. Yaacov Ro'i, "Soviet-Israeli Relations, 1947-1954," in M. Confino and S. Shamir, eds., *The USSR and the Middle East* (New York: Wiley, 1973), p. 133.
75. *FRUS 1949*, 6:828-42.
76. Spiegel, *Other Arab-Israeli Conflict*, p.19.
77. *Ibid.*, p. 24.

4

MISSED OPPORTUNITIES AND ROADS NOT TAKEN: THE EISENHOWER ADMINISTRATION AND THE PALESTINIANS

Deborah J. Gerner

INTRODUCTION

AS THE FIRST U.S. PRESIDENT to take office after the division of Palestine and the creation of the State of Israel, Dwight D. Eisenhower was uniquely positioned to restore Arab faith in the United States through strong U.S. action to implement United Nations resolutions on Palestine. Instead, due to a basic misinterpretation of the nature of the conflict and an unwillingness by U.S. decision makers to acknowledge Palestinian national aspirations, no progress was made toward the achievement of Palestinian self-determination during the 1950s. Yet there is little question that the decisions made during the Eisenhower administration had a significant influence in establishing the subsequent terms of debate on Palestine, as well as diminishing the possibility of significant compensation and repatriation of Palestinians and delaying indefinitely the establishment of an "independent Arab state" in any part of mandatory Palestine.

The Eisenhower years were critical ones in formulating the policy goals and public attitudes that continue to influence U.S. policy toward the Palestinians. They were years of transition: It was during the Eisenhower administration, for example, that the political and economic reconstruction of the post-World War II world — begun under President Truman — was essentially completed.

By the end of the Eisenhower presidency, both the international political structure of a bipolar, Cold War world and the liberal international economic

---

This research was supported in part by University of Kansas General Research allocation #3877-XO-0038. Thanks to archivist David Haight of the Dwight D. Eisenhower Library for his assistance in locating little-known documents and for his continuing good humor and sympathy with the author's frustration that many crucial materials remain classified after more than thirty-five years. An earlier version of this study was presented at the 1989 annual meeting of the American Political Science Association.

system established at the Bretton Woods Conference were firmly in place. As both the leading nuclear and capitalist power, the United States was in a position of unprecedented dominance. However, it lacked the international experience to use this power to influence affairs directly. Instead, it worked behind the scenes through the United Nations whenever possible, laundering U.S. policy preferences by giving them a veneer of international support. This strategy was frequently employed on issues related to Palestine.

This period was also significant within the Levant. Syria, Lebanon, and Jordan were among the Arab states that gained formal independence in the immediate post-World War II period as the European colonial powers withdrew from the Arab territories of the former Ottoman Empire. These new Arab governments faced massive problems of economic and political development and frequently faced domestic turmoil. As the international influence of war-damaged Britain and France declined, the United States sought to take over some of their responsibilities while avoiding actions that might be interpreted as explicit challenges to the European powers. The State of Israel was only a few years old, and was still technically at war with surrounding Arab countries whose leaders and populations viewed as illegitimate the process that had led to its creation.

The Palestinians were scattered and demoralized. Many were spread throughout areas controlled by Israel, Jordan, and Egypt — lands which had been theirs only a few years earlier. Others were living as refugees in nearby Arab countries, wanting and waiting to return to their homes. The political activism shown by the Palestinians in the 1930s and 1940s was greatly diminished. "For a decade or more following the 1948 Palestine war," Malcolm H. Kerr comments, "the shock of defeat and dispersion . . . caused a considerable decline in enthusiasm and activity [among Palestinians]; and the tendency of rival Arab states to try to co-opt the Palestinian cause for their own advantage reinforced the decline."[1] At the same time, Arab nationalism was gaining in power and credibility: The charisma of Gamal Abdel Nasser helped Egypt establish itself in a leadership position within the Third World, and pan-Arabism became the word of the day. With the death of Stalin in March 1953, the Soviet Union turned its attention to the formation of alliances in the Middle East after decades of only minimal interest. These factors — the rise of nationalism, changes in superpower involvement, the establishment of new political entities, unresolved regional conflicts — produced an unstable situation.

Dramatic changes were also occurring within the foreign policy structure of the United States government. The dominance of a relatively small group of foreign policy elites was challenged both by the public and by the newly expanded foreign policy bureaucracy created in the 1940s and 1950s.[2] Prior to World War II, foreign policy was a relatively low priority for the United States, except for interventionist activities in the Western hemisphere.[3] Most decisions were made by a small group of people. By the 1950s, this was no longer the case. Both the breadth and depth of U.S. involvement in foreign policy issues had increased, placing strains on a bureaucratic structure not originally

Missed Opportunities and Roads Not Taken   83

constructed to handle either the heavier workload or the high visibility.[4] In the societal arena, the foreign affairs interests of lobbies, the mass public, the media, and the business sector began to be articulated more emphatically. For the Middle East, this public pressure involved both the well-organized and often emotional appeals from pro-Zionist groups and the quiet lobbying of large multinational oil and construction companies with billions of dollars contingent on continued stable relationships with the Arab world. Weapons manufacturers found themselves in the middle, often pushing for arms sales to mutually antagonistic U.S. allies. Although Eisenhower himself appeared relatively immune to electoral pressures and lobbying efforts,[5] this was not always true for members of Congress or for the foreign policy bureaucracy.

As president, Eisenhower sought out advice and information on foreign policy from three major sources: the secretary of state, the National Security Council (NSC) and, following the creation of the position in 1953, the White House staff secretary (whose responsibilities included the management of top-secret security communications).[6] In particular, Eisenhower utilized the NSC to a far greater extent than had Truman, "formalizing, developing, and expanding the structure and procedures of the NSC and in effect creating an NSC *system* of which the Council was itself the primary but by no means the most significant portion."[7] Eisenhower also created the position of Special Assistant to the President for National Security Affairs (commonly referred to as the National Security Adviser) to work directly for him, linking the activities of the NSC and the White House.

This plethora of new players within and beyond government diminished somewhat the ability of the chief executive to control unilaterally the course of foreign policy in all its details, but the president and his closest advisers continued to have a significant impact on both the general direction and the specific choices that were made. Among foreign policy advisers, John Foster Dulles — the secretary of state from the beginning of the Eisenhower administration until his retirement due to cancer in 1959 — stands out. No other single person had as great an impact on Eisenhower's decision making as Dulles; his influence lingered even after his death. This was particularly true for areas in which Dulles had a particular interest or expertise, such as the Middle East:

> Dulles . . . was no stranger to the Arab-Israeli problem and had played an important role in facilitating the establishment of the state of Israel. As acting head of the U.S. delegation to the 1948 Paris General Assembly session, where admission of the provisional Government of Israel was being debated, Dulles successfully lobbied for a change in U.S. plans to postpone until the following year's session consideration of Israel's admission and to support the creation of an independent Arab state in Palestine. . . .
>
> Headed by Secretary of State [George C.] Marshall, the U.S. delegation had agreed to vote to postpone recognition by the General Assembly of Israel's admission. Instead, Marshall and his principal aide, Dean Rusk, advocated the U.N.'s acceptance of the plan drawn up by Chief Mediator Count Folke

Bernadotte (just before his assassination by Menachem Begin's *Irgun* terrorists), calling for a division of the old state of Palestine into Arab and Jewish sectors. Once Marshall was called to Washington to deal with the Berlin-blockade crisis, Dulles assumed charge of the delegation and, with support from delegates Eleanor Roosevelt and Ben Cohen, the U.S. delegation voted for the admission of Israel into the U.N.[8]

Dulles was strong-willed, influential, and independent of everyone except the president. The department he headed, however, was none of these. Damaged by McCarthyism and congressional budget cuts, in turmoil and demoralized by the bureaucratic changes brought on by Wristonization,[9] the State Department was hardly in a position to challenge its powerful head or to assert strongly the views of its regional experts. Initially, these departmental weaknesses led to a situation in which the old-time foreign service officers and other experts in the State Department had little ability to affect the course of U.S. decision making. The Arabists felt particularly ignored. Later, however, Dulles became more willing to use the range of knowledge and expertise available to him:

> When he first started as Secretary of State . . . [Dulles] tended to think that if he could just get rid of the onerous business of running the Department of State, that he could conduct our foreign policy much more effectively. . . .
>
> And then he explained later, perhaps five or six years later — "You know, I used to think that I could run the State Department better if I were off in an isolated corner of a building some place. I've changed my mind about that. I realize now that when I take up a problem in a staff meeting and we discuss it from every angle, this stimulates my thinking and it encourages me to see all of the aspects of the problem."[10]

Still, there remained a gap between the secretary and the Department of State personnel, and Eisenhower relied most heavily on the former. The importance of Dulles should not, however, be construed to mean Dulles acted autonomously or in directions inconsistent with Eisenhower's intent. Eisenhower, not Dulles, remained in control. "No one, none of my Cabinet officials, made as much of an effort to keep in absolute concord as did Dulles. He was insistent in knowing exactly what his mission and instructions were," reported Eisenhower.[11]

Together these elements — the international and regional systems, the increased foreign policy interest of the general population, the changes in governmental structure, and the particular individuals holding top decision-making positions — created the decisional milieu in which U.S. policy toward the Palestinians came to be formulated. The international and domestic contexts provide both the framework for what is possible and also set constraints on how the state can operate. The policy options available to decision makers, given this "objective" environment, have been labeled a state's "opportunity set." However, the way in which "the state *actually acts* or deals with its environment depends upon a number of factors: the sets of opportunities that the characteristics of the sub-environments 'objectively' provide the state, how the state perceives its environment, its willingness to take a particular course of action, and so on."[12] Because of the fluidity of the decisional milieu in the 1950s, examination of the Eisenhower administration's actions can illuminate general patterns in the process of foreign policy creation, as well as provide evidence about the roots of specific policies still in existence today.

This essay begins by describing briefly the overall foreign policy goals and objectives of the United States during the Eisenhower administration, and how these general attitudes and intentions influenced official U.S. actions toward the Palestinians. The perspectives of President Eisenhower and Secretary of State Dulles are given particular attention. It then examines the impact of several key policy choices made by the United States on issues affecting the Palestinians directly or indirectly. These decisions include U.S. support of UN resolutions critical of Israel, efforts to promote the Unified Plan for Jordan Valley Development, and the funding of the United Nations Relief and Works Agency for Palestine Refugees in the Near East (UNRWA). The focus is on foreign policy *outputs* rather than on the decision making *process*, although obviously both are important. An advantage of this approach is that although we may not be able to interpret the motivations or cognitive processes of an individual correctly, nor have full information on the interaction dynamics of a group of decision makers, the record of the actual choices and actions of these individuals and groups *is* now in large part available and can be analyzed.[13]

U.S. FOREIGN POLICY GOALS

The basic foreign policy orientation of the Eisenhower administration was set by the Eurocentric, anticommunist ideology of President Eisenhower and Secretary of State Dulles. All foreign policy goals — global expansion of economic liberalism, promotion of democracy, maintenance of peace internationally, support for the U.S.-dominated United Nations, establishment of collective security arrangements — were subsumed under this general approach and, if conflict occurred, anticommunism generally won out.[14]

This prevailing orientation is very clear when one examines the administration's stated policy goals for the Middle East. Two primary motivations are consistently mentioned as affecting decisions: the desire to protect essential supplies of petroleum for U.S. allies in Europe and the need to minimize Soviet involvement in the region.[15] Because the Palestinians had no direct control of oil, nor any significant military or political power that might serve to enhance or thwart Soviet interests, they were essentially invisible from the standpoint of this approach.

The concern with Middle Eastern petroleum has been part of U.S. calculations since shortly after oil exploration began in Bahrain in 1927. President Roosevelt's decision in February 1943 to declare Saudi Arabia "vital to the defense of the United States" and therefore eligible for Lend-Lease assistance in part reflected a desire to assure U.S. and European access to petroleum resources, as did U.S. actions in Iran in 1953. Repeatedly, Eisenhower returned to this concern, at one point writing in his personal diary:

> **13 March 1956**: The oil of the Arab world has grown increasingly important to all of Europe. The economy of European countries would collapse if those oil supplies were cut off. If the economy of Europe would collapse, the United Sates would be in a situation of which the difficulty could scarcely be exaggerated.[16]

Similarly, keeping the Soviet Union out of the Middle East was a theme raised repeatedly by decision makers in the Eisenhower administration. In a public address in 1954, Eisenhower spoke of his concern about communism:

> The principal and continuing factor [in the world today] is the persistently aggressive design of Moscow and Peiping, which shows no evidence of genuine change despite their professed desire to relax tensions and to preserve peace. Continuing, also, is the breadth and scope of the Communist attack; no weapon is absent from their arsenal, whether intended for destruction of cities and people or for the destruction of truth, integrity, loyalty.[17]

Dulles was even more outspoken; his hardline anticommunism permeated virtually every action he took and every public statement he made. Certainly Dulles's preoccupation with communism underlay his concern over Nasser's doctrine of Arab nationalism; this in turn affected his attitudes toward the Palestinians. To Dulles, Nasser's acceptance of economic and military assistance from the Soviet Union was a clear sign that Egypt was on the path toward becoming a Soviet satellite, and he feared this would provide opportunities for Soviet involvement in other Arab countries or groups that looked to Egypt for guidance.

This interpretation led to disagreements between Dulles and various State Department experts who wanted to use support for Arab nationalism as a way to improve U.S.-Arab relations. There was an important difference of opinion, for example, between Dulles and Assistant Secretary of State for Near Eastern, South Asian, and African Affairs Henry Byroade:

> Byroade's cables criticized Dulles's new policy [after Nasser had obtained aid from the Soviet Union in 1956] and argued that Washington should try harder to reconcile with Nasser. He thought Egypt's acceptance of Soviet aid did not imply sympathy for Moscow and felt the Dulles approach "suggests we continue to judge Egypt solely by whether — measured by our own criteria — she is for us or for the Soviets." Washington seemed to expect the Middle East states to be totally in the Western camp, but "neutralism exists over a large portion of this part of [the] world. If we fail to develop means of fruitful cooperation with this large body of people and continue to consider them as being either in enemy camp or as 'fellow travelers' I fear that before too long we will begin to appear in [their] eyes ... as being the unreasonable member of [the] East-West struggle."[18]

Dulles's view prevailed, as it usually did, but it cut off a possible avenue for constructive discussions on the Palestinians.

These two principal objectives — protection of petroleum and containment of communism — colored the U.S. assessment of all regional foreign policy issues. Finding a resolution to the Arab-Israeli dispute and the Palestine issue, for instance, was important only insofar as the failure to do so might damage U.S. and Western relations with the Arab world, make Arab states susceptible to Soviet influence, and risk the security of Middle Eastern oil sources. In the 1950s, many in the Foreign Service felt that "the question of the future status of the Palestinians was one that, unless it were resolved promptly, would pose a far greater threat to the U.S. and Western influence in the area than would any overt moves by the communist bloc."[19] Yet the policies made in Washington did not reflect this sense of urgency.

A third factor influencing U.S. actions was the U.S. relationship with former European colonial powers. Eisenhower wanted the United States to take a public anticolonial position as a way of improving ties with the newly independent states in Africa, the Middle East, and Asia. At the same time, France and Great Britain were both important Cold War allies, and Eisenhower did not want to alienate them unnecessarily. Only when Britain and France forced the issue, as they did during the Suez crisis, was the United States compelled to take a public position in opposition to its European friends. Great Britain and France remained influential in the Middle East in the 1950s, although their authority began to diminish, and the United States frequently appeared willing to restrict its own actions, particularly regarding Palestine, in deference to Europe's prior involvement.

From the beginning, the Eisenhower administration had an explicitly stated objective of pursuing an "evenhanded" approach in the Middle East, developing and maintaining strong ties with all anticommunist countries rather than following the Truman administration's policy of favoring Israel. In the spring of 1953, Secretary of State Dulles went on an extensive fact-finding mission to the Near East and South Asia. Shortly after his return, Dulles spoke in a radio address to the American people about his observations, concerns, and conclusions:

> Closely huddled around Israel are most of the over 800,000 Arab refugees, who fled from Palestine as the Israeli took over. They exist mostly in makeshift camps, with few facilities either for health, work, or recreation....
>
> The United States should seek to allay the deep resentment against it that has resulted from the creation of Israel. In the past we had good relations with the Arab peoples....
>
> Today the Arab peoples are afraid that the United States will back the new state of Israel in aggressive expansionism. They are more fearful of Zionism than of communism, and they fear lest the United States become the backer of expansionist Zionism....
>
> We cannot afford to be distrusted by millions who could be sturdy friends of freedom....

Israel should become part of the Near East community and cease to look upon itself, or be looked upon by others, as alien to this community. To achieve this will require concessions on the part of both sides.[20]

These basic motifs — Palestinians as refugees, the acceptance of Israel as part of the Middle East, the U.S. desire for positive relations with Arab states, the need for concessions from all parties to the Arab-Israeli conflict, and the need for U.S. economic assistance to the region — would be reiterated publicly throughout the years that followed. Missing, however, was any recognition of Palestinian identity as a national group.

National Security Council policy statements

The themes of Dulles's 1953 radio address are also expressed in the policy documents of the National Security Council. Within the first six months of his presidency, Eisenhower approved a new National Security Council document, NSC 155/1, on "United States Objectives and Policies with Respect to the Near East." Six general objectives for the Middle East were indicated:

- Availability to the United States and its allies of the resources, the strategic positions, and the passage rights of the area, and the denial of such resources and strategic positions to the Soviet bloc.
- Stable, viable, friendly governments in the area, capable of withstanding communist-inspired subversion from within, and willing to resist communist aggression.
- Settlement of major issues between the Arab states and Israel as a foundation for establishing peace and order in the area.
- Reversal of the anti-American trends of Arab opinion.
- Prevention of the extension of Soviet influence in the area.
- Wider recognition in the free world of the legitimate aspirations of the countries in the area to be recognized as, and have the status of, sovereign states; and wider recognition by such countries of their responsibility toward the area and toward the free world generally.

With specific reference to Palestine, the United States should:

- Make clear that Israel will not, merely because of its Jewish population, receive preferential treatment over any Arab state; and thereby demonstrate that our policy toward Israel is limited to assisting Israel in becoming a viable state living in amity with the Arab states and that our interest in the well-being of each of the Arab states corresponds substantially with our interest in Israel . . . .
- Seek progress in solving the Arab refugee problem through: (1) resettlement in neighboring Arab countries; (2) to the extent feasible, repatriation to the area now controlled by Israel; (3) to the extent feasible, emigration to countries outside the Near East; (4) settlement of problems concerning development projects, blocked Arab funds, and compensation for Arab refugee property.

- Use our influence to secure Arab-Israel boundary settlements, which may include some concessions by Israel.[21]

Subsequent NSC policy statements, while differing in details or emphasis, maintain this overall perspective. For example, NSC 5428 is almost identical to NSC 155/1, with the same six general objectives, except that it includes an extensive "Supplementary Statement of Policy on the Arab-Israel Problem" that specifies three additional objectives:

- To deter an armed attack by Israel or by the Arab states, and if an armed attack should occur to force the attacking state to relinquish any territory seized.
- To reduce current Arab-Israeli tensions and promote an eventual clear-cut peace between the Arab states and Israel.
- To alleviate the Arab refugee problem.[22]

This supplement reflects U.S. concern over the increased tensions between Israel and the Arab states, the greater Soviet involvement in the region, and the apparent inability of the United Nations to deal with the conflict, and in general suggests a more detailed awareness of the complexity of the issues to be resolved.

NSC 5428 was the guiding document for the following three and one-half years, until it was superseded in January 1958 by NSC 5801/1.[23] The Arab-Israeli conflict dominates the introductory remarks of NSC 5801/1, indicating that conflict's continuing impact on U.S. relations with the Arab world. The key goals remain the same: establishing permanent boundaries (although without the mention of possible concessions by Israel found in NSC 155/1); dealing with the Palestinian refugee problem through repatriation, resettlement, compensation, and rehabilitation; settling jurisdiction over Jerusalem; dividing the water resources of the Jordan River; setting limits on immigration into Israel; and lifting or relaxing the Arab boycott and the transit restrictions against Israel. The factors that led to the 1957 Eisenhower Doctrine are also reflected here. In particular, concern about Soviet influence is more pronounced than in the past, in response to increased Soviet commercial, political, and military ties with Arab states during the second half of the decade.

This policy statement remained operative only briefly; events in Lebanon, Jordan, and Iraq caused it to be revised less than nine months later. NSC 5820, partially declassified in 1987, reveals a clear shift in emphasis away from the Arab-Israeli conflict, and the deepening preoccupation with the Soviet Union foreshadowed in NSC 5801/1:

> The two basic trends in the area which have led to the weakening of the Western position have been the emergence of the radical pan-Arab nationalist movement and the intrusion of the USSR into the area. During the past three years, the West and the radical pan-Arab nationalist movement have become arrayed against each ther. The West has supported conservative regimes opposed to radical nationalism, while the Soviets have established themselves as

its friends and defenders. The virtual collapse during 1958 of conservative resistance, leaving the radical nationalist regimes almost without opposition in the area, has brought a grave challenge to Western interests in the Near East. . . .

[We] must reappraise our objectives and define those which are of such overriding importance that they must be achieved, if necessary, at the expense of others less essential. The critical importance of Near Eastern oil to our NATO allies requires that we make every effort to insure its continued availability to us and our allies. . . .

The most dangerous challenge to Western interests arises not from Arab nationalism *per se* but from the coincidence of many of its objectives with many of those of the USSR and the resultant way in which it can be manipulated to serve Soviet ends.[24]

Finally, NSC 6011 repeats the familiar U.S. objectives and positions *vis-à-vis* the Arab-Israeli conflict. By this point, any earlier sense of the Palestinians as a people was completely lost. They were "the refugees" (not even "*Palestinian* refugees"), a problem to be settled "within the context of the Secretary of State's speech of August 26, 1955."[25] From the perspective of the Eisenhower administration in its later years, once the refugees were compensated and successfully resettled, the problem would be solved.

EISENHOWER ADMINISTRATION'S APPROACH TO THE PALESTINE ISSUE

Recent research clearly indicates that top leaders in the United States in the 1940s had little interest in the establishment of a Palestinian state as proposed in UN Resolution 181.[26] It was far easier to support King Abdullah's aspirations to rule Arab Palestine, especially since British and American leaders believed Abdullah would help maintain Western influence in the region. This policy preference continued in the 1950s. Jordan was a conservative monarchy, closely tied politically, economically, and militarily to Great Britain and the United States. It was predictable and controllable in a way that an independent Palestinian state, even one linked economically with Israel, might not be.

Thus the Eisenhower administration developed an explicit policy regarding Palestine and the Palestinians that was consistent with previous U.S. decisions. Jordan was to govern most of the portion of Palestine that the United Nations had intended to become an independent Arab state and was to speak for the Palestinians. Israel would be allowed to annex the remaining areas originally designated as part of the Palestinian state. Gaza, as always, was largely ignored, except during crisis situations; it was assumed that Egypt would continue to control that area. The official U.S. position was summed up neatly by Under Secretary of State Walter Bedell Smith's statement in 1953 to the Near Eastern and African Affairs Subcommittee of the Senate Foreign Relations Committee:

> The refugee problem is the principal unresolved issue between Israel and the Arabs: outstanding issues are generally listed as compensation to the refugees, repatriation of the refugees, adjustment of boundaries, and the status of Jerusalem and the Holy Places. None of these issues can be separated from the refugee problem.[27]

Obviously, this policy did not include an understanding of the Palestinians as a distinct national group with political rights. To the contrary, the Palestinians were viewed exclusively as a refugee population that needed to be resettled, repatriated, rehabilitated, compensated, and otherwise taken care of so that the Arab-Israeli dispute could be resolved and the United States could continue to forge political alliances both with conservative Arab states such as Jordan and Saudi Arabia and also with Israel.

This rejection of the political rights of Palestinians had a number of important implications. First, it meant that U.S. decision makers made few if any efforts to identify Palestinian groups or individuals who had the authority to speak on behalf of Palestinian self-determination. It is striking to note that while U.S. officials in Washington met regularly with representatives of the Israeli government, conversations with Palestinian leaders were all but nonexistent. The issue of Palestine was formulated in terms of the *states* in the region. This left little room for Palestinians to be viewed as anything but refugees — unfortunate, pitiful, and tragic — in dramatic contrast to the positive, inspiring portrayal of the Jewish Israelis that was presented. Second, because of the way the problem was defined, the United States focused its attention on improving conditions for the Palestinian refugees through economic development activities (e.g., the Unified Plan for Jordan Valley Development) rather than pushing strongly for refugee repatriation, which was the preferred Arab solution.[28]

Finally, the U.S. attitude indicated that, at least in Washington, the United States fundamentally misunderstood the Palestine situation. Although Arab leaders in the surrounding states might privately admit Israel was in the region to stay, they would not publicly acknowledge this without a dramatic gesture of compromise by Israel. Israel had no intention of making such a gesture and the United States seemed disinclined to force the issue. Furthermore, U.S. policy ignored the fact that any proposed solution that satisfied the leaders of Syria, Jordan, and other Arab states was useless unless it was also acceptable to the Palestinians themselves. It was the political aspirations of the people of Palestine, and their sense of betrayal by the United States and the UN, that had to be addressed.[29] These factors partially explain why U.S. efforts at settling the Arab-Israeli dispute were unsuccessful: They were based on the false premise that if economic issues could be addressed adequately, the political dimensions of the problem would be more easily resolved. In fact, little or no progress could be made on the economic front without attention to the political issues. James Baster, who served for a period as economic adviser on the staff of UNRWA, commented in 1954:

> A solution to the Palestine refugee problem has so far been sought on the assumption that resettlement of the displaced population by economic measures would improve the prospects for a political settlement. Experience suggests that a strategy based on exactly the opposite assumption would be more likely to produce results. . . . The deterioration of refugee morale is now proceeding so rapidly that unless effective action is soon taken many refugees will have to be written off for good as useful citizens of any country.[30]

The Political Situation in the Levant

From the beginning, the U.S. choice to ignore the national rights and aspirations of the Palestinians was reinforced by the political situation in the Levant. One factor was the actions of some of the Arab leaders, particularly King Abdullah. Abdullah's ambition to lead an expansive Arab state encompassing present-day Lebanon, Syria, and Jordan, as well as the mandate of Palestine, extended far beyond the reality facing him at the end of World War II. Thus, in 1947 and 1948 he entered into secret negotiations with Zionist leaders to split Palestine between Jordan and Israel, an agreement that assured him of at least the lands of the West Bank.[31] Other Arab leaders spoke rhetorically of the need for Arabs to regain all of Palestine, but provided little support for Palestinian self-determination in the part of Palestine still under Arab control.

The majority of the Israeli leadership was also unopposed to Jordan's annexation of the West Bank, as that action served to wipe the name "Palestine" off the map.[32] Without a Palestinian state, there were few pressures for Israel to return to the borders established by the UN partition plan (which called for a far smaller Israel than the territory it controlled as of the 1949 armistice agreements). King Abdullah was in no position to argue with Israel over exact boundary lines, particularly since he had already increased Jordan's territory dramatically. Furthermore, it was far easier for Israel to deal with the known quality of Abdullah, and later with his grandson Hussein, than with the less well known, but clearly nationalist, Palestinians. King Abdullah had proven himself willing to collaborate with the Zionist state to the benefit of both the state and the king. This could not be assumed of the Palestinians.

In the 1950s Palestinians were disorganized and fragmented. Some 160,000 remained in Israel after the 1948-49 war, mostly in the Galilee, the Little Triangle region, and the Negev. These Palestinians within Israel were residents without full rights of citizenship, subject to military law, and under constant pressure to leave.[33] Many other Palestinians were refugees, often with no means of livelihood; in 1953, nearly 900,000 depended on relief from UNRWA.[34] The rest had been and remained residents in the parts of Palestine not occupied by Israel: Gaza and the West Bank. All Palestinians were shattered by the creation of Israel and by the failure of the Arab armies to maintain control even of the lands allotted to the Palestinians in the UN partition resolution. There were, however, clear differences in the political and economic desires of the three groups:

> The lives and livelihoods of Arabs who suddenly found themselves under Israeli rule were restricted and precarious....
>
> The second group, those who fled their homes in numbers around 700,000 was divided by wealth and by geography according to where they ended up after the war.... [A]ll were torn by the desire to return to their homes and property and the need to begin new lives. The property owners among them were further divided on the issue of compensation....
>
> The original inhabitants of the West Bank and Gaza were torn between the desire to regain the rest of Palestine in order to restore the social and economic fabric of the country and the need to settle with Israel to forestall further loss of territory and their own possible eviction from their homeland.[35]

In addition, the British had banned many indigenous political institutions as a result of the 1936-39 revolt, and had deported the principal Palestinian leaders.[36] As a result, there was no organized, unified Palestinian voice or single political authority that was able to speak effectively to the international community on behalf of Palestinians or challenge the claim of King Hussein to rule Arab Palestine as well as Transjordan.

In short, decision makers in the United States faced no coordinated pressures against the U.S. policy of subsuming the Palestinian issue under a more general concern about Arab-Israeli peace. At the same time, these policy makers saw both pragmatic and ideological justifications for the decision to ignore Palestinian political rights. As a result, the Palestinians were reduced in U.S. eyes to just another refugee problem.

The creation of UNRWA

In the 1947 Palestine Partition Resolution, the United Nations had "accorded the Palestinians national rights in the provisions.... authorizing them to establish 'the Arab state.'" As W. Thomas Mallison points out, however, in subsequent resolutions "the United Nations emphasized the Palestinians' *de facto* role as individuals who were refugees and war victims. The United Nations actions of that period were designed to implement their individual right of return and achieve their elementary human rights."[37] Not until the late 1960s did the UN again acknowledge the Palestinians as a national group. Thus, general UN policy toward the Palestinians during this period was consistent with the U.S. position that the Palestinians were a refugee population deserving of certain basic human rights, but not a national group with the right to control their political destiny.

The United Nations Relief and Works Agency, whose initial responsibilities included the creation of schemes for integrating Palestinian refugees into the economies of their host states and providing short-term relief, was established upon the recommendation of an economic survey mission sent to the region in 1949 by the United Nations Conciliation Commission for Palestine.[38] The United States had been involved in UNRWA since its creation and U.S. funds sustained the agency throughout the 1950s. The amount of money involved, while by no means adequate for the need, was still significant. Eventually, this expenditure was questioned by the U.S. Congress, which wondered how long the obligation would continue. In fact, in 1960, the U.S. Congress sought to tighten control over the funds in the following manner:

> Sec. 407. In determining whether or not to continue furnishing assistance for Palestine refugees in the Near East, the President shall take into account whether Israel and the Arab host governments are taking steps toward the resettlement and repatriation of such refugees. It is the sense of the Congress that the earliest possible rectification should be made of the Palestine refugee rolls in order to assure that only bona fide refugees whose need and eligibility for relief have been certified shall receive aid from the Agency and that the President . . . should take into consideration the extent and success of efforts by the Agency and the host governments to rectify such relief rolls. [39]

One concern was the belief by some members of Congress that U.S. contributions to UNRWA — 70 percent of its total budget each year — did not give the United States any credit with the Arab states. Another was a sense that U.S. support of UNRWA allowed the principal parties to the conflict to avoid resolving the issues between them. Although both these points had some validity, they ignored the fact that the efforts of UNRWA contributed significantly to the stabilization of at least two U.S. allies: Jordan and Lebanon. What the Congress saw as an unresolved crisis — the continuing refugee problem and U.S. support for those refugees — could also be interpreted as maintenance of a status quo that was in some ways quite consistent with U.S. interests in the region. The 1960 statement by Congress is also interesting given the generally low level of congressional effort to influence U.S. policy on Palestine during the Eisenhower years. That lack of attention differed significantly from the intense congressional involvement regarding Palestine during the Truman administration, as well as the active role Congress took after the 1967 Arab-Israeli War.

By the mid-1950s, it had become clear to UNRWA personnel that the refugee problem was not going to be solved through development activities in the host states. At this point, UNRWA changed tactics and began working with the UN Education, Scientific, and Cultural Organization (UNESCO) to expand its elementary and secondary school system and its vocational training programs. At the same time, the UN General Assembly passed a resolution extending the life of UNRWA an additional five years, breaking the pattern of a year-by-year mandate.[40] This change in tactics led to an unexpected and ironic result:

> [An] agency designed by its most important sponsor, the United States, to sweep the refugee problem under the carpet by bringing about the absorption of the Palestiniáns in the Arab countries has, through its education programmes, contributed to the refugees' growing political maturity and national solidarity.[41]

Throughout the 1950s, the United Nations continued to address international concerns about the Palestinians by treating Palestinians only as a refugee community in need of short-term assistance. Although there was some recognition of the flaws in this formulation, the effort to resolve the Palestinian situation through economic rather than political means remained. In a conversation among Dag Hammarskjold, Cabot Lodge, and Christian Herter on 16 December 1957, Hammarskjold argued that the "Palestinian refugee problem" could not be solved by referring to it in that language because, in Herter's words:

> the mere use of that phrase brought up insuperable political difficulties. [Hammarskjold] felt that only through a large economic development fund could the gradual absorption of these refugees be effected without bringing in the political implications that a settlement of the refugee problem was the principal reason for the establishment of such a fund.[42]

It is not clear the extent to which the United Nations approach was directly determined by the U.S. position on Palestine, but certainly the dominance of the United States, Great Britain, and France in both the General Assembly and the Security Council was significant. UN and U.S. attention again focused on the Palestinians with the declaration of 1959 as World Refugee Year. Various national and global reports were generated to summarize the situation of all refugee groups around the world. While this served to keep the issue alive in the minds of policy makers, the focus on refugees *per se* served to blur the distinctions among diverse groups of people whose refugee status originated from very different causes.[43]

The United States and the "refugee problem"

Throughout the Eisenhower presidency, official U.S. public policy at the United Nations called on the Arab states and Israel to honor the 1949 armistice lines until permanent borders were negotiated, and supported the repatriation, compensation, resettlement, and rehabilitation of the Palestinian refugees. While this official policy line correctly reflected U.S. actions regarding border violations, it was a less accurate guide to U.S. refugee policy.

The United States frequently indicated in public that it would like Israel to permit significant numbers of Palestinians to return to their homes. The U.S. also repeatedly cosponsored UN resolutions on repatriation.[44] (About 8,000 Palestinians — less than one percent of all the refugees — were allowed to return to Israel as part of a family reunion plan that ended in March 1953.)[45] U.S. public support for repatriation often seemed formulaic and half-hearted, however; and it is clear that the principal foreign policy decision makers in the Eisenhower administration, like their predecessors under Truman, believed the majority of the Palestinian refugees should remain in the surrounding Arab states rather than return to Israel.[46]

As early as June of 1953, Dulles stated his belief that "Some of these [Palestinian] refugees could be settled in the area presently controlled by Israel. Most, however, could more readily be integrated into the lives of the neighboring Arab countries."[47] State Department personnel in 1953 thought in terms of repatriating no more than 100,000 Palestinians. This was considerably less than

15 percent of all refugees, but it was expected to be adequate to accommodate those who wished to return. According to one State Department official, "Most of the refugees . . . will settle in the Arab lands by preference once the UNRWA projects get underway and the psychological roadblocks to resettlement begin to crack and be removed one by one."[48] Later that same year, in a statement to the UN General Assembly, James P. Richards presented the issue of repatriation as something Israel ought to *consider*, rather than as a clear obligation:

> We also believe that the interests of both the Palestine refugees and of Israel herself make it important for Israel to take further steps with a minimum of delay in discharge of the responsibilities she has accepted for compensating the Palestine refugees, and that Israel would be well advised to renew consideration of the responsibility for and the possibilities of repatriation.[49]

Throughout this period, Israel consistently refused to consider the possibility of significant repatriation or transfer of territory. In a private conversation with U.S. officials in late 1955, Israeli Ambassador Abba Eban:

> emphatically reiterated [a long-standing position that] Israel would make no territorial concessions to the Arabs and derided Egypt's desire for land contiguity with other Arab states. He further indicated Israel would shortly be asking to hold discussions with us regarding the Secretary's August 26 proposal on financing compensation to refugees and strongly implied Israel would stand adamantly against any sizeable repatriation.[50]

Despite the official U.S. stance in favor of at least limited repatriation, and the private statements to the Israelis "that they must in some way accept the principle of repatriation,"[51] there is no evidence that U.S. decision makers considered using sanctions to pressure Israel on this point. Israel balked at the idea of repatriation, citing security concerns and economic constraints, and the United States did not push the issue.

While U.S. decision makers sent mixed messages on repatriation, the attitude on compensation for property left in Israel by Palestinian refugees was more straightforward: this was considered an essential element in any peace agreement. At the same time, the U.S. recognized that Israel's economy was in no position to support compensation if it was to maintain the standard of living expected by its U.S. and European immigrants. Thus, in August 1955, Dulles (speaking, as he put it, "with the authority of President Eisenhower") proposed that Israel be granted an international loan to help cover the costs of compensation. The United States was willing to underwrite the loan to a "substantial" extent.[52] Israel did periodically acknowledge the possibility of compensation for the Palestinians.[53] However, no action was taken to provide for such a transfer of funds, despite the U.S. offers of assistance. In frustration, the officer in charge of Israel-Jordan Affairs commented publicly:

> Still, nothing is heard of efforts to set aside this income [from Palestinian lands and property taken over by Israel] in transferable liquid assets against the day when compensation must be paid. Official tables of Israel's balance of

payments of foreign indebtedness make no mention, even by footnote, of the standing obligation by Israel to make future payment for property which she has taken over and from which she is deriving present benefit.[54]

In short, during the Eisenhower presidency there was public and private discussion by the United States about repatriation and compensation of Palestinians, but no progress was made on either issue.

Unified Plan for Jordan Valley Development (the "Johnston Plan")

Increased economic development in the Arab states that were expected to accept the Palestinian refugees was critical to the U.S. resettlement plans. On 14 October 1953, Eisenhower announced that he was sending Ambassador Eric Johnston to the Middle East as his personal representative. Johnston's task was to explore possibilities for the joint use by Jordan, Lebanon, Syria, and Israel of the Jordan River for irrigation systems and hydroelectric facilities. If the Jordan River could be used to expand the amount of arable land in the Arab states (particularly Jordan), Palestinian refugees could then be resettled without creating an unreasonable burden on their Arab hosts. This, rather than significant repatriation of Palestinians, was clearly the preferred U.S. solution.[55] The Johnston Plan was supported by the United States Information Agency, which in December 1953 began:

> a carefully-conceived educational campaign on the subject for the Arab states and Israel. The Voice of America broadcast a series of talks in Arabic on the history, geography, and possible development of the Jordan Valley. These scripts were later made available for magazine articles in the area. Pamphlets in Arabic were published by USIA's Near East Regional Service Center in Beirut. Ambassador Johnston was encouraged to make several speeches on the subject before audiences in the United States; these speeches were then transmitted to the area by USIA press and radio services. Motion pictures showing large hydro-electric and irrigation projects in the US were sent to the area for exhibit to government leaders, agriculturalists and engineers. USIA officers going to the area were specially briefed on the subject.[56]

The United States had great hopes for this approach. In his first progress report, Johnston wrote that the Jordan Valley project should be considered a central element in U.S. Middle East policy and "a means of constructing the foundation on which peace in the area may ultimately be built."[57] This attitude appears to have been widely shared within the administration.

The United States felt a certain urgency to develop a plan for the shared use of regional water resources. On 2 September 1953 Israel had begun construction of a canal at Banat Yaqub in the UN Demilitarized Zone near the Syrian border for the diversion of the waters of the Jordan River for its own development activities.[58] An investigation by General Vagn Bennike, the chief of staff of the United Nations Truce Supervision Organization, determined that this action constituted a violation of the Israel-Syria armistice agreement of 1949. Reactions in Israel to this ruling were hostile.[59] Israeli Foreign Minister Moshe Sharett rejected Bennike's request to stop work on the canal and said he would take the issue to the UN Security Council. The UN, however, was not sympathetic to Israel's arguments. After earlier private warnings were ignored, the United States formally told Israel on 19 October that if their construction work did not stop, the United States would withhold the aid allotted to Israel under the Mutual Security Aid program.[60] According to Edward Tivnan, "Eisenhower also threatened to cancel the tax exemption on charitable donations to the United Jewish Appeal and other Jewish organizations raising money in the US to help Israel in its massive resettlement program,"[61] although nothing came of this.

On 20 October, the United States deferred the transfer of $26.25 million in economic assistance to Israel. One week later, Israel agreed to suspend temporarily work on the diversion project; the U.S. aid was released to Israel the following day.[62] Although this U.S. action appears to have been taken in part out of concern for the success of the Unified Plan and its prospect for aiding Palestinian refugees, an additional motive, perhaps even the principal incentive, was the U.S. desire to affirm and strengthen the authority of the United Nations.[63]

Johnston made four trips to the Middle East over a two-year period to promote various versions of the Unified Plan. Ultimately, however, he was unable to gain its acceptance. Publicly, the Arab states rejected the plan for a number of reasons. First, the share of water to be granted to Israel was significantly greater than Israel's proportion of the region's population, despite the fact that the three major tributaries of the Jordan River sprang from Arab territories. Second, the plan would allow for the resettlement of only 100,000 Palestinians and thus did not seriously address the refugee problem it was promoted as solving. Some Arabs expressed concern that the proposed diversion of the Jordan River would lower the level of the Dead Sea which would harm salt and potash mining projects in Jordan and might increase the salinity of the river. There were fears that acceptance of the plan would be used to freeze the existing political situation (Israel's 1949 armistice boundaries). Also, there was suspicion of the United States for acting unilaterally rather than through the United Nations. Finally, it was clear that Israel's share of the water would strengthen Israel by enabling Zionist settlement in the Negev; the Arab states were not prepared to endorse any policy with such an effect.[64]

Although each of these reasons for rejection of the plan sounds credible, Johnston indicates that, by October 1955, the technical aspects of the proposal had been agreed upon by the professional advisers of all four states.[65] Domestic political concerns stood in the way of approval, however: The leaders of Israel and the Arab countries all felt their positions would be jeopardized if their constituencies knew they were willing to cooperate with the "other side." According to Johnston, "the Prime Minister of Syria said he would be assassinated in Damascus if he tried to do some of the constructive things suggested,"[66] and other politicians were equally reluctant to act publicly.

This rejection created an awkward situation for the United States. How could it best assist Jordan's development of water resources — deemed essential for the resettlement of Palestine refugees — without appearing to undercut the Unified Plan? Ultimately the United States agreed to support a Jordanian diversion project on the lower Yarmuk River that was "not inconsistent with the Unified Plan as it related to the lower Yarmuk."[67] By this point, for all practical purposes, the Johnston plan was dead. Meanwhile, after a brief delay, Israel resumed work at Banat Yaqub. This remained a sore spot for Israeli-U.S. relations. Although the United States continued to protest unilateral Israeli development of the Jordan River, it was unwilling or unable to take the actions necessary to stop Israel from doing so.[68]

United States position on boundaries

Unlike the clear disjuncture between public posture and actual policy on Palestinian repatriation, the U.S. position on boundaries was internally and externally consistent. The United States said repeatedly that it considered the 1949 armistice borders to be binding on all parties until permanent boundaries could be negotiated. Furthermore, throughout its first term in office, the Eisenhower administration stressed that permanent borders might require some minor adjustments in order to reunite Palestinian villages with their agricultural lands:

> I see no sentiment here [at the Department of State] reflecting a belief that the Armistice boundaries of Israel are sacrosanct but, on the contrary, there is a general belief that they must be modified to remove gross injustices at such points as Tulkaram and Qalqilya. . . . I believe no clear case exists that Israel owes territory to an existing Arab state; she does owe land, I think (whether by repatriation or by territorial cession, or both) to the Arab refugees.[69]

Particularly during the first term of the Eisenhower administration, there were serious problems with border violations by all parties. Whereas most incursions from Egypt or Jordan were by unorganized groups or by individual Palestinians crossing to retrieve property in Israel, pick crops, or visit family members, Israeli border crossings frequently involved formal military operations.[70] The United States was openly critical of such preplanned military maneuvers and on several occasions cosponsored UN General Assembly or Security Council resolutions critical of Israel. Israel consistently ignored these resolutions, just as it had ignored Bennike's ruling on the Banat Yaqub diversion canal in 1953. This caused increased tension between the United States and Israel, both because the inability of the UN to compel Israel to abide by its declarations damaged the UN's credibility in the eyes of the Arab countries and because Israel's actions were seen as counter-productive to regional stability and the prospects for peace.

After the Israeli raid on Qibya on 14-15 October 1953, for example, the United States cosponsored a UN Security Council condemnation expressing "the strongest censure of that action."[71] This led to some criticism within the United States of the UN statement. U.S. representative to the UN Henry Cabot Lodge was defensive in a letter to Barney Balaban of Paramount Pictures:

> As a matter of fact the resolution on the Kibya incident, while not worded as I would have worded it personally, is not as bad as some naturally excited people have said. It makes it quite clear that we do favor the development of a just and lasting peace in the Middle East which is what Israel must have. . . .
>
> There was some alarm, which I think was without foundation, about the wording of the resolution and it was even said that the use of the word "censure" was the strongest that had ever been used in a United Nations resolution. I have had this looked up and it is not the case. The United Nations used stronger language on its resolution on the Spanish question on April 29, 1946, on the observance in Bulgaria, Hungary and Romania of human rights and fundamental freedoms on November 3, 1950, on the repatriation of Greek children on December 15, 1952, and on the complaint of the Union of Burma regarding aggression against it by the government of the Republic of China on April 23, 1953.[72]

Six months later, on 28 March 1954, Israeli forces attacked the West Bank Palestinian village of Nahalin, drawing a sharp condemnation from Assistant Secretary of State Henry A. Byroade: "To the Israelis I say . . . you should drop the attitude of the conqueror and the conviction that force and a policy of retaliatory killings is the only policy that your neighbors will understand. You should make your deeds correspond to your frequent utterance of the desire for peace."[73]

As the Israeli military border crossings continued, U.S. officials began to lose patience. In his public statements following the Israeli attack against Gaza on 28 February 1955, Lodge reflected:

> We have three times previously in the Council made the point clear either in resolutions or statements that Israel's retaliatory actions are inconsistent with its charter obligations. Now we have been faced with the fourth incident, and we believe it most serious because of its obvious premeditation.[74]

Less than a year later, Lodge again found himself speaking critically at the United Nations regarding Israeli actions. This time it was the 11 December 1955 attack on Syrian outposts overlooking Lake Tiberias that led to a UN Security Council "condemnation" of Israel's "flagrant violation" of the cease-fire and armistice agreements:

> It is always deplorable for any government deliberately and willfully to plan and carry out an attack against its neighbor in violation of its solemn international commitment. What makes these particular deliberations more serious is the fact that a member of the United Nations — indeed, a member created by the United Nations — should now be before this Council for the fourth offense of this kind in 2 years. . . .
>
> Each of the incidents from Qibya in 1953, through Nahalin, Gaza and now in the Tiberias area, has resulted in a deterioration in the situation in Palestine. This is something that the Security Council cannot ignore.[75]

There were other Israeli and Arab border actions that were criticized by the United States, but these four stand out because of the severe condemnations they elicited from officials of the U.S. government, despite general U.S. public opinion supportive of Israel and critical of the U.S. censures.[76]

It is important to stress that these official U.S. statements were not "pro-Palestinian" as much as they were an effort to maintain the credibility of the United Nations and the legitimacy of the 1949 armistice agreements. They are significant as further evidence that the Eisenhower administration was not hesitant about criticizing Israel when it believed U.S. national interests were involved. This suggests that, at least for the 1953-61 period, explanations of U.S. decision making on Palestine that stress the impact of domestic pressures in favor of Israel are not particularly useful. Other factors, such as the U.S. concern to prevent "radical influence" in the Middle East and the views of individual decision makers, must be taken into account in order to understand U.S. policy toward the Palestinians during the Eisenhower years.

The Suez crisis and beyond

Much has been written about the 1956 Suez War: the events leading to the Israeli attack on Egypt; the secret plan for British and French involvement, ostensibly as mediators but in fact as participants; U.S. anger at the actions of its allies; and the actual course of the war.[77] While the entire Suez crisis affected the Palestinians, the U.S. response to Israel's refusal to withdraw from Gaza after the cease-fire agreement is most relevant here.

The United States worked intensely through the United Nations to resolve the Suez crisis. It sponsored the initial cease-fire resolution on 2 November 1956 and called upon Israel to pull its troops behind the 1949 armistice line immediately. A personal message from Eisenhower to Israeli Prime Minister David Ben-Gurion on 7 November reinforced the U.S. position. Meanwhile, the United States considered how else it could convey its dismay at Israel's attack and put pressure on Israel to withdraw from the areas it occupied. One suggestion was to hold up Israeli bank balances in the United States unofficially; however, this was judged impractical (as well as politically difficult) and was not pursued.[78]

It appeared initially that Israel would accede to U.S. and UN demands. But after three months, Israel still maintained military control of two areas: Gaza and Sharm al Sheikh. Eisenhower sent a blunt cable message to Ben-Gurion on 3 February 1957 urging Israel to withdraw its forces behind the General Armistice Line as called for by several UN resolutions or risk damage to U.S.-Israeli relations.[79] The following day the United States voted in favor of two U.S.-sponsored UN resolutions that had been tabled on 1 February. The first called on Israel to withdraw its troops behind the 1949 armistice lines; the second demanded that both Israel and Egypt observe the armistice.[80] Dulles then went public with administration criticisms of Israel in a press conference on 5 February and, a week later, sent a secret aide-mémoire to Ben-Gurion in which he warned Israel that it risked angering members of the United Nations with its continuing "occupation in defiance of the overwhelming judgment of the world community."[81]

As so frequently was the case with Middle East affairs during the Eisenhower administration, the issue took on an importance that transcended any immediate concern for Egypt or the Palestinians: How would the U.S. policy on Gaza affect Arab perceptions of the United States? Would it provide an entrée for the Soviet Union? How would Israel's blatant refusal to follow UN resolutions affect that organization's credibility around the world? On 16 February, the president met with several cabinet members to determine U.S. options:

> In considering various courses of action, I rejected, from the outset, any more United Nations resolutions designed merely to condemn Israel's conduct. . . .
>
> To prevent an outbreak of hostilities I preferred a resolution which would call on all United Nations members to suspend not just governmental but *private* assistance to Israel. As we discussed it, [Secretary of the Treasury] George Humphrey put in a call to W. Randolph Burgess, Under Secretary of the Treasury for Monetary Affairs, who gave a rough estimate that American private contributions [to Israel] were about $40 million a year, and the sale of Israel's bonds in our country between $50 and $60 million a year.[82]

Eisenhower took several actions. He made public Dulles's aide-mémoire on 17 February and, on 20 February, he contacted Ben-Gurion yet again.

> Thus, in the absence of an immediate and favorable decision by your Government, there can be no assurance that the next decisions soon to be taken by the United Nations will not involve serious implications. . . .
>
> I would greatly deplore the necessity of the United States taking positions in the United Nations, and of the United Nations itself having to adopt measures, which might have far-reaching effects upon Israel's relations throughout the world. Our position must, however, conform with the principles for which we have firmly stood in relation to these tragic events.[83]

The same day Eisenhower sent the telegram to Ben-Gurion, he and Dulles met with a large group of congressional leaders — Democrats and Republicans — who expressed great concern at the U.S. criticism of Israel. In justifying the actions of the administration, both men repeated familiar themes:

> Eisenhower warned the legislators that Russian influence among the Arabs would most certainly increase if the Israeli [sic] continued to resist the compliance order. Besides, there would be further interruptions in the supply of oil from the Middle East, with more disaster to the economy of Britain and the Western European nations. . . .
>
> Then Eisenhower stated flatly that he did not know how to protect American interests in the Middle East except through the United Nations. If the United States failed to support the United Nations on the Israel issue, he declared, it would be a lethal blow to the principles of the world peace organization.
>
> "Nobody likes to impose sanctions," the President concluded, "but how else can we induce Israel to withdraw to the line agreed on in the 1949 armistice?"

Dulles . . . told [the congressmen] that if Israel were allowed to defy the withdrawal order any longer, the basic principle of the United Nations forbidding any individual nation from taking the law into its own hands would become ineffective and worthless.[84]

These ideas were reiterated by Eisenhower in a radio and television address to the American people that evening:

Should a nation which attacks and occupies a foreign territory in the face of United Nations disapproval be allowed to impose conditions on its own withdrawal? If we agree that armed attack can properly achieve the purposes of the assailant, then I fear we will have turned back the clock of international order. We will, in effect, have countenanced the use of force as a means of settling international differences and through this gaining national advantage. . . . If the United Nations once admits that international disputes can be settled by using force, then we will have destroyed the very foundation of the organization, and our best hope of establishing a world order. That would be a disaster for us all.[85]

Eisenhower's words were not met with universal approval: 90 percent of the letters and telegrams to the White House after the speech were supportive of Israel.[86] Nevertheless, Eisenhower held to his position that Israel had to withdraw its troops.

The issue finally came to a head on 22 February. Charles Malik, foreign minister of Lebanon, introduced a UN resolution calling for a halt to all military and economic assistance to Israel, including by individuals.[87] Once it became clear that the United States would support this resolution, Israel acquiesced, albeit not before receiving repeated assurances regarding U.S. support of free navigation through the Gulf of Aqaba. Israel began its withdrawal of troops from Sharm al Sheikh and Gaza on 4 March, completing it by 7 March.

For the second time in his presidency, Eisenhower had directly challenged Israel's right to take actions contrary to UN resolutions in territory beyond the 1949 armistice lines. On both occasions there was congressional and public pressure to back down; and in both cases Eisenhower refused to oblige his critics. But there were important differences in the two cases. In 1953, U.S. economic assistance to Israel was actually halted, if only for eight days; in 1957 this was threatened but did not occur. In 1957, Israel actually did withdraw from Gaza, in accordance with UN resolutions; in 1953 it ceased work on the diversion canal only temporarily. Finally, whereas U.S. actions in 1953 could be argued to have been motivated in part by concern for Palestinian refugees (within the framework of U.S. desires to resettle them in Jordan and elsewhere), in 1957 the principal concerns were for limiting Soviet influence in the region, restoring European access to petroleum, and maintaining some legitimacy for the United Nations — in short, the traditional U.S. policy goals. The fact that Israel was occupying the territory of *Palestinian* Arabs does not appear to have been a significant factor for U.S. decision makers. William Stivers comments:

> The events of the immediate post-Suez period suggest what might have been accomplished if Eisenhower had used his leverage on behalf of the Palestinians. But there was a difference between using U.S. leverage for the immediate sake of Europe's oil and using it to fulfill the long-term requirements of regional stability. Ensuring Europe's oil demanded nothing more than a narrow realism. Coping with the Palestinian question demanded sensitivity toward the fate of an Arab people.[88]

That sensitivity — that willingness to look beyond short-run realist concerns — was missing.

The immediate post-Suez period was the last time the Palestinians were a foreign policy concern for the Eisenhower administration, even indirectly. The 1957 Eisenhower Doctrine was "designed to deal with the possibility of Communist aggression, direct and indirect [in the Middle East]."[89] It was explicitly *not* intended to address the Palestine question nor even the more general issue of Arab nationalism. Shortly thereafter, the United States found itself caught up in the internal problems of Lebanon, Iraq, and Jordan; and soon other issues — disarmament, Cuba, global economic relations — came to dominate the attention of foreign policy decision makers. Through a combination of inertia and deliberate design, Palestine sank to the bottom of the agenda.

CONCLUSION

The eight years of the Eisenhower administration witnessed a series of missed opportunities by the United States for a resolution of the Palestinian issue that would have been, if not optimal, at least better — for the Palestinians, for regional stability, for U.S.-Arab relations — than what actually transpired in subsequent decades. Despite an overall policy toward the Middle East that was explicitly and publicly "evenhanded" and "impartial," the Eisenhower administration was unwilling to mediate a resolution to the conflict between Israel, the Palestinians, and the Arab states.

> [In] the short run, Eisenhower achieved what he desired. Pro-Western regimes in the area remained pro-Western and European oil supplies remained secure. . . .
>
> Judged from a long-run perspective, Eisenhower's apparent successes quickly pale. The United States enjoyed unprecedented leverage in the Middle East; it would probably never enjoy such leverage again. This leverage was not put to full constructive use. The administration addressed no concerted effort toward resolving the Palestinian problem; and after 1956, no attempt was made to broker an Arab-Israeli peace. Eisenhower thus bequeathed to his successors a virulent conflict that would go, at best, into sporadic remission before the next explosive outbreak. His ability to bring about a settlement was greater than any president who followed; hence, his failure to act when he had the chance imposed heavy burdens on future US leaders.[90]

Two factors stand out among the many that account for this disappointing record. First, the Eisenhower administration followed the already established policy of rejecting Palestinian national aspirations and the right of the Palestinians to self-determination. This policy, which characterized the U.S. approach to Palestine under presidents Roosevelt and Truman, was given renewed vigor in the 1950s under Eisenhower. Second, the Eisenhower administration fundamentally misjudged the nature of the problem, believing that improvements in the economic well-being of Palestinian refugees would serve as adequate compensation for the loss of a homeland, and that Palestinians in the West Bank would be content to live indefinitely as Jordanians under the rule of a king. Neither assessment was accurate, and the lack of real, as opposed to token, acknowledgement of the political aspirations of Palestinians doomed from the beginning U.S. efforts to deal with the refugee issue. In 1953, only five years after Israel had been established and Jordan and Egypt had taken control of the West Bank and Gaza respectively, it was not too late realistically to envision both repatriation of Palestinians to Israel and changes in the 1949 armistice lines to allow for an independent Palestinian state. By 1961, Israel was stronger militarily and economically, larger in population, less willing than ever to compromise, and less vulnerable to U.S. pressure. The opportunity for a resolution of the Question of Palestine — never really desired by the Eisenhower administration — was lost.

NOTES

1. Malcolm H. Kerr, *The Arab Cold War, 1958-70*, 3d ed. (London: Oxford University Press, 1971), p. 133.
2. By the 1960s, this had turned into a full-fledged, if quiet, revolution. "Power was passing almost imperceptibly from the old Eastern Establishment to a new Professional Elite, from bankers and lawyers who would take time off to help manage the affairs of government to full-time foreign-policy experts" (I.M. Destler, Leslie H. Gelb, and Anthony Lake, *Our Own Worst Enemy: The Unmaking of American Foreign Policy* [New York: Simon & Schuster, 1984], p. 91). During the Eisenhower presidency there were precursors of this shift. This was particularly true for Middle East policy making that had previously been managed by a small group of individuals, many of whom had prior business experience in the region.
3. Peter J. Schraeder, ed., *Intervention into the 1990s: U.S. Foreign Policy in the Third World*, 2nd ed. (Boulder: Lynne Rienner Publishers, 1992).
4. Barry Rubin, *Secrets of State: The State Department and the Struggle over US Foreign Policy* (New York: Oxford University Press, 1985), p. 264.
5. Eisenhower repeatedly stressed to members of Congress, State Department personnel, and others in his administration that he did not intend to allow electoral politics or public pressure to affect his foreign policy decisions regarding the Middle East. The most severe test of this came during the Suez crisis. Eisenhower wrote his old friend Swede Hazlett: "We realized that [Ben-Gurion] might think he could take advantage of this country because of the approaching election and because of the importance that so many politicians in the past have attached to our Jewish vote. I gave strict orders to the State Department that they should inform Israel that we would handle our affairs exactly as

though we didn't have a Jew in America. The welfare and best interests of our own country were to be the sole criteria on which we operated" (personal letter from Eisenhower to Captain E. E. Hazlett, ret., 2 November 1956, File: November 1956, Miscellaneous 4, Box 20, DDE Diary Series, Dwight D. Eisenhower Papers as President of the United States, 1953-61, Ann Whitman File [hereinafter Diary Series], Dwight D. Eisenhower Library [hereinafter DDEL]; see also John Emmet Hughes, *The Ordeal of Power: A Political Memoir of the Eisenhower Years* [New York: Atheneum, 1963], p. 62).

     6.   Destler, Gelb, and Lake, *Our Own Worst Enemy*, p. 177.

     7.   Stanley L. Falk, "The National Security Council under Truman, Eisenhower, and Kennedy," *Political Science Quarterly*, vol. 79 (Sept. 1964), p. 418. See also Walter Millis, with Harvey C. Mansfield and Harold Stein, *Arms and the State: Civil-Military Elements in National Policy* (New York: Twentieth Century Fund, 1958).

     8.   Wilbur Crane Eveland, *Ropes of Sand: America's Failure in the Middle East* (New York: Norton, 1980), p. 64.

     9.   Wristonization refers to the 1954 merger of the foreign service officers corps and the civil service employees into a single personnel system. The process is named for Henry M. Wriston, whose report on the State Department led to the reorganization. In the short run, "the upheaval produced by 'Wristonization' exacerbated tensions in the department and undercut the effectiveness of both personnel tracks. Career civil servants who never had any desire for foreign service were sent to specialized posts in remote places. Career diplomats were shifted to technical jobs for which they were frequently ill-prepared." James A. Nathan and James K. Oliver, *Foreign Policy Making and the American Political System*, 2d ed., (Boston: Little, Brown, 1987), p. 38.

    10.   Francis O. Wilcox, interview by John Luter, 3 April 1972, Columbia Oral History Project, DDEL.

    11.   Dwight D. Eisenhower, interview, 1967, Columbia Oral History Project, DDEL.

    12.   Maria Papadakis and Harvey Starr, "Opportunity, Willingness, and Small States: The Relationship between Environment and Foreign Policy," in Charles F. Hermann, Charles W. Kegley, Jr., and James N. Rosenau, eds., *New Directions in the Study of Foreign Policy* (Boston: Allen & Unwin, 1987). Also see Harvey Starr, "'Opportunity' and 'Willingness' as Ordering Concepts in the Study of War," *International Interactions*, vol. 4 (1978), pp. 363-87; and Benjamin A. Most and Harvey Starr, *Inquiry, Logic and International Politics* (Columbia: University of South Carolina Press, 1989), ch. 2.

    13.   One difficulty faced by foreign policy scholars dealing with the post-WWII period is that relevant documents often remain partially or completely classified. Although most records of what actually occurred are now public, papers that document the process by which a decision was reached (the internal debates, the information on which a choice was based, and so forth) are less frequently available. Furthermore, due to the inconsistencies in declassification decisions, it is impossible to know whether the fact that a document remains classified indicates it contains truly revealing new information that could change our interpretation of a foreign policy decision, or if its classified status is due to other factors.

    14.   A good overview of Eisenhower's foreign policy orientation is found in Richard A. Melanson, "The Foundations of Eisenhower's Foreign Policy: Continuity, Community, and Consensus," in Richard A. Melanson and David Mayers, eds., *Reevaluating Eisenhower: American Foreign Policy in the 1950s* (Urbana: University of Illinois Press, 1987).

15. These two priorities are clear not only from public and classified policy documents of the period, but also from memoirs and interviews by, and biographies about, the main individuals involved in creating those policies. See Ambassador Raymond Hare, interview by John Luter, 16 June and 28 August 1972, Columbia Oral History Project, DDEL; Operations Coordinating Board, Report on the Near East (NSC 5820/1), 3 February 1960, File: Near East (1), Box 4, Subject Subseries, OCB Series, White House Office, Office of the Special Assistant for National Security Affairs: Records 1952-61, DDEL; Sherman Adams, *Firsthand Report: The Story of the Eisenhower Administration* (New York: Harper & Brothers, 1961); Dwight D. Eisenhower, *The White House Years: Waging Peace, 1956-1961* (Garden City, NY: Doubleday, 1965); Stephen E. Ambrose, *Eisenhower: The President* (New York: Simon & Schuster, 1984); Hughes, *Ordeal of Power*.

16. *The Eisenhower Diaries*, ed. Robert H. Ferrell (New York: Norton, 1981), p. 319.

17. Dwight D. Eisenhower, "Peace in Freedom," address made at the American Jewish Tercentenary Dinner at New York on 20 October 1954, *Department of State Bulletin* (November 1954), 30:676.

18. Rubin, *Secrets of State*, p. 90. Rubin is citing State Department records, 874.2614/6-1956, Byroade to Dulles and Dulles to Byroade, obtained through the Freedom of Information Act.

19. Eveland, *Ropes of Sand*, p. 59.

20. John Foster Dulles, "Report on the Near East," radio address delivered 1 June 1953, *Department of State Bulletin* (15 June 1953), 28:832, 834.

21. Statement of Policy by the National Security Council, NSC 155/1, "United States Objectives and Policies with Respect to the Near East," 14 July 1953, *Foreign Relations of the United States* (hereinafter *FRUS*) *1952-1954*, vol. 9: The Near and Middle East, pt. 1 (Washington, DC: U.S. Government Printing Office, 1983), pp. 399-406.

22. Statement of Policy by the National Security Council, NSC 5428, "United States Objectives and Policies with Respect to the Near East," 23 July 1954, *FRUS 1952-1954*, pp. 525-39. Portions of NSC 5428, in particular items 10 through 13 under "Courses of Action," remain classified.

23. Statement by the National Security Council, NSC 5801/1, "Long-Range U.S. Policy toward the Near East," 24 January 1958, File: NSC 5801/1 (1), Box 23, Policy Papers Subseries, NSC Series, White House Office, Office of the Special Assistant for National Security Affairs: Records, 1952-61 (hereinafter PPS/NSC), DDEL. Significant portions of NSC 5801/1 remain classified.

24. Statement of Policy by the National Security Council, NSC 5820, "U.S. Policy toward the Near East," 3 October 1958, File: NSC 5820 — Policy toward the Near East (3), Box 26, PPS/NSC, DDEL.

25. Statement of Policy by the National Security Council, NSC 6011, "U.S. Policy toward the Near East," 17 June 1960, File: NSC 6011, Box 29, PPS/NSC, DDEL.

26. Mary Wilson, *King Abdullah, Britain and the Making of Jordan* (New York: Cambridge University Press, 1987); [Acting Secretary of State] Robert A. Lovett to [U.S. Representative on the Palestine Conciliation Commission] Mark F. Ethridge, Washington, DC, 19 January 1949, *FRUS 1949*, vol. 6: The Near East, South Asia and Africa (Washington, DC: U.S. Government Printing Office, 1977), pp. 681-83.

27. Walter Bedell Smith, "Request for Extension of UNRWA Program for Palestine Refugees," *Department of State Bulletin* (8 June 1953), 28:823.

28. Repatriation, if desired, was also typically the preferred international solution for refugee problems, at least in the case of European refugees.

29. During the hundreds of years of the Ottoman Empire, the Arab areas did not have legal status as states, although a sense of communal identity was certainly present. The state boundaries that were established after the collapse of the Ottoman Empire were in some sense artificial, determined as much by European interests as by indigenous preferences. In this context, and given the remnants of a colonial mindset that found nothing odd about European states determining the political destinies of the rest of the world, it is easy to see how the United States could come to the conclusions it did.

30. James Baster, "Economic Aspects of the Settlement of the Palestine Refugees," *Middle East Journal*, vol. 8, no. 1 (1954), p. 66.

31. Avi Shlaim, *Collusion across the Jordan: King Abdullah, the Zionist Movement, and the Partition of Palestine* (New York: Columbia University Press, 1988), p. 617.

32. For a discussion of conflicting Israeli views in the 1940s and 1950s on the issue of a Palestinian state, see Simha Flappan, *The Birth of Israel: Myths and Realities* (New York: Pantheon Books, 1987); Benny Morris, *The Birth of the Palestinian Refugee Problem, 1947-1949* (Cambridge: Cambridge University Press, 1987); Benny Morris, *1948 and After: Israel and the Palestinians* (Oxford: Clarendon Press, 1990); and Shlaim, *Collusion*, especially ch. 16.

33. Ian Lustick, *Arabs in the Jewish State: Israel's Control of a National Minority*. Modern Middle East Series, no. 6 (Austin: University of Texas Press, 1980), p. 49.

34. Baster, "Economic Aspects," p. 55.

35. Wilson, *King Abdullah*, pp. 178-79.

36. For an excellent discussion of Palestinian politics during the British Mandate, see Ann Mosely Lesch, *Arab Politics in Palestine, 1917-1939*. Modern Middle East Series of the Middle East Institute (Ithaca, NY: Cornell University Press, 1979); also Issa Khalaf, *Politics in Palestine: Arab Factionalism and Social Disintegration, 1939-1948* (Albany: State University of New York Press, 1991); Baruch Kimmerling and Joel S. Migdal, *Palestinians: The Making of a People* (New York: Free Press, 1993), ch. 1-4; Yehoshua Porath, *The Emergence of the Palestinian-Arab National Movement, 1918-1929* (London: Frank Cass, 1974); and Yehoshua Porath, *The Palestinian Arab National Movement: From Riots to Rebellion, 1929-1939* (London: Frank Cass, 1977).

37. W. Thomas Mallison, "The United Nations and the National Rights of the People of Palestine," in Ibrahim Abu-Lughod, ed., *Palestinian Rights: Affirmation and Denial* (Wilmette, IL: Medina Press, 1982), p. 23.

38. Edward H. Buehrig, *The UN and the Palestinian Refugees: A Study in Nonterritorial Administration*. International Development Research Center, Studies in Development (Bloomington: Indiana University Press, 1971), ch. 1; Michael E. Jansen, *The United States and the Palestinian People* (Beirut: Institute for Palestine Studies, 1970), pp. 100-118; Morris, *Palestinian Refugee Problem*, ch. 9; Saadia Touval, *The Peace Brokers: Mediators in the Arab-Israeli Conflict, 1948-1979* (Princeton, NJ: Princeton University Press, 1982), ch. 4.

39. A quote in George Kent, "Congress and American Middle East Policy," in Willard A. Beling, ed., *The Middle East: Quest for an American Policy* (Albany: SUNY Press, 1973), pp. 291-92.

40. James J. Wadsworth, "U.N. Extends Mandate of Relief Agency for Palestine Refugees," statements made in the *Ad-Hoc* Political Committee of the UN General Assembly, 19 November, 24 November, and 26 November 1956, *Department of State Bulletin* (January 1955), 32:24-28.

41. Margaret Arake, *The Broken Sword of Justice: America, Israel and the Palestine Tragedy* (London: Quartet Books, 1973), p. 138.

42. Memorandum for the Secretary by Christian A. Herter, Subject: Conversation with Dag Hammarskjold on Monday evening, December 16, 1957, 22 December 1957, File: Miscellaneous Memorandum 1957 (1), Box 9, Series I: Chronological File, Christian A. Herter Papers, 1957-61, DDEL.

43. Office of Refugee and Migration Affairs, Bureau of Security and Consular Affairs, Department of State, *Refugee Problems: World Survey, 1958*, File: Refugees — Miscellaneous (2), Box 2, Robert K. Gray: Records, 1954-60, DDEL; Programs for Refugees and Displaced Peoples through CARE, October 1959, *ibid.*; U.S. Committee for Refugees, World Refugee Year, File: Department of State, January-August 1959 (2), Box 77, Subject Series, Confidential File, 1953-61, White House Central Files, DDEL.

44. See, for example, James P. Richards, "Continuation of Assistance to Arab Refugees," statement made in the *Ad-Hoc* Political Committee of the UN General Assembly on 4 November 1953, *Department of State Bulletin* (30 November 1953), 29:759-61; and Wadsworth, "UN Extends Mandate."

45. Buehrig, *UN and the Palestinian Refugees*, p. 15.

46. Immigration to the United States was not an option for most Palestinian refugees. Although the number of Palestinians admitted to the United States under the Refugee Relief Act of 1953 increased in the second half of the 1950s, the totals were still small: significantly less than 1 percent of the total refugee population. See Louise Cainkar, "Palestinian Women in the United States: Coping with Tradition, Change and Alienation," Ph.D. Diss., Northwestern University, 1988, ch. 3.

47. Dulles, "Report on the Near East," p. 832.

48. Parker T. Hunter, director, Near East Section, Department of State, to William A. Eddy, Arabian American Oil Company, 29 January 1954. U.S. State Department Confidential File, Palestine-Israel, 1950-54. The figure of 100,000 Palestinians to be repatriated is given by Hunter and numerous other sources, including a Memorandum by the Deputy Assistant Secretary of State for Near Eastern, South Asian, and African Affairs (Jernegan) to the Secretary of State, Subject: Need for Early Diplomatic Initiative by U.S. Government re Arab Refugees and Related Palestine Issues, 10 August 1953, *FRUS 1952-54*, p. 1272.

49. Richards, "Continuation of Assistance," p. 760.

50. Memorandum from Colonel Andrew Goodpaster to Governor Adams, 9 November 1955, *Declassified Documents 1987*, microfiche #781.

51. Staff Study on NSC 5801/1, 16 January 1958, File: 5801/1 (2), Box 23, PPS/NSC, DDEL.

52. John Foster Dulles, "The Middle East," address made before the Council on Foreign Relations, New York, 26 August 1955, *Department of State Bulletin* (5 September 1955), 33:378-80.

53. Department of State Position Paper, "Israel: Arab Refugees," prepared for the briefing book for Dulles's trip to the Middle East and South Asia, 5 May 1953, *FRUS 1952-54*, p. 1194.

54. Donald C. Bergus, "Palestine: Focal Point of Tension," address made before the Conference on Middle Eastern Affairs of the Middle East Institute, Washington, DC, 9 March 1956, *Department of State Bulletin* (26 March 1956), 34:504.

55. See Dulles's radio address, "Report on the Near East," pp. 831-35. There is a sense in which this TVA-style development project was a solution looking for a problem.

The Tennessee Valley Authority (TVA) had been a great success during the Depression; this created the expectation that it would work equally well in other places as an economic panacea for political troubles. For example, President Lyndon Johnson proposed a massive, U.S.-funded Mekong development project to try to win over the North Vietnamese. See Stanley Karnow, *Vietnam: A History* (New York: Penguin Books, 1984), pp. 418-19.

56. Progress Report on NSC 155/1, "United States Objectives and Policies with Respect to the Near East," 29 July 1954, File: NSC 155/1 — Near East (1), Box 5, PPS/NSC, DDEL.

57. Eric Johnston, "Report by the President's Special Representative to the President," 17 November 1953, *FRUS 1952-1954*, pp. 1418-23.

58. Stephen Green points out this was not the first time Israel had diverted Jordan River water. "In March, 1951, Israel had moved bulldozers and military units into the demilitarized zone on the Syrian border, and over the protests of the UN observers in the area and the U.S. State Department in Washington, began draining Lake Hula, which is part of the Jordan River system. Syrian villages were fired upon by the Israelis, and though Syrian troops moved closer to the border, they did not return the Israeli fire. U.S. Major General A. R. Bolling, Assistant Army Chief of Staff for Intelligence, noted at the time that 'apparently, Israel is prepared to risk military operations against any of the Arab states, and several recent Israeli actions appear to have been designed, at least in part, to provoke Arab initiation of hostilities.'" *Taking Sides: America's Secret Relations with a Militant Israel* (New York: Morrow, 1984), p. 78.

59. "Israelis Confirm Canal Work Halt," *New York Times*, 14 October 1953.

60. Memorandum of Conversation, Secretary of State John Foster Dulles, Israeli Ambassador Abba Eban, and others, Subject: Israel/U.S. Relations — Diversion of Jordan River, 25 September 1953, *FRUS 1952-1954*, pp. 1320-25; Verbatim Record of the Press and Radio News Conference of the Secretary of State, Washington, DC, 20 October 1953, *FRUS 1952-54*, pp. 1369-71.

61. Edward Tivnan, *The Lobby: Jewish Political Power and American Foreign Policy* (New York: Simon & Schuster, 1987), p. 37.

62. Harry N. Howard, "The Development of United States Policy in the Near East, South Asia, and Africa during 1953: Part II," *Department of State Bulletin* (1 March 1954), 30:328-33.

63. Both Eisenhower and Dulles were greatly committed to the United Nations. This comes through in a number of ways, including the attention the United States gave to UN actions. See Memorandum of Conversation, Pinhas Eliav, Second Secretary of the Israeli Embassy and James M. Ludlow, Office of United Nations Political and Security Affairs, Department of State, Subject: Palestine Items Before the Security Council, 4 November 1953; Henry Cabot Lodge, *As It Was: An Inside View of Politics and Power in the '50s and '60s* (New York: Norton, 1976); Verbatim Record, *FRUS 1952-1954*, p. 1370.

64. Letter from Stanley High to the President, File: DDE Diary, April 1954, Box 6, Diary Series, DDEL; Faiz S. Abu-Jaber, *American-Arab Relations from Wilson to Nixon* (Washington, DC: University Press of America, 1979), p. 45.

65. Memorandum of Conference with the President, 10 February 1956, File: February 1956, Goodpaster File, Box 12, Diary Series, DDEL; Eisenhower, *White House Years*, p. 23.

66. Memorandum of Conversation between Under Secretary of State Christian Herter and Eric Johnston, 6 April 1957, File: Miscellaneous Memorandum 1957 (2), Herter Papers, DDEL.

67. Robert Cutler, Special Assistant for National Security Affairs, Memorandum for the President, Subject: Jordan River Valley Development, 28 March 1958; File: General Robert L. Cutler, 1958 (3), Box 11, Administrative Series, Dwight D. Eisenhower Papers as President of the United States, 1953-61, Ann Whitman File, DDEL.

68. John Foster Dulles, Memorandum for the President, Subject: Near Eastern Policies, File: White House Correspondence — General 1956 (6), Box 4, White House Memorandum Series, John Foster Dulles Papers, 1952-59, DDEL.

69. Hunter to Eddy, p. 2.

70. National Intelligence Estimate: Israel (NIE-92), 18 August 1953, *FRUS 1952-1954*, p. 1287; David Hirst, *The Gun and the Olive Branch* (London: Faber & Faber, 1977), ch. 6.

71. "Attack by Israeli Forces," press release 572 dated 18 October 1953, *Department of State Bulletin* (26 October 1953), 29:552; James J. Wadsworth, "Security Council Censure of Action at Qibiya," statement made in the UN Security Council, 20 November 1953, *Department of State Bulletin* (14 December 1953), 29:839-41; Resolution 101 (1953), adopted by the United Nations Security Council, 24 November 1953, *FRUS 1952-1954*, pp. 1436-37.

72. Letter from Henry Cabot Lodge to Barney A. Balaban, Paramount Pictures, 27 November 1953, File: Henry Cabot Lodge 1952-53 (2), Box 23, Administration Series, Dwight D. Eisenhower Papers as President of the United States, 1953-61, Ann Whitman File, DDEL.

73. Henry A. Byroade, "The Middle East in New Perspective," address before the Dayton World Affairs Council, Dayton, Ohio, 9 April 1954, *Department of State Bulletin* (26 April 1954), 30:632.

74. Henry Cabot Lodge, "Egyptian-Israeli Dispute Before the Security Council," statement to UN Security Council, 29 March 1955, *Department of State Bulletin* (18 April 1955), 32:661.

75. Henry Cabot Lodge, "Security Council Condemns Israel for Action Against Syria," statement to UN Security Council, 12 January 1956, *Department of State Bulletin* (30 January 1956), 34:182, 184.

76. Green, *Taking Sides*, pp. 88-92.

77. Chester L. Cooper, *The Lion's Last Roar: Suez, 1956* (New York: Harper & Row, 1978); Green, *Taking Sides*, ch. 6; Keith Kyle, *Suez* (New York: St. Martin's Press, 1991); Selwyn Lloyd, *Suez 1956: A Personal Account* (London: Cape, 1978); Donald Neff, *Warriors at Suez: Eisenhower Takes America into the Middle East* (New York: Linden Press/Simon & Schuster, 1981); Cheryl A. Rubenberg, *Israel and the American National Interest: A Critical Examination* (Urbana: University of Illinois Press, 1986), ch. 3; Charles D. Smith, *Palestine and the Arab-Israeli Conflict* (New York: St. Martin's Press, 1988), chs. 6 and 7. For an Egyptian perspective, see Mohamed H. Heikal, *Cutting the Lion's Tail: Suez Through Egyptian Eyes* (London: André Deutsch Limited, 1986).

78. Memorandum of Conversation, President with Dulles, Under Secretary Hoover, Goodpaster and others, 30 October 1956, File: October 1956, Staff Notes, Box 19, Diary Series, DDEL.

79. Henry Cabot Lodge, "Question of Withdrawal of Israeli Forces from Egypt," statements made to the UN General Assembly, 17 and 23 January 1957, *Department of State Bulletin* (18 February 1957), 36:269-71.

80. Henry Cabot Lodge, "General Assembly Adopts Two Resolutions on Middle East Question," statements made in the UN General Assembly, 2 Feb. 1957, *Department of State Bulletin* (25 February 1957), 36:325-28.

81. Aide-mémoire of U.S. Secretary of State Dulles handed to Israeli Ambassador Abba Eban, 11 February 1957; reprinted in Milton Viorst, *Sands of Sorrow: Israel's Journey from Independence* (New York: Harper & Row, 1987), p. 288.

82. Eisenhower, *White House Years*, pp. 185-86.

83. Telegram from Dwight D. Eisenhower to David Ben-Gurion, 20 February 1957, File: Israel (2), Box 29, International Series, Dwight D. Eisenhower Papers as President of the United States, 1953-61, Ann Whitman File, DDEL.

84. Adams, *Firsthand Report*, pp. 281-82.

85. Dwight D. Eisenhower, "Question of Withdrawal of Israeli Forces from Egyptian Territory," radio-television address, 20 February 1957, *Department of State Bulletin* (11 March 1957), 36:389.

86. Paul Findley, *They Dare To Speak Out: People and Institutions Confront Israel's Lobby* (Westport, CT: Lawrence Hill, 1985), p. 119.

87. "American private gifts and purchases of bonds produced $100 million for Israel each year." Chester J. Pach, Jr. and Elmo Richardson, *The Presidency of Dwight D. Eisenhower*, rev. ed. (Lawrence: University of Kansas, 1991), p. 163.

88. William Stivers, "Eisenhower and the Middle East," in Melanson and Mayers, *Reevaluating Eisenhower*, pp. 215-16.

89. President [Dwight D.] Eisenhower, "President Asks for Authorization for U.S. Economic Program and for Resolution on Communist Aggression in the Middle East," message of the President to the Congress delivered before a joint session of the Senate and the House of Representatives, 5 January 1957, *Department of State Bulletin* (21 January 1957), 36:86. Other public statements on the Eisenhower Doctrine include John Foster Dulles, "Middle East Proposals," statement made before the House Committee on Foreign Affairs, 7 January 1957, *Department of State Bulletin* (28 January 1957), 36:126-30; Dulles, "The Communist Threat to the Middle East," statement made before a joint session of the Foreign Relations and Armed Services Committees of the Senate, 14 January 1957, *Department of State Bulletin* (4 February 1957), 36:170-74.

90. William Stivers, *America's Confrontation with Revolutionary Change in the Middle East, 1948-83* (New York: St. Martin's Press, 1986), p. 26.

5

THE KENNEDY-JOHNSON ADMINISTRATIONS AND THE PALESTINIAN PEOPLE

Zaha Bustami

"REVIVED IRREDENTIST ACTIVITIES by militant Palestinian Arabs who were backed by Syria and equipped with sophisticated weapons gravely intensified Middle East tensions in May 1967. These activities, in turn, set in motion the train of events which triggered the six-day Arab-Israeli War of June 5-10 [1967]." So starts the history of the Arab-Israeli conflict as written by and for the State Department, summarizing its activities during the administration of President Lyndon B. Johnson.[1] It is a revealing summary of events, precisely because it goes against the spirit of the Johnson administration's attitude towards the conflict. That administration was remarkable in its lack of attention to the Palestinian people as an element of the Arab-Israeli conflict. It regarded the conflict as one involving the states of the region, primarily Egypt and Israel. In that respect it failed to grasp the dynamics of a changing political situation in the Arab countries surrounding Israel. In its neglect of the Palestinian factor the Johnson administration also was remarkably different from its predecessor, the John F. Kennedy administration.

Until the end of the Johnson administration, little attention was given to Palestinians as political actors in the Middle East. They had yet to develop a political voice of their own.[2] The Palestine Liberation Organization, established in 1964, was considered a bureaucratic outfit serving the interests of its Arab patron state, Egypt.[3] Still, the future of the Palestinians remained, nominally at least, on the agenda of efforts to resolve the Arab-Israeli conflict. While Kennedy exerted a serious effort to address that issue, Johnson did not.

THE KENNEDY ADMINISTRATION

President Kennedy brought to office what seemed to many observers a new approach towards the Third World. Although he maintained the policy of containment and vigorous opposition to communism, including willingness to use military force, he showed a more sympathetic understanding of the needs of nations not aligned formally with either East or West.[4] He was particularly willing to lend an ear, as well as various forms of aid, to these nations. In the Middle

East, this policy led to improved U.S.-Egyptian relations, after years of tension between the two governments.

Still, Kennedy's creative courage failed him in dealing with what he, originally at least, considered the crucial factor in the Arab-Israeli conflict, the problem of Palestinian refugees. He also was the president who laid the firm foundations of what later became a close friendship between the United States and Israel. He left his mark in two ways. He launched the program of military sales to Israel, and he vocalized the now familiar expressions of American emotional and moral attachment to the Jewish state.

Kennedy came out of the 1960 election owing a significant debt to Jewish American voters, among a number of other ethnic groups. Over 80 percent of Jewish votes went to Kennedy, an almost "astronomical" figure.[5] They were critical to his victories in Illinois and New York. Kennedy's friendship with the Jewish American community carried a new tone. He was the first presidential candidate to praise the Zionist experience in strong emotional terms. "Friendship for Israel," he said before the national convention of the Zionist Organization of America in August 1960, "is not a partisan matter, it is a national commitment."[6] This expression became a common theme in his statements to Jewish American as well as Israeli leaders.[7]

On the other hand, Kennedy made the most significant U.S. initiative to address the issue of Palestinian refugees, along lines prescribed by United Nations resolutions, while also protecting the interests of the states of the region. His guide was paragraph 11 of the UN General Assembly Resolution 194 of 11 December 1948:

> [The General Assembly] *Resolves* that the refugees wishing to return to their homes and live at peace with their neighbours should be permitted to do so at the earliest practicable date, and that compensation should be paid for the property of those choosing not to return and for loss of or damage to property which, under principles of international law or in equity, should be made good by the Governments or authorities responsible.

This was an approach that Kennedy had supported years before he took office as president, and his warm relationship with the Jewish American community did not alter his commitment. Speaking before the National Conference of Christians and Jews in February 1957, Kennedy said:

> Let those refugees be repatriated to Israel at the earliest practical date who are sincerely willing to live at peace with their neighbors, to accept the Israeli Government with an attitude of *civitatus filia*. Those who would prefer to remain in Arab jurisdiction should be resettled in areas under control of governments willing to help their Arab brothers, if assisted and enabled to earn their own living, make permanent homes, and live in peace and dignity. The refugee camps should be closed.[8]

One year later, in a speech before the B'nai Zion organization in New York, he repeated a similar theme.

> . . . the books cannot be closed on the Arab refugee question. It must be resolved through negotiations, resettlement and outside international assistance. But to recognize the problem is quite different from saying that the problem is insoluble short of the destruction of Israel, or only by the unilateral repudiation of the 1949 borders or must be solved by Israel alone.[9]

After he took office, Kennedy was in a position to implement this vision that expected compromise from both Arabs and Israelis. His first step, a few months after he became president, was a series of letters in May 1961 to President Gamal Abdel Nasser of Egypt, King Saud of Saudi Arabia, King Hussein of Jordan, as well as to the presidents of Lebanon and Iraq.[10] In these letters, Kennedy expressed the willingness of the United States to help resolve the Arab-Israeli conflict, particularly the problem of Arab refugees, on the basis of repatriation or compensation. He suggested the United Nations Conciliation Commission for Palestine (UNCCP) as a suitable framework for the effort,[11] and solicited the opinions of the Arab leaders.

A description of the deliberations within the Egyptian government on the subject of Kennedy's letter provides a sad commentary on Arab politics during those days of the Arab Cold War.[12] Rather than addressing the issues raised, advisers to President Nasser looked for a possible trap. Deputy Foreign Minister Hussein Zul-Fiqar Sabri, for example, warned Nasser that Arab representatives in the League of Arab States already were discussing the letter. The trap, he warned, was that Arab states were invited to take the initiative in proposing a solution for the refugee problem "on the assumption that that would lead to the disintegration of the Palestine Question altogether."[13] He did not need to remind Nasser of Egypt's strained relationship with most of the other Arab addressees. He merely pointed out that a "defeatist spirit" already permeated these deliberations. By this he meant that Arab representatives worried that, given the choice, Palestinian refugees might choose to stay where they were, and Arab states would be helpless to reject this outcome since they had always insisted on implementing the UN resolution.[14] Mutual Arab suspicions, at the same time, prevented coordinating a joint position on the issue or a pragmatic revision of the official Arab demand that all refugees should be allowed to return to Palestine because that was their desire. With these concerns in mind, Sabri suggested that Nasser should sidetrack Kennedy with a counter-proposal, changing the terms of the discussion towards something other than a solution for the refugee problem.[15] This was the tone of Nasser's reply on 1 August 1961.[16]

The combination of suspicion about American intentions and narrow-minded concern with the politics of rival Arab states produced a reply from Nasser that was surprisingly conciliatory, if rather petulant, in tone. In seventeen pages, Nasser recounted the history of U.S.-Egyptian relations, laying the blame heavily on the United States for the past strain on these relations. He also blamed Jewish American votes for influencing the U.S. position on the Arab-Israeli conflict. Early in his letter, however, Nasser had informed Kennedy that he did not believe a total agreement in their views on the issue of Palestine was necessary for a potential understanding and improved relations between the two countries. Nasser then presented Egypt's case, effectively changing the topic of discussion from the problem of Palestinian refugees to the stability of the area and the security of its states. Specifically, he brought up the question of Israel's borders as determined by the Palestine Partition Resolution of the UN General Assembly in 1947. The failure of the United Nations to force Israel's withdrawal from territories beyond those specified in the Partition Resolution, as well as continued Jewish immigration to Israel, created a threat to the region. There grew in Israel, Nasser wrote, "pressure which is bound to explode" and spill beyond its borders.[17]

In this lengthy response, Nasser pointed out Egypt's fundamental position: a solution of the refugee problem cannot be separated from that of larger security and border problems associated with the Arab-Israeli conflict. Short of addressing the demand for Israeli border adjustment, a solution of the Palestine question along the lines suggested by Kennedy threatened to force the Arabs to recognize the status quo left by the 1948 war with little gain on their part, and with the possible threat of a number of Palestinian refugees dumped permanently in their lap. This Arab worry, commonly referred to as fear of the "liquidation of the Palestine problem," created strong resistance in the Arab camp to Kennedy's subsequent efforts to address the refugee issue.

Another potential stumbling block to Kennedy's efforts came up in his meeting with Israeli Prime Minister David Ben-Gurion on 30 May 1961. The discussion dealt with two subjects: Israel's budding nuclear program at Dimona, and a solution to the Arab refugee problem. Ben-Gurion assured Kennedy that Dimona would be used for research and peaceful purposes only.[18] On the second subject, Kennedy emphasized to the Israeli leader that his plan envisaged a three-way solution to the problem: repatriation, resettlement in Arab countries, and immigration to other parts of the world. He assured Ben-Gurion that repatriation would be carried out with adequate safeguards for Israel's security.[19] Ben-Gurion received this information with very little enthusiasm. He insisted that the Arabs would not agree to such a plan because they wanted repatriation for all refugees. In the end, he "reluctantly agreed" to allow the negotiations to proceed.[20] His reluctance masked considerable Israeli opposition to the idea, an opposition that would become more apparent as negotiations proceeded and Israel had to make its position clear without using possible Arab rejection as an excuse for avoiding commitment.

The Joseph E. Johnson initiative

Kennedy proceeded with his effort to find a solution to the problem of Palestinian refugees. His personal involvement grew weaker as time went by, and it would be misleading to consider the developments of the following two years as orchestrated by the President. Still, the proposed solution was his brainchild even if it found other nurturers within the administration. Support for the initiative, particularly in the State Department, derived from the perceived benefit to regional stability and American interests of a solution of the refugee problem. Besides the humanitarian appeal of such a solution, there was a belief that it might prove a stepping stone toward solving other aspects of the Arab-Israeli conflict and might be a way, even if it were to fail, to remove one bone of contention between Arabs and Israelis. U.S. officials apparently held the naive expectation that their efforts in this direction would at least place the responsibility of failure either on the Arabs or the Israelis, thereby freeing the General Assembly from further polemics on the issue.[21]

With prodding from the U.S. government, the UNCCP appointed a special representative to discuss a solution to the refugee problem with the states involved (Israel, Egypt, Jordan, Syria and Lebanon). The man selected was Joseph E. Johnson, president of the Carnegie Endowment for International Peace. The basis for his efforts would be paragraph 11 of Resolution 194. Throughout his mission, Johnson kept in close touch with U.S. officials, in the firm belief that only the United States was in a position to underwrite the financial cost of resettlement, as well as bring political pressure to bear on Israel should that be necessary.[22]

Johnson went to the Middle East in August 1961. He adopted a low key approach to his mission, avoiding publicity and emphasizing the fact-finding nature of his talks. The first serious obstacle appeared in Israel. Despite Johnson's careful avoidance of presenting any precise proposals, Israel was suspicious of the idea, implicit in his approach, of "free choice" for the refugees. Soon Ben-Gurion was telling the Knesset that

> Israel categorically rejects the insidious proposal for freedom of choice for the refugees, for she is convinced that this proposal is designed and calculated only to destroy Israel. There is only one practical and fair solution for the problem of the refugees: to resettle them among their own people in countries having plenty of good land and water and which are in need of additional manpower.[23]

The Knesset soon adopted a resolution stating that the Arab refugees should not be returned to Israeli territory, and that the sole solution to the problem was their settlement in the Arab countries.[24] Israeli Foreign Minister Golda Meir allowed that some repatriation might be possible in the future but only through the family reunification program.[25] This remained the Israeli position until the end of Johnson's mission.

Israel's position did not deter Johnson. Although he realized that the two sides viewed the refugee problem as part of the larger Palestine question, involving other problems, he remained convinced of the possibility of a step-by-step solution of the refugee question as an isolated issue.[26] Neither Israel's opposition to the principle of repatriation, nor Arab opposition, already heard in some quarters, to the process of selective repatriation, was enough for Johnson to abandon his mission.[27] In early 1962, Johnson won an extension of his mandate from the General Assembly.

He then carried to Israel the idea of a pilot project involving a small number of refugees, after an initial determination of preferences by the refugees about their future residence. The Israelis balked. They insisted on learning the specific number of refugees involved before giving an answer. When Johnson suggested the figure of 50,000 families, Israel reacted negatively.[28] The Israelis still considered the principle of repatriation a threat to their security, and they objected to the idea of providing the refugees with a free choice. They worried that the majority would choose repatriation.[29] Ironically, Jordan objected as well, and for exactly the opposite reason. The Jordanians feared that the majority of Palestinian refugees, given a free choice, would decide to settle in their present places of domicile, with the greatest burden falling on Jordan. Like Egypt, Jordan demanded that the question of the refugees be solved simultaneously with the territorial and security aspects of the Arab-Israeli conflict.[30] There may have been another side to the Jordanian concern, not revealed to Johnson. In July 1961 King Hussein complained to King Saud that he feared some attempt within the Arab League to prepare for a separate Palestinian entity on the West Bank.[31] A free choice to the Palestinians on the question of repatriation or resettlement was only one step away from a discussion of their future political status, where they might conceivably be given a choice to decide for themselves. This question was equally addressed in a landmark General Assembly resolution, the Partition Resolution, to which the Arab states often referred in their demands for a settlement of the conflict and which called for an independent Arab state in Palestine. Jordan might have preferred to leave this hornet's nest undisturbed by attaching conditions (such as the comprehensive settlement, in one package, of the whole question of Palestine) that were guaranteed to torpedo Johnson's efforts. In any event, Jordan specifically asked Johnson to discount its declared positions in the United Nations on the question of repatriation unless they were linked to an overall settlement of the conflict.[32]

Johnson persevered, encountering on the whole greater opposition with each step he took. On the basis of his talks, he provided the Arabs and Israelis with the blueprint of a plan, the text of which has not been released officially. The purpose of this offer was to solicit comments on the plan before any further step could be taken.[33] In his draft, Johnson made clear that he saw no likelihood of any early settlement of the larger Palestine question, but that gradual progress on the refugee question was possible. He believed that the wishes of the refugees must be given priority, but would not extend to a "free choice" by them. There was a need to safeguard the legitimate interests of the states concerned. He specifically stressed that Israel's existence could not be allowed to be threatened by the return of any refugee. Therefore, some qualifications were necessary: Any state to which a refugee expressed a desire to go was to have the final say on permission for that refugee to enter. In response to Israel's fear that Arab states would use extensive propaganda to influence the decision of the refugees in favor of repatriation, Johnson suggested several safeguards: The wishes of the refugees were to be ascertained confidentially by the United Nations, and the UN would shield them from external influence as they made their decisions; they would be told what choices were available to them, that their first choice might not be granted, and that their first choice was not necessarily the final option that they could exercise; they would be given the right of choosing any country they wished for their future domicile; they would be told as exactly as possible what their choice would entail for their future, particularly with regard to their return to a Jewish state; and, with regard to repatriation, the United Nations would oversee that repatriation and resettlement were undertaken simultaneously, and that any party could disengage from the process. Initial acquiescence would not be binding if, for example, a state's security became endangered. The plan would be implemented slowly and gradually, with small but unspecified numbers of refugees involved.

At this stage, Kennedy and his advisers decided that the time had come for a more direct role by the administration to ensure Israeli cooperation. Myer Feldman, Kennedy's deputy special counsel and his channel to Israel and the Jewish American community, was dispatched to Tel Aviv on a secret mission.[34] Feldman discussed the Johnson Plan in a six-hour meeting with Meir, and the result was discouraging. Meir expressed strong doubts about Arab intentions, arguing that the Israelis feared an attempt by the Arabs, especially Nasser, to influence the decision of the refugees through propaganda. After a futile request for a report on the Arab response to the plan, Meir asked for adequate time to discuss the ideas with other political parties. Feldman explained that the plan rested on the notion that no party was expected to make a formal commitment, other than to allow the operation to proceed gradually and in good faith. Meir handed Feldman a letter from Ben-Gurion to Kennedy, devoted to a lengthy discussion of the impracticability of the plan's proviso that no attempt be made to influence refugee votes.[35]

The State Department, which was equally involved in this secret diplomacy, interpreted the result of Feldman's talks with the greatest measure of optimism. It then turned to Cairo for its views. John Badeau, the U.S. ambassador in Cairo, was instructed to discuss the Johnson Plan with Nasser. The Department told Badeau that

> our study of Feldman's useful exploratory talks in Israel leads us [to] conclude that although Israel's leaders are understandably hesitant to state *carte blanche* [their] acquiescence in [the] implementation [of the] Johnson Plan equally they have apparently NOT repeat NOT found in Plan sufficient hazards to Israel to justify its immediate rejection. Objections set up by Ben Gurion and Mrs. Meir seem to us essentially diversionary. In short, we have come out of this phase just about where we might have expected. Having explored preliminary reactions on one side without meeting rejection, we think similar exploration should be carried out on other. By these we are NOT repeat NOT necessarily committed finally to proceed with the Johnson Plan at this time. Rather, we will have facts on which this government can determine whether [it is] worthwhile [to] commit [the] US to [the] Plan and [to the] attempt [to] proceed [with] its implementation.[36]

Egypt's response to the plan was noncommittal enough to keep the State Department's hopes up. Johnson was authorized to present a draft of his proposals at the UN General Assembly session in the fall.[37] There the plan began to unravel. Apparently both Israel and the Arab states hoped that the other party would be the first to reject the plan. Rejection, not cautious acceptance, had been the real content of their replies.[38] The Arab states presented a joint response to Johnson, indicating that while their comments should not be taken as a rejection of the plan, they did not consider it a suitable framework for a fruitful discussion since Israel had not declared its clear and unconditional acceptance of paragraph 11 in Resolution 194.[39] In fact, though, the Arabs, particularly Jordan, did not want that paragraph as a basis for UN action, and Syria was not inclined to reach agreement with Israel on the refugee or any other issue.[40] It was Syria that first rejected the plan publicly in a unilateral move that took the other Arab governments by surprise.[41] Its argument was that the plan addressed only the refugee issue, disregarding the other aspects of the problem. It described the plan as a first step towards the "liquidation of the Palestine problem" and "a Zionist-imperialist conspiracy."[42] Israel maintained its public ambiguity on the plan, even while stating that it had already indicated its disapproval when the plan was presented, and that resettlement was the only possible solution to the refugee problem. In the meantime, the Knesset reiterated its resolution of November 1961 rejecting the principle of repatriation for Palestinian refugees.[43]

The secrecy that had surrounded the Johnson Plan at its inception disappeared with these developments. Then followed what could best be described as a campaign of "distorting rumors" about the content of Johnson's proposals.[44] Much of this effort came from Zionist organizations and their friends in the United States, who tried to generate opposition to the Plan.[45] Specifically, the Department of Information and Public Relations of the American Zionist Council distributed a memorandum, on 14 November 1962, to local Zionist council chairmen and key community leaders on "The Arab Refugee Issue in the U.N."[46] It characterized Johnson's initiative as a poll to be taken among the refugees to determine their choices. It further accused Johnson of offering no plans for resettlement.

Kennedy met with top officials from the State Department in early December. A decision was made not to seek implementation of the Johnson Plan at the time. The plan had not been endorsed publicly by any of the states involved in the conflict, and was facing increasing opposition from Zionist lobbying groups in the United States.[47] On 31 January 1963, Johnson presented his resignation to the United Nations.

The decision to shelve the Johnson Plan did not mean, however, that Kennedy gave up completely on an attempt to solve the refugee problem. Negotiations continued, this time with U.S. diplomats playing the role of intermediaries. There was one major distinction to the new American effort: the administration now spoke with two voices. Through its emissaries, the State Department sought to maintain the spirit, if not the letter, of the Johnson proposal. Repatriation and resettlement were equally viable options. In his direct talks with Israeli leaders, however, Kennedy accepted the Israeli argument. He discounted repatriation and suggested that resettlement of the refugees in Arab countries was the likely fate for most of them. His half-hearted approach to the problem, and broad hints to the Israelis that they did not need to offer a compromise, led to the failure of this American effort as well.

Kennedy met with Golda Meir in Florida in December 1962. The Israeli leader presented her country's point of view on a number of regional issues, warning the President that "there is a constant shadow of Nasser's ambitions in the Middle East," in conjunction with the Soviet Union.[48] Turning to the question of refugees, she complained that not all Arabs living in Israel were "peaceful citizens." She cited their opposition to "development programs" that sometimes required the removal of Arab houses to make way for new roads or other facilities. In one recent case in an Arab village, she complained, "we were accused of taking something away from the Arabs. They said they would put their women and children right in front of any bulldozers brought in. This is the sort of line they always take."[49] In return, Kennedy assured her that the United States had a "special relationship" with Israel in the Middle East "really comparable only to that which [the United States] has with Britain over a wide range of world affairs." It was to protect Israel's interests, however, that the United States had to maintain its ties with the Arab world. He added that it was quite clear that, in the case of an invasion, the United States would come to the support of Israel. "We have that capacity and it is growing," he said. In return for this friendship, he invited Israel to consider the interests of the United States by moving on the refugee question (and abstaining from reprisal raids, one of which had occurred recently, against Syria). However, he went on to add that obviously Israel could not accept a flood of refugees. Since the Arabs had their troubles as well, "may be no compromises are possible," he said. He described as an almost impossible quest what the United States had been seeking through the Johnson Plan. His judgement, therefore, was that the great majority of refugees would resettle. "We have not made any progress on the Johnson Plan and that is gone," he said. Still, he told Meir that they should keep trying for a settlement to the refugee problem. Wistfully, Meir noted how helpful it would be if only the Arabs took a similar position.[50]

Armed with this understanding of the President's attitude, Israel felt more confident in its subsequent discussions with the State Department. In a meeting with Ambassador Walworth Barbour in Tel Aviv, Ben-Gurion and Meir started with what seems to be a novel approach. They asked that once agreement on the refugee issue is reached, the subject would be closed forever. An agreement did not imply a direct understanding, much less a treaty, between the Arabs and the Israelis. It was understood that the United States would continue to play the role of intermediary and, according to the American ambassador, "what may be possible is [an] understanding between Israel and U.S. and between Arabs and U.S."[51] Meir clarified that Israel was not referring to a time after the operation to resolve the issue was under way. Rather, all talk of the refugee issue must cease from the very beginning of the operation. Ben-Gurion went one step further, emphasizing "that once, after all these talks, [the U.S. government] can say 'there is an agreement,' at this point all mention of refugee problem must end."[52] Since there were no qualifications to this request, it apparently included a ban on further discussion of the problem by the United States itself. Once there was a U.S. judgement that some form of an agreement had been reached, the book on the refugee problem would be closed forever regardless of what happened later. In addition, the Israelis questioned the current estimate of 1.2 million refugees. According to them, there were reports that the local population in Jordan and other countries had joined the refugee camps after they were established in their countries. Therefore they requested that a representative of the U.S. embassy in Tel Aviv meet with a representative of the Israeli Foreign Ministry to arrive at a working, agreed estimate of total bona fide refugees, apparently with no input from either Arab governments or the refugees themselves.[53] In return, Jews who left Arab countries for Israel, and the property they left behind, should be considered under General Assembly Resolution 194 as well. Though few Jews, Ben-Gurion admitted, would want repatriation, some probably wished to return to old Jerusalem. The main question, in Ben-Gurion's opinion, remained what he described as the Israeli understanding with President Kennedy. Most of the Arab refugees must go to Arab countries. He also wanted to know in advance the number of refugees the United States wanted Israel to take.[54] Already the idea of allowing the refugees to exercise a choice, albeit a highly qualified one, was eroding. Even as Meir softened the discussion to say that specific numbers were not important at that stage, she added that the number Israel would repatriate would be "more symbolic than substantial." When Barbour tried to raise the issue of ascertaining the wishes of the refugees, the Israelis countered by a proposal to give preference to requests for family reunion. This pragmatic approach, they said, would provide a "significant number for several years." Later, they said, as mutual confidence grew, more thought could be given to determining other preferences.[55]

Upon receiving the information, the State Department expressed a number of reservations. The idea that a "total seal of silence" would surround the actual operation and that there would be no further mention of the refugee problem in the UN or in Arab news media was "unrealistic."[56] Although the Department interpreted this position as applying only to the Arab side and as a way of removing the refugees from under the influence of Arab propaganda, it still felt such an all-inclusive ban was not reasonable. While it agreed to the idea of having a representative of the embassy in Tel Aviv receive Israel's arguments about the inflated numbers of refugees and believed there might be some merit to them, it still wanted to know the upper limit of refugees Israel would agree it could safely receive. In other words, a more forthcoming Israeli position was desired. On the question of Jews who left the Arab world, the State Department insisted that "these have NOT repeat NOT been covered by UN resolutions."[57] Also, the suggestion of proceeding with the operation on the basis of family reunion was not acceptable. Barbour was instructed to tell the Israelis, if they raised the subject again, that thus limiting the scheme was neither practical nor viable.

The State Department's discussions with Arab representatives did not fare much better. Although less is known about the details, the Arabs apparently continued to insist that the refugee problem could not be separated from the Arab-Israeli conflict as a whole.[58] Before the State Department could do much more on the subject, President Kennedy was assassinated, and the administration changed hands.

Kennedy's legacy

An account of the Johnson Plan would not be complete without reference to other developments in U.S. relations with the region. President Kennedy's legacy lies less in his attempts to solve the Arab refugee problem than his initiation of a close relationship with Israel. At the same time that discussion of the Johnson Plan was taking place, secret negotiations also went on between the Israelis and the Kennedy administration over arms sales. Israel requested a shipment of Hawk missiles in Ben-Gurion's meeting with Kennedy in New York in May 1961. At first the administration was reluctant to approve a sale that would see the United States involved, for the first time, in the arms race between the Arabs and the Israelis. Feldman, however, argued strongly in favor of the sale in order to counter Soviet arms sales to Egypt.[59] This argument is not quite convincing because Israel at the time did not suffer a shortage of arms suppliers. Its two major sources of arms were Britain and France — indeed, the British produced a missile, the Bloodhound, roughly equivalent to the Hawk.[60] The reasons for the U.S. shift on arms sale must be sought elsewhere. Certainly competition with the Soviet Union was a major factor in the administration's calculations. It was a competition broader than strict arms sales calculations. The nature of Western superpower presence in the region as a whole was shifting, with the gradual waning of British and French influence and the gradual ascendancy of the United States. The sale of the Hawk missiles, which was negotiated for roughly one year before it received final approval from Washington, was a further step in this process. As the United States assumed the role of the major Western power in the Middle East *vis-à-vis* the Soviet Union, closer U.S.-Israeli relations were almost inevitable.

Kennedy therefore established the pattern for future U.S. relations in the region. Friendship with Israel, as well as with individual Arab states, developed apart from the dictates of the Arab-Israeli conflict. Negotiations over the Johnson Plan proceeded at the same time that the United States was negotiating arms sales to Israel. Although Kennedy, in his meetings with Ben-Gurion and Meir, tried to urge them towards greater cooperation with Johnson's efforts, there was no serious attempt to link stronger U.S. support for Israel with a solution to the refugee problem. Meanwhile, U.S. relations with individual Arab states developed following the dictates of inter-Arab rivalries rather than along the lines dividing Arabs and Israelis. The breakup of the Syrian-Egyptian union in

September 1961 was followed by an intensification of the Arab Cold War. One year later, Nasser engaged in armed conflict over Yemen with Saudi Arabia, the United States' most important Arab friend. Jordan and Syria each fought a bitter conflict with Egypt as well. There was no unified Arab position that the United States needed to confront as a result of its developing friendship with Israel. The relationship between the United States and major Arab states therefore reflected inter-Arab conflicts. Relations between the United States and Egypt gradually cooled, as Egypt's engagement in the Yemen war led to strengthened ties with the Soviet Union in order to obtain arms and other forms of assistance.

There is little doubt, however, that the Kennedy administration sincerely wished to resolve the issue of Palestinian refugees. Its experience in that respect was remarkable also in the way it set a pattern for subsequent U.S. initiatives relating to the Arab-Israeli conflict. A proposal of great potential consequence was developed with little regard to the regional calculations of each of the actors, and no desire to outweigh these calculations with some leverage from the United States. With little forethought or preparation, Johnson was sent on his way to negotiate over the most sensitive aspect of the Arab-Israeli conflict. There seemed to be little appreciation in Washington of the vehement Israeli opposition to the idea of Arabs returning to their homes in Palestine. There was equally little appreciation of the intense suspicion among Arab states to the idea of solving the refugee problem separately from a comprehensive peaceful agreement that would involve territorial adjustments. The failure of the Kennedy initiative became apparent in late 1963. On 20 November 1963, the UN General Assembly's Special Committee on Palestine approved a U.S.-sponsored resolution calling on the UNCCP to continue its efforts for the implementation of paragraph 11 of Resolution 194. The Israeli delegate to the United Nations declared that the resolution was "wholly unacceptable to Israel."[61] On the same day the Israeli Prime Minister Levi Eshkol protested the contents of the resolution to the U.S. ambassador in Tel Aviv. He pointed out that Israel objected to the draft because it involved "a choice by the refugees," because it gave greater weight to repatriation than to resettlement as a solution, and because Israel favored direct negotiations rather than third-party mediation to settle the "disputes" between it and its Arab neighbors.[62] A short time later, the UNCCP mentioned, in its report to the General Assembly on 3 December 1963, that the United States had been conducting a series of high-level quiet negotiations since the beginning of the year with Israel, Jordan, Lebanon, Syria and Egypt. On the same day, Arab delegates to the UN issued a joint statement denying that such discussions took place. The statement also noted that Arab governments considered repatriation the only solution to the refugee problem.[63] Although neither assertion was accurate, the statement reflected the unwillingness of any of these Arab states to appear "soft" on the Palestinian issue. Without a comprehensive approach to solve the problem, any Arab attempt to reach an understanding with Israel would be open to attack from rival Arab states.

Despite the sincerity of Kennedy's effort to solve the refugee problem, his initiative in that direction remained secondary to other American interests in the region. Upgrading the U.S.-Israeli relationship, for example, was more important, and Israel's refusal to cooperate on the refugee issue did not threaten that relationship. The Palestinians themselves had no voice in these discussions and they carried no international weight. As long as they lacked representation and leverage in regional politics, their fate remained in the hands of other parties, each concerned with its national interest.

In 1962-63, while negotiations over the refugee issue continued half-heartedly via the State Department, a dangerous arms race began between Israel and Egypt, involving heavy tanks, supersonic planes, advanced rockets and missiles, and Israel's nuclear reactor at Dimona.[64] With the shifting of superpower competition in the region into one pitting the United States, rather than Britain or France, against the Soviet Union, the Soviets played an increasing role in supplying Egypt while the United States began building its military relationship with Israel. The Hawk sale was one step in that direction, together with special payment arrangements for the weapons and increased nonmilitary foreign assistance to Israel.[65] This development further detracted attention from the refugee issue, and the momentum generated by the Johnson initiative disappeared.

Partly out of concern for the escalating arms race, however, and in order to emphasize the U.S. new role in the region as well as to reassure Washington's friends, Kennedy announced U.S. opposition to the threat or use of force anywhere in the Middle East.[66] The statement was broad enough to cover inter-Arab conflicts as well as the Arab-Israeli conflict:

> In the event of aggression, or preparation for aggression, whether direct or indirect, we would support appropriate measures in the United Nations and adopt other courses of action on our own to prevent or to put a stop to such aggression.[67]

This was Kennedy's last major statement on the Middle East. The refugee issue already had receded from the president's attention.

THE JOHNSON ADMINISTRATION

U.S.-Israeli friendship flourished under the administration of Lyndon B. Johnson. The Texan president, himself sympathetic to Israel, was surrounded by strong advocates of this friendship and of Israeli interests. Among these were the U.S. Representative at the UN Arthur Goldberg, Undersecretary of State for Political Affairs Eugene V. Rostow, and presidential speech writer and adviser John Roche. Israeli Ambassador Avraham Harman and Israeli Minister at the Embassy Ephraim Evron both enjoyed easy access to the White House and personal friendship with the President.[68]

Johnson showed little interest in the question of Palestinian refugees that had so concerned his predecessor. In fact, the Israeli position on that issue had become so acceptable in the United States as to form part of the Democratic Party platform on which Johnson was elected in 1964. The platform pledged "to encourage the resettlement of Arab refugees in lands where there is room and opportunity."[69] The refugee issue, for all practical purposes, was buried. More important, however, was the strong anti-Nasserist and, by extension, anti-Arab bias that permeated political discourse in the United States in the mid-1960s, both in Congress and in the executive branch.[70] Sympathy with Israel was one reason for this bias, as was the deteriorating relationship between Egypt on the one hand and the United States and its friends in the Arab world on the other. Another factor, far more difficult to pinpoint, was the U.S. position as a superpower confronting nationalist sentiment in the Third World, which at that stage was receiving strong backing from the communist states. The Arab world was one arena for this confrontation, Vietnam another. This created a siege mentality which easily translated into resentment toward Third World movements, such as President Nasser's Arab Nationalism. Strong distaste for these assertive nationalist sentiments existed even among American groups that had reservations about direct U.S. military involvement in Vietnam. Anti-Arab sentiment in the United States easily fed upon a rich residue of cultural antipathy towards Arabs and Muslims, and was nourished by supporters of Israel constantly portraying the Jewish state as an outpost of the civilized Western spirit surrounded by hostile aliens.

A more concrete calculation in Johnson's support for Israel was the feeling that such a policy would help gain the support of Jewish Americans who were among the most active groups in the Democratic Party, particularly in its antiwar contingent.[71] With the Israeli military victory in 1967 other branches of government, especially the Pentagon, grew more interested in cooperating with the Israelis to benefit from their experience in battling Soviet weapons.[72]

The story of the growing U.S. military support for Israel and its role before and after the 1967 War is beyond the scope of this study.[73] Most remarkable in this tale, however, is the almost complete blindness of the Johnson administration, as far as can be ascertained from records released to date, to the crucial factor that characterized the politics of the region in the mid-1960s — namely the birth of organized Palestinian activity. It was this activity that upset the overwhelming sense of complacency in the region and provided a fuse to the tensions latent in the Arab-Israeli conflict. The description of the developments leading to the 1967 War in the State Department's history quoted above does not reflect any deep understanding of the significance of the rise of Palestinian guerrilla organizations.

The establishment of the Palestine Liberation Organization (PLO) by decree from an Arab summit meeting within the League of Arab States in 1964 might have contributed to this oversight on the part of Washington. The Johnson administration looked upon the PLO in those early days as a bureaucratic outfit, a tool of Egyptian diplomacy and an outlet for empty rhetoric.[74] The establishment of the PLO, however, set in motion a series of events that, if not leading directly to the 1967 War, at least helped set the stage for the conflict. It was the establishment of the PLO that hastened the movement by Fateh towards military action against Israel.[75] Yasir Arafat was worried that the PLO might divert the support of the Palestinians which he hoped to gain for his fledgling network of activists, thereby further placing the question of Palestine at the mercy of Arab politicians. Following the Syrian coup on 23 February 1966, which brought the Baath Party to power, Egyptian-Syrian rivalry intensified, and support for the Palestinian cause was, as usual, one of its arenas. Syria allowed the Palestinian guerrillas to operate from its territories, and taunted Nasser for his helplessness in stopping Israeli reprisals. Although Israeli Defense Minister during the 1967 War, Moshe Dayan, denied that Palestinian guerrilla activities were a cause of the war, in a very real sense they were.[76]

The U.S. administration seemed oblivious to all this, concentrating its attention instead on the other, very real and very threatening, aspect of the rising tensions, the Israeli-Egyptian confrontation. The only attention it gave the matter was to counsel restraint on the government of Israel with respect to growing Palestinian activities shortly before the war. In a meeting in Washington between Evron and Rodger P. Davies, Deputy Assistant Secretary of State for Near Eastern and South Asian Affairs on 10 May 1967, Davies reminded Evron of the importance of stability and the continued Western orientation of Lebanon and Jordan.[77] On 22 May 1967, Johnson wrote to Soviet Premier Aleksei N. Kosygin, inviting his cooperation in containing the emerging crisis in the Middle East by controlling those "elements based in Syria" who were contributing to the tensions.[78] By then it was too late.

The 1967 War created a new status quo in the region, one which the Johnson administration did not oppose. Israeli occupation of additional territories was a new bargaining chip to counter the old Arab demand for revision of the 1948 borders. Now the United States was the party adopting a call for a comprehensive settlement and lasting peace for Israel, but in return for a revision of the new borders of 1967. This was the position stated by Johnson on 19 June 1967, later incorporated in Security Council Resolution 242.[79] The Palestinians did not receive great attention in these efforts, and they were addressed merely as refugees. Under the circumstances, this was a gross misreading of the new realities in the area.

The U.S. position on the refugees remained that of the pre-1967 era. (The whole issue, in those Vietnam War days, received very little attention.) In the final days of the Johnson administration a little-known initiative by Secretary of State Dean Rusk restated that position: repatriation or resettlement of the refugees. Rusk's proposals were offered in November 1968 to the Egyptian Foreign Minister Mahmud Riad and his Israeli counterpart Abba Eban, during the General Assembly session in New York. The purpose of the new American initiative was to provide a push for the stalling UN-sponsored mission of Gunnar Jarring.[80] The U.S. proposals included support for full Israeli withdrawal from Sinai and restoration of Egyptian sovereignty over it (apparently with no mention of other occupied territories), in exchange for a signed peace agreement with

Israel. UN forces would be stationed permanently in Sharm al Sheikh, with freedom of navigation in the Straits of Tiran and through the Suez Canal for ships of all nations including Israel. The initiative also suggested movement toward resolution of the refugee problem by allowing the refugees to state their preferences on repatriation or resettlement.[81] Egypt, while not rejecting the initiative, asked for Israel's withdrawal from all Arab territories occupied in 1967. The Israeli response did not accept the idea of a commitment to withdraw from any occupied territories specifically. Rather, secure and recognized boundaries were to be agreed upon through negotiations. The refugee problem should be addressed through an international conference, thereby denying that it was Israel's responsibility.[82]

Were one to base one's judgement solely on formal pronouncements and the written record, one might conclude that the position of the United States on the question of the Palestinians at the end of the Johnson administration was the same as it was when President Kennedy took office. Paragraph 11 of Resolution 194 was the basis for a solution. So much had changed in the region, however, as to make such a statement quite misleading. Palestinians in 1968 were a growing force in regional politics. Their demographic distribution had changed with the addition of the refugees who fled the 1967 hostilities. Jurisdiction over much of the territory suggested for either repatriation or resettlement had shifted with the Israeli occupation of the West Bank and Gaza. Above all, the idea of Palestinian nationhood was taking shape, thereby making irrelevant any attempt to solve the problem by treating Palestinians as refugees instead of as a people with clearly articulated national aspirations. The most important, and unfortunate, change, however, was in the nature of the U.S.-Palestinian relationship. In 1960 that relationship was largely neutral, if only because of the absense of a representative Palestinian political structure. In the following years American-Israeli friendship advanced to such an extent that, when the Palestinians finally developed that necessary structure, they found themselves and the United States on opposite sides. Ironically, though, the U.S. position on the Palestinians officially remains that they have a right to repatriation on the basis of UN General Assembly Resolution 194. In that respect, the Covenant of the PLO and the formal position of the U.S. Department of State are closer than many people suspect.

NOTES

1. U.S. Department of State, *The Department of State During the Administration of President Lyndon B. Johnson. November 1963-January 1969*, vol. 1, pt. 4, Lyndon B. Johnson Library (hereinafter LBJL), Austin, Texas, p. 1.
2. Interview with Lucius D. Battle, Assistant Secretary of State for Near Eastern and South Asian Affairs 1967-68, Washington, DC, 3 October 1989.
3. *Ibid.*
4. Mordechai Gazit, *President Kennedy's Policy Toward the Arab States and Israel. Analysis and Documents* (Tel Aviv: Shiloah Center for Middle Eastern and African Studies, Tel Aviv University, 1983), pp. 14, 28; Steven L. Spiegel, *The Other Arab-Israeli*

Conflict: Making America's Middle East Policy, From Truman to Reagan (Chicago and London: University of Chicago Press, 1985), p. 97.

5. Spiegel, *Other Arab-Israeli Conflict*, pp. 95-97.

6. Ernest Barbarash, ed. *John F. Kennedy on Israel, Zionism and Jewish Issues* (New York: Herzl Press for the Zionist Organization of America, 1965), p. 60.

7. *Ibid.*, pp. 65-66; Kennedy address before the Zionist Organization of America convention in 1962; Kennedy to David Ben-Gurion, 13 June 1962, National Security Council Files (hereinafter NSCF), Box 117-118, John F. Kennedy Library, Boston, MA (hereinafter JFKL).

8. Barbarash, *Kennedy on Israel*, p. 26.

9. Quoted in Gazit, *President Kennedy's Policy*, pp. 34-35.

10. *Ibid.*, p. 18; Muhammad Hasanayn Haykal, *Sanawat al-Ghalayan* (Years of Upheaval), pt. 1 (Cairo: Ahram Center for Translation, 1988) p. 532. Interestingly, neither Syria nor Israel was approached at this time.

11. The UNCCP was created in December 1948 to continue the work of the UN Mediator on Palestine (Count Folke Bernadotte), and to implement paragraph 11 of General Assembly Resolution 194, which also created the Commission. On the work of the UNCCP see David P. Forsythe, *United Nations Peacemaking: The Conciliation Commission for Palestine* (Baltimore, MD: Johns Hopkins University Press, 1972), p. 532.

12. For more information on U.S.-Egyptian relations in those years see Douglas Little, "The New Frontier on the Nile: JFK, Nasser, and Arab Nationalism," *The Journal of American History*, vol. 75, no. 2 (1988), pp. 501-527. See also William Stivers, *America's Confrontation with Revolutionary Change in the Middle East, 1948-83* (London: Macmillan Press, 1986), pp. 38-59.

13. Haykal, *Sanawat al-Ghalayan*, p. 537.

14. *Ibid.*

15. *Ibid.*

16. The text of Nasser's letter to Kennedy is reproduced in Haykal, *ibid.*, Appendix 32, pp. 892-99.

17. *Ibid.*, p. 985.

18. Gazit, *President Kennedy's Policy*, p. 39.

19. *Ibid.* The U.S. record of this meeting has not been declassified. Gazit relies on unnamed Israeli sources and his own recollection.

20. *Ibid.*

21. Forsythe, *United Nations Peacemaking*, p. 124.

22. *Ibid.*, pp. 125-26.

23. *Jerusalem Post*, 12 October 1961, quoted in *ibid.*, p. 127.

24. *Jerusalem Post*, 7 November 1961, quoted in *ibid.*

25. *Ibid.*

26. *Ibid.*, p. 128.

27. For example, Emile Ghory, addressing the United Nations on behalf of Hajj Amin al-Husseini's Arab Higher Committee, declared that unqualified repatriation was the only solution to the refugee question. *Ibid.*, p. 129.

28. *Ibid.*, p. 130.

29. *Ibid.*

30. *Ibid.*

31. King Saud to Nasser, 2 August 1961, in Haykal, *Sanawat al-Ghalayan*, pp. 549-50 (full text of the letter). At the time, Iraq was engaged in a battle of words with Nasser

and called for the establishment of a separate Palestinian state on the West Bank and Gaza. Nasser reassured King Hussein that he did not support that position.

32. Forsythe, *United Nations Peacemaking*, p. 130.

33. *Ibid.*, p. 133. Johnson hoped that the proposals eventually would be endorsed by the General Assembly in a resolution and implemented by the parties without a formal treaty. Forsythe apparently used a copy of the plan, and the following description relies on his account.

34. State Department to American Embassy in Tel Aviv, 16 August 1962, NSCF, Box 117-18, JFKL; Spiegel, *Other Arab-Israeli Conflict*, p. 113.

35. Feldman to Kennedy, 21 August 1962, NSCF, Box 118-119, JFKL.

36. Secretary of State Dean Rusk to Badeau, 22 August 1962, quoted in Spiegel, *Other Arab-Israeli Conflict*, p. 114.

37. Spiegel, p. 114.

38. Forsythe, *United Nations Peacemaking*, p. 135, reports that Israel was the first to indicate its rejection to Johnson. He cites an "unimpeachable source," apparently Johnson himself.

39. *Ibid.*, p. 136.

40. *Ibid.*

41. *Ibid.*, p. 137. Syria rejected the plan on 5 October 1962.

42. *Ibid.*, quoting Syrian Foreign Minister Khaled al-Azm to *Al-Sada al-Amm*, 6 October 1962.

43. *Ibid.*, pp. 137-38.

44. *Ibid.*, p. 139. The expression was used by a U.S. spokesman at the UN General Assembly.

45. Joseph E. Johnson, "Arab v. Israeli: A Persistent Challenge to Americans," *Middle East Journal*, vol. 18 (Winter 1964), pp. 8-9.

46. *Ibid.*, p. 9.

47. Spiegel, in *Other Arab-Israeli Conflict*, pp. 114-15, blamed the failure on the Arabs. Johnson himself blamed the Israelis and their American supporters. See Johnson, "Arab v. Israeli," pp. 12-13.

48. U.S. Department of State, Memorandum of Conversation between Kennedy and Golda Meir, 27 December 1962, NSCF, Box 117-118, JFKL.

49. *Ibid.*

50. *Ibid.*

51. U.S. Department of State, Report by U.S. Ambassador in Israel re: Meeting with Ben-Gurion on Palestine Refugee Issue, 3 April 1963, NSCF, Box 119, JFKL.

52. *Ibid.*

53. *Ibid.*

54. *Ibid.*

55. *Ibid.*

56. U.S. Department of State, Department of State Review of Talks on Palestine Refugee Issue in Amman, Cairo, Damascus and Tel Aviv, 13 April 1963, NSCF, Box 119, JFKL.

57. *Ibid.*

58. *Ibid.*

59. Spiegel, *Other Arab-Israeli Conflict*, p. 107.

60. U.S. Department of State. Dean Rusk (Washington) to Feldman (via American Embassy in Tel Aviv), 18 August 1962, NSCF, Box 118-119, JFKL. Feldman was in Israel to discuss the Hawk missile sale which had just been approved by Washington.

61. Leila S. Kadi, *The Arab-Israeli Conflict: The Peaceful Proposals 1948-1972* (Beirut: Palestine Research Center, 1973), p. 44.

62. *Ibid.*

63. *Ibid.*

64. Fred J. Khouri, *The Arab-Israeli Dilemma*, 2d ed. (Syracuse, NY: Syracuse University Press, 1976), p. 305.

65. Spiegel, *Other Arab-Israeli Conflict*, p. 109.

66. The statement came in a press conference in May 1963. Richard P. Stebbins, ed., *Documents on American Foreign Relations, 1963* (New York: Harper & Row, 1964), p. 268.

67. *Ibid.* See also John C. Campbell, "American Efforts for Peace," in Malcolm H. Kerr, ed., *The Elusive Peace in the Middle East* (Albany: SUNY Press, 1975), p. 281.

68. Donald Neff, *Warriors for Jerusalem: The Six Days That Changed the Middle East* (New York: Linden Press/Simon & Schuster, 1984), pp. 110-11; Spiegel, *Other Arab-Israeli Conflict*, pp. 128-29.

69. Quoted in Michael E. Jansen, *The United States and the Palestinian People* (Beirut: Institute for Palestine Studies, 1970), p. 156.

70. Neff, *Warriors for Jerusalem*, pp. 102-3; Lucius D. Battle, Oral History, 14 Nov. 1968, LBJL.

71. Neff, *Warriors for Jerusalem*, pp. 83-85, 169, 328.

72. Spiegel, *Other Arab-Israeli Conflict*, p. 127.

73. See Neff, *passim*, and Spiegel, pp. 130-165.

74. Battle interview, 3 Oct. 1989.

75. Alan Hart, *Arafat: Terrorist or Peacemaker?* (London: Sidgwick & Jackson, 1984), p. 168.

76. Dayan's statement is quoted in Patrick Seale, *Asad of Syria: The Struggle for the Middle East* (Los Angeles: University of California Press, 1988), p.128.

77. Department of State to Tel Aviv Embassy, 10 May 1967, Telegram 191818, LBJL.

78. Neff, *Warriors for Jerusalem*, pp. 113-14.

79. For Johnson's statement, see Neff, p. 307; Campbell, "American Efforts for Peace," p. 284.

80. Gunnar Jarring, Swedish diplomat, was appointed Special Representative of the Secretary General of the United Nations on the Middle East Question in November 1967. His efforts to reach agreement among the states of the region on methods to implement Security Council Resolution 242 remained fruitless.

81. Campbell, "American Efforts for Peace," pp. 286-87.

82. *Ibid.*, pp. 287-88.

6

NIXON'S MIDDLE EAST POLICY: FROM BALANCE TO BIAS

Donald Neff

RICHARD M. NIXON CAME TO POWER in 1969 less encumbered by reliance on the supporters of Israel or burdened by misconceptions of the Middle East than any president since Dwight D. Eisenhower. He had been vice president during the traumatic Suez crisis of 1956, a period of extraordinary tension between the United States and Israel and its American supporters.[1] He had also personally faced the outrage and political impact of Jewish groups over the years when he was delegated to go before them to explain Eisenhower's policies, which were widely misperceived as anti-Israel.[2] Nixon had also traveled in the region and he knew some of its leaders.

As a result, Nixon assumed the presidency better informed than any of his predecessors about the problems of the Middle East and their domestic repercussions, although he was largely ignorant of the Palestinian aspect of the conflict. In fact, in all of his memoirs, Nixon does not once refer to Palestinians. The closest he comes is a reference to "Palestinian guerrillas," the usual stereotype. But in 1969 that was hardly an oddity. Most Americans knew little about the Palestinian experience.

More interesting is the fact that, unlike Truman, Kennedy, or Johnson before him, Nixon had no political debts to Israel's powerful domestic supporters. He had received only 15 percent of the Jewish vote in the 1968 elections and he was keenly aware that in general he was distrusted by Jewish voters. Both in Israel and the United States, Jews believed Nixon did not like them — in fact, that he was an anti-Semite.[3] In addition, Jews at the time generally voted for liberal issues and opposed Nixon's Republican conservative policies. The result was, as his first national security adviser, Henry Kissinger, reported, that Nixon "considered himself less obligated to the Jewish constituency than any of his predecessors had been and was eager to demonstrate that he was impervious to its pressures."[4]

Indeed, at the beginning of his presidency, Richard Nixon gave every indication that he saw the Arab-Israel conflict — if not the Palestinian aspect of it — in comparatively clear terms and was determined to settle it without the traditional bow to the political influence of Israel's supporters in America. In his view, the foremost problem in 1969 — and the prime deterrent to peace — was that Israel had become intransigent after its stunning 1967 victory. Nixon had visited Israel just after the June conquest of lands from Egypt, Jordan, and Syria and he recorded in his memoirs:

> I was impressed by the courage and toughness of the Israeli leaders and people. But I was disturbed by the fact that their swift and overwhelming victory over the Arabs [in 1967] had created a feeling of overconfidence about their ability to win any war in the future, and an attitude of total intransigence on negotiating any peace agreement that would involve return of any of the territories they had occupied. Their victory had been too great. It left a residue of hatred among their neighbors that I felt could only result in another war, particularly if the Russians were to step up military aid to their defeated Arab clients.[5]

This reflects a grasp of the Arab dimension of the conflict, if not of its Palestinian component. Nixon's memoirs leave no doubt that he considered previous administrations — with the exception of Eisenhower's — as too pro-Israel, too prone to cave in to the political pressures of Israel's domestic supporters. He wrote:

> One of the main problems I faced . . . was the unyielding and shortsighted pro-Israeli attitude in large and influential segments of the American Jewish community, Congress, the media and in intellectual and cultural circles. In the quarter-century since the end of World War II this attitude had become so deeply ingrained that many saw the corollary of not being pro-Israel as being anti-Israeli, or even anti-Semitic. I tried unsuccessfully to convince them that this was not the case.[6]

It is apparent that Nixon, as president, was not only acutely aware of the incestuous triangle that had grown between Israel, its American supporters, and the White House, but that he was determined to steer his own course. He gave dramatic warning of this new independence in the White House by resorting to one of Washington's transparent political ploys just before his inauguration. He sent a special emissary to the Middle East to "study the problem." The real purpose was to send up a trial balloon to see how controversial a change in policy would be and to send a warning that it was coming. Nixon's choice for the preinaugural mission was former governor of Pennsylvania William Scranton, a politician who had no special interests in the region. It could not have come as a surprise to the president-elect when Scranton reported back in December that he had found U.S. policy should be "more evenhanded" in order to protect American national interests. As it was, he said, America was regarded throughout the region as caring only for Israel and its security.[7]

As predictable as Scranton's conclusion was the uproar that the remark incited from Israel and from Jewish Americans, who considered such a "more evenhanded" attitude as anti-Israel, even as proof of anti-Semitism. The Scranton mission was the public's first broad hint that the new president was determined to exercise a more balanced policy in the Middle East. This suspicion was quickly borne out several days later when Nixon pointedly did not disavow Scranton's remarks beyond having his press secretary observe that "Scranton remarks [are] not Nixon remarks."[8] The point was underscored when Scranton publicly repeated the remarks for the media after meeting personally with Nixon.[9]

For those naifs still in doubt about Nixon's attitude, the new president said at his first presidential press conference on 27 January:

> I believe we need new initiatives and new leadership on the part of the United States in order to cool off the situation in the Mideast. I consider it a powder keg, very explosive. It needs to be defused. I am open to any suggestions that may cool it off and reduce the possibility of another explosion, because the next explosion in the Mideast, I think, could involve very well a confrontation between the nuclear powers, which we want to avoid.[10]

Private observations of Nixon in these early days confirm Nixon's determination to steer a new course. Henry Kissinger noted in his memoirs that "the President was convinced that most leaders of the Jewish community had opposed him throughout his political career. The small percentage of Jews who voted for him, he would joke, had to be so crazy that they would probably stick with him even if he turned on Israel. He delighted in telling associates and visitors that the 'Jewish lobby' had no effect on him."[11] Nixon's attitude toward Scranton's remarks is also evident in a memo he wrote to Kissinger: "'Even Handedness' is the right policy";[12] his sense of independence shows in his remark, "We cannot let the American Jews dictate policy."[13] The evidence is overwhelming — both on the basis of Nixon's own testimony and his public comments and actions and of the observations of those around him — that he entered office in 1969 determined to steer a less biased and more balanced course in the Middle East.

Nearly six years later, when he was forced from office, the record showed a startlingly different result. Nixon had become the most pro-Israeli president up to that time. He had increased aid, both economic and military, to Israel to levels never before imagined. He had aligned America diplomatically closer to Israel than ever before, even to the point of demeaning the value of the U.S. veto in the United Nations by using it repeatedly to protect Israel.[14] He had become, in the end, Israel's protector, and he had made America, more than ever before, Israel's mightiest and most powerful friend in the international arena.

How to explain this extraordinary evolution from cool-eyed statesman to passionate partisan, this bizarre trajectory from objectivity to embrace, from balance to bias? I believe the answer can be largely found in four intertwining areas: in Nixon's error in choosing two incompatible men as his secretary of state and his national security adviser; in his misreading of the global competition with the Soviet Union and its influence on the Middle East; in his political weakness caused by the Watergate scandal; and in the effects of Henry Kissinger's pro-Israeli policies. Each of these, in its way, contributed to Nixon's abandonment of his original intentions to play a balanced role in the Middle East.

By historic bad luck, the four strands all came together with stunning force during the last days of the 1973 War in the Middle East when Nixon's presidency was crashing around him. This ill-fated confluence occurred just when Nixon had summoned the courage for a desperate attempt at finding peace, about which more later. It was to be his last. But by then the president was too weak and Kissinger too arrogant and powerful in his own right. Kissinger, as Nixon's secretary of state, deliberately ignored his master's instructions to work for an imposed peace. Nixon was too enmeshed in saving his own career to remonstrate, and a chance — however slight — for an evenhanded settlement was lost, perhaps forever.

THE KISSINGER-ROGERS FEUD

To examine this tragedy let us first look at Nixon's White House and how he fashioned it as uniquely his own. From the beginning he had left no doubt that he would make the major decisions in foreign policy and be the administration's principal foreign minister as well as president. As he wrote in his memoirs: "From the outset of my administration . . . I planned to direct foreign policy from the White House."[15] To this end, he deliberately chose a weak secretary of state, whose substantive duties he severely circumscribed, and considerably strengthened the National Security Council (NSC) as a White House alternative to the State Department. The strengthened NSC was meant to give him advice independent of the bureaucracy at State as well as provide him with a variety of options that he could control and launch as his own.[16]

The job of overseeing the reinvigorated NSC was given to a comparatively obscure Harvard professor, Henry Alfred Kissinger. Although Kissinger had written an influential book in 1957 called *Nuclear Weapons and Foreign Policy* that had earned him Washington's attention, his sudden ascension to such a high position was a jolting surprise. Not only was he an intellectual and a representative of that stuffy academic community Nixon so openly disdained, but, foremost, he was closely associated with Nelson Rockefeller. The relationship between Nixon and Rockefeller, the very embodiment of the detested Northeast establishment, was "that of a mongoose and a cobra," according to speechwriter William Safire.[17] Safire did not designate which was mongoose and which cobra, but his point was well made — they were not bosom friends.

Yet it was Rockefeller's man, Kissinger, that Nixon brought into the White House despite the fact that the two men did not know each other and had no reason to hold each other in high esteem. Traditionally, they had occupied different parts of the Republican political spectrum, had different friends, circulated in different circles. As Nixon observed in his memoirs: "I made my choice in an uncharacteristically impulsive way." The primary reason, said Nixon, was that he had a "strong intuition about Henry Kissinger." What that intuition was he does not say. But one of the things he thought worth noting was that as a White House team they made an unlikely combination that, as so often worked — "the grocer's son from Whittier and the refugee from Hitler's Germany, the politician and the academic . . . our differences helped make the partnership work."[18]

Of the many considerations that go into such an appointment, some of the major rational ones from Nixon's side include the fact that Kissinger was respected but not so well known that he would upstage the president; one of their early agreements was that Kissinger would maintain such a low profile that he would not even talk to the press.[19] More substantively, Kissinger shared Nixon's worldview about the Soviet Union and their ideas were compatible in other areas as well, including the necessity for a nation to be strong in order to be successful diplomatically. Their characters also complemented each other, with Nixon instinctual and decisive and Kissinger analytical and subtle. Foremost, Kissinger had the energy, both intellectual and physical, to galvanize the National Security Council and give Nixon the new thinking and imaginative alternatives he desired. Finally, and this is not as frivolous a consideration as it may sound, the appointment would shock Rockefeller's supporters, dismay Kissinger's Harvard colleagues, and stun the media. The ability to surprise and to arrogate is a power that presidents, for the most part, delight in. As Kissinger admitted in his memoirs: "One of my attractions for Nixon, I understood later, was that my appointment would demonstrate his ability to co-opt a Harvard intellectual; that I came from Rockefeller's entourage made the prospect all the more interesting."[20]

In these early days, before unwanted events intruded, Nixon had already carefully crafted a strategy and a structure for achieving his aims in foreign policy. On a scale of urgency, this did not include the Middle East. He worried about the area's explosiveness and was determined to pursue a balanced policy, but there were other regions of far more immediate concern that demanded his personal attention. Foremost was Vietnam, now in its fourth year of major American military involvement. Although Nixon was right in seeing it as a short-term problem, in the sense that it was obvious American troops could not stay there forever, it nonetheless had the highest urgency. The war's unpopularity was tearing up America, splitting families and the social fabric alike, and consuming the entire energy of the presidency and its security and foreign policy apparatus. Vietnam had to be addressed immediately. And there were other problems, as profound in their long-term implications. These included disarray within NATO and the emergence of Japan as the world's second economic power, and at the top of the list with truly global implications, two supreme challenges: China, the slumbering giant that had been ignored at America's own peril since the communist takeover in 1949, and the Soviet Union, America's nuclear equal and Cold War adversary for the past two decades.

It was these profound global problems that Nixon had decided to face, essentially without the aid of a secretary of state. Yet this decision left Nixon with a vacuum: he still had to have a secretary of state and he had to see that the Middle East did not explode. Nixon's solution to these exigencies was elegant in its Machiavellian way. It was to appoint a secretary who would be content to occupy the high position shorn of its traditional influence, a figurehead willing to assume the ceremonial duties of the office while Nixon exercised its power. At the same time, the man had to be a patriot of such character as to be willing to take on a task so thankless that no president — much less a secretary of state — had ever truly had the courage to face head on and wage the tooth-and-nail fight it would demand. That was the quest for peace in the Middle East, a goal that had eluded Western officials for most of the century.

The man chosen by Nixon was William Pierce Rogers, fifty-five at the time, an old if not close friend of Nixon's from the Eisenhower administration where he had served as attorney general.[21] By all accounts, Rogers was a proud, upright, and honorable man, a highly successful corporation attorney who was as reasonable in tone as he was conservative in dress. He was handsome, chivalrous, and secure: in a word, a member in good standing of the establishment. But he was not overburdened by ambition or imagination, nor was he committed to the long work hours that had become the White House fashion since the hectic Kennedy days.[22] He was a social creature who enjoyed the perks of power, the media attention, and the prestige of high office. He did not have that visceral hunger for glory, that burning in the belly, that so motivated Kissinger and others to perspire in pursuit of excellence. Nor did he have any experience in foreign affairs. In fact, it can be speculated with a high degree of confidence that Bill Rogers did not have the slightest idea how thorny and intractable was the Middle East problem. From the beginning, in Seymour M. Hersh's words: "Kissinger and many of his aides wrote him off as uninformed, even stupid, and a coward."[23]

Nixon's assignment for Rogers was a unique one. While Rogers would be secretary of state in name and preside over the vast bureaucracy of the State Department, it would be Nixon who would actually conduct the nation's foreign affairs with the help of a small National Security Council under Henry Kissinger. "I recognized that [Nixon] wanted to be his own foreign policy leader and did not want others to share that role," Rogers said later.[24] Rogers' job would be to tame State's "recalcitrant bureaucracy," in Nixon's words, and to carry out the ceremonial functions that take up so much of the secretary's time.[25] And he would have one substantive area: the Middle East.

For an established and not excessively ambitious man, it was a seemingly ideal arrangement coming toward the close of a distinguished career. He would once again serve his country, this time in one of the highest offices of the nation and with an assignment in which high honor beckoned. Any man who could solve the festering problem in the Middle East was assured of his place in history. It was a worthy challenge, and on its face not beyond conquest. He would have State's entire resources to bring to bear on one isolated problem — albeit one that included the entire Arab world. But mainly his efforts were toward countering the intransigence of Israel, a country of only 3 million or so people, a country, moreover, that was totally dependent on the good will and economic support of the United States. Finally, Rogers had much to bring to the problem:

honesty, integrity, objectivity, and experience in government, if not in the Middle East.

But he was lacking two essentials: the trust of the Israelis and the respect of Nixon's new National Security Adviser, Henry Kissinger. Rogers did not know that yet.

At the same time that Nixon assigned the Middle East exclusively to Rogers, he deliberately barred Kissinger from any influence on Middle East policy. Nixon explained this strange arrangement as being eminently practical and workable. "I did this partly because I felt that Kissinger's Jewish background would put him at a disadvantage during the delicate initial negotiations for the reopening of diplomatic relations with the Arab states." In explaining his decision to Kissinger, Nixon added: "You and I will have more than enough on our plate with Vietnam, SALT, the Soviets, Japan and Europe."[26]

For Bill Rogers, the road ahead looked clear and promising. With the president his personal friend and his writ as secretary of state so precisely spelled out, with his past achievements, social standing, and new high position all seemingly secure, there was no reason for Rogers to suppose that a Jewish immigrant toiling away in the basement of the White House would become his nemesis, the man who would one day drive him from office. At the time, Kissinger was forty-five, pudgy and ungainly, his bookish glasses sitting askew his nose, giving him a misleading look of professorial forgetfulness and mildness. He was anything but. Kissinger was acid-tongued, impatient, malicious, and tirelessly ambitious, driven by self-promotion and a level of intellectual arrogance that was notable even for Harvard.

Although Kissinger was officially barred from forming Middle East policy, not many months passed before it became one of the prime areas that served as the battleground for his repeated clashes with Rogers. The fact that Kissinger had little knowledge (but strong biases) about the region did not stop his interference. He had never visited an Arab country and had been to Israel only three brief times during the previous decade.[27]

Of the Palestinians, Kissinger knew little. Like Nixon, he perceived the conflict mainly in terms of the Arabs against the Israelis, of state against state within the context of the cold war. This was not a totally egregious misunderstanding: At the time the region was dominated by the war of attrition between Israel and Egypt and the Soviet Union's role in protecting Egyptian skies from Israeli aircraft attacks. In this dramatic atmosphere, the plight of the Palestinians and their festering and potentially dangerous grievances appeared not even to register on Washington's or Kissinger's radar. The only evidence in Kissinger's memoirs that he was aware of the Palestinians at all did not come until after he held a secret meeting with Anwar Sadat's national security adviser in the winter of 1973. Before that meeting with Mohammed Hafiz Ismail the name Palestinian does not appear in Kissinger's memoirs.

In briefing a British official in March 1973, a month after meeting Ismail, Kissinger included the Palestinians as a basic part of the conflict. He explained to the official that even after a settlement of Israel's borders with neighboring Arab states there would remain "the dispute between the Palestinians and Israel over the future of Palestine. . . . It is obvious [from my talks with Ismail] that a peace settlement ultimately depends on the Palestinians — who have the least incentive to settle anything."[28]

For Kissinger and official Washington, that was an enormously important insight to the conflict. But it came too late (the winter of 1973) to influence policy before the war that fall. And afterward, even if Kissinger took the Palestinians seriously, he was too closely allied emotionally and intellectually with Israel to heed the implications.

At the beginning, in 1969 when Kissinger knew little about the Palestinians, his ideas about the Middle East were superficial and biased, viscerally paralleling those of Israel's staunchest supporters, among whom he openly included himself. As his early biographers Marvin and Bernard Kalb reported, "He never concealed his strong concern about the Jewish state."[29]

Kissinger knew firsthand about anti-Semitism but was no devoted practitioner of Judaism. He had grown up in the Bavarian village of Furth, a town with a population of about 80,000 with 3,000 Jews. His father, Louis, a teacher, lost his job with the advent of the Nazis in the 1930s and Kissinger and other Jews were expelled from the *Gymnasium*. By the time Kissinger was fifteen, in 1938, the family, like many European Jews, had had enough and emigrated to New York. The move probably saved their lives. At the end of World War II, only seventy Jews showed up in Furth at the first postwar service; among the six million Jews killed by the Nazis, thirteen were Kissinger's relatives.[30]

In Manhattan, Kissinger prospered beyond even the usual expectations of the American dream. He survived the impoverishment of the new immigrant by working odd jobs to get through high school as a straight A student, served as a sergeant in the army, and then, in 1947, won a scholarship to Harvard. It was the start of a brilliant career as historian and nuclear strategist. But he never forgot his past. As he later explained: "Look, anyone who has been through what I've been through has some very special feeling for the survival of the state of Israel." He remembered that he lost "many of his relatives in the concentration camps" and he viewed Israel as "a place of refuge for those who survived."[31] Observed one of Kissinger's closest aides: "He's objective about Israel but not detached. How could he be? He has a strong sense of 'these are my people.' He's immensely proud to be a Jew. When he pleads for changes in Israeli policy, it's precisely because he wants Israel and Jewry to prosper. It tears his guts out to be accused of treachery to his own." When Jewish leaders at one point accused him of acting against Israel, Kissinger replied: "How could I, as a Jew, do anything to betray my people?"[32]

With such a searing background and such strong emotions, Kissinger was hardly an objective mediator on the Middle East. However, even with the best intentions — and there is no evidence that Kissinger ever displayed such toward Rogers — Kissinger never made any effort to restrain his counsel. He repeatedly interfered in Rogers' preserve in the most insidious ways, even to the point of approving wiretaps against Rogers' top aide and his own aides as well.[33] He would urge U.S. and foreign ambassadors alike to bypass Rogers and the State Department and come directly to him.[34] He set up a "back channel" via Central Intelligence Agency (CIA) communications so that ambassadors could communicate directly with him without Rogers or State knowing. In this shunting aside of Rogers, Kissinger was joined by the president himself. More than once Nixon privately advised a foreign envoy: "If you really want to get something done, call Henry."[35]

This extraordinary behavior in the White House began the first day after Nixon's inauguration and continued until Nixon and Kissinger had completely cut Rogers at the State Department from all substantive areas of foreign policy.[36] Any foreign official of any importance at all soon knew that the way to deal with Nixon's White House was to "see Henry." Soon private arrangements bypassing State were established with the Soviets, the Israelis, the Egyptians, the North Vietnamese, and the Chinese, among others. The arrangement obviously suited a president who had an almost paranoid dislike of the State Department. But Nixon never seemed aware — until it was too late — that in making Kissinger the "back channel" to the White House he was conferring on his security adviser unprecedented power. By cutting out the State Department and controlling access to the president, Kissinger soon had gathered to himself all the powers and prestige that should have normally pertained to Bill Rogers. Within a comparatively short time Kissinger had everything except the title of secretary of state. He would eventually get that too.

Kissinger's meddling in Middle East policy began in earnest when Rogers unveiled his proposals for peace in the region: the 1969 initiative based on the land for peace formula of UN Security Council Resolution 242. The initiative, which became known as the Rogers Plan, was heatedly opposed by Kissinger because implicit in it was the proposition that Israel would have to withdraw from the occupied territories in return for peace.[37] The Rogers Plan eventually died an unheralded death, much to Kissinger's satisfaction, essentially ending Rogers' role in foreign affairs and facilitating his departure in the summer of 1973.

By then, Kissinger's ruthless infighting against Rogers and his scornful attitude toward him were such an open scandal that they became a public embarrassment for the administration, and of course for the upright Rogers himself.[38] Rogers at one point had to suffer the ignominy of hearing Senator Stuart Symington describe him as a "laughingstock" because of his inability to control Kissinger's open defiance of him. All this, of course, did nothing to help the administration carry out a coherent Middle Eastern policy.[39]

Kissinger himself later contended: "Neither Rogers nor I mustered the grace to transcend an impasse that we should have recognized was not in the national interest. If we had been prepared to overcome our not inconsiderable egos, we could have complemented each other's efforts."[40] But it was not Rogers who carried on the rivalry. It was Kissinger, and he never could "overcome" his considerable ego. As a result, "In the end, [Nixon] probably spent as much time mediating between Rogers and me as between the Arabs and Israelis."[41]

Thus right from the beginning Nixon's grand plan for a balanced policy in the Middle East was essentially foiled by his choice of his top officials and his eccentric reorganization of foreign policy responsibilities between the State Department and the White House. Another secretary grounded in diplomacy and knowledgeable about the Middle East might have been able to fight off the intrusions of Kissinger and persevere with his task. Or another national security adviser less committed to Israel and more civilized in his behavior might have been able to tutor Rogers and help him carry out his plan. The plan itself was evenhanded and balanced, just what Nixon repeatedly said he sought. But its execution amidst the tawdry behavior by Kissinger and the ineptness of Rogers was impossible. Further, it should be noted that the plan did not address the issue of the Palestinians as a people.

EXAGGERATING THE GLOBAL CONFLICT

Richard Nixon had made his reputation as an anticommunist with his entry into politics in the 1940s and he had remained a hard-lining anticommunist throughout his political career. When he came to power, he wrote in his memoirs, he saw the world much the same as he had twenty years earlier. "As I looked at America's position in the world and examined our relations with other nations, I could see that the central factor in 1968 on the eve of my presidency was the same as it had been in 1947 when I first went to Europe with the Herter Committee: America now, as then, was the main defender of the free world against the encroachment and aggression of the Communist world."[42]

As a result of this rather simple mindset, when Nixon looked at the world he saw it mainly in terms of U.S.-USSR competition. It followed that regional conflicts were rooted mainly in this global context; local causes counted for less in explaining events.[43] Thus the Vietnam war, in Nixon's (and Kissinger's) view, was being fought as a proxy war with the Soviet Union. It was a conflict of communism versus capitalism, of East versus West, superpower versus superpower. The fact that the Vietnamese had their own internal disputes, their own grievances and aspirations, counted little in explaining the conflict. Similarly with the Middle East: Nixon saw it mainly in superpower terms, as did Kissinger. Recorded Nixon in his memoirs:

> The Soviets wanted to maintain their presence in the Middle East, not because of ideological support for the cause of Arab unity but because it was through Egypt and the other Arab countries that the Soviets could gain access to what the Russians had always wanted — land, oil, power, and the warm waters of the Mediterranean. As I commented to Bill Rogers, "The difference between our goal and the Soviet goal in the Middle East is very simple but fundamental. We want peace. They want in the Middle East."[44]

In this view, the Palestinians were not visible.

Up to this point, Nixon and Kissinger were in total agreement. But it was with Nixon's analysis of how to oust the Soviets that Kissinger disagreed. As Nixon saw it: "It was clearly in America's interests to halt the Soviet domination of the Arab Mideast. To do so would require broadening American relations with the Arab countries."[45] At the time, U.S. relations with the Arab states were practically nonexistent. Diplomatic ties with the major Arab countries, Egypt, Iraq and Syria, remained broken since the 1967 War. No effort had been made by the Johnson administration to repair them. The result was that America's relations were essentially confined to Israel, a state of affairs with which Israel was well satisfied, as was Kissinger. But it did nothing to help the diplomatic process toward peace between Israel and the Arabs.

Rather than make any effort toward the Arab states, much less the Palestinians, Kissinger felt the United States should let them stew until they came begging to Washington. "I thought delay was on the whole in our interests because it enabled us to demonstrate even to radical Arabs that we were indispensable to *any* progress and that it could not be extorted from us by Soviet pressure," Kissinger later observed. "The state department wanted to fuel the process of negotiations by accepting at least some of the Soviet ideas, to facilitate compromise. I wanted to frustrate the radicals — who were in any event hostile to us — by demonstrating that in the Middle East friendship with the United States was the precondition to diplomatic progress."[46]

No one ever accused Kissinger of being naive, so one must assume he was aware that such a strategy fitted exactly with Israel's policy. Delay was what the Jewish state sought. It had begun populating the occupied territories with Jewish settlements within months of the 1967 war's end.[47] The longer the impasse lasted, the longer Israel would have to transfer its population to occupied territory, hence the stronger any later argument that the land was Israel's by right of settlement.

Few who knew anything about the area agreed with Kissinger's analysis. The experts in the State Department and CIA, for instance, were sensitive to local issues and keenly aware that they were the core — if not the total dimension — of the conflict. The global issue of communism versus capitalism had little meaning in the region compared to the sharp and bloody conflicts erupting from such local issues as control of land and water. It was, in the eyes of the experts, Israeli dispossession of the Palestinians and its expansionism and intransigence that fed the conflict and gave it its passions and urgency.

"I constantly wrote cables trying to explain that it was a local conflict and that the Soviets were only there because we were so totally pro-Israel," recalled the CIA agent stationed in Cairo during the early 1970s, Eugene Trone.[48] Others wrote similar reports. But these messages were ignored by Kissinger.

Nixon showed more understanding, at least when he was not thinking exclusively in global or domestic political terms. He especially did not agree with Kissinger that a do-nothing policy was the way to achieve peace. In his view, which would be proved correct, it was the surest of all ways to bring about another war. As a result, he supported the State Department in urging an active American role in seeking peace, restraint in arms aid to Israel and, as Scranton had urged, a more evenhanded policy.[49]

When Kissinger proposed a go-slow policy by writing the president a memorandum arguing that U.S. delay would demonstrate to the Arabs how impotent the Soviets were in finding a solution, Nixon wrote back: "I completely disagree with this conclusion. . . . We have been gloating over Soviet 'defeats' in the Mideast since '67 — & State et. al. said the June war was a 'defeat' for Soviet. It was *not*. They became the Arabs' friend and the U.S. their enemy. Long range this is what serves their interest."[50] Nixon, in other words, wanted to woo the Arabs away from the Soviets; Kissinger was content to follow Israeli policy and let the Middle East impasse continue.

Kissinger also disagreed with the conclusion by Nixon and the State Department that the impasse in the Middle East was primarily due to Israeli intransigence. He blamed Arab radicals abetted by Soviet meddling.[51] But Nixon did not agree. He "leaned toward the departmental views that Israel's policies were the basic cause of the difficulty."[52]

Beyond these disagreements with Nixon, Kissinger was at loggerheads with the State Department over the fundamental question of whether Israel was an asset or a deficit to U.S. interests in the Middle East. Kissinger saw Israel as an ally, strong and democratic, that could act in concert to promote and protect America's position. This argument was less than persuasive to experts who had watched Soviet influence grow from nil in the mid-1950s to the pervasive strength it had achieved less than fifteen years later, mainly because of the diplomatic openings Arab grievances against Israel provided the Soviets. In addition, Palestinian guerrilla groups had grown explosively during the same period and by 1969 were directly striking at Americans as never before. In the view of the experts, the area was being radicalized in direct response to Israeli intransigence on the issues of withdrawal from captured lands and its refusal to grant self-determination to the Palestinians.[53]

That, in summary, is an outline of the views of Nixon, Kissinger, and the State Department on the Middle East at the start of the Nixon presidency. The global-versus-local argument was eventually resolved, as we shall see, in favor of the global view, a policy that ignored justifiable Palestinian complaints and hindered the prospects for peace. This proclivity toward the global view on the part of American policy makers, especially in the White House, has been perhaps the single greatest contributor toward prolonging the conflict in the Middle East. Yet this astigmatic view has afflicted every administration, causing great miscalculation and plain errors, and providing Moscow with greater opportunities than any other source.

An illuminating example of this tortuous process is provided by the Baghdad Pact, that ill-gotten alliance led by Britain and encouraged by America to arm the "northern tier" of Muslim nations against the USSR in the early 1950s. In seeking to contain the Soviets, the Baghdad Pact managed to accomplish the reverse: it provided the motivation for Moscow to make its historic "Czech" arms deal with Egypt in 1955 and thus establish its first real outpost in the region. Although historians have generally explained this seminal event as being motivated by Moscow's traditional desire to penetrate the region, that does not answer the question of why the Kremlin moved at this time. The evidence strongly indicates that it was the forming of the Baghdad Pact itself that goaded Moscow into acting. As Foreign Minister V.M. Molotov let slip at the time, Moscow's major concern was to oppose the Baghdad Pact. It was not to arm Egypt against mounting Israeli attacks, although these were increasing at the time, but to encourage Egypt and therefore other Muslim states to stay out of the pact.[54] To win Egypt over, Moscow provided it with the arms the West would not.

The fact that Moscow did indeed desire influence in the Middle East provided an additional reason to justify its action but that does not explain the timing. Certainly there were few encouragements for the Soviets to try to penetrate the region at the time. The Arabs were unlikely targets for conversion to communism and there was no tradition of amity between the parties. Quite the reverse; there was bad blood going back centuries between the Muslim Turkish Empire and czarist Russia. And Moscow could barely afford to aid its East European satellites, much less expand into the Middle East. (Just how difficult the Soviets' role was is clear now. After almost forty years of major Soviet presence in the region, communism fares no better among the Arabs than before. Indeed, as a political force communism remained outlawed almost everywhere in the Arab world, up to the time of the collapse of communism itself.)

Despite this, the Czech arms deal was immediately portrayed by Israel — and many policy makers in London and Washington — as proof that the Soviets were planning to take over the Middle East. Following from that argument was a self-serving corollary that Israel quickly propounded: Israel deserved the West's backing because it was the one state in the region that could be counted upon to oppose communism. Needless to say, Israel's American supporters also supported this concept — and no one more than Henry Kissinger. But to experts on the region it was a misconception, a false reading of the reality on the ground.

The reality was that the Arabs, in particular Egypt and Syria, had no love for the Soviets. But under aggressive attacks from Israel, they had no other place to turn for the purchase of weapons for defense of their homelands.[55] The Kremlin in turn was not motivated by Egypt's main interest, defense against Israel, but by self-defense against the Baghdad Pact. In the event, the arms deal was a brilliant geopolitical achievement, as it did get the Soviets into the region, certainly the greatest single setback to U.S. policy in the Middle East up to that time.[56]

It was this issue of global vs. local problems that in large part caused Nixon's undoing in the Middle East. His worldview was so determined by the rhetoric of the Cold War that it overcame his common sense and all the facts to the contrary. How strong was this instinct was dramatically displayed in the first major Middle

East crisis he faced during his presidency. This occurred in 1970 when Black September suddenly exploded in Jordan, threatening Americans and nearly toppling America's friend, King Hussein. Nixon, with Kissinger's active encouragement, viewed it as a straight-out fight with Moscow. In fact, it was about as local in genesis and execution as any regional conflict could be in those days of the superpowers.

The crisis was solely rooted in the emergence of the Palestinian guerrillas. They had grown dramatically — without the help of Moscow — after the 1967 War. That conflict had shown the Palestinians that the Arab countries were not capable of protecting their homeland. Jordan had lost all of the West Bank, where a million Palestinians were now forced to live under Israeli military occupation. Once again, a flood of Palestinian refugees had been created, this time 323,000 new refugees on top of the 726,000 who were made homeless by the 1948-49 war.[57] The ranks of the guerrillas were swollen with new members. But the Soviets (no more than the Arabs, much less the West) had not shown the slightest interest in aiding the guerrillas.[58] They were on their own.

The result was a dramatic increase in terrorism and an open challenge to Hussein's throne in Jordan, where many of the refugees had been driven and where the major guerrilla groups had their headquarters. For Washington, the crisis began on 6 September 1970, with a series of hijackings of jet passenger planes that eventually resulted in three jetliners and 421 travelers held captive in the desert outside of Jordan's capital of Amman. Many of the hostages were American and Nixon was obviously anxious to free them. No president likes to appear impotent, much less Nixon with his macho posturings and tough-guy talk. Nixon publicly vowed action, but within the White House it was clear from the beginning that no one had the slightest idea how to fight against an amorphous, ragtag guerilla group in the Middle East any more than how to fight the Viet Cong.

Bill Rogers was experienced enough to recognize the near hopelessness of the situation. His suggestion at the start of the crisis was that Washington send the Palestinians a message reassuring them America meant them no harm. In this way, he thought, a dialogue might be opened. Kissinger was appalled. He wanted action, although what kind of action was not clear. His suggestion was that stiff notes be sent to the major Arab governments, warning them that no harm should come to the American hostages.[59] Those governments, of course, were as helpless against Palestinian terrorism as was the United States, but this subtlety did not seem to faze Kissinger.

With no one having any clear ideas about solving the crisis, Kissinger filled the vacuum by taking charge. He set up the dramatically titled WSAG, the Washington Special Actions Group, on 9 September. Membership of WSAG included the State Department's area specialists and policy analysts plus representatives of the CIA and the Pentagon, and any other expert who could contribute to the solution of problems as they emerged. But it was Kissinger who ran it. He was determined that the United States project a "powerful image."

This was attempted the next day, 10 September, when Nixon authorized placing the 82nd Airborne Division on "semi-alert" at Fort Bragg, North Carolina, and six C-130 cargo planes were flown to Incirlik air base in Turkey for possible evacuation of the American hostages. The next day the aircraft carrier *Independence* was ordered to sail off the coast of Lebanon with its task force of four destroyers; two more destroyers were ordered to join the group on 12 September and four more C-130s were ordered to Turkey with an escort of twenty-five F-4 Phantom warplanes.

What the point was of all these aggressive moves in combatting a handful of guerrillas in Jordan's desert never became clear. Nonetheless, these military actions reflected Kissinger's stated belief that the Soviet Union was trying to take advantage of the hijacking drama. "In my view," wrote Kissinger, "the Kremlin was playing the Jordan crisis. . . . It made formally correct noises but did nothing constructive to reverse the drift toward crisis."[60] In fact, the extent of Moscow's involvement in the early days of the crisis was confined to urging Iraq and Jordan to practice restraint. There was no evidence at all that it had anything to do with the crisis or that it was in any way trying to utilize it for its own ends.[61] Yet from this time onward, Kissinger and Nixon consistently cast it in global terms, of superpower against superpower. It was a popular stand as congressional elections approached in November.

The guerrillas' heady success in holding the three marooned jetliners and openly defying the United States raised their ambitions to unrealistic levels. They directly challenged King Hussein and tried to take over his country. Large-scale fighting broke out in Jordan on 17 September between royal troops and the guerrillas, mainly members of the Popular Front for the Liberation of Palestine, the PFLP. Then Syria gave signs of entering the fray on the guerrillas' side, causing panic in Washington.

Kissinger's reaction was to ask the Israelis for help. As Syria was an ally of the Soviet Union, Nixon warned at a meeting of editors of the *Chicago Sun-Times* that America would not tolerate interference by Moscow, although there had been no indication of such meddling. Nixon's remarks were supposed to be off the record but he was not displeased when the *Sun-Times* ignored the ground rules and ran a headline declaring: "Nixon Warns Reds: Keep Out."[62] The Kremlin's reaction was secretly to assure Nixon the next day that it had no intention of interfering.[63] Nonetheless, Nixon and Kissinger continued to act throughout as though their actions were dictated by aggressive Soviet moves. Nixon wrote in his memoirs a highly tortured version of what he thought was going on:

> One thing was clear. We could not allow Hussein to be overthrown by a Soviet-inspired insurrection. If it succeeded, the entire Middle East might erupt in war: the Israelis would almost certainly take preemptive measures against a Syrian-dominated radical government in Jordan; the Egyptians were tied to Syria by military alliances; and Soviet prestige was on the line with both the Syrians and the Egyptians. Since the United States could not stand

idly by and watch Israel being driven into the sea, the possibility of a direct U.S.-Soviet confrontation was uncomfortably high. It was like a ghastly game of dominoes, with a nuclear war waiting at the end.[64]

All subsequent research shows that the Soviets, rather than inspiring the insurrection, were as surprised by it as was Washington. If anything, they did all they could to calm the atmosphere.[65] For instance, when Nixon dramatized his words by sending the Sixth Fleet to the eastern Mediterranean, the Soviets docilely got out of the way to avoid a confrontation.[66] As for Nixon's bizarre claim that America could not watch "Israel being driven into the sea," there is no accounting for such apprehensions except as a cynical ploy to win domestic support. At no time was Israel's security threatened by the civil war. Quite the reverse: there were a number of State Department officials worried that Israel might take advantage of the fighting to try to snatch away additional territory while the Arabs fought among themselves. Talcott Seelye, a career foreign service officer who headed State's special task force during the crisis, was one of the skeptical diplomats. He recalled: "To us it was clear that what the Israelis wanted to do was to capitalize on this opportunity to extend their territory. We turned them down."[67]

Despite these facts, there was an external dimension to the crisis — Syria. When Syrian tanks began rolling into northern Jordan on 18 September, King Hussein panicked and beseeched Washington for help, preferably by the U.S. Air Force, but even, if necessary, by Israeli planes.[68] Kissinger immediately proposed the Israelis be encouraged to threaten Syria and in return he got Nixon to promise that the United States would protect Israel from any retaliation by the Soviet Union. Wrote Kissinger later: "If Israel acted, everyone [in WSAG] agreed that the United States should stand aside but block Soviet retaliation against Israel. . . . [O]ur forces were best employed in holding the ring against Soviet interference with Israeli operations."[69]

The Israelis, of course, were already acutely interested in what was going on at their frontiers and had moved military units just in case. By Kissinger's own testimony, all he asked them to do was to fly a reconnaissance mission over Jordan to report on the Syrian tanks. This was a mission that the planes of the Sixth Fleet could have perfectly well performed, but the usually strutting Kissinger was suddenly worried about the lack of American strength. "To be effective unilaterally we would have to commit our entire strategic reserve; we would then be stretched to near the breaking point in widely separated theaters and naked in the face of any new contingency." On the other hand, Israel, in Kissinger's view, was in an ideal situation. "If the situation in Jordan got out of control it could be remedied only by a massive blow against Syria, for which Israeli armed forces were best suited."[70]

Only fourteen years earlier, Western nations had tried to act in concert with Israel in a major military operation and it had ended in disaster during the Suez crisis. Yet here Kissinger was once again caught up in the mystique that the Jewish state could — and would — be used as the West's cat's-paw in the

Middle East. How reluctant Israelis were to assume this task was quickly revealed when Kissinger asked them to fly a reconnaissance mission and be prepared for air and land strikes against Syria if it became necessary. They first hesitated, then demanded a number of assurances, most importantly a commitment that the United States would protect Israel from any Soviet or Egyptian reaction.[71] As the Kalb brothers report in their biography of Kissinger: "Nixon gave his approval. Their understanding was historic: Israel would move against Syrian forces in Jordan; and if Egyptian or Soviet forces then moved against Israel, the United States would intervene against both."[72]

But the Israelis wanted more than assurances. They wanted the pledge to block Russia and Egypt in writing and they wanted a promise of additional weapons. As we have already seen, Nixon and his advisers had already agreed to provide the defense against Soviet or Egyptian troops. As for new weapons, that was no problem as dramatic increases in weaponry to Israel soon proved.[73] While all this bargaining was going on, the crisis suddenly ended. Jordanian royal troops, emboldened by firm U.S. pledges of help, engaged the Syrian tanks and sent them scurrying back across the border, the last one by 23 September. The question of Israeli military strikes became moot.

King Hussein's success in preserving his throne was quickly characterized by Kissinger as being due to U.S. policy. This was true to the extent that Washington's stance buttressed Hussein and intimidated Syria, causing it eventually to withdraw its tanks.[74] However, Kissinger and Nixon then overdramatized the conflict by characterizing it as a global crisis in which the United States, with Israel's help, thwarted the Soviet Union. This distorted beyond recognition Moscow's role which most analysts now agree was limited to cautioning Syria, and greatly exaggerated Israel's contribution. Nonetheless, it was the administration's first "victory" in foreign policy and Nixon and Kissinger exploited it as much as they could. Neither Nixon nor Kissinger was bashful about proclaiming his own role in bringing about the end of the crisis. (When King Hussein was asked later by Ambassador Dean Brown about Kissinger's memoir version of his own actions during the crisis, the king dryly replied: "I thought I had something to do with the war.")[75]

In this euphoric atmosphere, deep appreciation of Israel's actions was expressed. Although the fighting ended before Israel's promise to commit forces was actually tested, Kissinger called Israeli Ambassador Yitzhak Rabin and effusively thanked him. "The President will never forget Israel's role in preventing the deterioration in Jordan and in blocking the attempt to overturn the regime there. He said that the United States is fortunate in having an ally like Israel in the Middle East. These events will be taken into account in all future developments."[76]

Israeli leaders left no doubt that their country would have mobilized its forces in the face of Syrian tanks moving into Jordan anyway, but Prime Minister Golda Meir's coordination with Washington, though limited and conditional, was cited thereafter by Kissinger as evidence of the value of Israel as a strategic ally.

There was little attempt made to differentiate between the often conflicting national interests of the United States and Israel, or to recognize the regional nature of the conflict. Instead, Nixon and Kissinger emphasized the contest with Moscow and the benefits of cooperation with Israel, a popular stand for an administration under fierce criticism for its Vietnam policies.

On this flawed reading of reality, the historic argument of whether Israel was a strategic ally was substantially won by Kissinger. Israel reaped the benefits. U.S. economic and military aid suddenly burgeoned to historic heights. In fiscal 1970, aid totaled only $93.6 million. It leaped to $634.3 million the next year and soared to $2.6 billion in 1974 following the 1973 War. The Nixon-Kissinger years set a dramatic new benchmark for aid to Israel. Levels continued to climb until 1985 when they settled at $3 billion, where they remain today.[77]

In his memoirs, Yitzak Rabin writes: "The story of Kissinger's contribution to Israel has yet to be told, and for the present [1979] suffice it to say it was of prime importance."[78] This contribution consisted of substantially more than economic and military aid. Its prime importance was in cementing the perception that the Middle East was an arena of the global conflict with the Soviet Union and, more important, that Israel was an ally that could be depended on in that strategic contest. (Of course, this perception denies the Palestinians any role in the politics of the region.) How successful Kissinger was became clear in 1983 when the Reagan administration enshrined in a formal agreement the concept that Israel was a "strategic ally" deserving special status by the United States.[79]

WATERGATE AND KISSINGER

Even without Watergate, Henry Kissinger's position was soon dominant in foreign affairs in the Nixon White House. This was because of the peculiar way Nixon had organized his foreign affairs apparatus and because of Kissinger's own successful efforts in undercutting the prestige of the secretary of state. Kissinger's power grew even greater as the Watergate scandal spread and eventually occupied almost all of the energies of the president and his immediate staff. Thus the weakening of Nixon and the strengthening of Kissinger were so intertwined that they are more comprehensibly treated as a synergism than as two separate phenomena.

Before Watergate, it was Black September in Jordan in 1970 that had most dramatically enhanced Kissinger's influence. Not only had he personally taken charge of U.S. actions during the crisis, but Secretary of State Rogers had been foolish enough to acquiesce in Kissinger's leading role. Rogers' passivity was emphasized when at the height of the crisis, on 20 September, the Sunday when Kissinger had asked the Israelis to intervene, Rogers had remained at home.[80] Kissinger further secured his ascendancy over Rogers by consistently undercutting the secretary's efforts at finding a peace formula between Israel and Egypt. For two years Rogers pursued an evenhanded plan based on UN Security Council

Resolution 242 and calling for an exchange of land in return for peace. But Israel repeatedly placed roadblocks against any negotiations and Kissinger just as repeatedly worked against Rogers by supporting Israel. By November 1971, Rogers finally admitted he had failed. America's mediation effort under Rogers was at an end and Nixon's ambitious policy of evenhandedness was essentially dead.[81]

Kissinger was gleeful. As he exulted in his memoirs: "By the end of 1971, the divisions within our government, the State Department's single-minded pursuit of unattainable goals — and the Soviet Union's lack of imagination — had produced the stalemate for which I had striven by design."[82] What Kissinger so proudly hailed as stalemate was specifically against his president's policy but in line with Israel's goal. Stalemate, as Nixon had foreseen, could only lead to war. But Kissinger somehow seemed to find that prospect less portentous than applying the pressure necessary to make Israel give up territory it had captured and held by force of arms.

Astonishingly, given his insubordination in the Middle East, Kissinger was rewarded by Nixon. On 2 December 1971, the national security adviser officially was granted the Middle East portfolio in yet another of the extraordinary deals Nixon encouraged behind Rogers' back. During a meeting with Israeli Prime Minister Golda Meir, Nixon agreed that Israel's substantive relations would bypass the State Department and be handled privately through Kissinger. All that the State Department and Rogers were now left with was pomp and ceremony, and public humiliation.[83]

Kissinger predictably used his new influence over Middle East policy to continue the stalemate that had existed since Israel's conquest of Arab territories in 1967. At the first Nixon-Brezhnev summit in May 1972, the Middle East barely came up; Nixon does not even mention it in his memoirs as a summit topic. But it was part of the final communique, which Kissinger negotiated on the U.S. side. As he recalled, "I sought the blandest possible Middle East formulation in the communique. . . . The upshot was a meaningless paragraph that endorsed Security Council Resolution 242 and put the two sides on record as favoring peace in the Middle East. Calling as it did for 'peaceful settlement' and 'military relaxation' in the area, it was practically an implicit acceptance of the status quo and bound to be taken ill not only in Cairo but elsewhere in the Arab world."[84]

Little did Kissinger know. Egyptian President Anwar Sadat took more than "ill" the continued stalemate. His furious response was to kick out some 15,000 Soviet advisers in Egypt, thereby denying him Moscow's moderating counsel, and to decide that war was the only way to break the period of no war-no peace.[85] It was an extreme action but the only realistic alternative open to the Egyptian leader given Kissinger's obstructionist policies.

By the time of the second Nixon-Brezhnev summit in June 1973 the Soviets already had reason to believe that Egypt was planning to go to war and therefore Chairman Leonid Brezhnev was considerably concerned about the Middle East.[86] Brezhnev waited until after everyone had gone to bed on the last night of the summit before he demanded an unscheduled meeting. Obviously agitated, the Soviet leader heavily hinted — but could not reveal the source of his knowledge — that war would break out if a settlement was not found in the Middle East. Then he proposed what Moscow had consistently suggested in the past: an imposed settlement by the two superpowers. He proposed that the agreement could even be kept secret between the two leaders. The "principles" Brezhnev proposed were withdrawal of Israeli troops from the occupied territories, recognition of national boundaries, free passage of ships through the Suez Canal, and international guarantees of the settlement.[87]

Nixon and Kissinger, however, called these rather mild conditions "Arab terms." Nixon listened for somewhere between three hours (Nixon's report) or an hour and a half (Kissinger's) and then turned the Soviet leader down flat. Whatever the time period, both men agreed that Brezhnev was passionate and insistent in his presentation. Oddly, neither of them in his memoirs gives consideration to the fact that Brezhnev knew a war was coming and that his passion was well justified. Instead, Kissinger wrote off the performance as "egregiousness," claiming it was "a blatant attempt to exploit Nixon's presumed embarrassment over Watergate." Anyway, admitted Kissinger, "For Nixon to force the issue at the height of Watergate hearings would have added the allegation of engaging in a diversionary maneuver to the charge of betraying an ally."[88] Slightly more than three months later, war would erupt in the Middle East.

Between the two summits of 1972 and 1973, two important events had occurred that cemented Kissinger's position as America's foreign policy czar. One was Watergate and the other was Kissinger's final triumph in the enervating and unrelenting conflict with William Rogers. By the beginning of 1973, relations between Kissinger and the secretary of state had, in Kissinger's words

> soured beyond recovery. . . . I was too arrogantly convinced of my superior knowledge, Rogers was too insistent on his bureaucratic prerogative, for the acts of grace that would have permitted both of us to escape the treadmill on which we found ourselves, and more important, to serve the nation better. By the beginning of Nixon's second term, the pattern was frozen. Rogers and I had no social contact. Officially, we dealt with each other correctly without being forthcoming. I was the preeminent Presidential adviser; Rogers controlled the machinery by which much of our foreign policy had to be carried out.[89]

To add to the disarray, Watergate had erupted. By the summer of 1973 the poison of the scandal had spread from a minor break in the previous summer at the Democratic headquarters in the Watergate complex in Washington, DC, into a full-scale assault on the White House itself. Nixon's two top aides, H.R. Haldeman and John Ehrlichman, and his attorney general, Richard Kleindienst, had all been forced to resign because of their attempts to cover up White House complicity. Another aide, John Dean, had the country in thrall with his incredibly detailed recollection of events, few of them favorable to the president. The poison was spreading to the president himself. Nixon was dumbfounded by the tragedy. "The President lived in the stunned lethargy of a man whose nightmares had come true," observed Kissinger. "The disintegration of a government that only a few weeks earlier had appeared invulnerable was shocking to observe." He added: "The country seemed in a 'suicidal mood.'"[90] Kissinger confided to Alexander Haig that Nixon was "isolated, secretive, paranoid." But such was the neurotic atmosphere in the White House that Haig was "never sure whether Kissinger was describing himself or Nixon."[91]

The result of this disintegration was, as Kissinger wrote without exaggeration, that "I, a foreign-born American, wound up in the extraordinary position of holding together our foreign policy and reassuring our public." He added: "Nixon's attention span for foreign policy was also declining. He would sign memoranda or accept my recommendations almost absentmindedly now, without any of the intensive underlining and marginal comments that in the first term had indicated he had read my papers with care."[92] The time period Kissinger was referring to was the spring and summer of 1973. From that time forward, Kissinger must take, as his comments imply, prime responsibility for the course of U.S. foreign policy.

His responsibility became official on 22 August when Nixon finally ended the intolerable cat-fighting between Kissinger and Rogers by announcing that his new secretary of state would be Henry Kissinger. The president had informed Kissinger only the previous day of his promotion while they were in the swimming pool at San Clemente. It obviously was not a happy moment for the beleaguered president; he did not even mention it in his memoirs. But Kissinger did, recalling: "He told me matter-of-factly, while floating on his back, without warmth or an expression of anticipation of close cooperation."[93]

Among all the other global problems pressing in on America at the time of Kissinger's assumption of primacy in U.S. foreign policy, the Middle East in particular was heating up. The Arabs and Soviets were clambering for America to discard its Kissinger-sponsored policy of delaying a final settlement. King Faisal Abdulaziz of Saudi Arabia had also grown impatient. The Saudi leader had not only agreed several months earlier to help finance Egypt's coming war, he also still had hopes of averting it.[94] To that end he had sent his oil minister, Sheikh Ahmed Zaki Yamani, to Washington in April 1973 to meet with Kissinger and other high officials to warn that if a settlement was not achieved Saudi Arabia would invoke the oil weapon. No one took Yamani seriously — the *Washington Post* editorialized that "it is to yield to hysteria to take such threats as Saudi Arabia's seriously."[95] Israeli officials also pooh-poohed the idea. Foreign Minister Abba Eban declared: "There isn't the slightest possibility [of a boycott]. The Arab states have no alternative but to sell their oil because they have no other resources at all."[96]

Throughout the summer leading up to the autumn war Saudi Arabia repeatedly tried to warn the administration that it meant business, big business. Nixon contented himself by paraphrasing the Israelis: "Oil without a market . . . does not do a country much good," and Secretary of the Treasury George P. Shultz, who later became a secretary of state even more devoted to Israel than Kissinger, dismissed the Saudi warning as "swaggering."[97] King Faisal went to the point of enlisting a small group of prominent American oilmen to try to make the administration see the seriousness of his threat. But no one listened. Kissinger would not even grant them an appointment.[98]

When war broke out on 6 October, Kissinger was more than ever in charge. Nixon at that time was completely consumed by Watergate and by a subsidiary scandal involving his vice president. The first of a string of criminal indictments flowing from Watergate was just being handed down by the courts against White House aides, and Nixon was confronted with the additional embarrassment that Vice President Spiro Agnew was plea bargaining to escape prison for taking illegal payoffs while he was governor of Maryland.[99] Clearly, Nixon would have to appoint a new vice president. It was a traumatic period during which Nixon's overwhelming concern was his own survival. As Nixon recalled in his memoirs, "The immensely volatile situation created by the outbreak of this war could not have come at a more complicated domestic juncture."[100] When war broke out, Nixon was licking his political wounds in his Florida retreat at Key Biscayne. He was to take little direct action in the pursuit of U.S. policy during the war, except for one courageous effort toward the end. But beyond providing his imprimatur, Nixon essentially followed the advice of Kissinger throughout.

Kissinger's total commitment to Israel during the war is a well-known story, told most eloquently in his own words in his memoirs. In his concern to help Israel Kissinger worked day and night, so totally that the biggest economic threat by a foreign country ever to face the United States was overlooked by the secretary of state. That was the oil boycott King Faisal of Saudi Arabia had been threatening for months. He finally imposed it on 19 October, the day after President Nixon sought $2.2 billion in emergency aid for Israel in the middle of the war. The inflammatory nature of Nixon's request, particularly to proud King Faisal, should have been obvious to everyone, but Kissinger claims that "I can find no record that anyone warned of an Arab reaction."[101] His claim has a disingenuous ring — he tries to share blame with nameless others who did not warn Nixon, but it was, after all, specifically Kissinger's responsibility to make such a warning. Although he implies the matter simply slipped his mind — not exactly an excuse for a secretary of state — his memoirs unintentionally indicate a far more credible reason. Kissinger, like the Israelis, thought so little of the Arabs and was so arrogantly sure of the West's strength that he did not believe the Arabs had the courage or business acumen to carry out the boycott.[102]

In the event, the boycott struck a stupendous blow against the United States and the global economy, bringing about the greatest peaceful transfer of wealth in history and basic changes in the way people live around the world. Kissinger's personal responsibility for this disaster could hardly be exaggerated.

Another error of historic dimensions occurred toward the end of the war. The Soviet Union, anticipating that events in the Middle East were building toward a superpower confrontation, invited Kissinger personally to fly to Moscow to work out a settlement. Although Nixon's presidency was unraveling, the president for this brief moment ascended above his crushing personal problems and proposed a daring settlement. In sending his instructions to Kissinger as the secretary arrived in Moscow, Nixon wrote that on reflection Brezhnev had been right at the previous June summit when he made his impassioned plea for an imposed peace. Nixon instructed Kissinger to pass on to Brezhnev the following verbal message:

> The Israelis and Arabs will never be able to approach this subject by themselves in a rational manner. That is why Nixon and Brezhnev, looking at the problem more dispassionately, must step in, determine the proper course of action to a just settlement, and then bring the necessary pressure on our respective friends for a settlement which will at last bring peace to this troubled area.[103]

In the analytical part of the message for Kissinger's eyes only, Nixon perceptively argued that the coming end of the war was a unique time to achieve a settlement. He wrote that even Israel's interests would be served if the United States now applied "whatever pressures may be required in order to gain acceptance of a settlement which is reasonable and which we can ask the Soviets to press on the Arabs." Nixon then listed the obstacles to peace, according to Kissinger: "Israel's intransigence, the Arabs' refusal to bargain realistically, and [U.S.] preoccupation with other initiatives." He then addressed one of the biggest problems of all: "U.S. political considerations will have absolutely no, repeat no, influence on our decisions in this regard. I want you to know that I am prepared to pressure the Israelis to the extent required, regardless of the domestic political consequences."[104]

The message was, as even Kissinger admitted, "a remarkable feat of concentration considering the Watergate storm raging around him." But it was more than that. It was the product of much pondering and analyzing that had reached the conclusion that this was the only realistic strategy for achieving a settlement. But to this considered and thoughtful message, Kissinger's response was that it amounted to "an unnerving surprise" that caused him "extreme displeasure." In an irritable return message to Nixon, Kissinger declared he could not carry out his instructions in the present emergency circumstances. Perhaps, he suggested, "we can pursue the course the President has in mind after a ceasefire made with Israeli acquiescence, but not before."[105]

At any other time, the secretary might not have gotten away with such preemptory remarks about the president's desires. But this occurred on another of Watergate's extraordinary days of tumult — that of the "Saturday night massacre" when Nixon had fired his attorney general, Archibald Cox, in response to which two other top officials, Elliot Richardson and William Ruckelshaus, had resigned. Kissinger's insubordination was overlooked in the ensuing national uproar.

This represented the last time Nixon sought to carry out the "more evenhanded" policy with which he had so optimistically begun his presidency. After this, his fortunes continued their inexorable plunge until he was finally driven from office ten months later.

Kissinger, of course, went on as America's foreign policy master through the rest of Nixon's unserved term under Gerald Ford, which finally ended in 1977. During that time Kissinger continued his policy of strong support of Israel, bringing the two countries ever closer as "allies." He capped this accomplishment with the most extraordinary agreement ever signed by the United States, called Sinai II, on 1 September 1975. It was the largest surrender of U.S. treasury and diplomatic support ever rendered by Washington to another country.

The Israelis agreed to return to Egypt the Sinai oil fields they had captured in 1967 and to withdraw between twenty to forty miles east of the Suez Canal, still leaving nine-tenths of Sinai under their control. In return, Kissinger committed the United States to a dizzying array of give-aways to Israel, starting with a promise of $2 billion in annual aid, access to America's latest weapons, guarantee of Israel's oil needs, and a host of other promises. These included two significant diplomatic concessions, one to coordinate fully on diplomatic developments and the other a promise not to "recognize or negotiate with the Palestine Liberation Organization as long as the Palestine Liberation Organization does not recognize Israel's right to exist and does not accept Security Council Resolutions 242 and 338."[106]

These far-reaching promises not only committed the United States to the unique position of economically and militarily underwriting Israel's existence but they also diplomatically coordinated — practically to the point of subordination — America's policies to those of Israel. As Israeli Defense Minister Shimon Peres said at the time without exaggeration: "The . . . agreement has delayed [an international conference at] Geneva, while . . . assuring us arms, money, a coordinated policy with Washington and quiet in Sinai. . . . We gave up a little to get a lot."[107]

CONCLUSION

From a Palestinian point of view, the interesting component of this cornucopia of handouts given Israel by Kissinger is the promise not to talk with the Palestine Liberation Organization. Certainly the initiative for this far-reaching commitment came from the Israelis. But it is indicative that by this time, after six years in power, Kissinger was sensitized to the Palestinians — not, however, to help them, but to protect Israel from their claims to a homeland. He obviously recognized the immense implications of a U.S. refusal to talk with the Palestinians' only organized representative, the PLO. By so doing he perpetuated his policy of delay, which in reality was a policy aimed at rejecting any solution until the Arabs and Palestinians surrendered totally to Israel's dictates.

That Kissinger, after his interminable "shuttles" to the Middle East, became keenly aware of the Palestinians there can be no doubt. The proof is not only in the Sinai II agreement but in the historic "Saunders' Document," the recitation of

Nixon's Middle East Policy: From Balance to Bias

U.S. policy provided by Assistant Secretary of State Harold Saunders to Congress on 12 November 1975. In it, Saunders asserted that in many ways the Palestinian dimension was the "heart of the conflict." He added: "The legitimate interests of the Palestinian Arabs must be taken into account in the negotiating of an Arab-Israeli peace."[108]

This policy statement came less than three months after Kissinger had seen to it that Israel was completely aligned with the United States in the Sinai II agreement. With Israel so fortified, Kissinger presumably calculated that Israel would be ready to face the intractable Palestinian problem. Instead, Israel and its American supporters raised such an outcry at this description of the Palestinians that Kissinger quickly distanced himself from Saunders — although Kissinger himself had helped draft the paper.[109] The political heat on the White House was too fierce. Kissinger dismissed the Saunders Document as an "academic and theoretical exercise" and thus the Palestinians were left in limbo by the U.S. government.[110] Thereafter, Kissinger ignored the Middle East and the Palestinians for the rest of his time in Washington. He had done enough.

NOTES

1. However, Nixon did not display, even in his later years, any indication that he had the slightest understanding of how heroically Eisenhower had acted in the Suez crisis or, indeed, any understanding of what the crisis was about. In his memoirs (p. 179), Nixon writes: "In retrospect I believe that our actions were a serious mistake . . . . I have often felt that if the Suez crisis had not arisen during the heat of a presidential election campaign a different decision would have been made." Nixon makes it sound as though Eisenhower chose the easy course when, in fact, it was the most difficult of all in terms of alienating voters and traditional friends. It was precisely because of the timing of the crisis — in the middle of the 1956 presidential campaign — that Eisenhower's stand became even more courageous than it inherently was. He stood up to Israel's American supporters and the vocal friends of Britain and France and still determined on an independent and wise U.S. policy. It is hardly likely that Eisenhower would have taken any other action at any other time. Nor did Henry Kissinger understand the Suez crisis any better than did Nixon. He too thought Eisenhower had played "to the gallery," and the crisis had been "mishandled"; see Kissinger, *White House Years* (Boston: Little, Brown, 1976), p. 347.

2. See, for instance, *New York Times*, 20 October 1954.

3. Henry Kissinger repeatedly said outside of Nixon's hearing that "the man is an anti-Semite," although he was more diplomatic in his memoirs; see Bob Woodward and Carl Bernstein, *The Final Days* (New York: Avon Books, 1976), p. 169; and Henry Kissinger, *Years of Upheaval* (Boston: Little, Brown, 1982), pp. 202-3. Even such a true believer as William Safire, one of Nixon's admiring chief speechwriters for nearly seven years, finally concluded that charges of anti-Semitism were "apparently so" — that is, true; see Safire, *Before the Fall* (Garden City, NY: Doubleday, 1975), p. 577.

Yet the available evidence does not support such a charge, which is usually buttressed by reference to Nixon's excessive language, not to his actual actions. Nixon was a lifelong politician who not only remembered old enemies but thought in terms of voter blocs — and tended, carelessly, to express his frustration and hatreds against political groups. Thus he is on record cursing just about every group in America: the media, bureaucrats, lawyers, leftists, artists, the Northeast establishment — "fucking academics" and "goddamn Ivy Leaguers" — as well as Catholics, Jews, Wops and any other group a politician daily confronts; see Woodward and Bernstein, *Final Days*, pp. 169-70.

By general consensus, Nixon's actions displayed no prejudice toward Jews. His administration contained many — chief among them in the White House Kissinger, Safire, and advisers Arthur Burns, Ed David, and Leonard Garment — and in his personal relations Nixon displayed no self-consciousness around Jews. As Safire recalled: "Nixon treated the relatively many Jews around him [in the administration] with no Jewish consciousness on his part — there seemed to be no plus or minus to being a Jew in the Nixon White House." Safire, *Before the Fall*, p. 577.

Probably the shrewdest reading of what were likely Nixon's true attitudes comes from Arthur Burns, who had dealt with him since the Eisenhower administration. Burns doubted Nixon was an anti-Semite. But he believed there were deep strands of prejudice in the man. These, Burns believed, were a reflection of Nixon's generally low regard for mankind in general — not for any group in particular (Woodward and Bernstein, *Final Days*, p. 170). Perhaps more telling about Nixon's attitude toward Jews is one outstanding fact: Jews throughout Nixon's journey to the White House had abundantly shown they did not like him and would not vote for him, yet that did not keep him from appointing them to high positions.

4. Kissinger, *White House Years*, pp. 559-64; also see Nixon, *The Memoirs of Richard Nixon* (New York: Filmways, 1978), p. 481.
5. Nixon, *Memoirs*, p. 283.
6. *Ibid.*, p. 481.
7. *New York Times*, 10-14 December 1985.
8. *New York Times*, 12 December 1985, and *Facts on File 1968*, 28: 529.
9. *New York Times*, 14 December 1985.
10. William B. Quandt, *Decade of Decisions: American Policy toward the Arab-Israeli Conflict* (Berkeley: University of California Press, 1977), p. 82.
11. Kissinger, *White House Years*, p. 564.
12. *Ibid.*, p. 563.
13. Seymour M. Hersh, *The Price of Power: Kissinger in the Nixon White House* (New York: Summit Books, 1983), p. 214.
14. The first U.S. veto to protect Israel came on 10 September 1972, when the United States vetoed a UN Security Council resolution condemning Israeli attacks inside Lebanon and Syria. The vote was thirteen to one with one abstention. It was only the second time since the founding of the United Nations that the United States had used its veto. (The first also came during the Nixon administration, on 17 March 1970 over Southern Rhodesia.) During the next sixteen years, the United States, which once had been so circumspect in employing its veto, used it twenty-four more times to protect Israel. See U.S. UN Mission, "List of Vetoes Cast in Public Meetings of the Security Council," 4 August 1986.
15. Nixon, *Memoirs*, p. 340.
16. Quandt, *Decade of Decisions*, p. 73.
17. Safire, *Before the Fall*, p. 28.
18. Nixon, *Memoirs*, pp. 340, 341.
19. Kissinger, *White House Years*, p. 15.
20. *Ibid.*, p. 12.
21. Hersh, *Price of Power*, p. 33.

22. A number of Rogers' former aides, while praising his integrity, remarked in interviews on what can kindly be described as his disinclination to work long hours.
23. Hersh, *Price of Power*, p. 33.
24. *Ibid.*, p. 32.
25. Nixon, *Memoirs*, p. 339.
26. *Ibid.*, p. 477.
27. Kissinger, *White House Years*, p. 341; see pp. 341-47 for a summary of his parochial views on the history of the Arab-Israeli conflict. In interviews, a number of U.S. diplomats and intelligence officials commented on how limited Kissinger's knowledge was in the early years about the region and particularly about the Arab countries.
28. *Ibid.*, p. 222.
29. Marvin Kalb and Bernard Kalb, *Kissinger* (Boston: Little, Brown, 1974), p. 188.
30. The Kalbs, pp. 31-35, say twelve of Kissinger's relatives were killed but Kissinger, in *Years of Upheaval*, p. 203, puts the figure at thirteen.
31. Kalb and Kalb, *Kissinger*, p. 188.
32. Edward R. E. Sheehan, *The Arabs, Israelis, and Kissinger: A Secret History of American Diplomacy in the Middle East* (New York: Reader's Digest Press, 1976), p. 173.
33. Safire, *Before the Fall*, p. 404.
34. *Ibid.*, p. 167; Hersh, *Price of Power*, p. 114.
35. Hersh, *Price of Power*, pp. 42, 41.
36. Kissinger, *White House Years*, p. 29. The first incident was a fairly minor one involving Ambassador Henry Cabot Lodge. But more substantively, as early as 17 February 1969, Nixon and Kissinger held a private meeting with Soviet Ambassador Anatoly Dobrynin from which Rogers was excluded, as he was from subsequent meetings (Hersh, *Price of Power*, p. 40).
37. Kissinger, *White House Years*, p. 374.
38. The shoddiness of Kissinger's behavior is by now so well documented that it barely needs citation. Everyone, friend and foe alike, agrees that his behavior was crude and brutish. See, for instance, his friend, speechwriter Bill Safire, *Before the Fall*, pp. 402-8, and his foe, Seymour Hersh, *Price of Power*, pp. 40-44.
39. Hersh, *Price of Power*, pp. 213-14.
40. Kissinger, *White House Years*, p. 374. By equating his behavior with that of Rogers, Kissinger gives himself more credit for civility than he deserves. The fact is that Rogers acted as a gentleman throughout; that is not a phrase anyone has ever used to describe Kissinger's behavior.
41. Kissinger, *White House Years*, p. 349.
42. Nixon, *Memoirs*, p. 343.
43. Quandt, *Decade of Decisions*, p. 79.
44. Nixon, *Memoirs*, p. 477.
45. *Ibid.*
46. Kissinger, *White House Years*, p. 354.
47. Ann Lesch, "Israeli Settlements in the Occupied Territories," *Journal of Palestine Studies*, (Autumn 1978), 8(1):100-119. By the end of 1967, according to *Facts on File 1967*, Israel had expropriated 838 acres for new settlements, expelled hundreds of Arabs from the Jewish Quarter in the Old City of Jerusalem, razed Palestinian refugee towns at Tiflig and near Jericho as well as 144 homes in Gaza, and secretly embarked on a major plan for founding four large settlements in Arab Jerusalem. It was only in 1971 that Israeli Housing Minister Zeev Sharef revealed details of the Jerusalem settlements (*Facts on File 1971*, 31:123).

48. Eugene Trone, interview with author, Washington, DC, 9 February 1986.
49. Quandt, *Decade of Decisions*, p. 79.
50. Kissinger, *White House Years*, p. 564.
51. *Ibid.*, pp. 563, 354.
52. *Ibid.*, p. 564; also see Nixon, *Memoirs*, p. 786.
53. Quandt, *Decade of Decisions*, p. 121.
54. See for instance Molotov's comments in *New York Times*, 2 November 1955.
55. Donald Neff, *Warriors at Suez: Eisenhower Takes America into the Middle East* (Brattleboro, VT: Amana Books, 1988), p. 93.
56. The magnitude of the failure explains why British and U.S. officials seldom referred to the Soviet move as a riposte to the Baghdad Pact. To do so would have admitted that the strategy behind the pact had been a monumental miscalculation. But among themselves Washington experts at the time recognized, even if they did not publicize, that the Soviets were acting to counter the Baghdad Pact. A major top-secret study of the deal observed that the Kremlin's major objective was to oppose "Western policies in the area, particularly the efforts of the US and UK to develop anti-Communist defense arrangements and to retain their bases"; see Special National Intelligence Estimate, "Probable Consequences of the Egyptian Arms Deal with the Soviet Bloc," U.S. State Department, *Foreign Relations of the United States, 1955* (Washington, DC: U.S. Government Printing Office, 1989), 14:583. The major "anti-Communist defense arrangements" at the time were embodied in the Baghdad Pact.
57. UN A/6797*, "Report on the Mission of the Special Representative to the occupied territories, 15 Sept. 1967."
58. Alan Hart, *Arafat: Terrorist or Peacemaker?* (London: Sidgwick & Jackson, 1985), pp. 277 and 355. According to Hart, it was not until 1971 that the Soviets took any serious interest in the Palestinian guerrillas.
59. Kissinger, *White House Years*, pp. 607-8.
60. *Ibid.*, p. 606.
61. Hersh, *Price of Power*, p. 237; Quandt, *Decade of Decisions*, pp. 124-25.
62. Kissinger, *White House Years*, pp. 614-15; Nixon, *Memoirs*, p. 483.
63. Nixon, *Memoirs*, p. 483.
64. *Ibid.*, p. 483.
65. Quandt, *Decade of Decisions*, p. 124.
66. Hersh, *Price of Power*, pp. 240-241.
67. Talcott Seelye, letter to author, 27 October 1987. Also see Donald Neff, *Warriors against Israel: How Israel Won the War to Become America's Friend* (Brattleboro, VT: Amana Books, 1988), p. 40, and Hersh, *Price of Power*, pp. 244-45.
68. Quandt, *Decade of Decisions*, p. 116; Kalb and Kalb, *Kissinger*, p. 202; and Peter Snow, *Hussein* (London: Barrie & Jenkins, 1972), p. 228. For a brief discussion of Hussein's motives, see Patrick Seale, *Asad* (Berkeley: University of California Press, 1989), pp. 159-60.
69. Kissinger, *White House Years*, pp. 611, 620.
70. *Ibid.*, p. 620. In fairness to Kissinger, Nixon and the Joint Chiefs of Staff also opposed using U.S. forces; see Quandt, *Decade of Decisions*, p. 117. The difference is that Kissinger pushed for Israel's involvement from the beginning and seemed consciously determined to ally America with the country.
71. Quandt, *Decade of Decisions*, p. 117.
72. Kalb and Kalb, *Kissinger*, p. 206.
73. Yitzhak Rabin, *Rabin Memoirs* (Boston: Little, Brown, 1979), p. 188.

74. Seale, *Asad*, p. 160. Seale disputes the general interpretation that Syria withdrew the tanks because Asad as defense minister refused to send in planes because of his dispute with Prime Minister Salah Jadid. In fact, argues Seale, Asad was already in de facto control of Syria and had allowed the tanks to enter Jordan to protect the Palestinians from a massacre but not to threaten Hussein. He ordered the tanks out when the United States and Israel showed they might intervene.
75. Quote from a friend of the king who declined to be identified.
76. Rabin, *Rabin Memoirs*, p. 189.
77. Clyde R. Mark, Foreign Affairs and National Defense Division, "Israel: U.S. Foreign Assistance Facts," Congressional Research Service, 1989.
78. Rabin, *Rabin Memoirs*, p. 261.
79. Bernard Gwertzman, "Reagan Turns to Israel," *New York Times Sunday Magazine*, 27 November 1983. Also see John M. Goshko, *Washington Post*, 22 November 1983.
80. Kissinger, *White House Years*, p. 622.
81. Neff, *Warriors against Israel*, p. 71.
82. Kissinger, *White House Years*, p. 1289.
83. *Ibid.*
84. *Ibid.*, p. 1247.
85. Neff, *Warriors against Israel*, p. 100.
86. The Soviets by this time were supplying Egypt with numerous weapons. Egyptian officials had flown to Moscow in February 1973 and concluded a successful arms deal to be paid for by Arab gulf states; see Neff, *Warriors against Israel*, p. 111.
87. Nixon, *Memoirs*, p. 885.
88. Kissinger, *Years of Upheaval*, pp. 298-99.
89. *Ibid.*, p. 419.
90. *Ibid.*, pp. 105, 125.
91. Woodward and Bernstein, *Final Days*, p.36.
92. Kissinger, *Years of Upheaval*, pp. 125-26, 415-16.
93. *Ibid.*, p. 423.
94. Robert Lacey, *The Kingdom* (London: Hutchinson, 1981), p. 398.
95. *Washington Post*, 20 April 1973.
96. Lacey, *The Kingdom*, p. 400.
97. Sheehan, *Arabs, Israelis, and Kissinger*, p. 68.
98. Lacey, *The Kingdom*, p. 402.
99. *Facts on File 1973*, 33:743, 818-19.
100. Nixon, *Memoirs*, p. 922.
101. Kissinger, *Years of Upheaval*, p. 873.
102. See, for instance, his sarcastic remarks in *ibid.*, p. 874.
103. *Ibid.*, p. 551.
104. *Ibid.*, p. 550.
105. *Ibid.*, p. 552.
106. Sheehan, *Arabs, Israelis, and Kissinger*, pp. 190-92, and Quandt, *Decade of Decisions*, p. 273. Text of the Memorandum of Understanding and its secret addenda are in Sheehan, App 8.
107. Sheehan, *Arabs, Israelis, and Kissinger*, p. 192. At the time, Peres refused to be identified in the *Time* article where Sheehan found this quote, but I know Peres was the source because I was *Time*'s Jerusalem bureau chief in 1975 and Peres made the remark to one of my reporters.
108. Quandt, *Decade of Decisions*, p. 278.

109. Sheehan, *Arabs, Israelis, and Kissinger*, p. 213; Quandt, *Decade of Decisions*, p. 278.
110. Sheehan, *Arabs, Israelis, and Kissinger*, p 213.

7

THE CARTER ADMINISTRATION AND THE PALESTINIANS

Janice J. Terry

JIMMY CARTER, AS HAD ALL RECENTLY successful presidential candidates, campaigned on a strongly pro-Israeli, anti-Palestinian platform. Throughout the campaign, Carter adhered to the Kissinger formulation of "No negotiations with the PLO until it recognizes U.N. Resolution 242 and the right of Israel to exist." In 1973, when he was governor of Georgia, Carter had visited Israel; as a politician and a devout Christian, he had consistently expressed his deep sympathy with and commitment to the Jewish state.[1] In addition, Carter had jumped on the bandwagon of politicians and Zionist lobbyists who successfully pushed for stronger legislation to restrain U.S. companies from complying with Arab boycott regulations regarding Israel. Although the Arabs viewed the boycott as yet another weapon in the arsenal to fight for Palestinian rights, it was portrayed in the United States as purely anti-Semitic in concept. With the backing of major U.S. corporations, the Republican Ford administration had sought to water down any antiboycott legislation. During the campaign, the Democratic party and Carter used the boycott issue to good advantage and thereby garnered considerable Jewish financial and political support.[2]

As president, Carter might well have been expected to steer a course along strictly pro-Israeli and anti-Palestinian lines. However, several factors mitigated against the continuation of policies that completely rejected or ignored the legitimacy of Palestinian rights. In contrast to both his immediate predecessor and successor, Carter was very much a "hands-on" president. Carter was widely read and his rigorous schedule included close personal attention to written reports, briefing books and memos. Hamilton Jordan, chief staff aide and perhaps Carter's closest adviser, noted that the best way to convince Carter on any given issue was to marshal arguments in writing.[3] He was open to debate over crucial issues and showed considerable flexibility and willingness to change previously held opinions. The Carter administration received information and advice from numerous sources that had indirect and direct contact with the Palestinians. In particular, William Quandt of the National Security Council (NSC) offered balanced advice regarding the Arab-Israeli conflict and the necessity of addressing Palestinian grievances.

Once in office, the Carter administration, like Ford's and Bush's administrations, initiated a "reassessment" of the Middle East situation. However, Carter was very much an active participant in this reassessment, eliciting and listening to a wide variety of opinions regarding the Palestinians. To gauge the Carter administration's attitudes and subsequent policies toward the Palestinians it is instructive, first to look briefly at the input it received from both Israeli and Palestinian supporters and second to describe the actions regarding Palestinian demands for self-determination adopted by the administration. The "openness" of the Carter administration toward the Palestinians immediately raised the red warning flag to Israel and its supporters in the United States. Indications that the administration might be moving away from a completely pro-Israeli stance and toward consideration of Palestinian rights elicited a predictable reaction from the Zionist lobby. Most Zionists viewed the struggle as a zero sum game in which recognition of the Palestinians — on any level — was a loss for Israel; recognition of, or negotiation with, the Palestinians was therefore totally unacceptable. As a result, the Zionist lobby acted not only as an advocate for pro-Israeli policies, but also as an anti-Palestinian pressure group.

The American Israel Public Affairs Committee (AIPAC) immediately marshaled its considerable resources to lobby the White House and Congress against any consideration of a Palestinian homeland.[4] AIPAC and other Zionist organizations also provided White House officials with a steady stream of anti-Palestinian and anti-PLO materials, including an extensive report on Middle East refugees in which the author, Joan Peters, argued that the number of Arabs displaced was equal to the number of Jews displaced.[5] When Carter publicly referred to Palestinian refugees having been forced out of their homes in 1948, AIPAC head, Morris Amitay, protested that the president might not have known the "actual facts" and enclosed heavily slanted information from the pro-Israeli *Facts and Myths, 1976* and I.L. Kenen.[6] Likewise, the Anti-Defamation League (ADL) of B'nai B'rith and others opposed any contacts with the PLO or any hearing of the PLO case before the U.S. public.[7]

In addition, officials within the Carter administration sometimes acted as direct liaisons to communicate the opinions and policies of the Israeli government and Zionist lobby to the president, State Department and National Security Council.[8] As the 1980 presidential campaign heated up, these types of direct exchanges between the White House and the Zionist lobby increased. Alfred Moses was brought in as a special adviser to act as a conduit with the Jewish community; however, he clearly viewed the position as a means not only of improving communications between the Jewish community and Carter, but as a means of influencing foreign policy. In a memo to Warren Christopher at the Department of State, Hamilton Jordan complained that Cyrus Vance (then Secretary of State) "seems to view this post predominantly as a political assignment. In contrast, Moses views the job predominantly as a post for contributing special perspectives and insights into policy formation and then effectively communicating administration decisions back to gain support in a critical constituency group."[9]

Clearly, the Palestinians could not hope to match such extensive ground-floor contacts or input into policy formation. (This remains the case today.) Similarly, opposition to the Palestinians and support for Israeli policies were even more pronounced in Congress, whose members consistently pressured Carter. Although it enjoyed a Democratic majority in Congress, Carter's administration failed to mobilize or to sustain congressional support for its domestic and foreign policies. This was particularly true with regard to the Palestinian case; key elements within the administration, and Carter in particular, desired more flexible policies toward the Palestinians, but the administration failed to muster adequate congressional support for clear-cut changes.

In face of heavy contravening pressures and precarious support from even Democrats on the Hill, it is not altogether surprising that Carter and his advisers sought to assuage and mollify supporters of Israel on the issue of the Palestinians. To address Jewish concerns, Carter, Vice-President Walter Mondale, Cyrus Vance, and National Security Adviser Zbigniew Brzezinski held a high-level meeting with key Jewish leaders in July 1977. By this time, the administration had dropped Kissinger's step-by-step procedure, instead espousing a comprehensive settlement reached through the Geneva Conference. Kissinger's tendency was to view the conflict as a piece in the global Cold War puzzle, but Carter saw the problem as predominantly a regional one. The Carter administration understood and accepted the fact that a comprehensive settlement necessitated a solution to Palestinian demands for self-determination.[10] Most Zionists opposed a comprehensive settlement, as it might force them into concessions they did not wish to make.

At the July meeting, the Jewish leaders emphatically voiced their concerns regarding a return to Geneva and a comprehensive settlement. They were also adamantly opposed to any negotiations with the Palestinians, preferring to consider agreements with the Arab governments. Brzezinski emphasized that the administration hoped to secure a comprehensive peace reinforced by security arrangements needed to forestall any Arab or Palestinian attempts to try to redraw the borders. Former ambassador to the UN Arthur Goldberg argued that only the United States could act as an intermediary and that all the parties involved had to accept Resolution 242 (indeed, Goldberg had largely been responsible for the acceptance of 242). Goldberg concluded that the ambiguities in Resolution 242 were not accidental but purposeful.

Carter listened to Jewish concerns and then voiced his own intentions regarding Israel and the Palestinians. First, he emphasized his commitment to the security and continued existence of Israel. Carter stressed that, in his opinion, a separate Palestinian nation would be a threat to peace and that other Arab nations, namely Egypt, Jordan, and Syria, were similarly concerned. Finally, Carter also emphasized that politically it would be easier for him to espouse the

Israeli cause but that such an approach would not bring about a peace settlement; a balanced, more open approach was needed.[11]

Although not stated overtly at the July meeting, the Carter administration's policy by the summer of 1977 may be summarized as follows: The assembly of the Geneva Conference, with attendance of all involved parties, including some form of Palestinian representation; the return of most of the occupied territories to the respective Arab nations; some form of Palestinian autonomy, preferably in conjunction with Jordan; full peace agreements between the Arab nations and Israel; and maintenance of the firm U.S. commitment to the security of Israel. The administration had not committed itself to any specific border realignments but definitely did not envisage an independent Palestine between Israel and Jordan, nor did it have firm recommendations on the issue of Jerusalem.

By the autumn of 1977, Anwar Sadat's personal initiative and subsequent trip to Israel undermined Carter's attempts to reconvene the Geneva Conference and, most importantly, it seriously damaged — perhaps destroyed — the possibility of a comprehensive settlement. Sadat was, in fact, continuing the step-by-step, separate peace approach begun by Kissinger under Nixon and maintained under Ford.[12]

Although still publicly committed to a comprehensive settlement, the Carter administration supported Sadat's efforts, while maintaining back door contacts with the Palestinians. These contacts took several forms. From the outset of Carter's presidency, numerous and increasingly active Arab-American organizations had sought meetings with the President and top-level officials. William Quandt generally supported such meetings, but Zbigniew Brzezinski, who sought to keep foreign policy matters closely within the purview of the National Security Council and Department of State, was reluctant to open up the consultative process. Representatives of the National Association of Arab Americans (NAAA) met with Midge Costanza, assistant for public liaison, and a representative from the NSC in February but did not discuss the Palestinians at that time. Only after considerable pressure from Arab Americans and sympathetic members of Congress did the White House seriously consider a meeting between representatives of Arab-American organizations and the president. Even after receiving Quandt's detailed reasoning in favor of such a meeting, Brzezinski replied "Talk to me. I am skeptical."[13] Brzezinski remained unconvinced and wrote, "I do not recommend that the President meet with this group. However, the Arab-American community is clearly beginning to organize itself and we will be hearing from them more often (and more effectively) in the future than in the past."[14] Only after some meetings of Arab Americans with lower level officials did pressure within the White House mount for a direct meeting with the president. Cyrus Vance met with representatives of NAAA and the Association of Arab-American University Graduates (AAUG) in November. During that meeting the Arab Americans stressed that the inclusion of the PLO was a *sine qua non* for the success of any peace process.

Finally, some six months after leaders of Jewish-American organizations had voiced their frank concerns regarding the peace process and the Palestinians, Arab-American leaders met with Carter. However, as the Arab Americans gathered for the 11:45 meeting on 15 December 1977, they were unaware that Carter was in the midst of a press conference during which he would announce that, owing to its continued rejection of Resolution 242, the PLO had excluded itself from the peace process.

Because the meeting was purposely arranged to include a wide variety of Arab-American groups, it did not focus solely on the Palestinians.[15] At the meeting, Carter emphasized that he had taken considerable political flak for his attempts to include the Palestinians in the peace process. He noted that in spite of Chairman Yasir Arafat's moderation, the executive committee of the PLO had not accepted Resolution 242 and could not therefore be included in the talks. When one Arab-American leader pointed out that the PLO rejected 242 because it made no mention of the Palestinians, Carter retorted that he did not care if the PLO had thirty pages of reservations as long as they accepted the resolution. Although the meeting with Carter continued for about forty-five minutes, the discussion involving the Palestinians was largely moot owing to the earlier public rejection of PLO participation in the peace process.

On the other hand, even as the process that included only Israel, Egypt, and the United States, moved haltingly toward Camp David, the administration kept open private channels of communications with the PLO. It is impossible to ascertain exactly how close the Carter administration came to direct and open negotiations, but meetings did continue. For example, George Ball and Landrum Bolling, president of the Lilly Endowment, briefed White House officials on meetings with Arab and Palestinian leaders. Writing that continued land seizures in the occupied territories were the key obstacle to peace, Bolling emphasized that Israeli dissidents and doves wanted a settlement with the Palestinians and that only the United States could exert enough pressure to bring Israel to negotiate with the Palestinians. Bolling also publicly affirmed the right of Palestinians to self-determination and advocated Israel's return to the 1967 borders.[16] Simultaneously, a few congressmen, notably Paul Findley and James Abourezk, kept the administration informed of their exchanges with PLO leaders, including Chairman Yasir Arafat. Although Carter responded that only acceptance of Resolution 242 would "open the possibility of direct discussions with them,"[17] other members of his administration continued to meet with Palestinians. In Europe, Issam Sartawi, the PLO European Counselor, twice met with U.S. Ambassador Milton Wolf.[18] However, after the meeting between Zuhdi Terzi, the PLO representative to the UN, and U.S. Ambassador to the UN Andrew Young became public knowledge, the ensuing political brushfire, fanned by the Zionist lobby, forced Young's resignation.[19] This came after a flurry of exchanges during which the PLO had agreed to accept 242 if it were stretched to include mention of Palestinian rights to self-determination. This potential breakthrough, that Carter strongly supported, failed when Israel, Egypt, Jordan, and Syria rejected it.

Many of these — and other — exchanges took place after Camp David. Why, after Brzezinski had said "bye-bye PLO" and the Palestinians had been excluded from Camp David, did these contacts continue? Simply because the Carter administration was still committed, in principle at least, to a comprehensive settlement. The problem was that the Camp David process was actually a continuation of the separate peace, step-by-step approach that had proved futile in the past. As the thirteen days at Camp David attest, the Carter administration worked hard to pave the road for an Arab-Israeli peace treaty but, for the Palestinians, the Framework for Peace in the Middle East proved to be a dead-end road.

Owing to the way in which the Framework for Peace was conceived and the basic equivocation and ambiguity of its language, the agreement led only to the Egyptian-Israeli Peace Treaty which was precisely that — a bilateral treaty between only two parties to the conflict. Prior to, during and following Camp David, the Palestinians, one of the two major protagonists, were not directly represented, nor were any of the three parties at Camp David prepared to represent their interests in a manner consonant with Palestinian political realities.

As a result, the framework failed to address directly Palestinian rights to self-determination, that is, an independent state; it divided the Palestinians into several separate entities; and it attempted to impose a settlement without the participation of the PLO, the sole legitimate representative of the Palestinian people.[20]

Although Carter contended that the agreement provided for the implementation of Palestinian national rights, a close analysis of the agreement's exact wording belies that contention. As Carter himself noted, the term "autonomy" had multiple meanings, particularly for Israeli Prime Minister Menachem Begin, who had at one juncture emphasized that "autonomy does not mean sovereignty."[21] Carter wanted Palestinian participation in future negotiations and the cessation of all new Israeli settlements in the occupied territories, but an independent Palestinian state was definitely not on his list of negotiating points for the Camp David meetings. After leaving office, Carter acknowledged that Begin probably would have rejected "the possibility of an independent Palestinian state."[22]

Although the negotiating parties have acknowledged that a verbal agreement regarding future Israeli settlements was reached at Camp David, they disagree over the terms of that agreement. Carter has continued to maintain that Begin promised not to build any new settlements during the time the talks leading to the implementation of the framework were in progress. Begin alleged that he only agreed to a three month freeze; at any rate, Begin did not even adhere to his own interpretation of the agreement, approving new settlements only weeks after signing the Egyptian-Israeli Peace Treaty. As there is nothing in writing and the framework does not even mention this crucial issue, both sides were free to make their own interpretations.

The building of new Israeli settlements in the occupied territories became one of the major points of contention among the parties to the settlement; the failure to deal directly and clearly with this issue was one of the major shortcomings of the agreement. Why Carter, knowing the crucial importance of this issue, failed to put the supposed agreement on settlements in writing remains more than a bit perplexing. It is probable that Carter and Sadat knew that Begin would refuse to sign an agreement calling for the freeze on new settlements; pressing the issue might well have caused the negotiations to collapse. By negotiating at Camp David, both Carter and Sadat had taken considerable political risks and they needed an agreement. For both leaders, a weak agreement, even with obvious omissions and ambiguities, was better than nothing. Consequently, the central issue of the settlements was left purposefully vague. Subsequently, Carter admitted this omission had been his biggest mistake in the negotiations.[23] The failure to resolve the settlement issue meant that basic Palestinian rights continued to be contravened and made Arab acceptance of the framework and the separate peace even more impossible.

In fact, the administration had consistently ignored or chosen to misinterpret the political realities in the Arab world. Not only Arab leaders, but high ranking U.S. diplomats had warned the administration that a separate peace or rejection of Palestinian self-determination was unacceptable to the Arabs. One career diplomat bluntly admonished Brzezinski over the "extraordinary misunderstanding about Arab attitudes toward the Palestinian state." He continued:

> . . . the Saudi position was clear: it was that there could be no peace in the Middle East unless the rights of the Palestinians are recognized; that this includes the right of self-determination; and that everyone knows the Palestinians want a state of their own.
>
> . . . The Arabs are convinced that there must be a state sooner or later or there will be no peace. In the interim a confederation with Jordan might work.[24]

The Carter administration failed to heed this clear and realistic appraisal.

Even after Sadat and Begin agreed to the Camp David Framework, Carter had to exert great personal effort to secure the peace treaty.[25] When negotiations toward the peace treaty were in danger of breaking down altogether, Carter, with no guarantee he would secure any agreement, traveled to Egypt and Israel to make a personal plea for the treaty. With the notable exception of Eisenhower, Carter has been the only president willing to put his reputation and credibility on the line in order to achieve a settlement in the Middle East.

Carter's March 1979 trip to the Middle East was an extraordinary political risk, taken against the recommendations of some of his top advisers. As early as January 1978, long before the next presidential election or Camp David, Senior Adviser Edward Sanders — a consistently pro-Israeli voice in the Carter White House — recommended adopting a lower diplomatic profile. In a clear exposition of the anti-Palestinian and pro-Israeli position, Sanders wrote:

> If involvement in the Sadat-Begin peace process is too public, the Administration runs the risk of being blamed whenever difficulties arise . . . We believe that a visible substantive American role is unnecessary . . .
>
> The President has scored markedly at home by voicing explicit opposition to an independent Palestinian state (any diminution of that position would be harmful). We believe that there would be no chance for peace today without Israeli strength and that continued maintenance of the Middle East military balance is essential to the smooth functioning of the peace process. . . . Needless to say, serious domestic problems could occur if assistance to Israel is curtailed.[26]

Sanders was in fact arguing for the continuation of the status quo: Israeli control over the occupied territories, no concessions whatsoever to the Palestinians, and the maintenance of Israeli military superiority. (In 1979, when Carter was supporting the aforementioned efforts to work out a new UN resolution including the PLO's formula to include mention of Palestinian rights to self-determination in 242, Sanders was one of the officials who advocated dropping all efforts to secure a UN resolution on Palestinian rights, vetoing "any resolution in that forum" and continuing the autonomy talks as provided for in the Camp David framework.)[27]

On the other hand, Hamilton Jordan encouraged Carter to take the initiative and suggested that a trip to see Sadat might well be the only way to secure a peace treaty. In an emotional appeal, Jordan wrote, "I just have a gnawing feeling now that the chance for peace is slipping away and that only you can save it."[28] Ignoring Sander's advice to keep a low profile, Carter subsequently followed through on Jordan's suggestion, thereby placing his political reputation on the line in order to secure the peace treaty.

Although the treaty dealt solely with substantive issues between Israel and Egypt, Begin and Sadat both signed an attached letter regarding continued negotiations for a comprehensive settlement.[29] This text repeated all of the errors of Camp David. It did not define autonomy; it did not mention the PLO as the representative of Palestinian rights; and it did not deal with the issue of Israeli settlements. Nor is it clear what "inhabitants" — Israelis, Palestinians, or both — were to receive autonomy. Finally, the use of the phrase "by mutual consent" attached to possible Palestinian participation left the door open for the Israelis to argue that they had the veto over any and all Palestinian representation. Thus, resolution of the basic issues was deferred yet again.

Carter managed to obtain a peace settlement between Israel and Egypt, but the treaty and attached agreements did not provide the means to secure Palestinian self-determination. If there were any doubts on the point, the remarks exchanged by the three leaders on the occasion of the signing of the treaty clearly demonstrated that resolution of Palestinian rights to self-determination was not central to the settlement. Carter never even mentioned the Palestinians; Sadat sidestepped the issue; and, as is perhaps superfluous to note Begin ignored the Palestinians altogether. In effect, the Carter administration permitted Begin to trade Sinai for a peace settlement with Egypt, potentially Israel's most potent military foe, and for continued control over Gaza and the West Bank.

Yet Carter remained personally committed to a comprehensive settlement, including some form of autonomy for the Palestinians. Carter had a vested interest in keeping negotiations alive and seemed to nurture a forlorn hope that Palestinian autonomy could be achieved under the provisions of the Camp David framework and the additions to the peace treaty. It was unfortunate, but scarcely unexpected, that no agreements on any substantive issues regarding the Palestinians were reached.

Had circumstances during his last year in office been different, Carter might have been able to move more forcefully on the Palestinian issue, but the last year of his administration was beset with domestic and international problems, most prominent being the Iranian revolution and hostage crisis.

During the election year, the White House continued to monitor U.S. public opinion toward the Palestinians. Although a wide variety of polls indicated sustained support for Israel coupled with some moderate increase in sympathy for various Arab states, support for the Palestinians remained minuscule compared to that for Israel. In a 1979 Harris poll, respondents were asked to agree or disagree to the following proposition:

> As the most powerful force among Palestinian Arabs, the PLO should be in on any negotiations about Gaza or the West Bank, even if the PLO are terrorists.[30]

Loaded as it was with value judgment and bias, the question elicited a predictable negative response. Fifty-seven percent of the respondents disagreed with the statement, yet even under these terms, 34 percent still felt the PLO should be included. On the other hand, the same poll indicated that 61 percent thought the Palestinians should be included in the negotiations, while 65 percent thought the PLO should recognize Israel's right to exist before being recognized by the United States. Given that the polls indicated no great grassroots support for the Palestinians, it was unlikely Carter — an incumbent president already beleaguered with a host of problems — could launch a successful drive to include the PLO in the negotiating process. In addition, he had to contend with strong contravening domestic pressure from the Zionist lobby, from his own advisers, and from within his own party.

The Carter administration had been on the right track when it moved for a comprehensive settlement with the resolution of Palestinian demands for self-determination. As the behind-the-scenes negotiations with the PLO indicate, the administration also came close to recognizing that the PLO was the sole legitimate political representative of the Palestinians, although it did not make the fact public knowledge. The Palestinians and Arabs had always argued that a separate agreement that excluded the Palestinians would not achieve peace. By foregoing its quest for a comprehensive settlement in favor of a quicker, and politically more expedient, step-by-step process, the Carter administration drove the negotiations over a protracted detour on a dead-end road. In the final analysis, the Camp David framework and separate Egyptian-Israeli treaty led, not to peace, but to the continuation of Israeli domination over the occupied territories and to the 1982 war in Lebanon, hence to the continuation of the Palestinian struggle for self-determination.

NOTE

1. For a discussion of this trip and Carter's commitment to Israel, see Jimmy Carter, *The Blood of Abraham: Insights into the Middle East* (Boston: Houghton Mifflin, 1985); see also Carter, *Keeping Faith: Memoirs of a President* (Toronto: Bantam Books, 1982). Most of the documentation for this study is based on the unpublished papers at the Jimmy Carter Library in Atlanta, Georgia (hereinafter JCL) and, unless otherwise noted, the subsequent citations are from those papers.

2. "1977 Report on Jewish Vote," Hamilton Jordan's Files, N.A. Box 35, JCL. The report may have come from the Office for Domestic Affairs or from a special adviser regarding ethnic and domestic affairs. It noted that in 1976 over 60 percent of the substantial donors to the Democratic party were Jewish and that even when Carter was a "long shot" he received 35 percent of his funding from Jewish donors; in the election, Carter received 75 percent of the Jewish vote.

3. Hamilton Jordan, *Crisis* (New York: Putnam's, 1982), p. 42.

4. Telegram, Morris Amitay [Head of AIPAC] to Jimmy Carter, 6 June 1977, Hamilton Jordan's Files, Box 34, JCL. See also the telegrams and letters in Box ND39, Box CO-42, White House Central Files (hereinafter WHCF), and Palestine Liberation Organization Name File.

5. Joan Peters, "Report on Middle East Refugees," Marked "Not for Publication," 1977, Stuart Eizenstat's Files, Box 235, JCL. Eizenstat was assistant to the president for domestic affairs. In an addendum to this report, Peters alleged that Syria had 100 percent employment and needed additional workers On the basis of this "evidence," she made the stunning but hardly original recommendation that the settlement of the Palestinian refugees in Syria and elsewhere in the Arab world would be the "sensible arrangement." Joan Peters is, of course, the author of the highly touted but thoroughly discredited history, *From Time Immemorial: The Origins of the Arab-Jewish Conflict over Palestine* (New York: Harper & Row, 1984).

6. Letter, Morris Amitay to Hamilton Jordan, 17 August 1977, Office of Communications, Gerald Rafshoon Collection, Box 4, JCL.

7. For example, see ADL letters opposing a visa for PLO spokesperson Shafik al-Hout in 1979 (Anti-Defamation League File, Name File, JCL).

8. Memo, Stuart Eizenstat to David Aaron, 29 December 1978, WHCF-CO-74 [Israel], Box CO-35, JCL. For example, in 1978, acting on the suggestion of Morris Amitay from AIPAC, Stuart Eizenstat of the Domestic Policy Staff approached David Aaron on the National Security Council about supplying technical data on the F-18 plane as a means to "help break the ice" with Israel. "In the spirit of Camp David," information on the F-18 was released to Israel late in 1978. Along the same lines, Eizenstat also received direct requests from AIPAC and from Ambassador Ephraim Evron for increased aid to Israel. Subsequently, Eizenstat facilitated Evron's meeting with the director of the Office of Management and Budget. Memo, David Aaron to Stuart Eizenstat, 9 January 1979, *ibid*;

Your Choice

ons

rn Rolls

Kenneths' Salon
707 West MLK
Austin
(512) 499-0474
H (512) 252-3363
Ask For "Fay"

Perms   *Braids*

Spiral   *Weaves*

Curl   *Extensi*

Cuts   *Co*

Memo, Stuart Eizenstat to director of Office of Management and Budget, 20 November 1979, WHCF, Box F030, JCL.

9. Memo, Hamilton Jordan to Warren Christopher, 8 April 1980, Hugh Carter's Files, Box 37, Office of Administration, JCL.

10. Farouk A. Sankari, "The Effects of the American Media on Public Opinion and the Middle East Policy Choices," *American-Arab Affairs*, (Spring 1987) 20:107-22. In a memo of talking points for the president, Brzezinski stressed that during the meeting with Jewish leaders, the word "homeland" should be avoided as it had associations with the Balfour Declaration. Likewise, he advocated avoiding the use of the term "defensible borders" as this implied the incorporation of most of the occupied territories, which the Arabs opposed. Memo, Zbigniew Brzezinski to Hamilton Jordan [for Carter], 5 July 1977, Hamilton Jordan's Files, Box 35, JCL.

11. "Notes on Meeting with Jewish Leaders," n.a. [possibly Joyce Starr], 6 July 1977, Stuart Eizenstat's Files, Box 235, JCL. An edited and shorter version of these notes is found in Memo, Joyce Starr (White House liaison on Soviet Jews and Jewish Community Affairs), for the Files, File ND16/CO1-7, Box ND39, JCL.

12. Louis J. Cantori, "Egyptian Policy," in Robert O. Freedman, ed., *The Middle East Since Camp David* (Boulder, CO: Westview Press, 1984), pp. 171-91. Cantori argues that the inclusion of the Soviet Union in the conference helped motivate Sadat to visit Israel. However, one could also argue that by this time, Kissinger had sold Sadat on the personal, domestic, and international benefits to be gleaned from his leadership role in the step-by-step process and in signing a separate peace.

13. Memo, William Quandt to Zbigniew Brzezinski, 26 August 1977, with Brzezinski's handwritten comment. Quandt wrote a similar memo, 27 July 1977. File NO16/CO1-7, Box ND39, JCL.

14. Memo, Zbigniew Brzezinski to Hamilton Jordan, 2 September 1977, AAUG/NAAA Name File, JCL.

15. The discussion of this meeting is based on: a 30 May 1989 telephone interview with Dr. Michael Suleiman, then president of AAUG and member of the delegation that met with President Carter; AAUG *Newsletter*, December 1977; *The Voice*, January 1978.

Although the notes on the meetings with Jewish Americans are open and available through the files of the Domestic Policy Staff, the notes on the meeting with Arab Americans are not in the Domestic Policy staff papers nor are they currently available in NSC materials. Oddly, the White House staff apparently considered meetings with Jewish Americans matters of domestic concern and meetings with Arab Americans matters of foreign policy or national security. The presidential diary does, however, make note of the meetings and those who attended (Presidential Diary, Box 21, JCL).

16. Letter, Landrum Bolling to Carter, 20 December 1978, Box ND40, JCL.

17. Letter, Carter to Abourizk, 2 October 1978, Palestine Liberation Organization Name File; see also Paul Findley Name File and WHCF, Box CO-35, JCL.

18. Various reports and protests about these meetings are found in Jody Powell's Files, Box 82, JCL.

19. See Alan Hart, *Arafat: Terrorist or Peacemaker?* (London: Sidgwick & Jackson, 1984), pp. 440-41, for a fuller discussion of the background to Young's resignation and the behind-the-scenes negotiations with the PLO.

20. Fayez A. Sayegh, in "Camp David and Palestine: a Preliminary Analysis," (New York: Americans for Middle East Understanding, 1979) provides a thorough study of the framework's language and content. Full text of the Framework for Peace is provided in Appendix 4 of Carter, *Blood of Abraham*.

21. Carter, *Keeping Faith*, pp. 300, 325-27, 377.
22. Carter, *Blood of Abraham*, p.169.
23. *Ibid.*
24. Letter, James E. Akins to Brzezinski, 24 September 1979, Box CO-8, JCL. Akins was a former U.S. Ambassador to Saudi Arabia.
25. "Into the Valley of the Shadow of Failure," *Events*, 23 March 1979.
26. Memo, Edward Sanders and Roger Lewis to Robert J. Lipshutz [White House Counsel] and Hamilton Jordan, 11 January 1978, Robert Lipshutz's Files, Box 6, JCL.
27. Memo, Edward Sanders to Carter, 15 August 1979, Hamilton Jordan's Files, Box 49, JCL.
28. Memo, Hamilton Jordan to Carter, 30 November 1978, *ibid.*
29. Joint Letter to President Carter from President Sadat and Prime Minister Begin, 26 March 1979, Department of State, *Selected Documents* no. 11, (Washington, DC: U.S. Government Printing Office, 1979). In this letter the signatories agreed to begin negotiations within one month of ratification of the peace treaty. According to the text:

> The purpose of the negotiation shall be to agree, prior to the elections, on the modalities for establishing the elected self-governing authority (administrative council), define its powers and responsibilities, and agree upon other related issues.
>
> ... [T]he objective of the negotiations is the establishment of the self-governing authority in the West Bank and Gaza in order to provide full autonomy to its inhabitants.

Jordan was to be invited to join the negotiations and the delegations of Egypt and Jordan could include Palestinians, "as mutually agreed." In the event Jordan refused, Egypt and Israel would hold the talks alone.

30. Lloyd Cutler, Oral Interview, Miller Center, 23 October 1982, JCL. Cutler was counsel to the president. Stuart Eizenstat has described the relationship between Carter and Begin as "like oil and water." Eizenstat speech, Temple Sinai, Washington, 22 February 1991.
31. Briefing Memorandum, Hodding Carter III [Department of State] to Ambassador Linowitz and Harold Saunders, Assistant Secretary of State, 27 June 1980, WHCF, Box CO-8, JCL.

8

THE REAGAN ADMINISTRATION'S POLICY TOWARD THE PALESTINIANS

Ann M. Lesch

ON 14 DECEMBER 1988 Secretary of State George Shultz announced that the U.S. government would open a "substantive dialogue" with the Palestine Liberation Organization (PLO) that would be conducted by the American ambassador in Tunisia.[1] Earlier that day, Yasir Arafat, the chairman of the executive committee of the PLO, had met the strict conditions for talks imposed by Washington. At a press conference in Geneva, Arafat affirmed

> the right of all parties concerned in the Middle East conflict to exist in peace and security . . . including the state of Palestine, Israel and other neighbors, according to the Resolutions 242 and 338. As for terrorism, I renounced it yesterday [at the UN General Assembly] in no uncertain terms and yet I repeat for the record that we totally and absolutely renounce all forms of terrorism, including individual, group, and state terrorism. . . . We want peace. We are committed to peace.[2]

That statement met the three conditions imposed by the United States. In a secret American-Israeli Memorandum of Understanding that was attached to the second Egyptian-Israeli disengagement accord of September 1975, Washington pledged that it would "not recognize or negotiate with the Palestine Liberation Organization so long as the Palestine Liberation Organization does not recognize Israel's right to exist and does not accept Security Council resolutions 242 and 338."[3] The Reagan administration added a third condition: the PLO must renounce the use of terror before the United States would talk with its leaders. Washington tied its hands in dealing with the Palestinian movement, rejecting even informal contact and meetings unless the PLO stated those three conditions in a public, authoritative, and unqualified manner.

Arafat's remarks were accepted as such an authoritative statement. Ronald Reagan, who was entering his last month as president, added to Shultz's announcement: "We view this development as one more step toward the beginning of direct negotiations between the parties, which alone can lead to a [comprehensive] peace."[4]

The turnabout was astonishing for an administration that had labeled the PLO a terrorist organization and had harshly criticized its leadership. Shultz had just refused to issue Arafat a visa so that he could address the UN General Assembly in New York. Arafat had intended to explain the peace proposals articulated by the Palestine National Council in November, but Shultz banned him, labeling Arafat as an accessory to terror. Moreover, the administration viewed the Middle East through the lens of the Cold War and identified closely with Israel's strategic aims. Those complementary approaches reinforced Washington's biases against the PLO and led to repeated efforts to separate solving the Palestine problem from dealing with the PLO. Previous PLO diplomatic initiatives were ignored, even when they linked their efforts to King Hussein of Jordan, a long-term American ally, and when they indicated that they hoped that a dialogue with the United States would lead to negotiations with Israel.

The American policy shift in December 1988 was thus not simply the result of Arafat's issuing a statement that could not be dismissed. Rather, the *intifada* ("shaking off") launched by Palestinians in the Gaza Strip and the West Bank a year earlier had compelled the Reagan administration to reassess its assumptions about Israel's capacity to maintain its security through territorial control. The uprising induced Shultz to undertake the only intensive diplomatic effort to resolve the Israeli-Palestinian dilemma during the entire eight years of Reagan's tenure. Earlier initiatives had been half-hearted and had generally been conducted at a sub-cabinet level. The intensity of the intifada and the subsequent Palestinian diplomatic moves finally convinced Washington that it had to respond to the Palestinian movement and had to recognize that the PLO had met the conditions that the U.S. had imposed. Thus the intifada not only crystallized Palestinian political thinking but also altered American policy.

Nevertheless, Washington would not promise to support the key Palestinian aspirations for self-determination and statehood. Nor would the U.S. promise to press Israel to open a similar dialogue with the PLO. Shultz stated emphatically at his press conference on 14 December 1988: "Nothing here may be taken to imply an acceptance or recognition by the United States of an independent Palestinian state."[5] Shultz maintained that negotiations rather than unilateral acts or declarations were the appropriate means for determining the status of the West Bank and Gaza Strip. The United States would neither endorse Israel's calls for annexation nor Palestinian demands for statehood.

Opening a dialogue was a necessary first step toward including the PLO in negotiations, even if it did not guarantee that outcome. Moreover, it eased the burden on the incoming administration led by then vice-president George Bush. A former diplomat commented: "I think Ronald Reagan is taking the political flak and giving George Bush an opportunity to start with a clean slate in the Middle East."[6] The dialogue had already begun when Bush took office; he could incorporate the new relationship into his Middle East diplomacy if he so chose.

REAGAN'S STRATEGIC CONCEPTION

Reagan assumed the presidency in 1981 with a clear, overriding preoccupation with the Soviet Union. He perceived local conflicts — whether in Asia, Africa, Latin America or the Middle East — as manifestations of the global Soviet threat. The Soviet invasion of Afghanistan and the fall of the shah in Iran were said to heighten the risks for the West in the vital Persian Gulf. Moscow's arms supplies to Syria and Libya and access to Syrian ports were cited as proof of the vulnerability of the eastern Mediterranean to Soviet penetration. Therefore, Secretary of State Alexander Haig focused on the Soviet threat during his first trip to the Middle East in April 1981.[7] He urged the leaders of Israel, Egypt, Jordan and Saudi Arabia to develop a "consensus of concern" that would create an informal military alliance to block Moscow's alleged effort to control oil resources and routes. Haig's views were a throwback to the approach of John Foster Dulles in the 1950s, who assumed that Israel and the Arab states shared Washington's preoccupation with Soviet designs and would set aside their differences in pursuit of that common purpose.

Just as Dulles fatally misperceived the Middle East political context, so did Haig misdiagnose regional concerns in the early 1980s. The Arab regimes along the Persian Gulf were anxious to receive American assistance in order to ward off Iranian subversion and attack, but they did not see Moscow as a direct threat. Moreover, they were disturbed by the military imbalance in the Arab-Israeli equation caused by Egypt's withdrawal from the Arab front. Heightened Israeli-Syrian tension in Lebanon and the Israeli air strike against the Iraqi nuclear plant in June 1981 led Jordan and Saudi Arabia to seek weapons to ward off a potential Israeli attack. Riyadh purchased American AWACs to defend the kingdom against Iran and Israel, not the Soviet Union; the Saudis did not share a "consensus of concern" with Tel Aviv.

The Arab regimes' hesitancy to embrace Haig's approach, in turn, reinforced the secretary of state's proclivity to view Israel as the linchpin of American strategy in the region.[8] Ariel Sharon, who became Israel's defense minister in mid-1981, welcomed the role of policeman in the Middle East and negotiated a Memorandum of Understanding, signed on 30 November 1981, which explicitly linked Israel to Washington's anti-Soviet posture. A former Carter aide noted that

> the relationship took a giant step forward during the Reagan Administration which saw Israel not as a post-Holocaust American moral obligation but, for the first time, as a strategic asset in the regional struggle against the Soviet Union for primacy in the Middle East.[9]

Haig assumed that establishing firm American-Israeli strategic relations would encourage Israel to take steps toward peace. The administration reaffirmed its support for the Camp David process, but focused on finalizing the Israeli withdrawal from Sinai rather than on reinvigorating the autonomy talks. Egyptian President Anwar Sadat had refused to continue those talks in mid-1980 when the Israeli government declared all of Jerusalem its eternal capital. Moreover, Washington appeared to tilt toward Israel's interpretation of autonomy, particularly when Reagan stated that Israeli settlements in the occupied territories were not illegal. Moreover, administration officials tended to see Palestinians as individuals and refugees, whose difficulties could be resolved by gaining civic rights in a West Bank federated with Jordan. They termed the PLO a terrorist organization and sometimes called it a Soviet puppet, labels which delegitimized the PLO as the Palestinians' representative body.

Even after Sadat and Israeli Prime Minister Menachem Begin decided in August 1981 to resume the autonomy talks, Washington showed little concern to encourage them. Haig delayed until January 1982 to travel to the region to promote the autonomy negotiations, apparently jogged into action by the possibility that Egypt would lose interest once it regained Sinai on 25 April. But that effort faded and Haig waited until late May, a month after Israel withdrew from Sinai, to talk about the autonomy negotiations.

During 1981-82, Washington felt urgency only on the Israeli-Syrian front. U.S. officials expressed sympathy for Israel's security requirements (in effect legitimizing the airraids against PLO bases) and for Israeli assistance to the Lebanese Forces that opposed Syria and the PLO. However, they became concerned at the heightened tension when the Israeli raids provoked Syria to move SAM-6 missiles into the Biqa Valley and to tighten its strategic ties with Moscow. Haig feared that an Israeli air strike against the missiles might precipitate a superpower confrontation and hastily dispatched a special envoy to the Middle East in May 1981. The war of nerves peaked when the Israeli air force bombed Beirut on 17 July and killed 300 civilians in a crowded residential quarter. Reagan then, and rather belatedly, threw his weight behind attaining a cease-fire to which both Israel and the PLO agreed on 24 July 1981. The border remained quiet until the spring of 1982.

The Reagan initiative

Haig was aware that Sharon wanted to attack Lebanon, both to destroy the PLO's political and military presence and to create a new Lebanese government sympathetic to Israel. Haig had restrained Sharon in December 1981, when an Israeli strike might have damaged Egyptian-Israeli relations and undermined the agreement to restore Sinai to Egyptian control. But Sharon built up Israeli forces along the Lebanese border in the spring of 1982 and launched raids against the PLO in an effort to provoke them into breaking the cease-fire. Sharon then used an attempt by the renegade Abu Nidal organization to assassinate the Israeli ambassador in London as the pretext for a full-scale invasion of Lebanon on 4 June.

The United States supported the UN Security Council's demand on 6 June that Israel withdraw from Lebanon immediately and unconditionally. Nonetheless, within hours the U.S. position was modified and Washington vetoed a second UN resolution on 8 June. Once the prospect of superpower confrontation was reduced by the Israeli-Syrian truce on 11 June, the Reagan administration began to champion key Israeli goals: Reagan backed the Israeli demand to remove all foreign forces from Lebanon, notably Syria and the PLO, and endorsed the candidacy of Bashir Gemayel, head of the Lebanese Forces, for president of Lebanon. Reagan also concurred with Israel's demand to control (directly or through surrogates) a forty-kilometer zone north of its border.[10] However, Washington opposed Sharon's drive to occupy Beirut and protested the Israeli siege and aerial bombardments of Lebanon's capital. Reagan was angry that, even after the U.S. mediator won Arafat's agreement to evacuate his forces, Sharon unleashed massive air and artillery strikes against Beirut. By the end of August, Israel had secured its core goals: Removal of the PLO leaders and forces from Beirut, and election of Bashir Gemayel as president of Lebanon. The United States strongly supported those results. U.S. Marines participated in the multinational force which supervised the evacuation of Palestinian troops from Beirut. Meanwhile, on the diplomatic front, Shultz had replaced Haig as secretary of state and Washington readied a peace initiative, the first undertaken by Reagan.

The plan that Reagan announced on 1 September 1982 was based on UN Resolution 242 as well as the Camp David accords. Citing the opportunities created by the respite in the civil war and the PLO evacuation of Beirut, Reagan stated: "We must also move to resolve the root causes of conflicts between Arabs and Israelis," especially "the homelessness of the Palestinian people." Reagan did not, however, merely refer to the Palestinians as refugees. He added, "the question now is how to reconcile Israel's legitimate security concerns with the legitimate rights of the Palestinians." He sought to reassure Israel by declaring that the United States would "not support the establishment of an independent Palestinian state in the West Bank and Gaza" and would endorse Israel's request for changes in the 1967 territorial lines so as to ensure its security. But he also tried to reassure the Palestinians by declaring that "we will not support annexation or permanent control by Israel," and by calling for "the immediate adoption of a settlement freeze by Israel."[11]

Reagan reaffirmed the concept of a five-year transitional period on the West Bank and Gaza, enshrined in the Camp David accords, as the way to guarantee "the peaceful and orderly transfer of authority from Israel to the Palestinian inhabitants of the West Bank and Gaza." He concluded that "it is the firm view of the United States that self-government by the Palestinians of the West Bank and Gaza in association with Jordan offers the best chance for a durable, just and lasting peace." The initiative thereby provided a clear conceptualization of the U.S. vision of a peace accord. The speech, however, had four notable omissions: Reagan did not refer to PLO representation in negotiations; to the fate of Palestinians living outside the occupied territories; to the status of the Golan Heights; or to the method of negotiation.

The Israeli cabinet immediately rejected Reagan's proposal and asserted that the withdrawal provisions in Resolution 242 did not apply to the West Bank and Gaza. Two weeks later, the Israeli army violated the truce and entered West

Beirut in the wake of the assassination of Bashir Gemayel. The Reagan administration was not surprised at Israel's criticism of Reagan's proposal but was shocked at Israel's attack on Beirut and outraged at the massacre of Palestinian civilians in the Sabra and Shatila refugee camps by Lebanese militiamen who had been allowed into the camps by the Israeli commanders. Washington quickly returned the Marines to Beirut in a revived multinational force in order to ensure that Israeli troops would leave the capital and to provide belated protection for Palestinian residents. The United States also pressed for Israeli-Lebanese negotiations to resolve their disputes.

In contrast to the Israeli government, Arab leaders were cautiously positive in their responses to Reagan's ideas. The Arab Summit at Fez on 8 September asserted the Palestinian right of self-determination and statehood under the leadership of the PLO; indicated that the Palestinian state would encompass only the territories occupied by Israel in 1967; and demanded the dismantling of Israeli settlements.[12] The Summit statement also noted that a brief UN-supervised transitional period was acceptable and that the Security Council should guarantee "peace among all states of the region." King Hussein of Jordan argued that the Fez plan was compatible with Reagan's concepts and Arafat refrained from rejecting Reagan's ideas. American credibility was damaged when Washington proved unable to protect Palestinian civilians in Beirut in mid-September, but the prospect that Reagan would commit his prestige to a comprehensive peace settlement encouraged the Arab leaders.

Strategic cooperation with Israel

Nonetheless, the Reagan Plan was never transformed into a coherent diplomatic strategy and faded away within months. Washington became preoccupied by the Israeli-Lebanese negotiations, reasserted the primacy of its anti-Soviet strategy, and reaffirmed the strategic alliance with Israel. Once again Reagan argued that Israel played a key role in containing communism. In a speech on 27 October 1983 he even called Syria a surrogate of the Soviet Union and blamed Moscow for encouraging violence in Lebanon.[13] Juliana Peck, in analyzing the speech, noted that Reagan referred briefly to his peace plan but placed primary emphasis on "Soviet proxies" against whom he might "unleash" Israel. She concluded: "his speech was characterized by a return to the old Reagan view of all problems everywhere being caused by the Soviet Union, and by an explicit polarization of the conflict between East and West, between Syria and Israel."[14] The Palestinians were again branded as terrorist bands that destabilized the region.

One cause for the shift was U.S. frustration over the lack of resolution of the domestic and international situation in Lebanon, where U.S. forces were increasingly endangered. The Israeli-Lebanese draft treaty of May 1983 allowed Israeli troops to remain in southern Lebanon and normalized diplomatic relations. Its implementation, however, was contingent upon Syrian troops also withdrawing from Lebanon. Since President Hafiz al-Asad had already rejected anything less than full Israeli withdrawal and opposed the normalization of Israeli-Lebanese relations, the situation on the ground remained stalemated. Shultz blamed the impasse on Asad instead of on faulty American negotiating techniques.[15] And Reagan looked for the Soviet hand behind Syria's stance.

Moreover, Syrian-supported splits in the PLO fractured the Palestinian movement and Lebanese groups confronted violently the Israeli occupation of southern Lebanon. In addition, as Israeli forces withdrew from the central sector during the summer of 1983, the U.S. Marines lost their neutral status as peacekeepers. They became directly involved in confrontations by the Lebanese army with Syrian-supported Druze and Shiite militia, a fatal shift from their peacekeeping role that led to the devastating attack on the Marine barracks in October and the total withdrawal of the American peacekeeping contingents in February 1984. The Israeli-Lebanese treaty sank in their wake.

Meanwhile, Washington continued to insist that King Hussein negotiate on behalf of the Palestinians. The Palestine National Council of February 1983 rejected that idea but approved the establishment of a confederation between Jordan and an independent Palestinian state. The king could not persuade the Palestinian leaders to enter talks under his auspices since Washington would not soften its stance on either representation or self-determination. The resulting diplomatic stalemate on the Palestinian front damaged further the credibility of moderate Palestinians, who were still reeling from the loss of their territorial base in Lebanon.

Reagan's speech in October 1983, cited above, did not analyze the regional causes of Washington's failure in Lebanon and the lack of progress on regional diplomatic issues. Rather, Reagan signaled that he was giving up the search for a comprehensive peace and returning to a one-dimensional approach that would rely on Israel. That approach was reinforced on 29 November 1983 when Reagan and the new Israeli prime minister Yitzhak Shamir signed a strategic cooperation accord that went well beyond the agreement initialed in late 1981. Three joint groups were set up: political-military, economic development, and, in 1986, security assistance planning. By 1987 more than twenty-four military technical agreements were made.[16] Israel was also designated a major non-NATO ally, which codified its *de facto* status and enhanced its ability to sell military equipment to the United States. In addition to high-level strategic coordination in the eastern Mediterranean and the Middle East, Israel provided covert support for Reagan's policies toward Iran and in Central America. Israel played a key role in the arms-for-hostages drama exposed in the Iran-Contra affair and provided arms directly to the Contras after May 1983. The Department of Defense, for example, paid Israel $10 million for arms and ammunition captured from the PLO in 1982.[17] When the Boland Amendment banned American aid to the Contras in mid-1984, the administration continued to pay Israel to arm them; in return, Washington agreed to support Israel's military and economic requirements. Such arms deals continued through 1986, despite the strains caused by the Pollard spy case, which revealed that a U.S. government employee had provided classified information concerning Arab military sites to Israel's intelligence service. An Israeli general termed the close U.S.-Israeli relationship "a force multiplier for Israel."[18] Arab leaders again worried that Washington's intense relationship with Israel was undermining United States credibility as a mediator, especially in reference to the Palestine question.[19]

The Hussein-Arafat Initiative

Nevertheless, King Hussein sought to test the American commitment to the peace process. Hussein was encouraged by the parliamentary elections in Israel in July 1984 that resulted in a National Unity Government between Likud and Labor; Labor's Shimon Peres would serve as prime minister until October 1986. Moreover, Reagan appeared headed for a landslide victory in the presidential election of November 1984. A second-term Reagan presidency would be potentially less subject to domestic political pressure. Thus, the timing appeared propitious for a renewed peace drive. Hussein maneuvered to establish a favorable context by restoring diplomatic relations with Egypt in September 1984 and hosting the Palestine National Council in November. The moderate Arab front crystallized when he signed an accord with Arafat on 11 February 1985 which called for

1. Total withdrawal from the territories occupied in 1967 for comprehensive peace as established in United Nations and Security Council resolutions.
2. Right of self-determination for the Palestinian people . . . within the context of the formation of the proposed federated Arab states of Jordan and Palestine . . .
3. Peace negotiations [to] be conducted under the auspices of an international conference in which the five permanent members of the Security Council and all the parties to the conflict [would] participate, including the Palestine Liberation Organization, the sole legitimate representative of the Palestine people, within a joint (Jordanian-Palestinian) delegation.[20]

For the first time, Arafat explicitly affirmed the land-for-peace formula at the core of Resolution 242. Moreover, he accepted the concept of a confederation with Jordan rather than a fully independent Palestinian state and agreed to Palestinian participation in a joint delegation with Jordan. Hussein and Egyptian President Husni Mubarak viewed the accord as a major breakthrough and expected a comparable response from Washington. Instead of highlighting Arafat's conceptual shift, however, the United States emphasized a procedural issue. Washington criticized the idea of negotiating at an international conference where the Soviet Union could play a significant role. Reagan wanted to exclude Moscow from any peace negotiations on the Middle East. As a result, even though Peres was cautiously supportive of an international conference, if only as a ceremonial cover for direct negotiations, the United States dug in its heels and insisted on retaining the Camp David framework. Moreover, Washington argued that Arafat had still not fully committed the PLO to Resolution 242 and demanded additional statements from him. Arafat responded on 14 May by stating that the PLO would accept 242 if the United States would endorse the Palestinians' right to self-determination.[21]

There appeared to be a breakthrough that month after Shultz visited the region and pursued the possibility of a meeting between an American diplomat and a joint Jordanian-Palestinian delegation.[22] The PLO submitted seven names, noting that some could be deleted if the United States objected to them. Washington did object to the presence of three high-ranking PLO officials on the list. Then the talks were almost torpedoed when the Israeli press leaked the names. Nonetheless, Assistant Secretary of State Richard Murphy prepared to meet with the remaining four, including two persons from the West Bank and Gaza.

The session, scheduled for August, was abruptly canceled even though Murphy and the Palestinians were present simultaneously in Amman. The circumstances surrounding the cancellation remain obscure, but apparently resulted from new American demands. The Palestinian and Jordanian participants had anticipated that, if Murphy were forthcoming in the meeting, they would issue a public statement affirming Resolution 242; but Washington suddenly requested that the Palestinians affirm 242 *prior* to the meeting, a step they were unwilling to take since they did not know yet what Murphy would offer. The cancelation of the meeting dealt a hard blow to both Hussein and Arafat. It reinforced arguments that the United States was not serious in its pursuit of negotiations and accelerated the renewal of violence in the fall and winter of 1985-86. In rapid succession, prospects for negotiations were dashed by the Palestinian assassination of three Israelis at Larnaca, the Israeli bombing of the PLO headquarters in Tunis, the hijackings of the *Achille Lauro* cruise ship and later an Egyptair plane, and attacks at the Rome and Frankfurt airports. Several of those operations were designed to discredit Arafat and force him to discard the diplomatic route.

In a last-ditch effort in early 1986, Hussein and Peres wrung from Washington reluctant approval of the idea of an international conference. Moreover, Arafat issued a declaration from Cairo in November 1985 renouncing terrorist tactics and the use of violence outside the occupied territories. But the PLO refused to adhere formally to Resolution 242 unless the United States accepted Palestinian self-determination in the form of a confederation with Jordan. With no positive response from Washington, the Hussein-Arafat accord collapsed amid recriminations on all sides.

As a result, even though Israel withdrew its troops from most of Lebanon in June 1985 and Egyptian-Israeli relations were restored to ambassadorial level in September 1986, the regional atmosphere remained heated. Moreover, the Israeli government became paralyzed: Once Shamir replaced Peres as prime minister in October 1986, he blocked any moves toward an international conference or even talks with Hussein. Washington had contributed to the stalemate as well as the weakening of Peres by failing to seize the diplomatic opportunities in 1984-85. Subsequently, the United States acquiesced to the impasse by muting references to a political resolution and talking, instead, about improving the "quality of life" for the Palestinians living on the West Bank and Gaza Strip. Additional U.S. aid funds were allocated for the territories even though Defense Minister Yitzhak Rabin's "iron fist" policy, instituted in August 1985, had a sharply negative impact on the very quality of life that Washington sought to improve. The American approach appeared to concede that Israel would rule indefinitely and that cosmetic improvements were the most that could be expected.

THE SHULTZ PLAN

American complacency was shattered by the intifada, which erupted in December 1987. Unlike the previous spasmodic outbreaks of demonstrations and strikes that had occurred frequently over the two decades of military occupation, the uprising gained momentum as time passed. New grassroots leaders and structures emerged to sustain and deepen the protests. In July 1988, Murphy admitted to Congress that the intifada had created a new reality and that "we have no doubt that the uprising in the West Bank and Gaza was caused, in large part, by a sense that the peace process had stalled."[23]

The intifada compelled Washington to address the Palestine question. Mubarak, Hussein and even Peres prodded Shultz to assume personal responsibility for the American diplomatic effort. From February until June 1988, Shultz traveled four times to the region — the only sustained, high-level shuttle diplomacy attempted during the eight years of Reagan's presidency. Shultz even presented to the parties a detailed, coherent plan that went beyond Camp David and included substantive elements sought by Mubarak and Hussein. He also set deadlines, in an effort to inject a sense of urgency into the mission and to stress the linkage among the various elements of the plan. As sketched prior to the first trip, the proposal involved:

1. The convening of an international conference by mid-April as an "event" to open negotiations, with the participation of Israel, Egypt, Syria, a Jordanian-Palestinian delegation, and the five permanent members of the Security Council;
2. By May 1, the start of six-months' negotiations for an interim phase of self-administration on the West Bank and Gaza Strip, including the election of an administrative council by the Palestinians;
3. By December 1988, the initiation of talks between Israel and the Jordanian-Palestinian delegation on the final status of the territories. Those talks would conclude within one year and the final status would take effect three years after the beginning of the interim phase. Final status negotiations would begin in December even if no accord had been reached on the interim phase.[24]

Shultz explicitly linked the interim and final phases. He knew that the Arab parties would hesitate to participate if only an interim phase was stressed; but he also risked an Israeli boycott by insisting that the interim stage could not stand alone. Shultz tried to mollify Israel by calling the international conference an opening ceremony without the authority to negotiate — much less impose — a settlement. Importantly, he fudged the issue of Palestinian representation.

Shultz soon discovered that he had underestimated both the intensity with which Shamir would oppose the plan and Shamir's effectiveness in checkmating Peres. The Israeli prime minister blocked a cabinet vote on the proposals in early March and brusquely rejected the plan by stating: "The only word in the Shultz plan I accept is his signature. Apart from that, the document does not serve the cause of peace." He added that the proposal "obligates me to resist [it] with all my power — and my power to resist is very great."[25] Shamir argued that Israel had satisfied 242's requirement to withdraw from territory occupied in 1967 when it withdrew from Sinai; retaining the West Bank and Gaza was essential for Israel on the grounds of security, history, and national identity. He rejected an international conference, which he felt would not only put Israel at a disadvantage numerically but also give Moscow a decisive role. Solving the question of Soviet Jewry and restoring diplomatic relations were necessary, he asserted, before Israel could agree to a Soviet presence at the negotiating table.

Although Shultz was miffed at Shamir's language, Washington did not chastise him publicly. Rather, the United States granted Shamir valuable new strategic prizes: A revised Memorandum of Agreement on joint political, security and economic cooperation and the accelerated delivery of seventy-five F-16 fighters. The administration wanted to emphasize the strategic relationship with Israel, both to counter anticipated congressional criticism of Shultz's peace plan and to reassure Israel that its security would not be undermined if a peace accord necessitated its relinquishing the West Bank and Gaza. But the latter message was lost. Instead, as an Israeli journalist commented, the message received was: "One may say no to America and still get a bonus."[26]

Thus, Shamir felt safe in ignoring Shultz's argument that Israel needed to rethink its concept of security and its relationship to the Palestinians. Shultz asserted that prior concepts of defense based on territory were outdated: "The location of borders is less significant today in ensuring security than the political relations between neighbors. Peace is the real answer to the problems of security."[27] He also raised the issue of "the ticking demographic time bomb"[28] of a Palestinian population living under Israeli occupation, disenfranchised and hostile to Israeli rule. Such arguments were irrelevant to Shamir.

Washington sent contradictory signals when officials used phrases that seemed to support — or at least sympathize with — Israel's actions to suppress the Palestinian uprising. In March, Shultz commented that Israel "has the duty to maintain order . . . with firmness and authority and in as humane a way as is possible."[29] Likewise, Murphy spoke of "brutal casualties *on both sides*" in the violence in the territories.[30] That language ignored the genesis of the uprising in the harsh "order" that Israel had maintained and the fact that, at that time, casualties were largely among Palestinians at the hands of Israeli soldiers. Such statements reassured Shamir that Washington would not object to the measures that the army was taking to subdue the intifada.

Palestinian representation

Shultz's proposals maintained the long-term U.S. posture that Palestinians should express their views through a joint delegation with Jordan. Shultz did not refer to the PLO and did not state whether Palestinians living outside the West Bank and Gaza Strip would be included at any stage.

Palestinians had boycotted Shultz during his visit to Jerusalem in October 1987, prior to the intifada. In contrast, two prominent Palestinians from the West Bank and Gaza (who had been included in the delegation to the aborted meeting with Murphy in 1985) journeyed to Washington in January 1988. They presented to Shultz the fourteen-point memorandum that had just been issued by Palestinians in the occupied territories that outlined the grievances and objectives of the intifada. That memorandum called on Israel to remove all constraints on Palestinian political activities, including the cancellation of the Israeli ban on contact with the PLO and the holding of the long overdue elections for municipal councils. The memorandum stressed interim goals that would alleviate the burdens of Israeli rule and prepare the atmosphere for comprehensive negotiations.

Shultz interpreted the Palestinian initiative as meaning that he could deal directly with West Bank and Gaza residents. During his first trip, he invited a dozen Palestinians to a meeting in East Jerusalem on 26 February. No one came. They maintained that Shultz should meet with a delegation of Palestinians that would include those living outside the occupied territories; that the meeting should be in Cairo or Amman, not Jerusalem; and that the Palestinians should be selected or approved by the PLO, not the United States. Shultz was taken aback by the boycott but delivered a conciliatory statement that sought to keep the door ajar:

> Palestinians must achieve control over the political and economic decisions that affect their own lives. Palestinians must be active participants in the negotiations to determine their future.[31]

In March, Arafat emphasized that the PLO must be represented in peace talks and that a joint Jordanian-Palestinian delegation was no longer acceptable. Arafat criticized Shultz for selecting the Palestinians with whom he would meet:

> He hasn't the right to choose the Palestinian delegation. It is a matter of dignity and integrity. Can I choose the American representative? OK, I'll deal with Mr. Jesse Jackson, who accepts self-determination for the Palestinian people. I have not the right to do so.

But Arafat also offered positive incentives for Shultz to promote negotiations. He stated that he accepted Israeli existence by accepting "all UN resolutions" including 242 and 338 and noted that, at the Palestine National Council in 1984, "we said land for peace." He concluded: "With whom am I going to make peace at an international conference? With my enemies, with the Israeli government."[32]

By late March, Shultz began to respond to the demand to include Palestinians living outside the occupied territories in the scope of his talks. He met on 26 March with two Palestinian professors who had American citizenship but were also members of the Palestine National Council. The State Department stressed that Shultz was simply meeting fellow Americans and that the meeting did not violate the ban on talking to the PLO. However, professors Ibrahim Abu-Lughod and Edward Said noted that they had consulted with Arafat before the meeting and that their comments reflected PLO views. The PLO spokesperson in Tunis called the meeting an "important political step."[33]

Said emphasized that they had impressed on Shultz the reality that there are "two national communities" in conflict and that they need to work toward mutual coexistence "on a footing of equality."[34] Shultz appeared to comprehend that argument. Thus, during his last trip he remarked, for the first time, that the Arab-Israeli conflict "is the competition between two national movements for sovereignty on one land"[35] and added that the competition was not a zero sum game. Zionism and Palestinian nationalism were interdependent in his view. They could live side by side — but separately — as neighbors in Israel and on the West Bank and Gaza. Shultz also began to humanize the Palestinian people:

> The Palestinians . . . are like human beings everywhere else. They have their aspirations, they have a desire to have a say about how they are governed just like people everywhere do. . . . They want economic opportunities, they want to see that their children have a chance to get a decent education, they want access to health facilities . . . a chance to . . . have control over that, to have an impact on how those things are structured. It is a very human instinct that everybody has . . . . So it isn't just the fact that you have a health facility or that you have an educational institution. You want to do it yourself. And that is a political act, and so I think people ought to have a little more control over the way in which their lives are arranged.[36]

Shultz appeared to understand that improving the "quality of life" under occupation was a non-starter and that self-rule was essential. He still balked at the establishment of an independent state, terming it unworkable and unnecessary. Nonetheless, his comments about the prospects for talks with the PLO were more forthcoming than in the past:

> We will be willing to talk to the PLO when the PLO in a clear, unambiguous way accepts Resolution 242 and 338 as the basis for peace, accepts the right of Israel to exist, and turns away from violence and terrorism . . . Under those circumstances we will talk to the PLO . . . Frankly I don't see what's so difficult about [those conditions]. They are just common sense.[37]

Moreover, Washington expressed optimism at the statement circulated by Bassam Abu Sharif, a close aide to Arafat, at the Arab summit conference in June 1988.[38] That statement emphasized the common suffering of Israelis and

Palestinians and their mutual desire for peace and security. Abu Sharif added that the PLO accepted Resolution 242 in the context of a UN resolution that recognized Palestinian national rights and also accepted the need for a transitional period before gaining independence. Although the statement was not an official PLO document, Murphy termed it "a potentially significant development":

> We are struck by its constructive tone and the positive points it raises, such as its emphasis on the existence of Israel and on the ultimate goal of the Palestinians being to attain lasting peace in which there is security for Israelis and for the Palestinian people. We also note its flat assertion that the conflict can only be solved by direct talks. The paper remains silent, however, on the issue of terrorism and simply restates the PLO's equivocal position on acceptance of UNSC Resolutions 242 and 338. It remains to be seen whether this article is authoritative and represents the position of the PLO. . . . Nonetheless, should events prove this article to have marked a beginning of a responsible, reliable, authoritative and realistic approach by the PLO to the peace process, then it would be welcome.[39]

In fact, Murphy almost met with a group of Palestinians from the territories and the diaspora in Cairo in August. The meeting was canceled at the last minute because two of the Palestinians were deemed by Washington to be too closely connected with the PLO. Soon after, Murphy stressed in a public address: "Palestinians must be represented in every phase of the negotiating process. Exactly how Palestinians will be represented remains an outstanding issue. But the Palestinians must be involved — who are both acceptable and credible."[40] Moreover, Shultz stated in September that Palestinians should play a role "in the negotiations themselves and they must approve the outcome."[41] Washington was inching toward recognizing the centrality of Palestinian representation to any diplomatic process. The shift appeared related not only to the conciliatory statements emanating from Palestinian leaders and Hussein's public disavowal of responsibility for the West Bank on 30 July but also to Washington's growing irritation with Shamir.

Deadlock

Shultz had initially set a deadline of 16 March for the parties to respond to his plan. No one answered except Shamir, who flatly rejected it. Shultz lamely concluded that nonresponse meant that the plan had not been rejected by the Arab states. Nonetheless, Murphy's statements in April employed the cliches that signal a faltering diplomatic effort: one should not talk of a "breakthrough" but "momentum" and "continuing efforts," he opined. The United States was trying "to create an opportunity for progress" and the Shultz plan was "the only game in town."[42] As Shultz started his fourth — and last — trip, he argued: "It is not my initiative or the U.S. initiative that's in trouble. It's the region that's in trouble. That's why I keep coming back."[43] But he sounded discouraged at the end of the shuttle when he commented in Cairo: "The U.S. will remain heavily involved," in close touch with the parties to help shape opportunities and encourage accommodation.[44]

Washington officials used increasingly astringent language toward Shamir. Murphy said that the Israeli prime minister must "set aside outdated rhetoric and illusions"[45] and Shultz argued that Shamir should "not reject every new idea."[46] By refusing to relinquish any territory, Shultz added, Israel guarantees that no Arab will agree to negotiate. On his arrival in Tel Aviv in June, Shultz asserted bluntly: "The continued occupation of the West Bank and Gaza and the frustration of Palestinian rights is a dead-end street. The belief that this can continue is an illusion."[47] By September, Shultz was directly blaming Shamir for the failure to get negotiations started. He criticized Israel for its actions to suppress the intifada, arguing that Israel must maintain law and order but must also find a way to respond to Palestinian grievances. Shultz asserted that Shamir cannot claim there is no one to talk to while simultaneously suppressing political expression and arresting or deporting even those Palestinians who have moderate views.[48]

Murphy was even more blunt: "Force is not the answer. Intimidation is not the answer. Deportation of Palestinians is not the answer."[49] He particularly criticized Israel for closing schools and universities, arguing that such measures disrupt lives and increase bitterness rather than promote peace. Former United States officials candidly expressed their concern that Israel's measures in the territories would erode American support and weaken the foundations for the strategic relationship.[50]

Such statements denoted Washington's frustration at Shamir's ability to stonewall. They may also have been designed to bolster the position of Peres and the Labor party in the Israeli parliamentary elections on 1 November. They further underlined the despair of an administration that had only a few months remaining in its term. Shultz's potential leverage was already minimal when he began his shuttle in February. By autumn, the actors in the region knew that they would soon deal with a new American administration which might have a different approach and agenda. Shultz's precise timetable and the linked interim and final status negotiations never had a chance to be taken seriously and carried out.

Even though Shamir would not alter his position, the United States explicitly renounced the use of financial or military leverage against him. The one unilateral step that Washington could take that would alter the diplomatic dynamics and open up new prospects for the incoming president was to address the U.S.-PLO relationship. Such a move would be less risky for a still-popular lame duck administration than for a new president. Nonetheless, Shultz vigorously resisted taking that final step.

The Palestine National Council declaration of 15 November stated that "the international conference shall be convened on the basis of Security Council resolutions 242 (1967) and 338 (1973)" and included a long paragraph that rejected "terrorism in all its forms."[51] The declaration referred three times to the need for "security and peace for every state in the region."[52] But the declaration did not state directly that the Palestinians accepted Israel's *right* to exist. Arafat nearly used those words in his joint declaration with a group of American Jews in Stockholm on 7 December in which, in explaining the PNC declaration, he maintained that the PNC "established the independent State of Palestine and accepted the existence of Israel as a state in the region."[53]

Shultz was still dissatisfied. He maintained that Arafat had not yet articulated the three requirements directly, but only inferentially and conditionally. Moreover, objections were raised within the State Department by the head of the anti-terror office and the legal adviser. Congress was also likely to criticize any shift toward contact with the PLO. On the other hand, foreign diplomatic intermediaries, particularly from Sweden and Egypt, urged Shultz to act on the PLO statements. Shultz finally and reluctantly accepted the wording that Arafat stated at the specially convened press conference on 14 December. Even then, Shultz indicated that he still did not trust the PLO. When asked if his previous accusation that Arafat was a terrorist was now expunged from the record, Shultz replied: "No, when we have our dialogue you can be sure that the first item of business on our agenda . . . will be the subject of terrorism."[54]

CONCLUSION

During nearly all of the eight years of the Reagan administration, the Israeli-Palestinian relationship was viewed by the president through the Cold War lens. The U.S.-Israeli partnership was consolidated on the assumption that Israel could serve as a first line of defense against Soviet penetration of the Middle East. That perspective was not questioned during the Israeli invasion of Lebanon, but began to be questioned in the ensuing months as Israeli behavior in Beirut and south Lebanon diverged from American expectations. The Reagan Plan of 1982 represented the administration's first attempt to articulate a comprehensive approach to regional issues. However, Washington's disinterest in the Palestinian dimension became evident when it focused instead on Israeli-Lebanese relations and dismissed the Hussein-Arafat initiative.

Only the intifada and subsequent explicit shifts in the PLO's diplomatic position compelled Reagan's officials to reassess the American stand. They began to state in public that the Palestinians comprise a nation that deserves to control their own lives and must both play a role in negotiations and approve the outcome of those negotiations. Dialogue with the PLO was the logical outcome of those shifts, but an outcome which the administration resisted until the last moment. That dialogue began too late to have an impact on Shultz's shuttle diplomacy, but it had the potential to alter the basis for the new administration's strategy. Nonetheless, its impact should not be overstated. Despite increasing criticism of Shamir's rejectionist stance, the United States was not prepared to use leverage to induce Israeli compliance. Nor was it ready to undertake comprehensive talks with the Palestinians and to contemplate the possibility of a Palestinian state.

NOTES

1. *New York Times*, 15 December 1988.
2. *Ibid.*
3. *Ibid.*, 18 September 1975.
4. *Ibid.*, 15 December 1988.
5. *Ibid.*
6. *Ibid.* Comment by Mayor Andrew Young of Atlanta, who had been fired as U.S. ambassador to the UN for meeting with his diplomatic counterpart representing the PLO.
7. Juliana S. Peck, *The Reagan Administration and the Palestinian Question: The First Thousand Days* (Washington, DC: Institute for Palestine Studies, 1984), p. 15. For critiques of the early Reagan years, see also Naseer Aruri, Fouad Moughrabi and Joe Stork, *Reagan and the Middle East* (Belmont, MA: Association of Arab-American University Graduates, 1983) and Ronald J. Young, *Missed Opportunities for Peace: U.S. Middle East Policy 1981-1986* (Philadelphia: American Friends Service Committee, 1987).
8. Peck, *Reagan Administration*, p. 20.
9. Stuart Eizenstat, "An American Perspective," in *Between Two Administrations: An American-Israeli Dialogue* (Washington, DC: Washington Institute for Near East Policy, 1989), p. 76.
10. Peck, *Reagan Administration*, p. 55.
11. Text and talking points of Reagan Plan in Aruri, Moughrabi, and Stork, *Reagan*, pp. 79-87. See also the analysis in Ann M. Lesch and Mark Tessler, *Israel, Egypt and the Palestinians: From Camp David to Intifada* (Bloomington: Indiana University Press, 1989), pp. 199-204.
12. Text in Aruri, Moughrabi, and Stork, *Reagan*, p. 93.
13. Peck, *Reagan Administration*, pp. 113-14.
14. *Ibid.*, p. 114.
15. *Ibid.*, p. 103.
16. Dov Zakheim, former deputy undersecretary of defense for planning and resources, "The Reagan Years: An American Net Assessment," in *Between Two Administrations*, p. 15.
17. Jonathan Marshal, "Israel, the Contras and the North Trial," *Middle East Report* (September-October 1989), 160: 34-35.
18. General Amnon Shahak, head of Israeli Defense Forces (IDF) military intelligence, "Challenges to Israeli Interests in the Middle East," in *Between Two Administrations*, p. 31.
19. See, for example, the concern expressed by former assistant secretary for Near Eastern affairs Harold H. Saunders, in "American Diplomacy and Arab-Israeli-Palestinian Peace Since 1967," in Samuel F. Wells, Jr. and Mark Bruzonsky, eds., *Security in the Middle East* (Boulder, CO: Westview Press, 1987), p. 303.
20. Young, *Missed Opportunities*, p. 142. For another analysis of that period, see Bruce R. Kuniholm, "The Palestinian Problem and U.S. Policy," in Wells and Bruzonsky, *Security*, pp. 184-214.
21. Young, *Missed Opportunities*, p. 146.
22. *Ibid.*, pp. 146-49 and 153.
23. Richard W. Murphy, "Review of U.S. Policy in the Middle East," *Current Policy*, no. 1097 (Washington, DC: Bureau of Public Affairs, U.S. Department of State, 27 July 1988), p. 4. For an analysis of the causes and demands of the intifada, see Ann M. Lesch, "Anatomy of an Uprising," in Peter F. Krogh and Mary C. McDavid, eds., *Palestinians*

under Occupation: Prospects for the Future (Washington, DC: Georgetown University Press, 1989), pp. 87-110.

24. *New York Times*, 10 March 1988: text of Shultz letter to Shamir; a similar letter was sent to King Hussein.
25. *Ibid.*, 12 March 1988.
26. Yoel Marcus in *Haaretz*, 7 April 1988, quoted in *Journal of Palestine Studies*, vol. (Summer 1988) 68:152. The text of the Memorandum of Agreement is provided in full in *Journal of Palestine Studies*, (Autumn 1988) 69:300-2.
27. Arrival statement in Cairo, 3 June 1988, *Documents and Statements: U.S. Policy in the Middle East* (Amman: American Center, June 1988), n.p.
28. *New York Times*, 11 March 1988.
29. *Al-Fajr*, 3 April 1988.
30. Richard W. Murphy, "An American Vision of Peace in the Middle East," *Current Policy*, no. 1067 (Washington, DC: Bureau of Public Affairs, U.S. Department of State, 18 April 1988), p. 1 (emphasis added).
31. *New York Times*, 28 February 1988; the views of West Bank residents are presented in *al-Fajr*, 28 February 1988.
32. *New York Times*, 12 March 1988.
33. *Al-Fajr*, 3 April 1988.
34. *Ibid.*
35. Arrival statement in Cairo, 3 June 1988, *Documents and Statements*.
36. Interview in Damascus, 6 June 1988, *ibid.*
37. Press conference in Cairo, 7 June 1988, *ibid.*
38. *Al-Ahram*, 21 July 1988.
39. Murphy, "Review of U.S. Policy," p. 3.
40. *Al-Fajr*, 11 September 1988.
41. *Al-Fajr*, 2 October 1988.
42. Murphy, "American Vision," p. 1.
43. Shultz interview on Israeli TV, 20 May 1988, *Documents and Statements*.
44. Press conference in Cairo, 7 June 1988, *ibid.*
45. Murphy, "American Vision," p. 1.
46. Shultz TV interview, *Documents and Statements*.
47. Arrival statement in Israel, 5 June 1988, *ibid.*
48. *Al-Fajr*, 2 October 1988.
49. *Al-Fajr*, 11 September 1988.
50. At a seminar in Israel in June 1988, Robert C. McFarlane, Reagan's national security adviser from October 1983 to December 1985, commented: "in recent months, Israel has resisted yielding any of the territory. While this is Israel's decision, there should be no misunderstanding that such a choice would have profound consequences for Israel's relationship with the United States....While the U.S. commitment to Israel's security is enduring, there is an expectation of reciprocal good faith on fundamental positions. Any departure from them weakens the trust upon which the relationship is founded." (*Between Two Administrations*, p. 5). Samuel Lewis, U.S. ambassador to Israel from 1977 to 1985, added that "television pictures of an increasingly callous occupation" contribute to a "significant erosion of the fabric of this alliance." *Ibid.*, p. 28.
51. Official UN English language text, Political Resolution adopted by the Palestine National Council, 15 November 1988. The statement on terrorism reads: "The Palestine National Council... once again states its rejection of terrorism in all its forms, including State terrorism, and affirms its commitment to its previous resolutions in that regard, to the resolution of the Arab Summit Conference at Algiers in 1988, to General Assembly

resolutions 42/159 of 1987 and 40/61 of 1985, and to the relevant passage in the Cairo Declaration issued on 7 November 1985" (p. 8).
52. *Ibid.*, pp. 6-8.
53. *New York Times*, 8 December 1988.
54. *Ibid.*, 15 December 1988.

9

THE BUSH ADMINISTRATION AND THE PALESTINIANS: A REASSESSMENT

Cheryl A. Rubenberg

INTRODUCTION AND BACKGROUND

THE COMMON PERCEPTION OF THE BUSH administration as being more "even-handed" than previous executives on the question of Palestine and supportive of a just and equitable settlement of the Israeli-Palestinian conflict has become a common cliche. However, this idea is not borne out by the evidence. In fact, the Bush administration maintained the historical consistency of U.S. policy toward the Palestinians including rejection of the Palestinian right to self-determination, to an independent state, and to leaders of their own choosing.[1] In addition, the view of the Bush administration as an American government at serious odds with Israel in the context of a declining U.S.-Israeli partnership is equally flawed. The reality of Washington-Tel Aviv relations during Bush's tenure evidenced few substantial differences from previous administrations although at times the rhetoric was less than friendly and occasionally overtly hostile. This chapter will examine in detail the Bush administration's policies toward the Palestinians including, of necessity, some aspects of the U.S.-Israeli relationship during the same period.

Evidence to support the contention that the Bush administration faithfully adhered to long-standing American policy on the Palestinians can be illustrated in numerous circumstances including its relentless campaign to discredit the PLO which involved strenuous efforts to block the Palestinian organization from membership in various international organizations; a cavalier disregard for massive Israeli human rights violations against Palestinians living in the Occupied Territories; a vision of "peace" between Israel and the Palestinians based on Israel's rejectionist view; invariable opposition to United Nations resolutions (in both the General Assembly and the Security Council where it made frequent use of its veto) in support of Israel against the Palestinians, even when virtually the entire international community backed the Palestinians; a successful U.S. offensive in the United Nations to repeal the 1975 resolution equating Zionism with racism;[2] U.S. diplomatic, economic, and logistical support for massive Soviet Jewish immigration to Israel, as well as Ethiopian Jewish immigration; deepening U.S.-Israeli strategic cooperation; and increasing amounts of financial assistance to the

Jewish state even though it pursued policies that contradicted stated U.S. principles.

As a consequence of the inauguration of low level talks between the U.S. and the PLO during the Reagan administration, there was an auspicious opportunity for the Bush administration to chart a new course and broker a genuinely just and lasting peace in the Israeli-Palestinian conflict.[3] President Bush and his secretary of state, James Baker, chose, however, to maintain traditional American rejectionism on the question of Palestine. In fact, on the important substantive issues, the diplomatic boundaries of this administration never exceeded the limits imposed by the hard-line, right wing Israeli government of Yitzhak Shamir.[4] *New York Times* correspondent Thomas Friedman commented on this phenomenon in September 1991 as Bush and Baker were pushing hard to organize the Madrid "peace" conference, noting: ". . .the Bush administration's whole approach to peacemaking is almost entirely based on terms dictated by Prime Minister Yitzhak Shamir . . ."[5] In addition, the U.S. terminated the U.S.-PLO dialogue in June 1990 and, when Bush left office in January 1993, prospects for a meaningful settlement were no closer than at any previous time, while the cycle of violence between Israelis and Palestinians was at an all-time high.[6]

THE UNITED STATES AND THE PLO

The Bush administration indicated quite clearly from the outset that it accorded little importance to the U.S.-PLO dialogue. In terms of priorities, Secretary of State Baker noted that "The existence of the dialogue should not lead anyone to misunderstand our overall policy or question our enduring support for the State of Israel."[7] Another senior U.S. official likewise explained the subordination of the U.S.-PLO dialogue to U.S.-Israeli joint interests stating that a "substantive U.S.-PLO dialogue, beyond the current meetings, is not likely to take place until [the] U.S. and Israel explore [the] possibilities of a new peace process, including an arrangement for Palestinian autonomy."[8]

The administration never appointed an official with a specific mandate for the talks with the PLO, choosing rather to conduct them through the U.S. ambassador to Tunisia, Robert Pelletreau. The U.S. insisted on meeting with low level PLO officials (with the exception of one secret and much criticized encounter between Pelletreau and Salah Khalaf, second in command in the PLO prior to his assassination on 14 January 1990). Substantively, the U.S. used its meetings with the PLO not so much to broker a just settlement between Israel and the Palestinians as to attempt to persuade the PLO to halt the *intifada* and to give up its claim as the sole, legitimate representative of the Palestinian people.[9] Finally, the administration terminated the dialogue eighteen months after George Bush assumed office.

In addition, and at the same time that a U.S. "peace" initiative was taking shape which included strong efforts to bypass the PLO in any negotiating process (see discussion below), the American government was engaged in vigorous action to block the PLO's bid for membership in various international organizations including the World Health Organization (WHO), the Food and Agricultural Organization (FAO), the International Labor Organization (ILO), the International Telecommunications Union (ITU), the UN Educational, Scientific, and Cultural Organization (UNESCO), and the International Atomic Energy Agency (IAEA). Also, the Bush administration exerted efforts to prevent the PLO from signing the four Geneva Conventions. In this regard, Assistant Secretary of State for International Organizational Affairs, John Bolton, told the Subcommittee on Near Eastern and South Asian Affairs of the Senate Foreign Relations Committee: ". . . Secretary Baker made it clear in his 1 May [1989] statement that: (1) we oppose the PLO's efforts as a matter of principle; and (2) the inevitable result of any enhancement of the PLO's status in an international organization would be the complete termination of United States funding for that organization. . . ."[10]

In November 1989, the U.S. issued a sharp warning to the Food and Agricultural Organization that the U.S. would pull out of the organization if it recognized the PLO.[11] Bowing to U.S. pressure not to grant the PLO full membership but nevertheless desirous of assisting the Palestinians in some way, the FAO passed a resolution that endorsed a PLO role in providing technical assistance to farmers in the Occupied Territories.[12] Slightly over a month later the U.S. announced that it was sharply cutting its funding of the FAO — from $61.4 million to $18 million.[13]

On 23 April 1990 the U.S. repeated previous threats to stop paying contributions to UN bodies that admitted the State of Palestine or upgraded the PLO's status[14] — a warning that came just two weeks before the opening of the World Health Organization's Assembly, to which the PLO had applied for full membership.[15] The WHO bowed to U.S. threats and shelved indefinitely the PLO's application.[16] However, it did pass a resolution increasing direct assistance to Palestinians in the Occupied Territories.[17]

The U.S. also exerted strong pressure against Switzerland in July-August 1989 to stop the PLO's effort to sign the Geneva Conventions.[18] The PLO was denied the right to sign. Moreover, in an October letter to Frederico Mayor, director-general of UNESCO, the U.S. voiced strong objections to the possible admission of the PLO to UNESCO.[19] The PLO application was denied.

Other efforts to delegitimize the PLO included U.S. government pressure on the Council on Foreign Relations to cancel PLO Executive Committee member Yasir Abed Rabbo's invitation to speak before the organization.[20] Moreover, on learning that members of the PLO delegation to the UN would take part in a speaking event, the State Department announced that doing so would be considered improper "political activity" and could lead to the revocation of the delegation's visas.[21] Also, the U.S. repeatedly denied requests from Yasir Arafat for visas to speak at the United Nations.

During this same period, the U.S. cast the first of a series of "nay" votes in the General Assembly and vetoes in the Security Council. It also exercised strong pressure on Security Council members to withdraw various resolutions, thus avoiding use of its veto but accomplishing the same purpose. For example, in the Bush administration's first week in office it utilized strong pressure on Council members to force the withdrawal of a resolution deemed too critical of Israel's human rights violations in the Occupied Territories.[22] On 17 February 1989 the U.S. vetoed a UN Security Council resolution deploring Israeli actions in the Occupied Territories while the other 14 Security Council members voted for the resolution.[23] On 20 April 1989 the U.S. voted against a UN General Assembly resolution condemning Israel's policies in the Occupied Territories and stressing the need for an international conference. The vote was 129 to 2 (the U.S. and Israel).[24] On 31 August the U.S. abstained on a Security Council resolution that deplored Israel's deportation of Palestinians and called on Israel to respect the Geneva Conventions in the Occupied Territories.[25] Although the U.S. abstention was considered by many a great victory for the Palestinians, it clearly did not deter subsequent Israeli deportations which reached their apogee in December 1992 when the "dovish" Israeli Labor government of Yitzhak Rabin deported 413 Palestinians *en masse* — the largest group ever to be expelled at one time. On 6 October 1989 the U.S. and Israel cast the only two negative votes (140 to 2) against another General Assembly resolution condemning Israel's policies against the Palestinians in the Occupied Territories.[26]

On 16 February 1990 the U.S. abstained on a resolution passed by the United Nations Commission on Human Rights affirming the applicability of the Fourth Geneva Convention to the Occupied Territories and calling on the Israeli government to cease settling Jewish immigrants in these areas.[27] Subsequently the U.S. "explained" its abstention by stating that while the Bush administration objected to new settlements in the Occupied Territories " . . . we have not determined that it is productive to address the legal issue. . . . we are concerned that the [resolution] . . .while upholding the principle of freedom of emigration, also refers to the 'Right of Return'[for Palestinians] . . . we also object . . . to the use of the phrase 'Palestinian and Arab territories' . . . we do not accept the implied prejudgment of their status. . . . "[28] On 16 May the U.S. voted against a World Health Organization resolution condemning Israel for conditions of health care in the Occupied Territories. The vote was 67-2 (the U.S. and Israel).[29]

In May 1990, in the context of massive Soviet Jewish immigration to Israel and extensive Israeli settlement building in the Occupied Territories, including East Jerusalem, to house these and other settlers, the U.S. successfully pressured the Security Council to drop a resolution terming Jewish settlement in the Occupied Territories and East Jerusalem illegal.[30] In the same month, in the context of escalating Israeli human rights violations and massive repression in the Occupied Territories, U.S. pressure in the Security Council killed a proposed resolution to send a UN observer force to the territories and subsequently killed a compromise resolution that would have sent a special UN envoy to investigate the violence—all done at Israel's behest and to the detriment of the Palestinians.[31] Then on 31 May the U.S. vetoed a Security Council resolution to send a special commission of inquiry to the Occupied Territories.[32] The Bush administration's defense of Israel in the face of virtually universal condemnation of Israel's massive human rights violations against Palestinians in the Occupied Territories is highly revealing and indicative of the depth and strength of the structural alliance between Israel and the U.S. — a connection that the U.S. clearly would not jeopardize to protect Palestinians.

THE U.S. "PEACE" INITIATIVE PRIOR TO THE GULF WAR AGAINST IRAQ

The first policy statement from the Bush administration on the Palestinian-Israeli conflict came on 10 February 1989 from Vice President Daniel Quayle who told a meeting of the B'nai B'rith Anti-Defamation League: "I am here to tell you that the Bush Administration shares your basic outlook. . . . The first principle of U.S. Middle East policy remains strong and unwavering support for Israel's security . . . [and] I want to assure you that . . . the Bush-Quayle years . . . will . . . continue to strengthen and deepen our strategic alliance with Israel."[33]

In early March Secretary of State Baker broadly outlined what would become the administration's "two-tier" approach to the Arab-Palestinian-Israeli conflict.[34] This strategy involved separating the Israeli-Arab state and the Israeli-Palestinian (excluding the PLO) negotiations. It was the antithesis of the concept of a comprehensive settlement that enjoyed an international consensus (with the exception of the U.S. and Israel) and which was formally expressed in the 1983 UN General Assembly Resolution 38/58.[35] The U.S., instead, aimed at separate, bilateral agreements with particular emphasis on the Israeli-Arab state track.

The initial Bush-Baker diplomatic effort centered around a proposal put forth by Israeli Prime Minister Shamir in April 1989 in response to an administration request for an Israeli initiative.[36] Indeed, the so-called "Shamir Plan" constituted the parameters of the Bush administration's Middle East peace efforts throughout the entire four years of this administration — even after the Gulf War which objectively altered a number of other significant factors in the region. Prior to the Gulf War, the U.S. focused on the aspect of Shamir's plan that concerned elections, strongly encouraging the Palestinians to participate in such elections, while after the war the U.S. emphasized the Israeli idea of bilateral negotiations and worked to promote talks between Israel and the Arab states and between Israel and a delegation of non-PLO Palestinians from the West Bank and Gaza. The basics of Shamir's proposals were first elaborated in April 1989 and included four points: (1) the Camp David accords were to constitute the basis of any peace process; (2) the Arab states were called on to end the economic boycott and the state of belligerency against Israel and to enter into direct, bilateral negotiations based on exchanging "peace for peace" (rather than land for peace); (3) the Arab "refugee" problem was to be resolved in a humanitarian manner through the contribution of financial and other resources from countries other than Israel; and (4) elections were to be held among the "Arabs of Judea,

Samaria, and Gaza" to produce a delegation which would participate in negotiations on an interim settlement in which a self-governing administration would be set up.[37] On 5 April 1989 Prime Minister Shamir met in Washington with Secretary of State Baker who called the Israeli proposals "very encouraging."[38] The following day President Bush met with Shamir and expressed endorsement of the election proposal stating in addition that "we do not support an independent Palestinian state . . ."[39] The administration encouraged the Israeli prime minister to develop a more elaborate and detailed election scheme.

On 14 May 1989 the Israeli government released a follow-up proposal to its original election plan. This embellished twenty point scheme was premised on the following conditions: No negotiations with the PLO; no Palestinian state; free elections in the Occupied Territories in order to produce a delegation which would negotiate "for a transitional period of self-rule," to be followed by negotiations between Israel and Jordan for a peace agreement.[40]

The Palestinians responded by spurning Shamir's proposals and reiterating their own position on peace in a letter signed by West Bank leaders and made public in Jerusalem on 27 April 1989. The Palestinians' main demands included negotiations with the PLO; recognition of "the Palestinians as a people with a right to a secure life and an independent state," and UN administration of the Occupied Territories during the period of transition.[41]

In spite of the Palestinian reaction to Shamir's proposals, however, the Bush administration's response was extremely positive and, as noted above, those proposals became the basis of U.S. policy in the next four years. The American stance was articulated by Secretary of State Baker in an address to the American Israel Public Affairs Committee [AIPAC] on 22 May 1989:

> . . . President Bush believes, and I believe, that on these issues, there can be only one policy and that is *continuity*. American support for Israel is the foundation of our approach to the Middle East . . .
>
> . . . [The U.S. believes in a peace] based on United Nations Security Council resolutions 242 and 338 . . . negotiations must allow the parties to deal directly with each other, face-to-face. A properly structured international conference could be useful *at an appropriate time* [emphasis in original]. . . . the United States does not support annexation or permanent Israeli control of the West Bank and Gaza, nor do we support the creation of an independent Palestinian state. . . .
>
> The Israeli proposal is, in our view, an important and positive start down the road toward constructing workable negotiations. . . .
>
> For the Palestinians, now is the time to speak with one voice for peace. Renounce the policy of phases in all languages, not just those addressed to the West. Practice constructive diplomacy, not attempts to distort international organizations, such as the World Health Organization. Amend the covenant. Translate the dialogue of violence in the intifadah into a dialogue of politics and diplomacy. Violence will not work. Reach out to Israelis and convince them of your peaceful intentions. You have the most to gain from doing so,

and no one else can or *will* do it for you. Finally, understand that no one is going to "deliver" Israel for you. . . . [42]

One month later President Bush sent Prime Minister Shamir a letter endorsing Secretary Baker's speech.[43]

As regards Mr. Baker's apparent middle ground between opposition to Israeli annexation and an independent Palestinian state, analyst Walid Khalidi aptly remarked: "There is only a spurious symmetry in denying *both* Israeli and Palestinian sovereignty in the Occupied Territories. Denial of Palestinian sovereignty is denial of the minimal turf of survival. It is denial of the territorial imperative that operates even in the animal kingdom. Denial of Israeli sovereignty is denial of triumphalist maximalism. It is denial of the fruits of conquest."[44] Moreover, Mr. Baker's admonitions to the Palestinians were patronizing and wholly negative. The U.S. position was not a constructive stance toward a just and lasting peace.

In what subsequently became known as the "point and assumption game," Egypt put forth in July 1989 a ten point proposal in response to Israel's four point and twenty point plans.[45] This was followed by a five point proposal offered by the U.S. to Israel and Egypt.[46] The five points became known as the "Baker Plan" and contained the following "understandings": That Israeli and Palestinian delegations will conduct a dialogue in Cairo; that Egypt will consult with all parties, i.e. Palestinians, Israelis and the U.S.; that Israeli participation would be contingent on acceptance of the proposed Palestinian participants; and

> that the Government of Israel will come to the dialogue on the basis of the Israeli Government's May 14 initiative. The United States further understands that the Palestinians will come to the dialogue prepared to discuss elections and the negotiating process in accordance with Israel's initiative. The U.S. understands, therefore, that Palestinians would be free to raise issues that relate to their opinions on how to make elections and the negotiating process succeed. . . . [47]

Clearly, the American plan was tailored to suit Israel's interests. Subsequently, the PLO, Egypt and Israel each proffered a set of "assumptions" regarding Baker's five points.[48] However, despite the apparent diplomatic flurry, Israel's fundamental dictums regarding "peace" — i.e., no negotiations with the PLO, no Palestinian state, no right of return for Palestinians, no discussion of Jerusalem, and "elections" to select individuals to participate in negotiations on autonomy — remained the bottom line of Israel's — and the United States' — peace plan.

Moreover, by the Spring of 1990 it became apparent that Israel was refusing to implement its own election proposal — a stance that resulted in growing frustration and irritation on the part of President Bush toward Prime Minister Shamir. Then, a 1 March statement by Secretary of State Baker tying U.S. approval of an Israeli request for $400 million in loan guarantees to help settle Soviet Jewish immigrants to an Israeli halt in construction of settlements in the Occupied Territories, led to a hardening of the position of the Shamir government, and consequently increasing "tensions" in the U.S.-Israeli relationship. Most important, movement toward an Israeli-Palestinian accord came to a virtual halt while at the same time Israel engaged in a frenzy of new settlement construction.

The intensity of Israeli settlement building was connected to two interrelated factors: (1) an ideological imperative that drove the Jewish State to create ever more "facts on the ground" in order to establish its permanent control over what it defined as *Eretz Israel* (a land mass that included the West Bank, the Gaza strip, and East Jerusalem as well as Israel within the "green line") and (2) the need to absorb and settle as quickly as possible the massive numbers of Soviet Jewish immigrants who were weekly flooding Israel.[49]

Immigration (together with land acquisition) is one of the pillars of Zionist objectives and Soviet Jews have long been considered a most valuable immigrant pool. In the context of the disintegration of the Soviet Union and Moscow's desire to gain favor with the U.S. in order to secure aid, loans, credit, trade and investment, the Soviet Union acceded to American pressure on behalf of Israel and permitted an unprecedented number of Jews to leave. In 1989, 71,200 Jews left the Soviet Union; in 1990, 187,000 emigrated; and between 1 January and 31 July 1991, 113,000 more departed.[50] The vast majority of these went to Israel and it was estimated that within the following five years as many as one million more would arrive.[51]

These huge numbers of immigrants inextricably altered the nature of the Palestine-Israel conflict — most significantly by the construction of new settlements to house them, a process which involved the use of Palestinian land and water resources in the West Bank, East Jerusalem, and the Gaza Strip as well as in Israel proper. By June 1991 Israeli confiscation of Palestinian land was estimated at 70 per cent of the West Bank and 50 per cent of the Gaza Strip. Construction of settlements and infrastructure in these areas were significantly accelerated in 1990-91 with expenditures in that fiscal year (ended 1 April 1991) at $500 million.[52] Israel's intention to transform Arab East Jerusalem into a Jewish enclave was evidenced in its plan to settle 195,000 Jews there by the end of 1991, a situation that marginalized the Palestinian population of approximately 150,000 and was designed to effectively remove the issue of East Jerusalem from the "peace" agenda.[53]

In addition, the immigration of Soviet Jews deeply affected Palestinian economic life. As part of its effort to transform the West Bank and Gaza into the Jewish State, Israel has pursued deliberate policies since 1967 to keep the economies of these areas underdeveloped and to tie them to its own economy in structural relations of dependence and subordination that have included severe restrictions on economic development and the consequent employment of 40 per cent of the West Bank's labor force and 50-60 per cent of Gaza's inside Israel.[54] New immigrants from the Soviet Union replaced many Palestinians from the territories who worked in Israel contributing significantly to the pauperization of Palestinians — a process that was greatly accelerated after the Gulf War, and was institutionalized in the Spring of 1993 with the permanent sealing of the territories by the Labor government of Prime Minister Yitzhak Rabin.

Israel's massive settlement drive in the Occupied Territories was the most obvious example of Israel's real intentions regarding the Palestinians. Israeli analyst Amiram Goldbloom wrote in this regard that the new settlements, many of which were pointedly set up during Secretary Baker's visits to the Middle East in his efforts to move the peace process forward, had enormous political significance in that "they are intended to prove to the Palestinians, and . . . to the Arab world, that the Israeli government thumbs its nose at the U.S. efforts to advance peace in the region . . . . The government is now mobilized to torpedo any chance for peace."[55] Goldbloom also noted that while the Israeli government continually justifies its settlement of the West Bank, East Jerusalem, and Gaza by saying that it is unacceptable that any area should be "Judenrein," in fact the real objective is to make all of *Eretz Israel* "Arabenrein."[56] Another Israeli analyst, Danny Rubinstein, expanded on Goldbloom's appraisal writing that the intention of the Israeli government "is clearly visible on the ground — to push the Palestinians into a corner from which there is no exit, thus compelling them, sooner or later, to pick up and leave."[57]

Palestinian scholar Walid Khalidi has written pointedly of the meaning of settlements to Palestinians:

> Continued settlement activity is the single most lethal threat to the prospects of Israeli-Palestinian coexistence . . . . Thus the envisaged U.S. financial support for the mass emigration of Soviet Jews to Israel combined with the non-reaffirmation of the illegality of the settlements raises the question of the seriousness of American purpose in sponsoring the peace process and constitutes a potential death blow of American provenance to the process itself.[58]

A more direct statement came from PLO spokesman, Bassam Abu Sharif, who told reporters in Tunis that Israel's resettlement of Soviet Jews in the Occupied Territories is "an act of war against the Palestinian people [and that] such an action can only beget similar reactions — that is, acts of war."[59]

Nevertheless, the U.S. persisted with its "non-reaffirmation" of the illegality of settlements. For example, on 16 February 1990, when the UN Human Rights Committee endorsed a resolution calling on Israel not to settle Soviet Jews in the Occupied Territories, the U.S. abstained.[60] Indeed, the following day Jordan's King Hussein expressed concern that the U.S. abstention indicated a reduction in Washington's opposition to Israeli settlements.[61]

Sensing that its credibility with the Arab states as an impartial broker was increasingly coming into question, the Bush administration began to exert some mild pressure on Israel regarding the settlement of Soviet immigrants in the Occupied Territories. As noted above, Secretary Baker announced on 1 March 1990 that the American government would back $400 million in loan guarantees for the housing of Soviet Jews in Israel only if Israel stopped settlement building in the Occupied Territories.[62] Also, President Bush made several statements to the effect that the settlements were a serious, even the main, obstacle to peace. In response, Israeli Prime Minister Shamir took a defiant and resolute stand, in one instance stating publicly: "There are no settlements in Jerusalem. It is part of Israel and it will never be divided again."[63] And further, that new Jewish neighborhoods in East Jerusalem would be expanded with "as many Soviet Jewish immigrants as possible."[64] Three days later Israeli Housing Minister David Levy announced construction of 2,000 new West Bank apartments to house Jewish immigrants.[65]

Thus began the cycle of increasing tensions between Washington and Tel Aviv even though the U.S. repeatedly sought to placate its tiny belligerent ally. For example, in mid-March 1990 the U.S. backtracked from its already weak position on both settlements and Jerusalem when Secretary Baker wrote a letter on Jerusalem to one of Israel's ardent supporters in Congress, Rep. Mel Levine (D, CA), stating that "Clearly, Jews and others can live where they want, East or West, and the city must remain undivided."[66] Israel, however, continued its defiance of the U.S., beginning in early April construction of five new settlements, and later in the month, of several more. On 13 June Israeli Prime Minister Shamir publicly blamed the U.S. for stirring up "Arab hostility" in the territories; and at the same time, laid down new, more restrictive conditions for peace talks, saying that Israel would not negotiate with any Palestinian who opposed limited autonomy for the Occupied Territories and stipulating that there could be no role in the talks for any Palestinian from East Jerusalem.[67] Another Israeli official said that Baker's formula for talks was "no longer relevant" while Foreign Minister David Levy averred that Baker's plan had "distorted" the Israeli peace initiative and called on the U.S. to "get back to basics" with Israel."[68] Secretary Baker responded by expressing impatience with the peace process and suggesting that if positive peace moves from the Middle East actors were not forthcoming, the U.S. might disengage. It was in this context that Baker made his famous comment to Israel: "When you're serious about peace, call us," and gave the White House telephone number.[69]

However, to interpret this U.S.-Israeli tiff (or any other) as indicating a more favorable U.S. attitude toward Palestinian rights is a serious misjudgment. In fact, in the very same week (on 20 June), the U.S. suspended the dialogue with the PLO, marking the end of 18 fruitless months of talks. The ostensible reason for the termination was the PLO's failure to condemn a 30 May attempted raid on Israel by the Palestine Liberation Front (PLF), and its subsequent refusal to submit to the U.S. demand to expel Abul Abbas, leader of the PLF, from the PLO's Executive Committee. The real reason was U.S. capitulation to relentless Israeli pressure on the Bush administration to discontinue the dialogue.

Indeed, PLO officials went to considerable lengths to find a compromise formula that would satisfy the U.S. demand for Abul Abbas's expulsion. Thus, on 23 June, the PLO announced that Abul Abbas was prepared to accept disciplinary action from the PLO Executive Committee and, moreover, that he had stated that Chairman Arafat could "take any measure he sees as necessary to protect the national achievements of our people." Abul Abbas also stated that he had given Arafat a file on the attack to show that the raid had been aimed at military targets.[70] In addition, there was a scramble by "moderates" in the PLO to devise compromise formulas in further attempts to restore the dialogue.[71] The Bush administration, however, made no response to the Palestinian entreaties.

On the other hand, as has been discussed above, the U.S. was equally persistent in shielding Israel from any condemnation by the United Nations for the continuous terrorism it practiced against the Palestinians living in the Occupied Territories (as well as those Palestinians subjected to its punishing military attacks in Lebanon). For example, it was in this same period that efforts in the Security Council to either send an observer force to the Occupied Territories to protect Palestinians or to dispatch a special envoy to investigate Israeli practices against them, failed as a consequence of U.S. pressure in response to Israeli opposition, after which the U.S. used its veto against a resolution to send a special commission of inquiry to the Occupied Territories.

Throughout July 1990 there were continuous Palestinian efforts to restart the talks with the United States. In an attempt to appear responsive to the PLO (in its effort not to antagonize the entire Arab world), the Bush administration, working through Egypt, informed the PLO that the U.S. would be willing to resume the dialogue if the PLO accepted a U.S. demand to discipline Abul Abbas.[72] Subsequently, Chairman Arafat indicated that the PLO was willing to discipline Abul Abbas, but only after the U.S. agreed to resume the talks as well as to expand them. Speaking for Arafat, Yasir Abed Rabbo stated: "We want a real dialogue, not a mailbox to send questions and wait for answers."[73] The U.S. replied that the PLO must discipline Abul Abbas before it would restart talks and that the dialogue would not be expanded to suit the Palestine Liberation Organization. Arafat rejected these humiliating demands and accused the U.S. of "supporting Israel without limit."[74]

PLO efforts to reestablish a dialogue with the U.S. were brought to a halt with the 2 August 1990 Iraqi invasion of Kuwait followed by its 8 August annexation. Prior to these Iraqi moves, Baghdad had been supportive of the PLO — a much appreciated strategic alliance given the long-standing hostility of Syria toward Arafat and Damascus' desire to control PLO decision making; the 1988 Jordanian "disengagement" from Palestinian politics; and Egypt's questionable motives with regard to Palestinian interests. Baghdad frequently hosted meetings of the PLO Executive Committee and it was the only Arab state to make even a rhetorical threat against Israel — a situation that greatly appealed to the Palestinian masses.[75] On 5 and 9 August Yasir Arafat met publicly with Saddam Hussein in Baghdad, meetings that were widely misinterpreted as indicative of PLO support for Iraqi aggression against Kuwait. The PLO position on the Gulf situation was clearly articulated in a statement from the organization:

> The Palestinian stand was based on the need to reach an Arab solution and reject foreign intervention . . . *It did not seek a solution in favor of one party at the expense of another, but rather a solution that safeguards the security*

and safety of Iraq, Kuwait, Saudi Arabia, the Gulf and the entire Arab region. . . .[76] [emphasis added]

Nevertheless, following U.S. and Israeli government lines, the media significantly distorted the PLO's position. For example, the *Los Angeles Times* wrote that the PLO "may have written themselves out of the diplomatic script" by supporting Iraq, a stance that will make it nearly impossible for resumption of the U.S.-PLO dialogue.[77] Revealingly, the *Washington Post* reported that Israel saw the Gulf crisis as a "windfall" in that Arafat was pushed further away from a rapprochement with the U.S.[78] And, indeed, the U.S. chose to interpret the PLO position in that light and to use the false allegations to justify its traditional negation of the PLO.[79]

THE U.S., ISRAEL, AND THE PALESTINIANS DURING THE GULF WAR

From August 1990 through January 1991, American interests in the Middle East were primarily directed at cobbling together, then holding together, a coalition of Arab states in support of American objectives vis-a-vis Iraq. This necessitated maintaining a certain apparent distance from Israel and satisfying some minimal — mainly symbolic — Arab demands regarding the Palestinians. Thus, after Israeli border police fired without provocation into a group of Palestinian worshipers at al-Aqsa Mosque on the Haram al-Sharif in Jerusalem on 8 October, killing seventeen and wounding more than one hundred individuals,[80] the U.S. supported UN Security Council Resolution 672 which "Condemn[ed] especially the acts of violence committed by the Israeli security forces" . . . and endorsed "the decision of the Secretary-General to send a mission to the region."[81] Israel condemned the resolution and refused to receive a UN mission which prompted a second resolution, 673, passed on 24 October " . . . Deplor[ing] the refusal of the Israeli government to receive the mission . . .[and] Urg[ing] the Israeli government to . . . comply fully with resolution 672."[82]

While Israel was enraged that the U.S. did not veto these resolutions, the U.S. stance did not reflect a new policy concerning the massive human rights violations Israel was perpetrating against the Palestinians. In fact, the U.S. had worked very hard at the Security Council to prevent the passage of a much stronger resolution sponsored by the non-aligned countries and supported by a majority of the Council members, including France and Britain. The U.S. also worked hard and successfully to prevent the inclusion of a clause calling for the UN team to propose ways of protecting the Palestinians living in the Occupied Territories.[83] Moreover, the U.S. effectively delayed the vote on Resolution 673 in order to give Israel time to comply with the stipulations in Resolution 672.

In an additional attempt to maintain some ostensible distance from Israel in the interest of holding the Arab coalition together, the U.S. further delayed approval of Israel's request for $400 million in loan guarantees for housing for Soviet immigrants. Nevertheless, Israel forged ahead with new construction in the Occupied Territories enraging the Palestinians and making the U.S. relationship with its Arab partners quite embarrassing.[84] Also aggravating the Bush administration and complicating U.S. relations with its Arab state allies, Prime Minister Shamir publicly attacked two pillars of U.S. policy — the sale of arms to the Arab states and efforts to arrange Israeli-Palestinian peace talks.[85] He, moreover, declared that it was necessary for the Jewish State to keep "the land of Israel from the sea to the Jordan for the generations to come . . ."[86] Still, the U.S. sought to protect Israel, successfully postponing meetings of the Security Council on 7 and 10 December that were scheduled to discuss an international conference for solving the Palestinian-Israeli conflict.

In another attempt to maintain its Arab coalition, the U.S. declined to veto Security Council Resolution 681 deploring Israel's deportation of four Palestinians. However, the resolution was debated for over a month and went through several drafts in which it was successively diluted to avoid the American veto. Following its passage, Israel declared that "the fate of this resolution will be like the fate of other resolutions which are now in the UN archives" (which it was, and with typical U.S. acquiescence), while the PLO called it "insufficient and disproportionate compared to the volume of aggressions committed by Israel."[87]

THE U.S. PEACE INITIATIVE AFTER THE GULF WAR

In the aftermath of the Gulf War and the strong stand the U.S. took against Iraq's occupation of Kuwait, some analysts have argued that the credibility of the U.S. as the leader of the "new world order" would mandate that it act consistently and in a principled manner by taking an equally strong position in opposition to Israel's occupation of the West Bank, Gaza, and East Jerusalem, and by working to bring about a just solution to the Palestinian issue. This, however, constituted a serious misunderstanding of the nature and purpose of American foreign policy. So consistent has the U.S. been in its antipathy to basic Palestinian interests that to have expected a change at this time was unrealistic. Moreover, the consistency of U.S. policy toward the Palestinians is congruent with long-standing U.S. "national interests" in the Middle East as they have been traditionally defined by the ruling elite as well as with the typical means utilized to secure those interests, which include opposition to all nationalist movements, firm support for Israel's interests (in the context of the belief that Israel serves as an important "strategic asset" to U.S. regional objectives), and a strong preference for "stability" or the status quo.[88] In addition, as a consequence of the dissolution of the Soviet Union and its Eastern European alliances, the U.S. stood alone as a hegemonic power in a unipolar world which meant that it had much greater leverage over regional political issues and could impose its geopolitical will with far greater ease than previously. Thus Israel's power in the region (already preeminent) was strengthened, the Arab states fell in line with U.S. wishes, and the Palestinians were left without any significant support. Indeed, President Bush remarked — without so much as a murmur from his audience — in an interview with journalists from Morocco, Egypt, Saudi Arabia, and Kuwait that the PLO had "lost credibility" as a consequence of its siding with Iraq, and he dismissed the possibility of a resumption of the U.S.-PLO dialogue.[89]

During the Spring and Summer of 1991, following the end of the Gulf War, the U.S. undertook an intensive venture to catalyze an Arab-Palestinian-Israeli peace process. Between March and July 1991 Secretary of State Baker made five trips to the Middle East in a kind of shuttle politics reminiscent of Henry Kissinger's efforts in the post-1973 war period. Yet, in spite of the flurry of "American" diplomacy, the 1989 Shamir Plan remained the basis of Baker's efforts.[90]

The Bush administration repeatedly reiterated U.S. opposition to an independent Palestinian state in the West Bank and Gaza as well as its opposition to recognition of the PLO or to the organization's inclusion in the negotiating process. This stance was manifested in the strong pressure exerted by Secretary of State Baker on West Bank and Gaza residents to find a group of non-PLO Palestinians to join a Jordanian delegation to negotiate with Israel about some form of "autonomy" for the Palestinians.[91] In reality, United States' objectives in advancing a peace strategy were narrowly conceived and focused more on process than substance. The U.S. sought to bring about an end to the Arab states' economic boycott of Israel, to terminate the Palestinian intifada, to get the various parties (the Arab states, Israel, and a group of non-PLO Palestinians) to the negotiating table, and to cement a stable pro-American status quo in the region.[92] Indeed, Washington admitted openly that it had "no plan" to resolve the differences between Israel and the Palestinians when a conference was convened.[93]

The Palestinian position on the evolving peace process was presented by West Bank and Gazan leaders, led by Faisal Husseini and approved by the PLO leadership in Tunis, to Secretary of State Baker in Jerusalem on 12 March 1991 during Baker's first post-war trip to the region. In it the Palestinians laid out the principles under which they were willing to participate in a peace process including recognition of the PLO as their sole, legitimate representative; the goal of an independent Palestinian state alongside Israel in the West Bank, Gaza, and East Jerusalem; existing UN resolutions as the basis of a peace process; and an international conference as the mechanism for advancing the peace process.[94] Subsequently Palestinians from the territories, with the approval of the PLO in Tunis, submitted to Secretary Baker a series of memoranda elaborating on the meaning and modalities of these basic points as well as presenting a series of written questions designed to ascertain U.S. intentions. The U.S. avoided any concrete promises to the Palestinians while at the same time accepting Israel's demands concerning the peace process that included: no negotiations with the PLO, a veto over the composition of the Palestinian delegation which in any case could contain no Palestinians from East Jerusalem or from the diaspora, no independent Palestinian state, and no right of return for Palestinians. Nevertheless, the U.S. managed to induce the Palestinians to take part in the evolving peace process.

In addition to the fundamental and far-reaching concessions that the PLO had made at the November 1988, 19th Palestine National Council, the Palestinians continued to make attempts to participate in the peace process and/or to affect it substantively — all to no avail. For example, Bassam Abu Sharif, a close advisor to Arafat, gave a television interview in which he offered a number of concessions and, most importantly, suggested that the borders of the Palestinian state could be negotiated.[95] This surprising offer was ignored by the U.S. and Israel. Also, in an interview with *Le Figaro,* Arafat proposed to participate in direct negotiations with Israel — an offer that was quickly rejected by U.S. and Israeli officials.[96] Several days later, in an interview with the *Toronto Star,* Arafat tendered a detailed peace plan for solving the Israeli-Palestinian conflict and said that the PLO would accept a UN buffer zone on the Palestinian side of the border between Israel and the future Palestinian state.[97] This too was disregarded. Instead, the U.S. forged ahead with a peace plan that involved two basic elements: (1) a truncated international conference, and (2) Shamir's 1989 plan for elections in the Occupied Territories and bilateral talks with the Arab states.

The U.S. proposal for an international conference was designed to meet Israel's substantive needs while providing the Arab states with some figurative cover that would allow them to attend. In the American plan, the very antithesis of UN Resolution 38/58 on an international conference, the United Nations was to be represented by an "observer" who would have no functional role in the talks, the conference would only be reconvened provided both sides were agreeable, and then only to hear reports of progress but not to interfere in the talks in any way. What this meant in effect was that: (a) the conference would be chaired by the U.S., along with a weakened Soviet Union, and not by the United Nations; (b) the UN and the Europeans would have only token observer roles; (c) the conference would be largely symbolic without any binding power and with follow-up meetings indeterminate; (d) relevant UN resolutions would serve merely as a "basis for talks" rather than being binding; (e) the conference would set the stage for separate, bilateral talks between Israel and individual Arab states; and (f) the Palestinians would achieve none of their fundamental objectives.[98]

Despite its favorable features for Israel, the Jewish State rejected the American proposal.[99] Israel insisted that the conference be simply a one-day ceremonial opening to direct talks between Israel and its Arab state neighbors. Israel also made it clear that the Jewish State would not exchange territory for peace — thus negating Resolutions 242 and 338 (the territories for peace formula),[100] and again demanded a veto over the composition of a Palestinian delegation which it insisted could only participate as part of a Jordanian delegation and could contain no Palestinians from East Jerusalem, those living in the diaspora, or affiliated with the PLO.

On the other hand, in mid-July 1991 Syria accepted the U.S. proposal. After Syria's agreement to participate in the U.S. proposed conference, Israel came under considerable pressure to accept. Thus, in early August Israel gave a conditional "yes" to attend such a conference;[101] however, its agreement came with several stipulations including the repeated demand that Israel have a veto over the composition of the Palestinian delegation and that Israeli sovereignty over the West Bank, East Jerusalem, and Gaza remain absolute. Israel then reinforced its position through public declarations and the rapid construction of new settlements.[102]

With the Syrian and Israeli agreement to attend a peace conference, the stage was set, since Egypt and Jordan had previously signalled their willingness. Also, once Syria accepted, Lebanon, under a pro-Syrian government, fell into line too. Thus pressure on the Palestinians to participate became intense, and by the end of August they had reduced their demands for joining the conference to the following:

> Assurance that the aim of the conference be to implement Resolutions 242 and 338, be aimed at ending the occupation, and at Israel's withdrawing from all Arab lands occupied in 1967, including Arab East Jerusalem.
>
> Recognition of Palestinians' political rights.
>
> Palestinian participation on the basis of a PLO decision without outside intervention.
>
> Discussion of the status of East Jerusalem at each stage of the negotiations with the residents of East Jerusalem taking part in the negotiations at each stage.
>
> Immediate cessation to settlement activities on occupied lands, especially in Jerusalem.[103]

In response, the U.S. sent the Palestinian leaders in the Occupied Territories a "letter of assurance" in mid-October outlining basic U.S. positions on the issues of concern to the Palestinians—what became known as the "terms of reference" for the conference.[104]

The terms of reference, however, did not augur well for the Palestinians. Although the settlement to be attained was to be based on Resolutions 242 and 338, the U.S. made no mention of the "land for peace" principle, conceding instead the parties' right to differing interpretations of the resolutions, especially on the issue of Israeli withdrawal from the West Bank, Gaza, and East Jerusalem.[105] Also, as noted above, the United Nations would have a minor (if any) role in the process; and although the aim of the negotiations was supposed to be a comprehensive Arab-Israeli settlement, there was to be no binding link between the different fronts, which meant that Israel could play one front against the other. The absence of a link between the negotiating fronts was complicated by the specific timetable set for the Palestinian-Israeli negotiations. The Palestinians had to negotiate in two separate stages—the first to reach agreement on "interim self-government arrangements" in the Occupied Territories, and the second to reach a final settlement based on Resolution 242 that would begin only in the third year of the interim period. Moreover, the extent of the Palestinian self-government was not specified and was to be agreed upon during the negotiations. There was no reference to Palestinian self-determination or statehood. Also, there would be no autonomous Palestinian delegation facing the autonomous Israeli delegation. Rather, the Palestinians would be part of a joint Jordanian-Palestinian team, none of whom could come from East Jerusalem, the diaspora, or be affiliated with the PLO.[106] In addition, the U.S. warned the Palestinians that they would be held responsible if they did not join or, later, if they pulled out of the peace process. Moreover, the U.S. also gave no indication that it was willing to put pressure on Israel to adhere to UN resolutions or to stop other practices anathema to the Palestinians.[107]

The "peace" conference opened in Madrid, Spain on 30 October 1991 with a group of non-PLO Palestinians (who lived neither in East Jerusalem nor the diaspora and who were "approved" by Israel) participating in a joint Jordanian-Palestinian delegation. Each delegation gave an address and the conference recessed indefinitely on 1 November. The first round of bi-lateral talks commenced for one day in Madrid on 3 November, and thereafter successive rounds were held in Washington D.C. By November 1992 seven sessions of the peace conference had been held; Mr. Shamir had been replaced by the Labor Party and a new prime minister, Yitzhak Rabin; George Bush had been defeated by William Clinton who would assume office in January 1993; and the Palestinians were no closer to the achievement of any of their fundamental objectives than they had ever been. Moreover, when there were contentious issues during the course of the talks, the Palestinians were held responsible.

For example, after the fourth round of talks (24 February through 4 March 1992) during which the Palestinians presented a detailed plan for the interim period arrangements leading to the establishment of an independent state, the Bush administration severely chastised them in public, blaming them for stalling the peace process, violating the rules of the game, and seeking publicity. The public display of American anger at the Palestinians was a not-so-subtle form of pressure to force the delegation to toe the line set by the U.S., disengage itself from the PLO, and not to pull out from the talks. All of this placed the Palestinians under even more pressure, including growing opposition among the masses in the Occupied Territories and growing dissention within the PLO over the negotiating strategy or lack thereof. In practice, the Palestinians had already dropped an important tactic from their strategy by agreeing to pursue the negotiations on the interim period without first securing a halt to Israeli settlement construction. The demand for more concessions and the public humiliation from the Bush administration only made the Palestinian situation worse.[108]

THE U.S.-ISRAELI STRATEGIC ALLIANCE

The full picture of the extent of the bias of the Bush administration against the Palestinians can only be comprehended by some analysis of the depth and intimacy of the relationship between the U.S. and Israel during this period. Though the media made much of the seemingly strained relations between

Washington and Tel Aviv, in fact the problem was much more personal than political. President Bush was not fond of Israeli Prime Minister Yitzhak Shamir with his openly defiant attitude (of "official" U.S. policy), and he made little secret of his dislike of the Israeli leader. Also, the Bush administration was relatively open about its wish to see a Labor Party victory in the June 1992 elections in Israel. But that the so-called "rift" between the two countries was not serious was evident in numerous circumstances.

For example, some analysts had considered the Bush administration's September 1991 decision to defer Israel's request for $10 billion (up from the original $400 million) in loan guarantees for Soviet Jewish housing as a sign that there were deep differences between the U.S. and Israel and that the administration was going to push Israel to withdraw from the territories and return them to Arab control. But as the *New York Times* noted ". . . nobody in Washington is challenging Israel's need for the loan guarantees."[109] In fact, the delay in approval of the loan guarantees was designed with two purposes in mind: (1) to influence domestic Israeli politics to bring about a Labor victory, and (2) to ensure that the Arabs came to the conference table by making the U.S. appear as an impartial mediator. Indeed, no one in the American government was considering forcing Israel to return to the Palestinians the 70 per cent of West Bank land and 50 per cent of Gazan land it had confiscated, or to turn over to Palestinians the more than 200 settlement locales illegally constructed by Israel, or to ask the 225,000 Jewish settlers to leave the West Bank, Gaza, and East Jerusalem. Nor was the U.S. even demanding that Israel relinquish the 75 per cent of West Bank water that it diverts to Israel.[110] In reality, the U.S. was interested in no more than supporting Israel's old "autonomy" concept for the Palestinians.[111]

The issue of the loan guarantees was resolved in Israel's favor on 11 August 1992 with President Bush's announcement that the U.S. was now prepared to provide the $10 billion in loan guarantees.[112] This was done, even though Mr. Rabin never promised to cease settlement construction; instead, he made a highly ambiguous distinction between "security" and "political" settlements, and said only that additional political settlements would not be built. Nevertheless, the Bush administration did not again raise the issue of settlements as an obstacle to peace.

It is also notable that throughout the "difficult" years of the Bush-Shamir relationship, Israel remained an important "strategic asset" to American Middle East objectives — even in an era in which the Arab states were virtually flocking to the American fold! In fact, the U.S. strengthened its military relationship with Israel, provided it additional weapons, and made no effort to require the Jewish State to dismantle its massive stock of chemical, biological, and nuclear weapons — all despite much talk about regional "arms control."[113]

The continued strength of the U.S.-Israeli relationship was additionally reflected in the amount of economic assistance that flowed to Israel during the Bush administration. For example, for FY 1991, total U.S. aid to Israel was $5.147 billion. And every year thereafter the amount of economic aid from the

Bush administration to Israel increased.[114] Another important indicator of the closeness of the U.S.-Israeli relationship during this period was the extensive and eventually (16 December 1991) successful effort made by the Bush administration to repeal the 1975 United Nations General Assembly resolution equating Zionism with racism.

The intimacy of the U.S.-Israeli relationship was further evidenced in the number and position of high officials in the Bush administration with strong pro-Israeli sentiment. Thus, the American group at the Madrid conference was made up of the top Middle East advisors who had surrounded the administration since its inception. While, publicly, only one person was identified as having pro-Israeli sentiment, three others came to the Bush administration from the Washington Institute for Near East Policy, a pro-Israeli think tank founded in 1985 by Martin Indyk, a former deputy director of research for the American Israel Public Affairs Committee — the registered pro-Israel lobby.[115]

CONCLUSION

This chapter has clearly demonstrated that the Bush administration maintained the historic U.S. hostility to fundamental Palestinian rights and interests. In spite of a relatively activist diplomacy in pursuit of a regional peace, especially after the Gulf War, the basic principles of American policy toward the Palestinians remained intact—i.e., no right of self-determination, no independent state, no right to leaders of their own choosing, and no right of return. Conversely, despite apparently strained relations between the U.S. and Israel throughout the Bush administration (at least until the election of the Labor Party and Yitzhak Rabin in June 1992), the important underpinnings of the relationship remained unchanged and were even intensified — e.g., the acceptance of Israel as a strategic asset or surrogate power, enormous quantities of financial assistance, deep military and intelligence cooperation, pro-Israeli American individuals determining U.S. foreign policy on the Middle East, etc. The American position was pointedly articulated by Secretary Baker when he addressed the AIPAC conference on 22 May 1989 and admonished the Palestinians to "understand that no one is going to 'deliver' Israel for you."[116]

NOTES

1. See Cheryl A. Rubenberg, "U.S. Policy Toward the Palestinians: A Twenty Year Assessment," *Arab Studies Quarterly*, (Winter 1988), 10(1):1-43 and Cheryl A. Rubenberg, "The U.S.-PLO Dialogue: Continuity or Change in American Policy." *Arab Studies Quarterly*, Vol. 11, no. 4 (Fall 1989) pp. 1-58.

2. For the official U.S. position, see "Statement of U.S. Policy on the Repeal of the UN 'Zionism is Racism' Resolution by the Assistant Secretary of State for International Organizational Affairs, Washington D.C., 30 March 1990," reprinted in *Journal of Palestine Studies*, (Summer 1990), 19(4):183-188.

3. See for example the analysis by Dan Kurtzer, Deputy Assistant Secretary of State for Middle East Negotiations, "The Bush Aministration," *Policy Forum Report* (a publication of the pro-Israeli think tank, the Washington Institute for Near East Policy), Washington, DC, December 1989, reprinted in *Journal of Palestine Studies*, (Spring 1990), 19(3):183-185.

4. For a good general analysis, see Walid Khalidi, "The Half Empty Glass of Middle East Peace." *Journal of Palestine Studies*, (Spring 1990), 19(3):14-38.

5. Thomas L. Friedman, "A Window on Deep Israeli-U.S. Tensions," *New York Times*, 19 September 1991, p. A9.

6. See for example the analysis by Carol Rosenberg, "Surge in Violence in Occupied Lands Gives Rise to Vigilantism," *Miami Herald*, 29 March 1993.

7. The quote from Secretary Baker was given by Vice President Daniel Quayle without citation. See "Vice President Daniel Quayle, remarks to the Anti-Defamation League, Palm Beach, Florida, 10 February 1989," reprinted in *Journal of Palestine Studies*, (Spring 1989), 18(3):188.

8. Quoted in "The First Year of the Bush Administration and the Arab-Israeli Conflict: A Chronology," *Journal of Palestine Studies*, Vol. 19, no. 3 (Spring 1990) 19(3):119-120, cited in *New York Times*, 6 March 1990.

9. The U.S. effort to persuade the PLO to relinquish its claim as the sole, legitimate representative of the Palestinians was disclosed by PLO executive committee member 'Abdullah al-Hurani. It was revealed in *Foreign Broadcast Information Service*, 21 August 1989 and reprinted in *Journal of Palestine Studies*, (Spring 1990), 19(3):124. Also see "The First Year of the Bush Administration: A Chronology," p. 120 citing *New York Times*, 22 March 1989 and *Washington Post*, 22 March 1989. The U.S. effort to use the talks to end the intifada was also noted in "The First Year of the Bush Administration: A Chronology," p. 120 citing the *Los Angeles Times*, 23 March 1989.

10. "Statement of U.S. Policy on the Repeal of the UN 'Zionism is Racism' Resolution by the Assistant Secretary of State for International Organizational Affairs, Washington D.C. 30 March 1990" (originally published by the State Department's Bureau of Public Affairs as Current Policy No. 1269), reprinted in *Journal of Palestine Studies*, (Summer 1990), 19(4):183-188.

11. "The First Year of the Bush Administration: A Chronology," p. 128, cited in *New York Times*, 29 November 1989.

12. "The First Year of the Bush Administration: A Chronology," p. 128, cited in *New York Times*, 30 November 1989.

13. "The First Year of the Bush Administration: A Chronology," p. 129, cited in *New York Times*, 10 January 1990.

14. "The First Year of the Bush Administration: A Chronology," p. 128, cited in *Washington Post*, 27 November 1989.

15. "Palestine Chronology 16 February-15 May 1990," *Journal of Palestine Studies*, (Summer 1990), 19(4):207, cited in *Washington Times*, 24 April 1990.

16. "Palestine Chronology 16 February-15 May 1990," p. 211, cited in *New York Times*, 11 May 1990.

17. "Palestine Chronology 16 May-15 August 1990," *Journal of Palestine Studies*, (Autumn 1990) 20(1):197, cited in *New York Times*, 18 May 1990.

18. "The First Year of the Bush Administration: A Chronology," p. 124, cited in *New York Times*, 9 August 1989.

19. "The First Year of the Bush Administration: A Chronology," p. 126, cited in *Washington Post*, 6 October 1989.

20. "Edward Said's Interview on PLO Dealings with the U.S., *Al-Qabas*, Kuwait, 7 October 1989 (Excerpts)," reprinted in *Journal of Palestine Studies*, (Winter 1990), 19(2):146-151.

21. "The First Year of the Bush Administration: A Chronology," p. 126, cited in *Washington Post*, 6 October 1989.

22. "Vice President Daniel Quayle, remarks to the Anti-Defamation League, Palm Beach, Florida, 10 February 1989," p. 188. Also see "The First Year of the Bush Administration: A Chronology," p. 118, cited in *New York Times*, 2 February 1989.

23. "The First Year of the Bush Administration: A Chronology," p. 119, cited in *New York Times*, 18 February 1989.

24. "The First Year of the Bush Administration: A Chronology," p. 121, cited in *New York Times*, 21 April 1989.

25. "UN Security Council Resolution 641 (1989) on Deportations, New York, 30 August 1989," reprinted in *Journal of Palestine Studies*, (Winter 1990), 19(2):134-135. Also see the *Washington Post*, 31 August 1989.

26. "UN General Assembly Resolution No. 44/2 (XLIV), 'The Uprising (Intifada) of the Palestinian People,' New York, 6 October 1989," reprinted in *Journal of Palestine Studies*, (Winter 1990), 19(2):140-141.

27. "United Nations Commission on Human Rights, 'Resolution on Israeli Settlements in the Occupied Territories,' Geneva, 16 February 1990," reprinted in *Journal of Palestine Studies*, (Spring 1990), 19(3):150.

28. "Explanation of U.S. Vote on the UN Commission on Human Rights Resolution, 'Israeli Settlement in the Occupied Territories,' by the U.S. Permanent Representative to the United Nations in Geneva, Geneva 16 February 1990," reprinted in *Journal of Palestine Studies*, (Spring 1990), 19(3):193-194.

29. "The First Year of the Bush Administration: A Chronology," p. 122, cited in *Foreign Broadcast Information Service*, 17 May 1989. For an analysis of the dreadful health situation in the Occupied Territories and the ways in which Israel uses medicine (or the withholding thereof) as a political weapon against Palestinians, see Dr. Martin L. Rubenberg, interview with, "Medicine as a Political Weapon," *American-Arab Affairs*, (Spring 1990), (32):71-80.

30. "Palestine Chronology 16 February-15 May 1990," pp. 211 and 212, cited in *Washington Times*, 10 May 1990. Also see "Palestine Chronology 16 May-15 August 1990," pp. 196-97, cited in *New York Times*, 18 May 1990.

31. "Palestine Chronology 16 May-15 August 1990," pp. 199-220, cited in *Los Angeles Times*, 25 May 1990, *Washington Post*, 25 May 1990, and *Washington Post*, 27 May 1990.

32. "Palestine Chronology 16 May-15 August 1990," p. 202, cited in *Washington Times*, 1 June 1990 and *Los Angeles Times*, 2 June 1990.

33. "Vice President Daniel Quayle, remarks to the Anti-Defamation League, Palm Beach, Florida, 10 February 1989," *Journal of Palestine Studies*, (Spring 1989), 18(3):186-190.

34. "The First Year of the Bush Administration: A Chronology," p. 120, cited in the *New York Times*, 14 March 1989.

35. That consensus was most clearly expressed in UN General Assembly Resolution 38/58 passed on 13 December 1983 calling for an "international conference" under the auspices of the Security Council with the U.S., the Soviet Union, Israel, the PLO, Syria, Lebanon, Jordan, and Egypt participating on equal footing in conformity with certain principles including: (1) the right of self-determination and the right to an independent state

for the Palestinians; (2) the right of the PLO to represent the Palestinians; (3) the inadmissibility of the acquisition of territory by force; (4) the exchange of land for peace; and (5) the right of all states in the region to exist within secure and internationally recognized borders. For analysis and documentation, see Cheryl Rubenberg, "U.S. Policy Toward the Palestinians."

36. There are two versions of the Shamir plan — one is a "twenty point" version which appears to be an elaboration on an earlier "four point" version. For a full text of the first version (which was originally printed in the *Jerusalem Post Weekly* on 23 April 1989), see "The Shamir Four-Point Plan," *Journal of Palestine Studies*, (Summer 1991), 20(4):149-150. For a full text of the elaborated plan, see "Israeli Government Election Plan, Jerusalem, 14 May 1989," *Journal of Palestine Studies*, (Autumn 1989), 19(1):145-148. For a detailed analysis of Shamir's proposals see Khalidi, "The Half Empty Glass," *op.cit.*, pp.15-38.

37. "The Shamir Four-Point Plan," *op. cit.*

38. "The First Year of the Bush Administration: A Chronology," p. 121, cited in *New York Times*, 6 April 1989.

39. "The First Year of the Bush Administration: A Chronology," p. 121, cited in *New York Times*, 7 April 1989.

40. *Ibid.*

41. "Text of a letter signed by West Bank leaders rejecting Israel's election plan, Jerusalem, 27 April 1989" (the text originally appeared in *al-Fajr* 1 May 1989), *Journal of Palestine Studies*, (Summer 1989), 18(4):155-167.

42. "James A. Baker, address to American Israel Public Affairs Committee, Washington D.C., 22 May 1989," reprinted in *Journal of Palestine Studies*, (Summer 1989), 18(4):172-176.

43. "The First Year of the Bush Administration: A Chronology," p. 123, cited in *New York Times*, 7 July 1989. The letter was sent on 30 June 1989 but not revealed until 7 July.

44. Khalidi, "The Half Empty Glass of Middle East Peace," p. 34.

45. "Egypt's Ten Point Response to Israel's Election Plan, Cairo, 2 July 1989," reprinted in *Journal of Palestine Studies*, (Autumn 1989), 19(1):144-145. It should be pointed out that, as a consequence of Jordan's 1988 "disengagement" from Palestinian affairs, Egypt became the designated party to "represent" the Palestinians, or, more specifically, to persuade the PLO to give a "green light" to non-PLO Palestinians from the West Bank and Gaza to dialogue with Israel about elections. For a good analysis of this, see Khalidi, "The Half Empty Glass," pp. 24-29.

46. "Secretary of State James Baker's 'Five-Point Framework for an Israeli-Palestinian Dialogue,' Washington D.C., 10 October 1989," reprinted in *Journal of Palestine Studies*, (Winter 1990), 19(2):169-170.

47. *Ibid.*

48. For the PLO's "assumptions," see "PLO 'Assumptions' with Regard to Baker's Five Points, Tunis 1 December 1989," reprinted in *Journal of Palestine Studies*, (Winter 1990), 19(2):158-159. For Egypt's, see "Egypt 'Assumptions' with Regard to Baker's Five Points, Cairo, 5 December 1989," reprinted in *Ibid.*, p. 159. For Israel's, see "The Israeli Government's 'Assumptions' with Regard to Baker's Five Points, Jerusalem, 5 November 1989," reprinted in *Ibid.*, pp. 161-162.

49. For several analyses of the Soviet immigration and settlement construction issues, see Amiram Goldbloom, "Are Settlements An Obstacle to Peace?"

New Outlook (Tel Aviv), (June/July/August 1991), 34(4):7-9; Alon Ben-Meir, "Israeli Settlements: A National Imperative," *Miami Herald,* 9 June 1991; Danny Rubinstein, "Burying Peace," *New Outlook,* (June/July/August 1991), 34(4):6; Peretz Kidron, "Partial Settlement Freeze," *Middle East International,* (7 August 1992), (431):7.

    50. The figures on Soviet emigration are given by Michael M. Phillips, "Jewish Leaders Fear a Cutoff In Emigration," *Miami Herald,* 21 August 1991, p. 15A. The issue can be looked at in a slightly different way. The Israeli journal *New Outlook* (Tel Aviv), (December 1990/January 1991), 34(1) states that 200,000 people immigrated to Israel in 1990 including 185,000 from the Soviet Union. And, "This was the largest annual immigration figure since 1951." *Ibid.,* p.25. In addition to Soviet Jews immigrating to Israel, in 1991 a large number of Ethiopian Jews arrived.

    51. See for example the analysis by Geoffrey Aronson, "Soviet Jewish Emigration, the United States, and the Occupied Territories," *Journal of Palestine Studies,* (Summer 1990), 19(4): 30-45.

    52. Amiram Goldbloom, "Are Settlements an Obstacle to Peace?," *New Outlook,* (Tel Aviv), (June/July/August 1991), 34(4):7-9.

    53. See the analysis and statistics provided by Hanan Ashrawi, "Israel's Real Intentions," *The Palestinians After the Gulf War: The Critical Questions* (Washington, D.C.: The Center for Policy Analysis on Palestine, 1991), pp. 19-25. On 3 October 1991 the Israeli weekly *Kol Ha'ir* (Hebrew) revealed details of a secret master plan of the Israeli Housing Ministry for the construction of 4,000 homes for Jews in the heart of Arab East Jerusalem. See *Miami Herald,* 5 October 1991. Population figures for Jerusalem are always somewhat variable. One source notes that there are 500,000 inhabitants in Jerusalem of whom 71.7 per cent are Jews; 25.4 per cent are Muslims; and 2.9 per cent Christian. See John N. Tleel (World Council of Churches), "Ecumenical Life in Jerusalem," *Al-Fajr* (Jerusalem-Palestinian Weekly-English), 28 September 1992, p. 9.

    54. Cheryl A. Rubenberg, "Twenty Years of Israeli Economic Policies in the West Bank and Gaza: Prologue to the Intifada," *Journal of Arab Affairs,* (Spring 1989), 8(1).

    55. Goldbloom, "Are Settlements an Obstacle to Peace?" p.9.

    56. *Ibid.,* p.8.

    57. Danny Rubinstein, "Burying Peace," *New Outlook,* (June/July/August 1991), 34(4):6. .

    58. Khalidi, "The Half Empty Glass of Middle East Peace," p. 33, emphasis in original. On the issue of American interference with Soviet Jewish emigration, the Israeli analyst Boaz Evron commented aptly: "We all know that Israeli and Zionist Organization emissaries have left no stone unturned in persuading the nations of the world to bar entrance to Jewish refugees, in order to force them to come to Israel, the one country which most of them would not otherwise choose as their destination. After all, it is clear to all of us that if the choice was theirs, 97 per cent of them would 'drop out'." Boaz Evron, "Captives of [Israeli] Immigration," *Yediot Ahronot* (Hebrew), 4 April 1991, translated by Israel Shahak, "From the Hebrew Press: Monthly Translations and Commentaries from Israel," Washington, D.C., American Educational Trust, (June 1991), 3(6).

    59. "Palestine Chronology 16 February-15 May 1990," p. 191, cited in *Los Angeles Times,* 23 February 1990.

    60. "Palestine Chronology 16 February-15 May 1990," *Journal of Palestine Studies,* (Summer 1990), 19(4):189, cited in *Foreign Broadcast Information Service,* 20 February 1990.

61. "Palestine Chronology 16 February-15 May 1990," p. 189, cited in *Foreign Broadcast Information Service*, 20 February 1990. For a good analysis of Jordanian foreign policy, especially Jordan's extensive efforts to accommodate the U.S. and conclude peace with Israel, see Madiha Rashid al Madfai, *Jordan, the United States and the Middle East Peace Process 1974-1991* (Cambridge, England: Cambridge University Press, 1993).

62. "Palestine Chronology 16 February-15 May 1990," p. 193, cited in *New York Times*, 2 March 1990.

63. "Palestine Chronology 16 February-15 May 1990," p. 194, cited in *Washington Post*, 6 March 1990.

64. *Ibid.*, p. 195.

65. "Palestine Chronology 16 February-15 May 1990," p. 196, cited in *Washington Times*, 9 March 1990.

66. "Palestine Chronology 16 February-15 May 1990," p. 198, cited in *New York Times*, 13 March 1990.

67. "Palestine Chronology 16 May-15 August 1990," p. 205, cited in *Washington Post* and *New York Times*, 14 June 1990.

68. "Palestine Chronology 16 May-15 August 1990," p. 205, cited in *New York Times* and *Washington Post*, 14 June 1990.

69. "Palestine Chronology 16 May-15 August 1990," p. 205, cited in *New York Times*, 14 June 1990.

70. "Palestine Chronology 16 May-15 August 1990," p. 208, cited in the *New York Times*, 24 June 1990.

71. "Palestine Chronology 16 May-15 August," p. 211, cited in *Washington Post*, 30 June 1990.

72. "Palestine Chronology 16 May-15 August 1990," p. 212, cited in *Washington Post*, 5 July 1990.

73. "Palestine Chronology 16 May-15 August 1990," p. 213, cited in the *New York Times*, 13 July 1990.

74. "Palestine Chronology 16 May-15 August 1990," p. 215, cited in *Washington Post*, 16 July 1990.

75. See, for example, George T. Abed, "The Palestinians and the Gulf Crisis," *Journal of Palestine Studies*, (Winter 1991), 20(2):129-42.

76. "PLO Statement on the Gulf Crisis, Tunis, 19 August 1990," *Journal of Palestine Studies*, (Autumn 1990), 20(1):165-168.

77. "Palestine Chronology 16 May-15 August 1990," p. 223, cited in the *Los Angeles Times*, 14 August 1990.

78. "Palestine Chronology 16 May-15 August 1990," p. 220, cited in *Washington Post*, 6 August 1990.

79. See the analysis in Cheryl A. Rubenberg, "The Gulf War, the Palestinians, and the New World Order," in *The Gulf War and the New World Order: International Relations of the Middle East*, edited by Tareq Y. Ismael and Jacqueline S. Ismael (Gainesville: University Press of Florida, 1994). pp. 317-346.

80. For an extensive discussion of this situation, see "Special File: The Haram al-Sharif (Temple Mount) Killings," *Journal of Palestine Studies*, (Winter 1991) 20(2):134-159. Initially, Israel claimed that the police had fired in response to provocations and life-threatening stonings by the Palestinians; however, documentary evidence (including a video tape taken by a by-stander) demonstrated otherwise. Finally, on 17 July 1991 Israeli Judge Ezra Kama issued a report saying that Israeli police had provoked the violence on the Haram al-Sharif. His ruling contradicted the Israeli police's own report which had

exonerated the policemen of blame and which had claimed that Palestinians had provoked the incident by throwing stones at Jews worshiping at the Western wall. "Chronology 16 May-15 August 1991," *Journal of Palestine Studies*, (Autumn 1991), 21(1):196, cited in *New York Times*, 18 July 1991.

81. The text of Security Council resolution 672 is reproduced in "Special File: The Haram al-Sharif Killings," pp. 154-55.

82. The text of Security Council resolution 673 is reprinted in *ibid.*, pp. 154-155.

83. See the analysis in *ibid.*, pp. 152-153.

84. The *New York Times* reported in September that 7,000 to 8,000 new settlers had moved to the territories. "Chronology 16 August-15 November 1990," p. 214, cited in *New York Times*, 23 September 1990.

85. "Chronology 16 August-15 November 1990," p. 222, cited in *Washington Post*, 16 October 1990.

86. "Chronology 16 November 1990-15 February 1991," *Journal of Palestine Studies*, (Spring 1991), 20(3):172, cited in *Foreign Broadcast Information Service*, 18 & 19 November 1991.

87. For a text of the resolution and analysis of the context of its passage as well as Shamir's quote (which originally appeared in the *Jerusalem Post*, 21 December 1990), see "UN Security Council Resolution 681 on Protecting Palestinians in Israeli Occupied Territories, New York, 20 December 1990," *Journal of Palestine Studies*, (Spring 1991), 20(3):134-136. For the PLO quote, see "Chronology 16 November 1990-15 February 1991," p. 183, cited in *Foreign Broadcast Information Service*, 24 December 1990.

88. Rubenberg, "U.S. Policy Toward the Palestinians: A Twenty Year Assessment."

89. "Chronology 16 February-15 May 1991," *Journal of Palestine Studies*, (Summer 1991), 20(4):198, cited in *Washington Post*, 10 March 1991.

90. Rubenberg, "U.S. Policy Toward the Palestinians: A Twenty Year Assessment," and Rubenberg, "The U.S.-P.L.O. Dialogue: Continuity or Change in American Policy."

91. Serge Schmemann, "Baker Makes Case to 3 Palestinians for October Talks," *New York Times*, 3 August 1991, and Henry Kamm, "Palestinians Call Issues Unresolved," *New York Times*, 3 August 1991.

92. See the analysis by Thomas L. Friedman, "Bush Makes Aid to Israel Subject to Conditions," *New York Times*, 6 October 1991, p. E3.

93. Thomas L. Friedman, "U.S. Hopes Sessions on Mideast Create a New Atmosphere: Won't Push Its Own Plan," *New York Times*, 27 October 1991.

94. "Palestinian Nationalists from the Occupied Territories, Memorandum to Secretary Baker, Jerusalem, 12 March 1991," *Journal of Palestine Studies*, (Summer 1991), 20(4):163-164.

95. "Chronology 16 February-15 May 1991," p. 200, cited in *Foreign Broadcast Information Service*, 14 March 1991.

96. "Chronology 16 February-15 May 1991," p. 202, cited in *Washington Post*, 19 March 1991.

97. "Chronology 16 February-15 May 1991," p. 204, cited in *Foreign Broadcast Information Service*, 26 March 1991.

98. See the analysis by Haim Baram, "A Jubilant Shamir Gets What He Wanted," *Middle East International*, (26 July 1991), (405):3.

99. Thomas L. Friedman, "Israel Rejects Baker's Plan for Talks," *New York Times*, 16 May 1991, p. A6.

100. In August 1992 the newly elected Israeli prime minister, Yitzhak Rabin, declared that Israel now would recognize Resolution 242 but that it would only give up "some

kilometers" of the Golan Heights and would "never come down from the Heights." Clyde Haberman, "Israel Tells Arabs It Accepts U.N.'s Land-for-Peace Plan," *New York Times*, 26 August 1992. Also, Israel declared that it would never withdraw from Jerusalem and that it would "not budge one inch" from the West Bank and Gaza. Clyde Haberman, "Rabin Strongly Criticizes Palestinian Negotiators," *New York Times*, 3 September 1991.

101. Serge Schmemann, "Israelis Give U.S. Conditional 'Yes' on Mideast Talks," *New York Times*, 2 August 1991.

102. Thomas L. Friedman, "Shamir is Unyielding on Makeup of Palestinian Delegation," *New York Times*, 25 July 1991.

103. "Five-Point Palestinian Document Submitted to Secretary Baker, Jerusalem, 2 August 1991," reprinted in *Journal of Palestine Studies*, (Autumn 1991), 21(1):169-170.

104. "U.S. Letter of Assurances to the Palestinians," reprinted in *Journal of Palestine Studies*, (Winter 1992), 21(2):118-119, reprinted from *Mideast Mirror*, 24 October 1991. In principle, this memorandum was supposed to be secret, not public. Nevertheless, it found its way, in substance, into the press.

105. This analysis borrows heavily from the discussion by Camille Mansour, "The Palestinian-Israeli Peace Negotiations: An Overview and Assessment," *Journal of Palestine Studies*, (Spring 1993), 22(3):5-6 ff.

106. *Ibid.*, p.5.

107. See the analysis by Lamis Andoni, "The Washington Talks: Deadlock or the End?" *Middle East International*, (6 March 1992), (420):3.

108. See the analysis by Lamis Andoni, "US Attacks Palestinians," *Middle East International*, (20 March 1992), (421):5-6; and Mansour, "The Palestinian-Israeli Peace Negotiations," pp. 13-16.

109. The first quote is from Friedman, "Bush Makes Aid to Israel Subject to Conditions," and the second is from Thomas L. Friedman, "A Window on Deep Israel-U.S. Tensions," *New York Times*, 19 September 1991, p. A9.

110. The statistics may be found in Thomas L. Friedman, "Peace Talks But No Dove," *New York Times*, 20 October 1991; and *Report on Israeli Settlement in the Occupied Territories*, (May 1991), 1(3):1,6.

111. Israel was clear that it would permit Palestinians administration over only such things as "garbage collection, local police authority, traffic, and education," but absolutely no control over land, water, security, immigration or ultimate authority. See Thomas L. Friedman, "Peace Talks But No Dove."

112. Andrew Rosenthal, "With Rabin Beside Him, Bush Lauds Israelis," *New York Times*, 12 August 1992.

113. See the data and analyses by Joel Brinkley, "U.S. Begins Storing Military Supplies in Israeli Bunkers," *New York Times*, 1 June 1991; Donald Neff, "An Empty Gesture," *Middle East International*, (14 June 1991), (402):6; Joel Brinkley, "Book on Israel's Atomic Arms Goes Beyond US Estimates," *New York Times*, 20 October 1991 reporting on a new book by Seymour M. Hersh, *The Samson Option*. Also noteworthy in regard to Israel's nuclear weapons is the September/October 1991 special issue of the Israeli journal *New Outlook* (Tel Aviv), 34(5), entitled "The Middle East: Approaching the Nuclear Edge?"

114. Since 1949, Israel has received more than $46 billion in U.S. assistance. For additional analysis, see *Report on Israeli Settlement in the Occupied Territories*, a Bimonthly Publication of the Foundation for Middle East Peace, Washington, D.C. beginning in January 1991 with Volume I, no. 1. Also see *Breaking the Siege* (The Newsletter of the Middle East Justice Network), (June-July 1991), 3(2).

115. Alfonso Chardy, "U.S. Policy Parallels Group's Ideas," *Miami Herald*, 19 June 1989; Steve Niva, "The Bush Team," *Middle East Report*, (May/June 1989), (158):31; *ibid*, pp. 4-5; and Rubenberg, "The U.S.-P.L.O. Dialogue: Continuity or Change in American Policy," pp. 34-36.

116. "James A. Baker, Address to American Israel Public Affairs Committee, Washington D.C., 22 May 1989," reprinted in *Journal of Palestine Studies*, (Summer 1989), 18(4):176.

10

THE CLINTON ADMINISTRATION AND THE PALESTINE QUESTION

Joe Stork

PRESIDENT BILL CLINTON WAS surely as surprised as anyone who saw him on the podium in the White House garden on 13 September 1993, nudging Yasir Arafat and Yitzhak Rabin together for what has been momentarily immortalized as "The Handshake." As candidate and as president, Clinton had adopted a pose and rhetoric that might have been (or might as well have been) scripted in the cubicles of the Israeli Foreign Ministry. The most constructive gloss one could put on his administration's policy over many months of Israeli-Palestinian negotiations in Washington was that its reflexive and inflexible endorsement of Israeli goals and maneuvers had created a strong incentive for Israelis as well as Palestinians to short-circuit those talks in order to move towards some sort of settlement.

When Bill Clinton took over the presidency from George Bush in January 1993, his Middle East agenda was largely fixed, at least in strategic terms. The center of gravity of this agenda remained the Persian Gulf. Ever since the Iranian revolution of 1979, U.S. policy in the region as a whole (including its Arab-Israeli and Palestinian components) was largely derivative of the need to check hostile local powers — first Iran and then Iraq — from exercising significant hegemony over the politics and trade and investment decisions of Saudi Arabia and the small princedoms on the Arab side of the Gulf. For most of this period since 1979, Washington was able to indulge its "strategic relationship" with the annexationist Likud regimes in Tel Aviv at virtually no cost to its ties with the conservative Arab oil producers, mainly on account of their understandable focus on the outcome of the long war between Iran and Iraq.

A shift in Washington's stance towards Israel's Palestine policies had begun as a result of the Palestinian *intifada* that erupted in late 1987-early 1988. By the end of 1988, even the fiercely pro-Israel Reagan administration felt the need to open talks with the Palestine Liberation Organization. But this "dialogue" was put at the service of Israel's game plan: talk inconclusively about procedures while Israeli force was systematically applied to crush Palestinian resistance and initiatives.[1]

The major disruption to this complacent pattern came with the Gulf crisis and war of 1990-91, which had the effect of turning the "peace process" charade into actual negotiations. This involved a brief season of discord between the U.S. and Israel, from September 1991 through June 1992, the significance of which should be appreciated but not exaggerated in terms of assessing the policy of the current incumbent in the White House.

The Bush administration's efforts to stage the Madrid talks and subsequent negotiations represent at bottom a U.S. acknowledgement of the "linkage" issue—that is, the insistence of Palestinians and other Arabs that the political future of the Persian Gulf can not be entirely separated from the dynamics of the Palestinian-Israeli-Arab state conflict. A prime concern of U.S. policy in the Middle East is to dominate the political agenda there, and this is a major reason why the U.S. opted for war as the means of choice to confront Iraq's aggression. To have accepted the "Arab solution" approach of Jordan's King Hussein (among many others) would have been to share the power to set the agenda. Linkage in this sense had to be rendered presumptuous and invalid.

The extent of popular support in the Arab world for Iraq and against Kuwait, Saudi Arabia and the United States — i.e., against the prevailing hierarchies of power and privilege — captured the attention of the custodians of power in Washington. True, no political firestorm erupted to devour any of the Arab allied regimes, but the legitimacy of the existing order was clearly vulnerable. Once Iraq, and by extension its partisans among the Palestinians and other Arabs, had been defeated, linkage could flourish — on terms largely set by Washington. But Washington's control of the agenda would have to extend to Israel as well.[2]

With the convening of the Madrid conference in October 1991, with the ensuing bilateral and multilateral negotiations involving Israel, the Palestinians and most Arab states, and finally with the election of Yitzhak Rabin's Labor-led government in Israel in June 1992, the recalibration of U.S.-Israeli relations required by the Gulf War and the end of the Cold War was well on track, from Washington's vantage point. By the fall of 1992, Bush's defense chief Dick Cheney was proposing to elevate Israel to NATO status in terms of access to classified military technologies, in return for Rabin's decision not to oppose a proposed sale of F-15 fighter-bombers to Saudi Arabia (which had been endorsed by Bill Clinton as well).[3] With Rabin in office, the first $2 billion in loan guarantees were signed over on exceptionally favorable terms, allowing Standard & Poors to upgrade Israel's debt rating (and borrowing clout) from triple B minus to triple B.[4]

There is every reason to think that Bill Clinton and his campaign advisors appreciated the favor President George Bush and Secretary of State James Baker had done the next administration, regardless of who won the election. The campaign saw predictable Democratic carping about "unfair pressures" on Israel to make "one-sided concessions," but the Democratic and Republican party platforms were virtually interchangeable.[5] Considering the rancorous relations between Bush/Baker and Shamir, the U.S. presidential campaign of 1992 was remarkable mainly for the invisibility of Middle East policy and U.S.-Israel relations as an issue.

This relative absence of the Palestinians as an issue in the campaign reflected a bipartisan appreciation that the factors underlying the Bush/Baker Middle East agenda following the Gulf War were still operative. The Persian Gulf clearly dominated the Pentagon's scenarios of future armed interventions. Between 1988 and 1992, U.S. forces overseas had dropped by 42 percent in Europe, 31 percent in the Pacific and 25 percent in the Western hemisphere but increased by about 30 percent in the Persian Gulf region.[6] In the event of hostilities there requiring U.S. intervention, Washington would have to minimize political stresses on its ties with Saudi Arabia and other friendly regimes.

The Clinton administration thus came into office with a clear but unspoken mandate from the "national security" strategists: get a settlement of the Israeli-Palestinian conflict. The terms of the settlement were incidental, so long as it had some durability and would serve the purpose of absorbing political shocks in the event of a major crisis requiring U.S. military intervention in the region. With Yitzhak Rabin at the helm in Israel, Washington had someone who appreciated this U.S. imperative. After all, Rabin, as ambassador to Washington in the Nixon/Kissinger period, was the key architect from the Israeli side of the U.S.-Israeli "strategic relationship" in its formative period, and appreciated the end of U.S. patience with the belligerent intransigence of the Likud.

Clinton himself appears to hold no strong personal views about the Israel-Palestine conflict — neither the pro-Zionist zealotry of Ronald Reagan nor the oil industry inclinations of Bush and Baker. His personal political compass in this regard is steered strictly by utilitarian considerations, more influenced by the fact that Jewish donors accounted for an estimated 60 percent of his non-institutional campaign funds than by any strong conviction regarding Israel.

In such circumstances, one would hardly look for bold appointments at any of the Middle East desks. And any such inclination would have been quickly canceled by the preemptive complaints that greeted Clinton's early foreign policy and national security appointments. Both Pentagon chief Les Aspin and CIA director James Woolsey came bedecked with testimonials to their past service with the Washington Institute for Near East Policy (WINEP) and the Jewish Institute for National Security Affairs. On the other hand, Warren Christopher and Anthony Lake, the new Secretary of State and National Security Advisor, were tainted by their employment in the Carter administration. Lake's top deputy, Sandy Berger, was Jewish enough, but a bit too friendly to American Friends of Peace Now. Some of the fragmenting of Israeli political consensus as a result of the intifada was showing up in the U.S. political establishment. The problem for the most powerful Jewish organizations, wrote Thomas Friedman, was that "their monopoly on representing Jewish positions is being broken."[7]

In order to help offset these concessions to reality embodied in the first-tier appointments, the partisans of Israeli-U.S. strategic solidarity pressed the Clinton administration for appointments of solidly pro-Israel persons to posts directly concerned with the Middle East. The administration would work to implement the post-Gulf War U.S. agenda in the region, but in a way that would challenge as little as possible the status quo as it pertained to Israel. This was Clinton's message to the Israelis and their partisans in the U.S. with the appointment of Martin Indyk to the Middle East desk in the National Security Council, Samuel Lewis to Policy Planning at the State Department, and Dennis Ross as special coordinator for the peace talks. Indyk, a former research director at the chief Israel lobby organization, AIPAC, and executive director of the pro-Israel spin factory, WINEP, is not a particularly deep thinker, but he is an articulate proponent of Israeli concerns and dedicated to the fullest possible meshing of Israeli and U.S. policy and public relations gears. In an article in *Foreign Policy* (Summer 1991), Indyk harped on the tired theme that the PLO could be safely ignored in any post-Gulf War arrangements. He ended a "think tank" paper written around the same time with the revealing proposition that the U.S. was, after the Gulf War, "in a position to lay down the law" in the Middle East.[8] Lewis had been U.S. ambassador to Israel for nine years. Ross had been a prominent WINEP fixture before working at the State Department under Baker, and was slated to take over Indyk's job at WINEP.

Together these appointments signalled that Israeli interests would get the utmost consideration, and that Israel should try to get the most favorable possible deal from the Palestinians, with U.S. support. Indyk reportedly remarked on one occasion that the U.S. should not be "evenhanded" but rather persuade the Palestinians to accept the positions advanced by Israel.[9] But the rejectionism of Likud could have no place in the circumstances of the "new order." This much was implicit in Indyk's mid-May "dual-containment" speech to his old WINEP colleagues: "promoting Arab-Israeli peace in the west will impact our ability to contain the threats from Iraq and Iran in the east." In other words, the U.S. ability to maintain a hegemonic position in the Persian Gulf requires some measure of Israeli-Arab and Israeli-Palestinian accommodation.

The Clinton administration's first opportunity to define its approach to the Palestine conflict erupted in mid-December, with Rabin's mass expulsion of more than 400 Palestinians accused of being supporters of Hamas, the militant Palestinian Islamist group which had launched a series of deadly attacks against Israeli military personnel. Lebanon's refusal to accept the men turned the incident into a major political standoff. The Bush administration supported UN Security Council Resolution 799, requiring Israel to readmit the men. The initial position of the Clinton administration, once it took the reins of the state in late January, reportedly was to press Israel to bring back half of those expelled immediately, and the rest within a short period of time. What the Clinton administration settled for however, bore the handprints of Indyk and Lewis: following secret talks only with the Israelis, the State Department announced that Israel would offer to take back only 100 of the expellees immediately, half of the rest in September, and the remainder by the beginning of 1994. The U.S., in return, would oppose further UN Security Council action. The proponents of this deal on the U.S. side reasoned that this was as much "political traffic" as Israel could bear, and that to push Rabin any further would risk the survival of his government. He was, after all, the Israeli political leader most in tune with U.S. priorities. Rabin, for his part, described the negotiations as producing "an infrastructure of understanding" with the new administration.[10]

The issue of the expellees remained unresolved, and an irritant to U.S. policy, but not to the point of provoking pressures on Israel. When Rabin visited Washington in mid-March, 1993, Clinton promised "our best efforts" to maintain current levels of U.S. military aid, and claimed he did not raise with Rabin the matter of the expellees. At the same time, it appears that Washington declined a number of Israeli requests for military cooperation, including a proposal to make Haifa a homeport for the U.S. Sixth Fleet.[11] But the Palestinian delegation still refused to reconvene in Washington, and the multilateral talks in other venues were disrupted as well.

In Israel the security situation continued to deteriorate following the December expulsions, to the point where Rabin was forced to return home early from his U.S. trip in mid-March. Murderous clashes between Palestinians and Israelis inside Israel as well as in the Occupied Territories led Rabin on 30 March to declare emergency measures which sealed the border between the Occupied Territories and Israel (including annexed Jerusalem), drastically affecting economic life and basic subsistence for tens of thousands of Palestinians.

The Clinton administration declined to criticize this sweeping act of collective punishment, though occasions were not lacking. Egyptian President Husni Mubarak, on the eve of his first meeting with Clinton in early April, told an interviewer that he would press for further steps on the expellees. "The Palestinians now want a small step within the package to take place," Mubarak said plaintively. "If President Clinton could agree with it and discuss it with Prime Minister Rabin, I think it would help a lot." The Clinton team was unrelenting. "The ball is very clearly in the Palestinian court," said an unnamed U.S. official, adding in his best "laying down the law" manner that "The time has come for the Palestinians to decide on the basis of the significant package and understanding that got worked out . . . to come to the table, and that's it."[12] Clinton adopted the same tone in a press conference with Mubarak following their talks, saying Rabin had done "enough to get people back to the table." Mubarak faintly praised Clinton for doing "the maximum."[13]

Clinton did state his readiness to restart talks with the PLO, which Mubarak noted was already happening anyway through the delegation. A few days later, Clinton publicly suggested that Israel accept Faisal Husseini as a leading member of the official delegation. This formula, along with a non-public U.S. promise to request that Saudi Arabia renew funding of Palestinian projects in the Occupied Territories, got the Palestinians back to Washington for a round of talks in May. According to Palestinian sources, though, Saudi aid was not forthcoming, despite a U.S.-brokered meeting in Cairo between Faisal Husseini and Saudi foreign minister Saud bin Faisal, leading Palestinians to suspect a U.S. hand on the Saudi tap.

Prior to the renewal of Israeli-Palestinian bilateral talks in May, the New York Times dutifully articulated the not-so-subtle Indykian version of events: "So far in the quid pro quo that is a part of negotiations, the concessions have come from Israel. Next week, Israeli and American officials say, it is time for a significant gesture from the Palestinians." Other accounts reported that U.S. officials were advising the Palestinians to strike a deal soon; otherwise they would be facing a Likud regime under Benjamin Netanyahu.[14]

In its efforts to get over the obstacle presented by the expellees, the Clinton administration promised it would elevate the U.S. role from that of "honest broker" to "full partner." Whose partner the Clinton administration was supposed to be was left unspoken, but the first exercise in partnership was fairly transparent. In the midst of the ninth round of talks, in May, the U.S. side tabled its own draft of principles of agreement, which the Palestinian side quickly rejected. The Israelis spoke of having some problems with the text, but it later became known that Rabin had been shown a draft of the draft 36 hours before it was presented in Washington, and had strongly objected to certain features. He crossed out the phrase "territories for peace," for instance, and the U.S. team dutifully modified the draft.[15]

The Palestinian delegation continued to press Washington to clarify the positions implicit and explicit in the U.S. draft of principles, positions which the Palestinians regarded as inconsistent with the terms of reference of the negotiations, as contained in the invitations to Madrid. According to Hanan Ashrawi, they presented the State Department with a list of ten questions, such as "Does the U.S. consider Palestinian territory to be 'occupied'?" and "Does the U.S. consider Jerusalem to be part of these territories?" According to another delegation member, the U.S. refused to answer the questions directly, evidently considering them impertinent. The exchange, according to this participant, went something like this:

"Our position is well known."

"When does it come into play?"

"This is not the right time."

A tenth round commenced in mid-June, and a second U.S. draft of principles was brought to the parties on 30 June. This one was slightly more elaborate than the earlier one, but even more tentative as a U.S. proposal: It was presented on plain paper, without any kind of letterhead or identification. And the elaborations proved even more disturbing to the Palestinians than the vacuity of the earlier text. The problems, from the Palestinian side, centered around the presentation of unspecified "territory" as subject to the competing claims of sovereignty of "any interested party" — presumably including Jordan as well as Israel. The U.S. responded that the drafts did not represent U.S. positions but were simply efforts to find an acceptable neutral language. The Palestinians, seeing less and less daylight between the Israeli positions and these U.S. "expressions," urged (without success) that the draft at least revert to the language contained in the $10 billion loan guarantee — i.e., "land not under Israeli control on June 4, 1967."

As the tenth round broke up with no movement, the Israelis and the U.S. blamed the Palestinians for insisting that the difficult issue of East Jerusalem be addressed now. The Palestinians retorted that Israel's draconian closure policy, in effect since the end of March, had pushed Jerusalem to the forefront. This was the economic, civic, cultural and social center of the West Bank. Israel had expanded Jerusalem's borders to the point where closure put the only Palestinian cosmopolitan area out of bounds for the vast majority of the West Bank residents (Palestinians, that is; Israeli settlers were under no restriction), and effectively divided the West Bank into northern and southern sectors, rendering transportation and communication between communities extremely difficult, costly and for all practical purposes virtually impossible. Commerce and services had been severely disrupted for the entire West Bank, with no end in sight. The Palestinians were further perturbed by U.S. spokespeople in UN agencies and committees raising objections to boilerplate formulations of the occupied territories as "including East Jerusalem," and feared this signalled a de facto change of U.S. policy regarding the future status of the city.

By early July, the talks in Washington had every appearance of having degenerated into the wheel-spinning that characterized the U.S.-sponsored "peace process" over the last two decades. The Palestinian constituency needed some strong encouragement to continue. The genuine and widespread popular enthusiasm for the talks that existed after the opening Madrid round had clearly dissipated. Popular support had eroded — not because of the Islamist Hamas or Iran or any of the other bogies of the hour, but because, after nearly two years, the talks had produced not even a framework for negotiation, while the economic and security situation on the ground had deteriorated badly.

If Washington had been seriously interested in boosting moderate and secularist forces among the Palestinians and throughout the region, it would have given some sign that it supports a settlement of the Palestinian-Israeli conflict that meets minimum standards of justice, one that appreciates the risks in the realignments taking place within Palestinian communities under the boot of repression and serious economic deprivation. What Washington gave instead was Christopher's threat that he and Clinton had many other things to attend to if the Israelis and Palestinians did not "want peace."[16]

July saw a tour of the region by Dennis Ross, Martin Indyk and Aaron Miller, designed to pave the way for a trip by Christopher himself at the end of the month. The U.S. goal was to secure the agreement of both sides to some version of the draft declaration of principles the State Department was peddling. The three peddlers returned empty-handed. Several individuals closely involved in the negotiations — Hanan Ashrawi and Saib Erakat on the Palestinian side, Shimon Peres on the Israeli side — spoke openly of a need to scrap the Camp David/Madrid formula of phases and move directly to final status negotiations, perhaps in the context of a Jordanian-Palestinian confederation.[17] More than half of Rabin's cabinet came out in support of direct talks with the PLO.[18]

Christopher's trip was postponed when heavy fighting broke out along the Israeli-Lebanese border. A series of deadly attacks by Lebanese guerrillas against Israeli troops in Lebanon triggered shelling across the border, followed by Israeli attacks purposefully designed to force hundreds of thousands of Lebanese to flee north towards Beirut, leaving southern Lebanon a "free fire zone." Even after the Rabin government openly proclaimed its purpose of generating a massive refugee flow, a flagrant violation of the rules of war, the U.S. posed no objection. Christopher's decision to postpone his trip in effect gave the Israelis additional days to work their purpose.

When Israel's heavy application of military power failed to suppress the fighting, Washington stepped in. As with the U.S.-Israeli agreement in early February around the Hamas expellees, the U.S. brokered a deal that pulled Rabin out of the political hole which he himself had dug. This time, however, Syria was a party as well, and the resulting deal, never made public, was much less favorable to Israel. Syria secured the Lebanese Hizbullah's agreement to halt shelling of Israeli territory, but only so long as Israel did not shell Lebanese villages, and Hizbullah expressly retained the right to attack Israeli military forces inside Israel's so-called "security zone" in northern Lebanon. It was precisely such attacks that had led to this eruption of fighting in the first place.

The process of arranging the ceasefire, though, produced a Christopher version of "shuttle diplomacy," in which he made several trips between Jerusalem and Damascus carrying messages between Rabin and Hafiz al-Asad. U.S. sources later put out the word that Christopher also made a "decoy" trip to Damascus solely for the purpose of making the PLO think that important progress was being made on the Israeli-Syrian track, and that the Palestinians would have to soften their positions on issues like Jerusalem in order not to be left out of the diplomatic game.[19]

While Christopher, like Ross and Indyk before him, made no headway in getting the Palestinian delegation to subscribe to the U.S. draft agreement of principles, there were developments on another front. During Christopher's stop in Cairo, Mubarak forwarded to the Americans a proposal that would virtually short-circuit the formal Palestinian demand that issues like sovereignty and Jerusalem not be entirely deferred. However, as recently as 3 July, the PLO Executive Committee had reaffirmed its decision not to consider the U.S. draft. Therefore, the new proposal prompted several leading Palestinian peace delegation members to go to Tunis to meet with Arafat, resignations in hand. In the words of an unnamed "senior Palestinian official": "Mr. Christopher has in his hands a Palestinian document which does not have the support of the majority of the Palestinian leadership, nor the majority of the Palestinian negotiating team."[20]

By the end of August 1993, the PLO and the Israeli government revealed that they had directly negotiated a draft declaration of principles over the course of 11 months of secret negotiations in Norway. President Clinton, at a 10 September news briefing, remarked that "we have been aware for some time, I don't remember the exact date, but we've known for quite a while about the discussions in Norway." Along with other imprecisions, the extent of the "we" in that statement is not at all clear. This and similar remarks by high U.S. officials betray a great need to take some credit for the directly negotiated agreement. But any U.S. knowledge of the Norway talks, or at least of the seriousness of the Norway talks, must have been confined to a group of U.S. officials commensurately as small as those Palestinians and Israelis who were aware of what was going on. It is certainly unlikely that the American "Likudniks" — Indyk, Ross and Lewis — would have kept the Oslo process secret from their Israeli counterparts, had they been aware of it.

Certainly the intransigent U.S. position in the Washington talks helped motivate the Palestinians to produce the declaration that was signed on 13 September. Was this intransigence designed to encourage an Oslo scenario?[21] One knowledgeable Palestinian observer thinks this is unlikely. "The individuals who masterminded Madrid had the intent of creating an alternative Palestinian leadership," says Rashid Khalidi. "If it were up to Ross and Indyk and Lewis, things would still be where they were a year ago."[22] "The Americans made some errors of judgement about what the Israelis would or would not accept," according to Nabil Shaath, a leading advisor to Yasir Arafat. "When the Jericho idea was presented to the United States, President Clinton and Secretary Christopher were mildly interested, but the team in charge of the peace process totally rejected it. That is why we took it to the Israelis directly."[23]

It still seems a bit premature to say, as Yasir Arafat did within days of the 13 September ceremony, that "the Palestinians have an important friend in the White House," despite Clinton's telephone call to Hafiz al-Asad urging the Syrian president to silence Palestinians in Syria opposed to the agreement. At the White House ceremony Clinton reportedly promised Rabin to consider selling Israel high tech military items that had so far been restricted.[24] Every issue except mutual (and still unequal) recognition remains to be negotiated in the plethora of committees and councils that will be established under the terms of the declaration. There is no evidence that the Clinton administration's one-sided concept of "full partner" has undergone any substantial alteration. The Washington "Likudniks" continue to be the U.S. aides working directly on the negotiations to come. There is no indication that Martin Indyk, for instance, has altered his view that the U.S. role is not to be "evenhanded" but to persuade the Palestinians to accept Israeli positions.

The story of the Clinton administration and the Palestinian question remains to be written in the policies and approaches that will or will not emerge under the fresh circumstances of the PLO-Israel accord.

NOTES

1. On this period see Joe Stork and Rashid Khalidi, "Washington's Game Plan in the Middle East," *Middle East Report* 164/165 (May-August 1990).
2. For an elaboration of this argument, see Joe Stork, "Dinosaur in the Tar Pit: The U.S. and the Middle East after the Gulf War," in Phyllis Bennis and Michel Moushabeck, *Altered States: A Reader in the New World Order* (New York: Olive Branch Press, 1993).
3. *New York Times*, 15 September 1993; *Armed Forces Journal International*, January 1993.
4. *Financial Times*, 22 January 1993.
5. For the relevant paragraphs of the party platforms and a Clinton fundraising letter to Jewish voters, see the *Journal of Palestine Studies*, vol. 22, no. 1 (Autumn 1992), pp.166-69.
6. See the figures cited by David Morrison in *National Journal*, 6 February 1993.
7. *New York Times*, 5 January 1993.
8. "The Postwar Balance of Power in the Middle East," in Joseph S. Nye, Jr. and Roger K. Smith, *After the Storm: Lessons from the Gulf War* (Lanham, MD: Madison Books, 1992), p. 109.
9. *Washington Jewish Week*, 24 December 1992.
10. *Financial Times*, 2 February 1993.
11. *Jerusalem Post International Edition*, 27 March 1993.
12. *New York Times*, 5 April 1993.
13. *New York Times*, 6 April 1993.
14. *New York Times*, 2 and 5 May 1993.
15. *Jerusalem Post International Edition*, 29 May 1993.
16. *New York Times*, 5 July 1993.
17. *New York Times*, 16 and 17 July 1993.
18. *Financial Times*, 5 July 1993.
19. *New York Times*, 7 September 1993.
20. *New York Times*, 10 August 1993.
21. *Issues* (Paris), September 1993, pp.1-3.
22. Interview, October 1993.
23. *Los Angeles Times*, 8 September 1993.
24. *Los Angeles Times*, 15 September 1993.

11

AMERICA'S PALESTINE POLICY*

Ibrahim Abu-Lughod

ALTHOUGH THE QUESTION OF PALESTINE has always been at the core of the Arab-Israeli conflict, the extent to which various works that address the foreign policy of the United States toward Palestine and the Palestinians have consistently entangled that question with the Arab-Israeli conflict is quite astonishing. The entanglement has been, analytically speaking, so basic as to produce a fusion of the Question of Palestine, which remains salient, with the general Arab-Israeli conflict. Equally important to observe is the extent to which the Question of Palestine in fact has become subordinate to that of the Arab-Israeli conflict. The policy that has been systematically developed by the United States, consciously or otherwise, has sought either to subordinate Palestine to the Arab-Israeli conflict or to deconstruct the Question of Palestine and thus handle its constituent parts separately. Nowhere is the latter more evident than in the Camp David agreements of 1979. Although stating that Palestinians have legitimate — but undefined — rights, the agreements clearly called for resolving the issues associated with the "autonomy" of the so-called West Bank and the Gaza Strip, the "refugees," and so forth, without noting their connection with either Palestine or a Palestinian nation. Later schemes advanced by the Reagan-Shultz and the Bush-Baker administrations were premised on similar formulations and proposed solutions similarly in violation of the Palestinian right to self-determination.

While recognizing that the complex issues associated with the Arab-Israeli conflict were and remain pressing for policy makers, it is important to recall that it has been Israel's historic strategy not only to ascribe primary importance to the Arab factor, but additionally to impress upon the world community that its conflict in the Middle East has much more to do with the Arab states than with the Palestinians, the principal victims of the colonization of Palestine. Even as the *intifada* assumes worldwide importance and emphasizes anew the centrality of

---

*Editor's Note: Abu-Lughod's review, analysis and concerns about U.S. policy toward the Palestinians, written in 1990, were on target. Therefore, the essay was left intact, but an update was provided.

the Palestinian dimension of the conflict, Israel attempts, evidently without much success, to project the primacy of its conflict with the Arabs. Hence its persistent allegations of dire threats posed by the belligerent policies of either Syria, or Libya, or Iraq, and so on. Consciously or otherwise, America's policy has tended in fact, if not in theory, to accept the validity of Israel's strategy and perception. Also, America's varied economic, military, strategic, and political interests in the Arab world have tended to validate, for American policy planners and apologists, the centrality of the Arab states factor not only in resolving the issues of contention in the Middle East but also in promoting a particular foreign policy toward the states in the region. That perhaps may explain the overriding emphasis on an American Palestine policy that is essentially subordinate to that of America's Middle East policy in general.

In the narration that follows an attempt will be made to show that the United States pursued a very complex foreign policy toward Palestine in the period of the British Mandate and that, when Palestine was dismembered in 1948, the United States pursued a distinct policy on Palestine that inevitably led to the subordination of the Palestinian dimension in the struggle to that of the Arab-Israeli conflict, while simultaneously favoring a particularly hostile political outcome for the Palestine people. It will also be pointed out that the United States chose in subsequent years to pursue policies in the region as if the Question of Palestine had been obliterated, thus making it possible for the United States to address itself to derivative questions such as those of autonomy, refugees, and Jerusalem. Only when the Palestinians resumed their independent political expression and reassumed their central role in conducting their own struggle for independence did the United States make tentative steps toward a comprehensive policy toward the Question of Palestine.

Our purpose is clearly not to survey the history of American policy. But it is useful to summarize the principal issues addressed by that policy in order to provide the explanation for America's opposition to Palestinian self-determination.

AMERICAN POLICY ON PALESTINE

There is strong consensus among Palestinians, reinforced by considerable international endorsement, to the effect that the United States is opposed to Palestinian self-determination. By this is meant that the United States has pursued policies toward the Palestinians that entailed denial of the Palestinian national identity, opposed the right to be represented by legitimate national leadership, namely the Palestine Liberation Organization (PLO), and opposed the right to establish an independent and sovereign state in any part of Palestine. In theory, the United States government accepts the right of the Palestinians to return to their country (UN Resolution 194, 11 December 1948) but it is totally indifferent to its implementation, and in fact actively assists Israel in denying this right to the Palestinians.

Although Palestinian national consensus is evident on this issue, Palestinians and others differ as to the reasons and the historic bases of that hostile policy. What Palestinians, and others also, do not readily recognize is how consistent American policy has been over time on this issue. American opposition to Palestinian self-determination is all too evident today, but the reality is that the United States has consistently opposed Palestinian independence — the intimate connection of the idea of self-determination with President Woodrow Wilson notwithstanding. This was as true when the British Mandate was imposed as it is true today. For a variety of complex reasons, the United States has never accepted in principle or as a matter of policy the right of the Palestinian people to self-determination.

Studies of America's Palestine policy, few as they may be, clearly reflect the distinct phases that have characterized the evolution of the Question of Palestine since its emergence essentially in the second decade of this century. Palestinians, along with other Arabs, had hoped — largely as a result of their active involvement in the dismemberment of the Ottoman state — to benefit from Ottoman defeat and achieve independence. However, European powers, namely Britain and France, already had schemes for colonizing the areas where that independence was to be exercised. It is clear that the United States early on endorsed the Balfour Declaration, acquiesced with British-French designs, and accepted the imposition of the British Mandate on Palestine — the first significant violation of Palestinian self-determination. The provisions of the mandate recognized the legitimacy of the claim for the establishment in Palestine of "a National Home for the Jewish people," the corporate existence of the Jewish community in Palestine, while denying the Palestinians their political rights, especially their rights to self-government. While the United States explicitly endorsed these efforts, its concern was more specifically related to the achievement of a privileged status for itself and its citizens in a colonized Palestine. In other words, the United States sought to benefit from British imperialism's control of Palestine — which indeed it did. In the process, however, it also provided both moral and informational support for Zionism and its claims. It was totally indifferent to the fate of Palestine's Arab community.

A more active policy was suggested and pursued as World War II was coming to a successful end for the Allies. Both presidents Roosevelt and Truman were active in promoting policies for Palestine that presaged later policies that were extremely detrimental to the future of Palestine and the Palestinians. President Roosevelt showed malicious indifference to the Palestinian people by suggesting or entertaining proposals that sought the "transfer" of the Palestinians from Palestine to make room for the projected Jewish state. Although he is reported to have broached the subject of transfer with some of his advisers and is reported to have proposed a "bribe" to the Arabs (specifically to King Abdulaziz of Saudi Arabia) to facilitate such a transfer, mercifully he did not have the opportunity to act more seriously on that proposal. But the proposal in itself, and Roosevelt's willingness to think of it as a probable solution to the conflict in

Palestine, is a reflection of racial or ethnic prejudice toward Palestinian Arabs. For the proposal entails a view of the Palestinians as lesser people than the intended European Jewish immigrants, not fit for the kind of political future Zionism and its American supporters envisaged for Palestine. It certainly viewed the Palestinians as a commodity to be bartered for a few dollars. Although Roosevelt's idea of transfer was not put into effect than, it was to surface later as an attenuated solution to the problem of the Palestine refugees.

President Truman's policies are the most important of this second phase of America's Palestine policy. Under Truman incessant pressure was put on Britain to permit the influx of 100,000 European Jewish immigrants to Palestine which, in effect, caused a significant demographic revolution, to the detriment of the indigenous Palestinians. It was Truman who involved the United States in promoting the establishment of the Anglo-American Committee, which endorsed the right of European Jewish immigrants to settle in Palestine — rather than in the United States! Also, it was the Truman administration that pressured America's client states to support the United Nations General Assembly's recommendation of 1947 to partition Palestine, and thus helped immeasurably in legitimizing the effort to establish the Jewish state, with disastrous consequences for the Palestinians. And it was Truman who extended recognition to the State of Israel barely fifteen minutes after its declaration. In charting and pursuing such policies, President Truman was clearly concerned with the fate of European Jews, was excessively concerned with accommodating American Jews, and was not in the least concerned with the implications of such support for the Palestinians.

As Palestine was being successfully dismembered in 1948, America's Middle East policy, by then obsessed with the Cold War, took concrete shape. Its basic premise became quite explicit by 1949-50. First, the United States favored the annexation by Jordan of the Arab part of Palestine that remained outside Israel's actual military control. (The "Jordanian option" has resurfaced from time to time in subsequent years.) That same territorial policy in fact applied to Jerusalem, an area designated by the partition recommendation of the United Nations to come under international control. Although the United States did not explicitly abandon "internationalization" of Jerusalem, it acquiesced with its de facto annexation by both Israel and Jordan and later on (in 1967) by Israel alone.

Second, the United States, although seeming to endorse the Palestinian right to return, as evidenced by its sponsorship of UN General Assembly Resolution 194, first adopted in December 1948, in fact promoted various schemes premised upon the permanent settlement in the adjacent states of the more than 700,000 Palestinian refugees. In fact, the United States in 1949 and 1950 actively promoted a scheme for the settlement of 100,000 Palestinian refugees in Iraq, a scheme that was supposed to represent a population "exchange" with Iraqi Jews who were enticed (with the connivance of the government of Iraq at the time) to emigrate to Israel. Every "solution" to the refugee question that has been promoted by the United States since has been based on the settlement of the Palestinians in the Arab states. This was first given explicit expression by

Secretary of State John Foster Dulles in 1954 and has remained an unexamined postulate of American policy ever since.

These two principles affecting territorial jurisdiction and the disposition of people have constituted the basis of future American policy towards Palestine and the Palestinian people. Clearly, both principles are violative of the Palestinian right to self-determination.

As the United States pursued these Palestinian policies and sought to implement them, working with some Arab states, Israel, and internationally, both the environment and the reality on the ground were altered significantly with the emergence of the PLO in 1964. As it grew more effective and began to establish an institutional basis for the struggle, the PLO became an important object of hostile U.S. policy. It is reasonably clear that the United States has never accepted the PLO as the representative of the Palestinian people (despite President Carter's statement that the PLO "represents a substantial portion of the Palestinians"), nor has it acknowledged the political programs espoused by various Palestine National Councils.

As the PLO continued to demonstrate its effectiveness, its increasing legitimacy, and its singular role in promoting the national interests of the Palestinians, it elicited American policies that identified it not only as a "terrorist" organization but as an actual obstacle to the "peace" envisaged by the United States. In 1975, Secretary of State Henry Kissinger committed the United States not to "negotiate" with the PLO, and thus effectively cut off bilateral discussions between the two authorities, and his successor in office, Mr. Zbigniew Brzezinski, bade "bye bye PLO" in 1978, suggesting the end of any practical role for the Palestinians in any peacemaking process devised by the United States. Secretary of State George Shultz went even further when he suggested that it was up to the Arab states to "take care" of the PLO. The culmination of these hostile policy statements and actions came with the enactment of the notorious Anti-Terrorism Act of December 1987 (significantly two weeks after the outbreak of the Palestinian uprising), which called for the closure of all PLO offices in the United States and threatened to penalize individuals who carried out activities or spent money intended to advance the interests of the PLO in the United States.

This brief outline indicates America's broad policy toward Palestine and the Palestinians. The United States has been — and is — unalterably opposed to the Palestinian right to self-determination in all its aspects. That was true of the mandate period and it is true today. It is also obvious that the United States, on a policy level, does not accept the indivisibility of the Palestinians as a people and thus is prepared to deal with them only as distinct units: as refugees, West Bankers, PLO people, and so on. Hence, its complex policies have called for, supported, promoted, and sustained the subordination of the Palestinians of the West Bank and Gaza to Israel and Jordan, the destruction of the Palestine Liberation Organization, and the settlement of the Palestinians of the diaspora in the countries of their residence.

America's Palestine policy of today essentially calls for the Bantustanization of the West Bank and Gaza (the homeland concept) and the Armenianization of the Palestinians of the diaspora. Under such conditions, there is clearly no need for a national political representative of the Palestinian people — thus the pursual of initiatives calculated to bring about the demise of the PLO. Former president Ronald Reagan's peace plan gave clear expression to these policies which, in their broad outline, constitute the basis of the Bush administration's policy of peace for Palestine. A careful analysis of the minutes of the short-lived "dialogue" carried out by Ambassador Robert Pelletreau, Jr. and the PLO delegation in Tunis reveals quite clearly that the United States has not entertained any thought of reversing that policy and replacing it with a policy premised upon the acceptance of the Palestinian self-determination.

FACTORS AFFECTING AMERICAN POLICY

It is useful to note an important paradox at this juncture. The popular and historic perception of the United States in Palestine (as in other Middle East countries) is that it has generally supported people who have been subject to European colonialism and has endorsed their right to self-determination, meaning independence. This perception underlies the persistent and historic appeal of Palestinian (and other Third World) leadership to America's apparent historic support for self-determination, as called for by President Woodrow Wilson. The fact that the United States has never endorsed such a principle in its engagement with the Question of Palestine (except in its applicability to Jewish self-determination), and that it has pursued policies in Central and Latin America and elsewhere that have violated that same principle has not discouraged Palestinian leaders from their belief in the validity of the principle of self-determination as a basis of American foreign policy. When it became clear that various administrations have bypassed the Palestinians altogether and have unfailingly supported Zionist-Israeli policies that have brought about Palestinian dispossession, exile from their historic national soil, and Israeli occupation, the explanation of such policies tended to emphasize the unique and powerful role that Jewish communities play in the domestic politics of the United States. A cursory examination of Palestinian and Arab political discourse on the issues associated with the policies of the United States toward either the Question of Palestine or the Arab-Israeli conflict would clearly suggest that the policies that have been so supportive of Zionism and Israel reflect the powerful influence of Jewish groups. I think it is fair to suggest that most Arab and Palestinian analysts and their supporters tend to accept this hypothesis. This has led many an Arab leader and group, including some Palestinian leaders and supporters, to work for an alternative "lobby" to counteract such pressure. An alternative explanation, generally espoused by "leftist" writers, tends to emphasize America's global hegemonic role and Israel's alleged utility as an instrument of American policy in dominating the Arab Middle East. This viewpoint envisions countermeasures that would unite Palestinian-Arab constituencies with other anti-imperialist forces in civil society. Both explanations of course have some validity, but neither explains America's specific policy toward Palestine or the Palestinians within the broader context of America's historic policy toward the Third World, including Central and Latin America, its policies toward national liberation movements globally, and its specific racial and ethnic policies and their relationship to foreign policy.

Public opinion polls taken on the eve of the 1948 war between Palestine's two antagonistic communities revealed quite clearly that the American public was generally so uninformed on the issues of contention between the two communities as to withhold support from both of them. Only a very active minority of less than 20 percent felt sufficiently informed as to declare its support for Palestine's Jewish community and withhold that support from the "Arabs." The polls clearly reflected either a conscious or unintended bias of polltakers who portrayed the conflict as an Arab-Jewish one. Rarely if at all were Palestinians as such identified as the antagonists of the Jewish-Zionist aspirants for a Jewish state in Palestine. The responses clearly reflected the same bias.

But what became gradually clear is that whatever support was given to Palestine's Jewish community reflected an understanding that the Jewish settlers of Palestine were Europeans — pioneering, democratic, ambitious, and so on — in conflict with an undifferentiated mass of Arabs who were, if anything was known about them, Muslim, fanatical, backward, nonwhite, and so on. In other words, the Jews of Palestine who were calling on America's support were more or less imbued with the same values and attitudes as Americans. That was in part what Zionists had conveyed in their incessant educational and political work in the United States and Western Europe. American policy as such tended of course to reflect the value concerns of the policy makers. Scholars of the so-called Arab image in the United States would maintain that there are significant, deep-seated racial, ethnic, and religious prejudices against the Arabs that have been perpetuated in textbooks, churches, movies, and the like to such an extent that such prejudices inevitably had a significant impact on the process of policy formation relevant to Palestine. There should be no question that Woodrow Wilson's support for the principle of self-determination of people did not go beyond the shores of Christian Europe and certainly did not extend to the masses of Asia and Africa, including the Palestinian Arabs. Perhaps America's complex policy toward the Arab people today has been shaped with the same ambivalence. The suggestion that is being made is clear: on religious, ethnic, and perhaps racial grounds, the United States has historically denied the applicability of the right to self-determination to the Palestinian people.

One can even go further. American policy has consistently been hostile to Arabs and Muslims in general, particularly those Arab-Muslim leaders who adopted radical policies seeking the restructuring of the social and economic sectors of the societies they led. Of course Arab and Muslim states that espoused domestic and foreign policy programs consistent with U.S. goals have fared somewhat better, but even these have not been viewed with any particular esteem. The hostility with which various American administrations have viewed Gamal Abdel Nasser of Egypt, Muhammad Mussadegh of Iran, and Yasir Arafat, and the epithets used to characterize Muammar Qaddafi, Saddam Hussein, and Ayatollah Khomeini, have been more offensive than the particular circumstances have warranted. The affiliation of the Palestinians with the Arab people and to some extent with Islam has brought long-standing American cultural and religious prejudices into play.

The second consideration relates to the affiliation of the Palestinians with the people of the Third World. Although we can identify limited instances of some official American support for some people in the Third World, it seems clear that in general the United States has pursued policies and engaged in activities that have been quite detrimental to Third World interests. Those policies and activities have included repeated military interventions in Central America, economic exploitation in Latin America, political subjugation of Cuba and the Philippines, and actual rendering of military support to colonial powers such as France and Portugal that sought the perpetuation of their colonial relationships in Africa and elsewhere. Third World people have eventually become much more conscious of the historic role of the United States as an imperial power affiliated with the general system of imperialism, a role that has become especially evident in the era of decolonization. In the context of the Cold War, and anxious to "stabilize" recently independent countries, the United States has pursued policies that tended to support authoritarian and generally corrupt Third World regimes — a course of action that has engendered intense hostility among the people in those areas. As a Third World people, the Palestinians, especially in the period following the dismemberment of Palestine and the founding of the PLO, identified with and supported the struggle of other Third World people and movements of national liberation and of the oppressed generally. In that context, the United States identified the Palestinians as part of the general Third World public that is clearly opposed to its clients, including Israel. Thus, the American hostile policy toward the Palestinians, originally formulated to render support to Zionism (and Israel) and nourished by negative cultural, ethnic, religious, and national factors, was simply reinforced and solidified as a consequence of Palestinian identification with radical movements.

The third, related, consideration is the specific attitude of the United States toward national liberation movements that have sought the achievement of their goals by revolutionary means. An examination of American attitudes and policies towards such movements reveals quite clearly general support for the European adversaries of Asian and African national liberation movements. America's support for France in its war against Algeria, for Portugal in its war against national liberation movements in Mozambique, Angola, and Guinea Bissau, as well as U.S. support for the South African regimes against the African National Congress (ANC) and South West African People's Organization (SWAPO) made it inevitable that the United States would adopt a similar policy towards the Palestinian movement of national liberation. The fact that such movements developed integrated strategies of national liberation that included "armed struggle" made them all anathema to U.S. policies. It will be recalled that the ANC was classified by the apartheid regime as a terrorist organization and that the United States accepted that designation, as it accepted Israel's view of the PLO as a terrorist organization.

In conclusion, it is fair to suggest that America's Palestine policy is not likely to improve in the near future. Palestinians tend to think that America's policy can change for the better with better communication, with stronger lobbying, with "image" improvement and clarification of views and with the presentation of "reasonable" Palestinian goals. If anything is clear from our presentation, it is the following: whereas American policy has been consistently hostile to the Palestinians and opposed to the fulfillment of their national aspirations, it is not hostile simply because it is subject to Jewish influence or just because the Palestinians are Palestinians. Its hostility is rooted in deep cultural, ethnic, and racial values, in attitudes of the United States toward people of the Third World, and, perhaps equally important, in its attitude toward radical movements of national liberation. It is these considerations that in large part explain the incredible support that the United States has rendered to Israel in its effort to suppress the Palestinians.

******

New American initiatives became necessary largely in response to three major developments. First, complex Palestinian developments: the intifada and the world-wide support for the Palestinians but also the PLO's evident weakness in the aftermath of the American success in gathering Arab support in the military attack on Iraq; second, the evident transformation of the region from one of challenge to American hegemony to one of total subordination; and third, the restructuring of the international system begun by the collapse of the Soviet system and its negative impact on Third World politics. These three developments contributed immeasurably to the collapse of the Palestinian challenge to both Israel and American policies in the region. Sensing opportunities for imposing the United States' authority over the region, both Secretaries of State, George Shultz and more significantly James Baker III, reformulated broad American principles of a settlement of the Question of Palestine as well as the Arab-Israeli conflict. Thus, the United States "accepted" discussions with the Palestine Liberation Organization, without violating Secretary Kissinger's promise of 1975 to Israel not to negotiate with the PLO, and it successfully obtained an essentially unconditional PLO acknowledgement of Israel's right to exist, and of Security Council Resolutions 242 and 338, as well as a renunciation of "terrorism." The United States then pursued its historic policy of legitimating Israel in the region without accommodating any aspect of the Palestinian right to self-determination. By December 1988, it became evident to the U.S. as well as Israel that the PLO had begun its disengagement from national liberation and intensified its efforts to complete the process of political settlement with Israel on the latter's terms, which the United States would support. It will be recalled that Yasir Arafat's Geneva declaration in the wake of the UN conference on Palestine (which was held in Geneva precisely because the United States rejected Mr. Arafat's application to enter the United States for the purpose of speaking at the United Nations) was essentially unconditional. Neither the United States nor Israel reciprocated in any form. Mr. Arafat's pursuit of the policy of accommodating both powers signified to the Bush Administration that its proposed solutions to the Question of Palestine would find Palestinian and Arab acceptance as well — hence Mr. Baker's initiative which brought about the Madrid Conference on terms that were consistent with America's historic policy on Palestine.

In its Palestinian part, the Madrid Conference was based on several premises. The first related to the non-participation of the PLO, even though it was then almost universally viewed as the legitimate representative of the Palestinian people. Second, the discussions were to revolve around specific issues, namely Israel's occupation of the West Bank and Gaza; an interim period of autonomy (a notion first broached in the Camp David agreement); the exclusion of Jerusalem from any immediate discussions; and the rejection of the concept that the Palestinians constitute a separate national community and thus excluding any role for the Palestinians of the diaspora (the majority of the Palestinians) in the determination of the Question of Palestine. Even the Palestinian participation in the Madrid Conference was conditional on their membership in the joint delegation — Jordanian/Palestinian. Perhaps what was most significant about those terms was the absence of any reference to the fact that Palestine itself is the national patria of the Palestinian people.

The PLO itself acknowledged that these conditions imposed by the United States were, in Mr. Arafat's words, "onerous" and "unjust." However, cajoled by Mr. Baker, the PLO felt compelled to authorize a West Bank/Gaza delegation to participate on the above terms for fear that it would otherwise be excluded from the so-called peace process. From Madrid to Oslo was a defeat for the Palestinians; from Oslo to Washington it was a rout; from Washington to Cairo (May 1994) it was a catastrophe, the second for the Palestinian people. The success of American (and Israeli) policies was total. Thus, the PLO in fact but not de jure (because the Oslo/Washington accords enabled the PLO to create an "autonomy" Authority) became the instrument of a policy imposed on it by the two powers. Also, the PLO has now de facto accepted a more ambiguous definition of Palestine which includes no more than 15% of the land of Palestine, and has for all practical purposes annulled its national Charter and thus accepted in fact that no part of Palestine may become an independent state, and it is clearly no longer able to render any meaningful support to the claims and rights of the Palestinians in exile. It is also clear that the Palestinians will not have much to say about the ultimate disposition of Jerusalem.

It is somewhat early to chart the outcome of the so-called Palestinian National Authority. But what is clear is that it neither has authority over its people nor over the land of Palestine. The land itself is largely Israel's and the Palestinians on it live in several distinct ghettoes which lack geographic contiguity or jurisdictional authority. Everywhere in the world today, the Palestinians live under control of others, as they have been. Although Palestinians are secure in their identity now (thanks, paradoxically, largely to the firm and successful struggle of the PLO as a national liberation movement), the loss of control has been effected with legal political assent. In that sense, the historic formulation of America's Palestine policy of negating the Palestinian right to self-determination is now on the verge of total success: Bantustanizing of Palestine, ghettoizing of the Palestinians, and Armenianizing of the Palestinians of the diaspora. How long will the Palestinians maintain their Palestinian identity in light of the various agreements which the PLO signed with Israel under America's tutelage?

BIBLIOGRAPHIC NOTE

Whereas many works on the Middle East conflict refer to America's policy, surprisingly there is no systematic analysis of that policy that covers the entire period. The mandate period that culminated in the dismemberment of Palestine is adequately covered in such works as Evan M. Wilson, *Decision in Palestine: How the United States Came To Recognize Israel* (Stanford: Hoover Institution Press, 1979); Dan Tschirgi, *The Politics of Indecision: Origins and Implications of American Involvement with the Palestine Problem* (New York: Praeger, 1983); and Muhammad K. Shadid, *The United States and the Palestinians* (New York: St. Martin's Press, 1981). American policy on the eve of the mandate and its concerns can be gleaned from a reading of *The Palestine Mandate: Collected United States Documents relating to the League of Nations Mandate for Palestine, to the Possible Future Independence of Palestine and to the Need for the Creation of a Separate Jewish State* (Salisbury, NC: U.S. Department of State, Division of Near Eastern Affairs, 1977, originally published as *Mandate for Palestine* [Washington, DC: U.S. Government Printing Office, 1927]). In my "North American Public Opinion and the Question of Palestine" in *International Journal of Islamic and Arabic Studies* (1989), 3(2):1-11, I discuss the findings of public opinion polls relevant to Palestine per se and cite the works of such scholars as Seymour Lipset, Fouad Moughrabi, Elia Zureik, and Michael Suleiman, who have dealt with the evolution of American public opinion on the Palestine as well as the Arab-Israeli conflict. My own assessment of continuities in American policy negating the Palestinian right to self-determination, especially following the dismemberment of Palestine, is based upon the reports, minutes of meetings, and memoranda issued by the Department of State in the period of 1949-50. These are to be found in *Foreign Relations of the United States 1949*, vol. 6 (Washington, 1977) and *Foreign Relations of the United States 1950*, vol. 5 (Washington, 1978). For illustration of America's support for the annexation of Arab Palestine to Jordan (the eventual Jordanian option) see, among others, pp. 608 and 170-71 (*1949*) and particularly the memorandum titled "Policy of the

United States with respect to Jordan: Policy Statement Prepared in the Department of State" (*1950*, p. 1094ff) which contains the following statement: "The major problems which confront Jordan today and which are of primary concern to the United States are the establishment of peaceful and friendly relations between Israel and Jordan and the successful absorption into the polity and economy of Jordan and Arab Palestine, its inhabitants and the bulk of the refugees now located there." The memo and other statements are clear on the need for annexation and for the settlement of the refugees in the Arab States. The following works are useful on some of these issues: Ambassador George McGhee (later assistant secretary of state for the Near East), *Envoy to the Middle World* (Cambridge, MA: Harper & Row, 1983), pp. 27-45 and 85, and Abbas Shiblak, *The Lure of Zion* (London: al-Saqi Press, 1986). Shiblak deals with the Iraqi government's role in facilitating the emigration of Iraq's Jewish population to Israel in 1949-50 and the U.S. embassy's support for the possible settlement of Palestinian refugees (about 100,000) in Iraq as a form of "exchange" for Iraq's Jewish emigrants.

Selected Bibliography

Abu-Jaber, Faiz S. *American-Arab Relations from Wilson to Nixon.* Washington, DC: University Press of America, 1979.

Abu-Lughod, Ibrahim, ed. *Palestinian Rights: Affirmation and Denial.* Wilmette, IL: Medina Press, 1982.

Abu-Lughod, Ibrahim, ed. *The Transformation of Palestine: Essays on the Origin and Development of the Arab-Israeli Conflict.* Evanston, IL: Northwestern University Press, 1971.

Adams, William C., ed. *Television Coverage of the Middle East.* Norwood, NJ: ABLEX Publishing Corporation, 1981.

American Center. *Documents and Statements: U.S. Policy in the Middle East.* Amman: American Center, June 1988.

Arab American Institute. *The Deadly Silence: A Report on the 1988 Presidential Candidates and Where They Stand on the Middle East.* Washington, DC: Arab American Institute, 1988.

Arake, Margaret. *The Broken Sword of Justice: America, Israel and the Palestine Tragedy.* London: Quartet Books, 1973.

Aruri, Naseer, Fouad Moughrabi and Joe Stork. *Reagan and the Middle East.* Belmont, MA: Association of Arab-American University Graduates, 1983.

Atiyeh, George N., ed. *Arab and American Cultures.* Washington, DC: American Enterprise Institute for Public Policy Research, 1977.

Baker, Ray Stannard and William E. Dodd, eds. *The Public Papers of Woodrow Wilson, War and Peace: Presidential Messages, Addresses, and Public Papers (1917-1924).* New York: Harper & Brothers, 1927.

Barbarash, Ernest, ed. *John F. Kennedy on Israel, Zionism and Jewish Issues.* New York: Herzl Press for the Zionist Organization of America, 1965.

Barlow, Elizabeth, ed. *Middle East Studies Association/Middle East Outreach Council Text Evaluation Project.* Ann Arbor, MI: Center for Middle Eastern and North African Studies, University of Michigan, 1991.

Bassiouni, M.C. *The Civil Rights of Arab-Americans.* Detroit, MI: AAUG, 1974.

Beling, Willard A., ed. *The Middle East: Quest for an American Policy.* Albany: SUNY Press, 1973.

Bennis, Phyllis and Michel Moushabeck. *Altered States: A Reader in the New World Order.* New York: Olive Branch Press, 1993.

Between Two Administrations: An American-Israeli Dialogue. Washington, DC: Washington Institute for Near East Policy, 1989.

Buehrig, Edward H. *The UN and the Palestinian Refugees: A Study in Nonterritorial Administration.* International Development Research Center, Studies in Development. Bloomington: Indiana University Press, 1971.

Carter, Jimmy. *The Blood of Abraham: Insights into the Middle East.* Boston: Houghton Mifflin, 1985.

Carter, Jimmy. *Keeping Faith: Memoirs of a President.* Toronto: Bantam Books, 1982.

Center for Policy Analysis on Palestine. *The Palestinians After the Gulf War: The Critical Questions.* Washington, DC: The Center for Policy Analysis on Palestine, 1991.

Cohen, Michael J. *Palestine and the Great Powers.* Princeton, NJ: Princeton University Press, 1982.

Cooper, Chester L. *The Lion's Last Roar: Suez, 1956.* New York: Harper & Row, 1978.

Curtiss, Richard H. *A Changing Image: American Perceptions of the Arab-Israeli Dispute.* Washington, DC: American Educational Trust, 1986. 2d ed.

Daniel, Norman. *Islam and the West: The Making of an Image.* Edinburgh: The University Press, 1966.

Eisenhower, Dwight D. *The White House Years: Waging Peace, 1956-1961.* Garden City, NY: Doubleday, 1965.

Esposito, John L. *The Islamic Threat: Myth or Reality?* New York: Oxford University Press, 1992.

Eveland, Wilbur Crane. *Ropes of Sand: America's Failure in the Middle East.* New York: Norton, 1980.

Feintuch, Yossi. *U.S. Policy on Jerusalem.* Westport, CT: Greenwood, 1987.

Findley, Paul. *They Dare to Speak out: People and Institutions Confront Israel's Lobby.* Westport, CT: Lawrence Hill, 1985.

Flappan, Simha. *The Birth of Israel: Myths and Realities.* New York: Pantheon Books, 1987.

Foreign Relations of the United States 1949. Vol. 6. Washington, 1977.

Foreign Relations of the United States 1950. Vol. 5. Washington, 1978.

Forsythe, David P. *United Nations Peacemaking: The Conciliation Commission for Palestine*. Baltimore, MD: Johns Hopkins University Press, 1972.

Frangi, Abdallah. *The PLO and Palestine*. Trans. by Paul Knight. London: Zed Books, 1983.

Freedman, Robert O. ed. *The Middle East Since Camp David*. Boulder, CO: Westview Press, 1984.

Friedman, Isaiah. *The Question of Palestine, 1914-1918: British-Jewish-Arab Relations*. New York: Schocken Books, 1973.

Gathorne-Hardy, Geoffrey Malcom. *The Fourteen Points and the Treaty of Versailles*. Oxford: Clarendon Books, 1939.

Gazit, Mordechai. *President Kennedy's Policy Toward the Arab States and Israel. Analysis and Documents*. Tel Aviv: Shiloah Center for Middle Eastern and African Studies, Tel Aviv University, 1983.

Gilboa, Eytan. *American Public Opinion and the Arab-Israeli Conflict*. Lexington, MA: D.C. Heath, 1987.

Godfried, Nathan. *Bridging the Gap between Rich and Poor: American Economic Development Policy toward the Arab East, 1942-1949*. Westport, CT: Greenwood, 1987.

Green, Stephen. *Taking Sides: America's Secret Relations with a Militant Israel*. New York: Morrow, 1984.

Griswold, William J. *The Image of the Middle East in Secondary School Textbooks*. New York: Middle East Studies Association of North America, 1975.

Grose, Peter. *Israel in the Mind of America*. New York: Knopf, 1984.

Hadawi, Sami. *Bitter Harvest: Palestine 1914-1979*. Delmar, NY: Caravan Books, 1979.

Hart, Alan. *Arafat: Terrorist or Peacemaker?* London: Sidgwick & Jackson, 1985.

Heikal, Mohamed H. *Sanawat al-Ghalayan*. (Years of Upheaval), pt. 1. Cairo: Ahram Center for Translation, 1988.

Heikal, Mohamed H. *Cutting the Lion's Tail: Suez Through Egyptian Eyes*. London: André Deutsch Limited, 1986.

Hentsch, Thierry. *Imagining the Middle East*. Montreal, Canada: Black Rose Books, 1992.

Hersh, Seymour M. *The Price of Power: Kissinger in the Nixon White House.* New York: Summit Books, 1983.

Hersh, Seymour M. *The Samson Option: Israel's Nuclear Arsenal and American Foreign Policy.* New York: Random, 1991.

Hogan, Michael J. *The Marshall Plan.* Cambridge: Cambridge University Press, 1987.

Hourani, Albert. *Islam in European Thought.* New York: Cambridge University Press, 1991.

Howard, Harry N. *The King-Crane Commission: An American Inquiry in the Middle East.* Beirut: Khayats, 1963.

Hudson, Michael C. and Ronald G. Wolfe, eds. *The American Mass Media and the Arabs.* Washington, DC: Center for Contemporary Arab Studies, Georgetown University, 1980.

Ismael, Tareq and Jacqueline Ismael. *The Middle East in the Aftermath of the Gulf War.* Gainesville: University Press of Florida, 1993.

Jansen, Michael E. *The United States and the Palestinian People.* Beirut: Institute for Palestine Studies, 1970.

Jordan, Hamilton. *Crisis.* New York: Putnam's, 1982.

Kadi, Leila S. *The Arab-Israeli Conflict: The Peaceful Proposals 1948-1972.* Beirut: Palestine Research Center, 1973.

Kalb, Marvin and Bernard Kalb. *Kissinger.* Boston: Little, Brown, 1974.

Kerr, Malcolm H. *The Arab Cold War, 1958-70.* 3d ed. London: Oxford University Press, 1971.

Kerr, Malcom H., ed. *The Elusive Peace in the Middle East.* Albany: SUNY Press, 1975.

Kern, Montague. *Television and Middle East Diplomacy: President Carter's Fall 1977 Peace Initiative.* Washington, DC: Center for Contemporary Arab Studies, Georgetown University, 1983.

Khalaf, Issa. *Politics in Palestine: Arab Factionalism and Social Disintegration, 1939-1948.* Albany: State University of New York Press, 1991.

Khalidi, Walid, ed. *From Haven to Conquest: Readings in Zionism and the Palestine Problem until 1948.* Washington, DC: Institute for Palestine Studies, 1971.

Khouri, Fred J. *The Arab-Israeli Dilemma.* Syracuse, NY: Syracuse University Press, 1985.

Kissinger, Henry. *White House Years*. Boston: Little, Brown, 1976.

Kissinger, Henry. *Years of Upheaval*. Boston: Little, Brown, 1982.

Krammer, Arnold. *The Forgotten Friendship: Israel and the Soviet Bloc 1947-53*. Urbana: University of Illinois Press, 1974.

Krogh, Peter F. and Mary C. McDavid, eds. *Palestinians under Occupation: Prospects for the Future*. Washington, DC: Georgetown University Press, 1989.

Kyle, Keith. *Suez*. New York: St. Martin's Press, 1991.

Lacey, Robert. *The Kingdom*. London: Hutchinson, 1981.

Lansing, Robert. *The Peace Negotiations: A Personal Narrative*. London: Constable, 1921.

Lesch, Ann Mosely. *Arab Politics in Palestine, 1917-1939: The Frustration of a Nationalist Movement*. Modern Middle East Series of the Middle East Institute. Ithaca, NY: Cornell University Press, 1979.

Lesch, Ann M. and Mark Tessler. *Israel, Egypt and the Palestinians: From Camp David to Intifada*. Bloomington: Indiana University Press, 1989.

Lloyd, Selwyn. *Suez 1956: A Personal Account*. London: Cape, 1978.

Lodge, Henry Cabot. *As It Was: An Inside View of Politics and Power in the '50s and '60s*. New York: Norton, 1976.

Louis, William Roger. *The British Empire in the Middle East, 1945-1951*. Oxford: Clarendon Press, 1984.

Louis, William Roger and Robert W. Stookey, eds. *The End of the Palestine Mandate*. Austin: University of Texas Press, 1986.

Love, Kennett. *Suez: The Twice Fought War*. New York: McGraw-Hill, 1969.

Lustick, Ian. *Arabs in the Jewish State: Israel's Control of a National Minority*. Modern Middle East Series, no. 6. Austin: University of Texas Press, 1980.

al Madfai, Madiha Rashid. *Jordan, the United States and the Middle East Peace Process, 1974-1991*. New York: Cambridge University Press, 1993.

Madrid, Robin, ed. *Statements and Position Papers of Major American Organizations on Middle East Peace*. Washington, DC: Washington Middle East Associates, 1986.

Manuel, Frank Edward. *The Realities of American-Palestine Relations*. Washington, DC: Public Affairs Press, 1949.

McGhee, George. *Envoy to the Middle World: Adventures in Diplomacy.* New York: Harper & Row, 1983.

Michalak, Laurence. *Cruel and Unusual: Negative Images of Arabs in American Popular Culture.* Washington, DC: ADC, 1988. 3d ed.

Miller, Aaron David. *Search for Security: Saudi Arabian Oil and American Foreign Policy, 1939-1949.* Chapel Hill: University of North Carolina Press, 1980.

Moore, John Norton, ed. *The Arab-Israeli Conflict: Readings and Documents.* Abr. and rev. ed. Princeton, NJ: Princeton University Press, 1977.

Morris, Benny. *1948 and after: Israel and the Palestinians.* Oxford: Clarendon Press, 1990.

Morris, Benny. *The Birth of the Palestinian Refugee Problem, 1947-1949.* Cambridge: Cambridge University Press, 1987.

Mouly, Ruth W. *The Religious Right and Israel: The Politics of Armageddon.* Chicago: Midwest Research, 1985.

Neff, Donald. *Warriors for Jerusalem: The Six Days That Changed the Middle East.* New York: Linden Press/Simon & Schuster, 1984.

Neff, Donald. *Warriors against Israel.* Brattleboro, VT: Amana Books, 1988.

Neff, Donald. *Warriors at Suez: Eisenhower Takes America into the Middle East.* Brattleboro, VT: Amana Books, 1988.

Nixon, Richard. *The Memoirs of Richard Nixon.* New York: Filmways, 1978.

Nutting, Anthony. *The Tragedy of Palestine from the Balfour Declaration to Today.* London: Arab League Office, 1969.

Nye, Joseph S., Jr. and Roger K. Smith. *After the Storm: Lessons from the Gulf War.* Lanham, MD: Madison Books, 1992.

Painter, David S. *Oil and the American Century.* Baltimore, MD: Johns Hopkins University Press, 1986.

Peck, Juliana. *The Reagan Administration and the Palestinian Question: The First Thousand Days.* Washington, DC: Institute for Palestine Studies, 1984.

Peters, Cynthia, ed. *Collateral Damage: The New World Order at Home and Abroad.* Boston: South End Press, 1992.

Peterson, J.E. *Defending Arabia.* New York: St. Martin's Press, 1986.

Pollard, Robert A. *Economic Security and the Origins of the Cold War, 1945-1950.* New York: Columbia University Press, 1985.

Porath, Yehoshua. *The Emergence of the Palestinian-Arab National Movement, 1918-1929*. London: Frank Cass, 1974.

Porath, Yehoshua. *The Palestinian Arab National Movement: From Riots to Rebellion, 1929-1939*. London: Frank Cass, 1977.

Quandt, William B. *Domestic Influences on U.S. Foreign Policy in the Middle East: The View from Washington*. Santa Monica, CA: The Rand Corporation, 1970.

Quandt, William B. *United States Policy in the Middle East: Constraints and Choices*. Santa Monica, CA: The Rand Corporation, 1970.

Quandt, William B. *Decade of Decisions: American Policy toward the Arab-Israeli Conflict*. Berkeley: University of California Press, 1977.

Rabin, Yitzhak. *Rabin Memoirs*. Boston: Little, Brown, 1979.

Rubenberg, Cheryl A. *Israel and the American National Interest: A Critical Examination*. Urbana: University of Illinois Press, 1986.

Rubin, Barry. *Secrets of State: The State Department and the Struggle over U.S. Foreign Policy*. New York: Oxford University Press, 1985.

Safire, William. *Before the Fall*. Garden City, NY: Doubleday, 1975.

Said, Edward W. *Orientalism*. New York: Vintage Books, 1979.

Said, Edward W. *Culture and Imperialism*. New York: Alfred A. Knopf, 1993.

Said, Edward W. and Christopher Hitchens, eds. *Blaming the Victims: Spurious Scholarship and the Palestinian Question*. London: Verso, 1988.

Seale, Patrick. *Asad of Syria: The Struggle for the Middle East*. Los Angeles: University of California Press, 1989.

Sha'ban, Fuad. *Islam and Arabs in Early American Thought: The Roots of Orientalism in America*. Durham, NC: The Acorn Press, 1991.

Shadid, Muhammad K. *The United States and the Palestinians*. New York: St. Martin's Press, 1981.

Shaheen, Jack G. *The TV Arab*. Bowling Green, OH: Bowling Green State University Popular Press, 1984.

Sharif, Regina. *Non-Jewish Zionism: Its Roots in Western History*. London: Zed Press, 1983.

Sheehan, Edward R.E. *The Arabs, Israelis, and Kissinger: A Secret History of American Diplomacy in the Middle East*. New York: Reader's Digest Press, 1976.

Sherry, Michael S. *Preparing for the Next War: American Plans for Postwar Defense, 1941-45*. New Haven, CT: Yale University Press, 1977.

Shiblak, Abbas. *The Lure of Zion*. London: al-Saqi Press, 1986.

Shlaim, Avi. *Collusion across the Jordan: King Abdullah, the Zionist Movement, and the Partition of Palestine*. New York: Columbia University Press, 1988.

Simon, Reeva S. *The Middle East in Crime Fiction: Mysteries, Spy Novels and Thrillers from 1916 to the 1980s*. New York: Lilian Barber Press, 1989.

Smith, Charles D. *Palestine and the Arab-Israeli Conflict*. New York: St. Martin's Press, 1988.

Snetsinger, John. *Truman, the Jewish Vote and the Creation of Israel*. Stanford, CA: Hoover Institution Press, 1974.

Snow, Peter. *Hussein*. London: Barrie & Jenkins, 1972.

Southern, R.W. *Western Views of Islam in the Middle Ages*. Cambridge, MA: Harvard University Press, 1962.

Spiegel, Steven L. *The Other Arab-Israeli Conflict: Making America's Middle East Policy, from Truman to Reagan*. Chicago and London: University of Chicago Press, 1985.

Stebbins, Richard P., ed. *Documents on American Foreign Relations, 1963*. New York: Harper & Row, 1964.

Stein, Leonard. *The Balfour Declaration*. London: Vallentine, Mitchell, 1961.

Stivers, William. *America's Confrontation with Revolutionary Change in the Middle East, 1948-83*. New York: St. Martin's Press, 1986.

Stoff, Michael B. *Oil, War, and American Security*. New Haven, CT: Yale University Press, 1980.

Suleiman, Michael W. *The Arabs in the Mind of America*. Brattleboro, VT: Amana Books, 1988.

Terry, Janice J. *Mistaken Identity: Arab Stereotypes in Popular Writing*. Washington, DC: American-Arab Affairs Council, 1985.

Tivnan, Edward. *The Lobby: Jewish Political Power and American Foreign Policy*. New York: Simon & Schuster, 1987.

Touval, Saadia. *The Peace Brokers: Mediators in the Arab-Israeli Conflict, 1948-1979*. Princeton, NJ: Princeton University Press, 1982.

Tschirgi, Dan. *The Politics of Indecision: Origins and Implications of American Involvement with the Palestine Problem*. New York: Praeger, 1983.

U.S. Congress. House. Subcommittee on Criminal Justice of the Committee on the Judiciary. *Hearings on Ethnically Motivated Violence Against Arab-Americans.* Washington, DC: U.S. Government Printing Office, 1988.

U.S. Department of State. *The Palestine Mandate: Collected United States Documents relating to the League of Nations Mandate for Palestine, to the Possible Future Independence of Palestine and to the Need for the Creation of a Separate Jewish State.* Salisbury, NC: U.S. Department of State, Division of Near Eastern Affairs, 1977, originally published as *Mandate for Palestine* [Washington, DC: U.S. Government Printing Office, 1927].

Umozurike, Umozurike Oji. *Self-Determination in International Law.* Hamden, CT: Archon Books, 1972.

Viorst, Milton. *Sands of Sorrow: Israel's Journey from Independence.* New York: Harper & Row, 1987.

Vogel, Lester I. *To See a Promised Land: Americans and the Holy Land in the Nineteenth Century.* University Park, PA: Pennsylvania State University Press, 1993.

Wells, Samuel F., Jr. and Mark Bruzonsky, eds. *Security in the Middle East.* Boulder, CO: Westview Press, 1987.

Wilson, Evan M. *Decision on Palestine: How the U.S. Came to Recognize Israel.* Stanford: Hoover Institution Press, 1979.

Wilson, Mary. *King Abdullah, Britain and the Making of Jordan.* New York: Cambridge University Press, 1987.

Woodward, Bob and Carl Bernstein. *The Final Days.* New York: Avon Books, 1976.

Young, Ronald J. *Missed Opportunities for Peace: U.S. Middle East Policy 1981-1986.* Philadelphia: American Friends Service Committee, 1987.

Zogby, James and Helen Hatab Samhan. *The Politics of Exclusion: A Report on Arab-Baiting in the 1986 Elections.* Washington, DC: Arab American Institute, 1987.

Zureik, Elia and Fouad Moughrabi. *Public Opinion and the Palestine Question.* New York: St. Martin's Press, 1987.

Contributors

Ibrahim Abu-Lughod is Professor Emeritus of Political Science (Northwestern University) and is now Vice President of Birzeit University, Birzeit, Palestine.

Hisham H. Ahmed PhD, a Political Scientist, presently is a visiting Fulbright Research Fellow at the Palestinian Academic Society for the Study of International Affairs (PASSIA) for the academic year 1993-94. He is also teaching at various Palestinian universities and colleges in addition to serving as President of the Palestinian Federation of the Blind in Jerusalem.

Zaha Bustami is Assistant Professor of History at New England College, Henniker, New Hampshire.

Deborah J. Gerner is Associate Professor of Political Science at the University of Kansas. Her articles on the Israeli-Palestinian conflict, foreign policy decision making, and the use of event data for studying international interactions have been published in *American Journal of Political Science, International Studies Quarterly, Arab Studies Quarterly, International Interactions, International Journal of Group Tensions, Journal of Arab Affairs*, and elsewhere. She is the author of *One Land, Two Peoples: The Conflict over Palestine*, 2nd ed., Westview Press 1994.

Fred H. Lawson is Associate Professor of Government at Mills College in Oakland, California. He is author of *The Social Origins of Egyptian Expansionism during the Muhammad 'Ali Period* (1992) and *Bahrain: The Modernization of Autocracy* (1989). His essays on United States policy toward the Middle East have appeared in *The International Journal of Middle East Studies, Middle East Report*, and *The Harry S. Truman Encyclopedia*.

Ann M. Lesch, Professor of Political Science and Associate Director of the Center for Arab and Islamic Studies at Villanova University, is the author of numerous studies on the West Bank and Gaza, including *Transition to Palestinian Self-Government* (Indiana, 1992) and *The Exiles* (The Link, 1993).

Donald Neff is the author of the *Warriors* trilogy on U.S. policy during the 1956, 1967, and 1973 wars in the Middle East. The first volume, *Warriors at Suez*, was a finalist for the American Book Award in 1981 and an alternate selection of the Book of the Month Club and the History Book Club. The other volumes are *Warriors for Jerusalem* (1984) and *Warriors against Israel* (1988). All three books are available through Amana Books, Brattleboro, VT.

Joe Stork is the editor of *Middle East Report* and cofounder of the Middle East Research and Information Project (MERIP), which publishes that magazine. His articles and reviews have also appeared in *World Policy Journal, The Nation, Le Monde Dioplomatique* and many other publications. He is a regular commentator on Middle East developments and U.S. policy for the Pacifica radio network.

Michael W. Suleiman is University Distinguished Professor, Department of Political Science, Kansas State University. He has written on American attitudes toward the Middle East, on Arab politics, and on the Arab-American community. Among his publications are *Political Parties in Lebanon* (1967); *American Images of Middle East Peoples: Impact of the High School* (1977); *The Arabs in the Mind of America* (1988); and *Arab Americans: Continuity and Change*, coedited with Baha Abu-Laban (1989).

Janice J. Terry is a graduate of the American University of Beirut and the School of Oriental and African Studies, University of London. She is the author of *The Wafd 1919-1952: Cornerstone of Egyptian Political Power* and *Mistaken Identity: Arab Stereotypes in Popular Writing*; she is also co-author of the texts *The Twentieth Century: A Brief Global History* and *World History* (2 vols.) She has published many articles on the Middle East in various journals and anthologies.

Index

Abdulaziz, King   50, 62, 153, 235
Abdullah, King   90, 92
Abdel Nasser, Gamal
   See Nasser, Gamal Abdel
Abed Rabbo, Yasir   197, 205
Abourezk, James   167
Abul Abbas   204 - 205
Abu Sharif, Bassam   187, 203, 209
Acheson, Dean   61, 64, 69, 74 - 75
Achille Lauro   183
American Israel Public Affairs
   Committee (AIPAC)   164, 200, 213, 226
American Jewish Congress   36, 41
Amitay, Morris   164
Amman   146, 183, 186
   See also Jordan
Anglo-American Committee of
   Inquiry on Palestine   70, 236
Anglo-American Convention   49
Anti-Defamation League of B'nai
   B'rith (ADL)   164, 199
Anti-Terrorism Act   237
al-Aqsa Mosque   206
Arab League   115, 118, 126
Arab summit   17, 126, 180, 187
Arab(s)   2, 4 - 5, 7, 10 - 20, 35 - 37, 47 - 48, 61 - 65, 67, 69, 71 - 74, 76 - 77, 81 - 84, 86 - 99, 101 - 102, 104 - 105, 113 - 128, 134, 138 - 140, 142 - 146, 148, 151, 153 - 156, 163 - 167, 169, 171 - 172, 177, 179 - 182, 189, 199, 202 - 205, 207 - 210, 212, 223 - 224, 233 - 242, 244
Arab-Israeli Conflict   9, 11, 15 - 21, 31, 61, 64 - 65, 73, 75 - 76, 83, 87 - 94, 96 - 97, 99 - 102, 104, 113 - 119, 121 - 128

Arafat, Yasir   17, 127, 167, 175 - 176, 179 - 180, 182 - 183, 186 - 187, 190, 197, 204 - 206, 209, 223, 230 - 231, 240, 242
al-Asad, Hafiz   180, 230 - 231
Ashrawi, Hanan   228 - 229
Aspin, Les   225
Association of Arab-American
   University Graduates (AAUG) 166
Atlantic Charter   28, 30, 50

Baghdad   68, 144 - 145, 205
   See also Iraq
Baghdad Pact   144 - 145
Baker, James   196 - 197, 199 - 201, 203 - 204, 208, 213, 224 - 226, 233, 241 - 242
Balfour, Arthur   11, 32 - 33, 41, 45
Balfour Declaration   14, 16, 27, 32 - 36, 38 - 42, 45 - 49, 235
Ball, George   167
Begin, Menachem   84, 168, 178
Beirut   36 - 37, 97, 178 - 180, 190, 230
   See also Lebanon
Ben-Gurion, David   101 - 102, 116 - 117, 119, 121 - 123
Bennike, Vagn   97, 99
Bernadotte, Count Folke   73, 84
Biltmore Program   50
Black September in Jordan   146, 150
Bolling, Landrum   167
Bolton, John   197
Brandeis, Louis   32 - 34, 40 - 43, 45, 47
Brezhnev, Leonid   151 - 152, 155

Britain 14, 31, 34 - 36, 38, 43 - 45, 49, 63, 65, 68, 70, 73, 76, 82, 87, 90, 95, 102, 121, 123, 125, 144, 206, 235 - 236
British Mandate over Palestine 14, 33, 44 - 45, 49, 61, 234 - 235
Brzezinski, Zbigniew 165 - 166, 168 - 169, 173 - 174, 237
Bush, George 164, 176, 195 - 201, 203 - 205, 207 - 208, 211 - 213, 223 - 226, 233, 238, 242
Byrnes, James 61
Byroade, Henry 86, 100

Cairo 119, 143, 151, 183, 186, 188, 201, 228, 230, 242
See also Egypt
Camp David 167 - 172, 177, 179, 182, 184, 199, 229, 233, 242
Carter, Jimmy 163 - 171, 177, 225, 237
Cecil, Lord Robert 33
Central Intelligence Agency (CIA) 71 - 72, 141, 143, 146, 225
Cheney, Dick 224
Christian Zionism 10
See also millenarian
Christopher, Warren 164, 225, 229 - 231
Clayton, Will 69
Clinton, Bill 211, 223 - 231
Congress 2, 5, 20, 46 - 50, 61 - 62, 64, 70, 83, 94, 126, 134, 157, 164 - 166, 184, 190, 204
Council of Four 37
Crane, Charles 38, 40 - 42, 48
Culbertson, William 68

Damascus 98, 205, 230
See also Syria
Davies, Rodger P. 127
Dayan, Moshe 127
Defense Department 181

Democrat(s) (Party) 59, 102, 125 - 126, 152, 163, 165, 224
deportation of Palestinians 189, 198, 207
Dulles, John Foster 83 - 88, 95 - 96, 101 - 103, 177, 237

Eban, Abba 96, 127, 153
Egypt 34, 62, 67 - 69, 82, 86, 90, 96, 99, 101 - 102, 105, 113 - 118, 120, 123 - 128, 134, 139, 141 - 143, 145, 147, 149 - 151, 153, 156, 165, 167 - 172, 175, 177 - 178, 182 - 184, 190, 201, 205, 207, 210, 227, 240
Egyptian-Israeli peace treaty 169
Eisenhower, Dwight D. 81, 83 - 90, 94 - 99, 101 - 105, 133 - 134, 138, 169
Erakat, Saib 229
Eshkol, Levi 124
Ethridge, Mark 64
Evron, Ephraim 125, 127

Faisal, Emir 36
Faisal, King 154
Fateh 127
FBI 20
Feldman, Myer 119, 123
Fez (plan) 180
Findley, Paul 167
Fish, Hamilton 46 - 47, 49
Ford, Gerald 156, 163 - 164, 166
Four Freedoms Declaration 28
Frankfurter, Felix 33, 40 - 42
French 16, 29, 31, 38 - 39, 68, 101, 123, 235

Gaza 19, 90, 92 - 93, 100 - 103, 105, 128, 171, 176, 179, 183 - 187, 189, 199 - 200, 202 - 203, 207 - 208, 210, 212, 233, 237 - 238, 242

Gemayel, Bashir 179 - 180
General Assembly 63 - 64, 71, 83, 95 - 96, 99, 114, 116 - 118, 120, 122, 124, 127 - 128, 175 - 176, 195, 197 - 199, 213, 236
Geneva Conventions 197 - 198
Glazebrook, Otis 36, 42 - 43
Golan Heights 179
Goldberg, Abraham 47
Goldberg, Arthur 125, 165
Gulf War 199, 202, 206 - 208, 213, 224 - 226

Haig, Alexander 153, 177 - 179
Hamas 226, 229 - 230
Hammarskjold, Dag 95
Haram al-Sharif 206
Harding, Warren 49
Harris poll 171
Herter, Christian 95, 142
Herzl, Theodor 34
Hizbullah 230
Holy Land 1 - 2, 10 - 15, 18
House of Representatives 28, 44, 46 - 47
House, Colonel Edward 33 - 34, 38, 40 - 41
Hughes, Charles E. 45
Hussein, King of Jordan 93, 115, 118, 146 - 149, 176, 180 - 184, 188, 190, 203, 224
Hussein, Saddam 205, 240
Hussein, Sherif 36
Husseini, Faisal 208, 227 - 228

Immigration and Naturalization Service (INS) 20
Indyk, Martin 213, 226, 229 - 231
intifada 17, 20 - 21, 176, 184, 186, 189 - 190, 196, 200, 208, 223, 225, 233, 241
Iran 67, 73 - 75, 86, 171, 177, 181, 223, 226, 229, 240

Iraq 31, 67, 69, 73, 75, 89, 104, 115, 143, 147, 177, 199, 205 - 208, 223 - 224, 226, 234, 236, 241, 244
Israeli settlements
See settlements

Jacobson, Eddie 59
Jarring, Gunnar 127
Jefferson, Thomas 27, 29
Jerusalem 5, 19, 36 - 37, 42 - 43, 61, 71, 89, 91, 122, 166, 178, 186, 198, 200 - 204, 206 - 212, 227 - 230, 234, 236, 242
Jewish lobby 135
See also Zionist lobby
Jews (Jewish) 2 - 3, 10 - 19, 32 - 37, 40 - 42, 44 - 50, 59 - 64, 72 - 73, 76 - 77, 84, 88, 91, 98, 106, 114, 116, 119, 122 - 123, 126, 133 - 135, 139 - 140, 143, 157, 163 - 165, 190, 195 - 196, 198, 201 - 204, 207, 209, 212, 217, 225, 235 - 239, 241, 243 - 244
Johnson, Joseph E. 116 - 118, 120, 123
Johnson, Lyndon 113, 125 - 128, 133, 143
Johnson Plan 119 - 121, 123
Johnston, Eric 97 - 99
Johnston Plan 97
Joint Chiefs of Staff 63, 70 - 71
Jordan 69, 82, 89 - 92, 94, 97 - 99, 103 - 105, 117 - 118, 120, 122, 124, 127, 134, 146 - 149, 165 - 166, 168 - 170, 176 - 183, 186, 200, 203, 207, 210, 228, 236 - 237, 243 - 244
Jordan, Hamilton 163 - 164, 170
Justice Department 20

Kennedy, John 113 - 116, 119 - 125, 128, 133, 138

Khalaf, Salah 196
Kibya
  See Qibya
King, Henry C. 36, 41 - 42, 48
King-Crane Commission 14, 16, 36 - 38, 40 - 44, 47 - 48
Kissinger, Henry 133, 135 - 157, 163, 165 - 166, 208, 225, 237, 241
Kremlin 73 - 75, 145, 147
Kuwait 205, 207, 224

Labor (Party) 59, 182, 189, 211 - 213
Lake, Anthony 225
Lansing, Robert 30, 35, 42, 44
League of Arab States
  See Arab League
League of Nations 13, 30, 37, 45, 49, 243
Lebanon 17, 21, 31, 37, 44, 69, 82, 89, 92, 94, 97, 103 - 104, 115, 117, 124, 127, 147, 172, 177 - 181, 183, 190, 205, 210, 226, 230
Levy, David 204
Libya 177, 234
Likud 182, 223, 225 - 226, 228, 231
Lloyd George, David 34, 39
Lodge, Henry Cabot 46, 95, 99 - 100
Lovett, Robert A. 63 - 64, 71

Madrid (conference) 21, 196, 211, 213, 224, 228 - 229, 231, 242
Malik, Charles 103
Marshall, George C. 69 - 70, 73, 83 - 84
Marshall Plan 69
McDonald, James G. 63 - 64
McGhee, George 64, 244
media 2, 9, 14, 18, 122, 134 - 135, 138, 206, 212
  See also press
Meir, Golda 117, 119, 121 - 123, 149, 151

millenarian(s) 2, 10 - 19
  See also Christian Zionism
Miller, Aaron 229
Miller, David Hunter 35, 43
missionaries 11 - 13, 49
Molotov, V.M. 145
Monroe Doctrine 29
Moslem(s)
  See Muslim(s)
Mubarak, Husni 182, 184, 227, 230
Murphy, Richard 183 - 186, 188 - 189
Muslim(s) 2, 10 - 13, 18, 126, 144 - 145, 239

Nasser, Gamal Abdel 82, 86, 115 - 116, 119, 121, 124, 126 - 127, 240
National Association of Arab-Americans (NAAA) 166
National Security Council 70, 83, 88, 136 - 138, 163 - 164, 166, 226
Nixon, Richard M. 133 - 139, 141 - 156, 166, 225
Norway 6, 230 - 231
  See also Oslo

Occupied Territories 195, 197 - 198, 200 - 206, 209 - 211, 227
Oslo 6, 231, 242
  See also Norway
Ottoman Empire 13 - 14, 30 - 31, 36, 38, 41 - 43, 82, 235

Palestine Liberation Front (PLF) 204
Palestine Liberation Organization (PLO) 17 - 18, 21, 126 - 128, 156, 163 - 164, 166 - 168, 170 - 171, 175 - 176, 178 - 183, 186 - 190, 195 - 197, 199 - 201, 203 - 211, 226 - 227, 230 - 231, 234, 237 - 238, 240 - 243

Palestine National Council (PNC) 176, 181 - 182, 186 - 187, 189, 209, 237
Palestinian National Authority 242
Palestinian refugees 64, 90 - 91, 93, 95 - 98, 103, 105, 114 - 116, 118, 120, 124 - 125, 146, 164, 236, 244
Paris Peace Conference 28, 36 - 37, 44
Party of God
See Hizbullah
Partition Resolution 93, 116, 118
Pelletreau, Robert 196, 238
Pentagon 60, 65, 126, 146, 225
Peres, Shimon 156, 182 - 185, 189, 229
PLO
See Palestine Liberation Organization
PLO Executive Committee 197, 204 - 205, 230
Popular Front for the Liberation of Palestine (PFLP) 147
press 9, 16 - 17, 97, 183
See also media
Protestant 2, 10 - 14, 19
public opinion 2, 5, 9, 15, 18 - 20, 101, 171, 239, 243

Qalqilya massacre 99
Qibya 99 - 100
Quandt, William 163, 166
Quayle, Daniel 199

Rabin, Yitzak 149 - 150, 184, 198, 202, 211 - 213, 223 - 228, 230 - 231
Reagan, Ronald 150, 175 - 182, 184, 190, 196, 223, 225, 233, 238
Reed, Edward Bliss 46 - 49
refugees
See Palestinian refugees

repatriation 75 - 76, 81, 88 - 89, 91, 94 - 97, 99 - 100, 105, 115 - 122, 124, 127 - 128
Republican(s) (Party) 102, 224
Riad, Mahmud 127
Richards, James P. 96
Rogers, William Pierce 138 - 142, 146, 150 - 153
Rogers Plan 141
Roosevelt, Franklin D. 28, 50, 59, 105, 235 - 236
Roosevelt, Theodore 29
Ross, Dennis 226, 229 - 231
Rossdale, Albert B. 46
Rostow, Eugene V. 73, 125
Rothschild, Louis de 32 - 33, 35
Rusk, Dean 127

Sabra massacre 21, 180
Sabri, Zul-Fiqar 115
Sadat, Anwar 139, 151, 166, 169 - 170, 177 - 178
San Remo 44
San Remo Agreement 44 - 45
Sanders, Edward 169 - 170
Sartawi, Issam 167
Saud, King 115, 118
Saudi Arabia 50, 62, 67, 69, 85, 91, 115, 124, 153 - 154, 177, 205, 207, 223 - 225, 227, 235
Saunders, Harold 156 - 157
Scranton, William 134 - 135, 144
Security Council Resolution 242: 127, 141, 150 - 151, 156, 163, 165, 167, 170, 175, 179, 182 - 183, 185 - 189, 200, 209 - 210, 241
Security Council Resolution 338: 156, 175, 186 - 189, 200, 209 - 210, 241
Security Council Resolution 672: 206

Security Council Resolution 673: 206
Security Council Resolution 799: 226
self-determination 14, 18, 20, 27 - 31, 33 - 39, 41 - 44, 49 - 50, 66, 68, 70, 81, 91 - 92, 105, 118, 135, 144, 164 - 165, 167 - 172, 176, 180 - 183, 186, 195, 211, 213, 233 - 235, 237 - 239, 241 - 243
Senate 28, 46, 91, 197
settlements 89, 143, 168 - 170, 178, 180, 198, 201 - 204, 210, 212
Shaftesbury, Lord 11
Shamir, Yitzhak 181, 184, 196, 198, 202, 211 - 213, 223 - 225
Sharett, Moshe 97
Sharon, Ariel 177 - 179
Shatilla massacre 21, 180
Shultz, George P. 175 - 176, 179, 181, 183 - 190, 233, 237, 241
Sinai II Agreement 156 - 157
Sixth Fleet 148, 227
Smith, Walter Bedell 91
Sokolov, Nahum 35
Soviet Union 30, 34, 65 - 67, 71 - 76, 82, 86, 89 - 90, 102, 121, 123 - 125, 135, 137, 139, 142, 144, 147 - 151, 154, 177, 180, 182, 202, 207, 209
Stalin, Joseph 50, 82
State department 4, 6, 13, 32, 44, 48, 60 - 65, 67 - 68, 71, 74 - 75, 84, 86, 95 - 96, 99, 113, 116, 119 - 123, 125 - 126, 128, 136, 138, 141 - 144, 146, 148, 151, 164, 166, 187, 190, 197, 226, 228 - 229, 243 - 244
Suleiman, Michael 173
Sykes, Sir Mark 32
Sykes-Picot Agreement 31

Syria 31, 36 - 38, 40, 44, 62, 69, 74, 82, 91 - 92, 97 - 98, 100, 113, 117, 120 - 121, 124, 127, 134, 143, 145, 147 - 149, 165, 168, 177 - 181, 184, 205, 209 - 210, 230 - 231, 234

Terzi, Zuhdi 167
Transjordan 31, 62, 73, 93
See also Jordan
Truman, Harry 59 - 62, 64 - 65, 69 - 70, 72, 75 - 77, 81, 83, 87, 94 - 95, 105, 133, 235 - 236
Tunis 183, 187, 203, 208, 230, 238
See also Tunisia
Tunisia 175, 196
See also Tunis
Turks 10, 37, 47, 70
See also Ottoman Empire

UN Conciliation Commission for Palestine 64
Unified Plan for Jordan Valley Development 85, 91, 97
See also Johnston Plan
United Nations (UN) 17, 28, 30 - 31, 59, 61, 63, 71, 81 - 82, 85, 89 - 90, 93 - 95, 97 - 98, 100 - 103, 114 - 116, 118 - 120, 124 - 125, 135, 182, 195, 197 - 198, 200, 205, 209 - 210, 213, 236, 242
See also various UN agency headings
United Nations Educational, Scientific, and Cultural Organization (UNESCO) 94, 197
United Nations Relief and Works Agency (UNRWA) 85, 92 - 94, 96
U.S. Congress
See Congress
U.S. Department of Defense
See Defense Department

U.S. Department of Justice
  See Justice Department
U.S. House of Representatives
  See House of Representatives
U.S. Department of State
  See State Department
U.S. Immigration and Naturalization Service
  See Immigration and Naturalization Service (INS)
U.S. Senate
  See Senate
U.S. Sixth Fleet
  See Sixth Fleet
USSR
  See Soviet Union

Vance, Cyrus   164 - 166

Wallace, Henry   59
Washington Institute for Near East Policy (WINEP)   213, 225
Watergate   135, 150, 152, 154 - 155
Weizmann, Chaim   32 - 33, 48, 59
West Bank   19, 92 - 93, 100, 105, 118, 128, 146, 171, 176, 178 - 179, 183 - 189, 199 - 200, 202 - 204, 207 - 208, 210, 212, 229, 233, 237 - 238, 242
Westermann, William   36

White House   5 - 6, 13, 38, 42, 59 - 60, 64, 83, 103, 125, 134, 136, 138 - 139, 141 - 142, 144, 146, 150, 152 - 154, 157, 164, 166 - 167, 169, 171, 204, 223 - 224, 231
Wilson, Woodrow   13 - 14, 27 - 45, 47 - 48, 50, 68, 235, 238 - 239, 243
Wise, Rabbi Steven   33, 35 - 36, 41
Wolf, Milton   167
World Health Organization (WHO)   197 - 198, 200
World War I   12, 14 - 15, 28 - 32, 43 - 46
World War II   15, 28, 61, 65, 67, 69, 77, 81 - 82, 92, 134, 140, 235

Yamani, Sheikh Ahmed Zaki   153
Young, Andrew   167

Zionism   10 - 11, 16, 33, 35, 48, 50, 60, 87, 187, 195, 213, 235 - 236, 238, 240
Zionist   11, 13 - 14, 16, 18 - 19, 32 - 50, 59 - 62, 72, 77, 83, 92, 98, 114, 120, 163 - 165, 167, 171, 202, 225, 238 - 239
Zionist lobby   3
  See also Jewish lobby